SIXTH EDITION

WORKING WITH FAMILIES

RENA SHIMONI
Bow Valley College

JOANNE BAXTER
Mount Royal University

PEARSON

Toronto

Vice-President, Editorial Director: Gary Bennett
Senior Acquisitions Editor: Carolin Sweig
Senior Marketing Manager: Loula March
Developmental Editor: Christine Langone
Project Manager: Rachel Thompson
Production Editor: Rashmi Tickyani, Aptara®, Inc.
Copy Editor: Karen Alliston
Proofreader: Tara Tovell
Compositor: Aptara®, Inc.
Photo and Permissions Researcher: Electronic Publishing Services Inc.
Art Director: Zena Denchik
Cover Designer: Bruce Kenselaar
Cover Image: Virinaflora/Shutterstock.com

10 9 8 7 6 5 4 3 2 1 [WC]

Library and Archives Canada Cataloguing in Publication

Shimoni, Rena, 1948-, author
    Working with families/Rena Shimoni, Joanne Baxter.—Sixth edition.

Includes bibliographical references and index.
ISBN 978-0-321-88380-3 (pbk.)

    1. Family social work—Textbooks.   2. Social work with children—Textbooks.
3. Families—Textbooks.   I. Baxter, Joanne Marlena, 1955-, author   II. Title.

LB1139.23.S55 2013   362.82   C2013-903968-6

ISBN 978-0-321-88380-3

Contents

About This Book

More often than not, people entering the early childhood field see children as the prime focus of their work. As they learn about their profession and begin to practise, they realize that in order to understand children, they need to understand the families of these children. Moreover, they learn that the well-being of children and the well-being of families are inextricably connected, and that early childhood professionals have an ethical responsibility to support families and promote their involvement in the care and education of their children. That being so, most educational programs for early childhood professionals and child and youth workers include at least one course on families. Scholars from many disciplines write about families—sociologists, psychologists, and anthropologists, to name but a few—and each discipline enriches the knowledge base with its own particular perspective. This book integrates all the relevant knowledge from that broad range of disciplines into a practical book for early childhood professionals.

We are pleased to be able to work with children and families. Both of us have come into the early childhood profession with a background in other "helping professions"—psychology and social work. We have practical experience working with families in a number of frameworks and have continued to be involved in the field as well as in the classroom. During the years we have taught courses on the family, we have collected stories and anecdotes about the families of our students, who have repeatedly told us that they are different from "textbook" families. We hope that, in this book, we have combined our theoretical knowledge with our professional experience, and added to these the wisdom gained from listening to our students.

The book is divided into three parts. Part 1, "Understanding Families," provides the conceptual framework for understanding families. We have attempted to use the most inclusive definition of families in this section, and have provided examples of nontraditional as well as traditional families. Part 2, "Facing Family Challenges," consists of 12 chapters devoted to the challenges families face today. Early childhood professionals are very likely, in the course of their careers, to work with children who have dealt with a death in the family or a divorce. Many children are from single-parent families, families who live in poverty, or families in which one of the members has special needs. Understanding these families' challenges will help the early childhood professional offer support in a nonjudgmental and empathic manner. Finally, Part 3, "Working with Families," offers a framework for early childhood professionals to apply their understanding of family in their efforts to involve families in the care and education of the children. This begins with an overview of parental involvement from a theoretical perspective, then proceeds to consider practices with parents from a family-centred approach.

We hope that our readers will share our interest in and respect for the diversity among us that is rooted in the various cultures from which we come. We have attempted to portray diversity by including excerpts from interviews with many of our students. There is a wide range in age, social class, culture, ethnicity, and religion represented in these interviews. Keep in mind, however, that the students are telling their own personal stories and speaking of their own personal beliefs and attitudes. Although they all recognize that their heritage has affected their beliefs, they do not necessarily represent a particular group or culture.

New to This Edition

Key points of revision in this new edition include the following:

- All of the "families" Chapters have been grouped together. "Culturally Diverse Families" (previously Chapter 14) is now Chapter 9, and "Modern Families" (previously Chapter 15) is now Chapter 10. They follow the other "families" Chapters: "Blended Families," "Single Parents," and "Teenage Parents."

- The section "Films/Videos," previously found in the Instructor's Manual, has been transferred to the textbook to enable students to access the information. Resources for films and videos now appear at the end of Chapters.

- The entire book has been updated with new references and research, reflecting current research and academic literature.

Supplements

Instructor's Manual (978-0-321-86640-0)   The Instructor's Manual includes Teaching Tips and Strategies; Discussion Questions; Student Activities and Exercises; and Group Work Activities and Exercises. This material is linked to the main sections of each chapter and includes page references to the textbook. It is available in PDF format from the Pearson Online catalogue to instructors who adopt the textbook.

CourseSmart for Instructors (978-0-321-86639-4)   CourseSmart goes beyond traditional expectations—providing instant, online access to the textbooks and course materials you need at a lower cost for students. And even as students save money, you can save time and hassle with a digital eTextbook that allows you to search for the most relevant content at the very moment you need it. Whether it's evaluating textbooks or creating lecture notes to help students with difficult concepts, CourseSmart can make life a little easier. See how when you visit www.coursesmart.com/instructors.

CourseSmart for Students (978-0-321-86639-4)   CourseSmart goes beyond traditional expectations—providing instant, online access to the textbooks and course materials you need at an average savings of 60%. With instant access from any computer and the ability to search your text, you'll find the content you need quickly, no matter where you are. And with online tools like highlighting and note-taking, you can save time and study efficiently. See all the benefits at www.coursesmart.com/students.

Pearson Custom Library   For enrollments of at least 25 students, you can create your own textbook by choosing the chapters that best suit your own course needs. To begin building your custom text, visit www.pearsoncustomlibrary.com. You may also work with a dedicated Pearson Custom Editor to create your ideal text—publishing your own original content or mixing and matching Pearson content. Contact your local Pearson representative to get started.

Acknowledgments

Our thanks are due to many people who have contributed to our understanding of family. First and foremost, our own families—our mothers and fathers, siblings, and grandparents; our husbands, Dave Baxter and Yakhim Shimoni; and our daughters, Orit, Galit, and Tammy Shimoni, and Chelsea and Carissa Baxter. Our colleagues at Mount Royal University College and Bow Valley College have, as always, offered support and ideas. In addition, early childhood colleagues who have used the book have provided ideas and input—Cathy Smey Carston, Jane Hewes, and Becky Kelley. Most of all, our students over the years have given us a window into the lives of many different kinds of families, so that we could enrich our understanding and sensitivity. To all, a warm thank-you.

A well-deserved thank-you is also extended to the crew at Pearson Canada for their encouragement and not-so-subtle prodding, but mostly for their faith in our ability. We have been delighted with the very positive feedback we have received about the book from students and instructors, and hope that the additions and changes we have made will meet the expectations of our readers. Thanks are due to the following instructors who reviewed the fifth edition of the text in preparation for the revision and the new chapters of the sixth edition: Ginnie Goblen, Nova Scotia Community College; Linda L. Hudson, Fleming College; Linda Leone, Camosun College; Dayan Perera, Assiniboine Community College; Jane Proudlove, Red Deer College; Sandy Schlieman, Algonquin College; Cathy Smey Carston, Mount Royal University; and Jinder Virdee, Seneca College.

Lastly, though perhaps unconventionally, we want to thank each other. This is the second book we have co-authored. We have gone through many stages of work together and have experienced the excitement, disappointments, stresses, and ultimate satisfaction at arriving at a worthwhile final product. We have now been collaborating for many years, including the updates, revisions, and enhancements to each of the five editions of this book. We have worked as co-teachers, co-authors, and friends, and hope that we will continue to do so for many years to come.

Authentic writing requires, in our view, that writers have direct experience with the subjects about which they write. In addition to our main roles at our respective colleges, Joanne has been actively involved in programs with children and families in the Calgary region; in developing and implementing accreditation guidelines for child care, family child care, and school-age care in Alberta; in developing a website resource for aides, family, and educational staff working with children with behavioural challenges; and most recently, in developing a provincial curriculum for early childhood educators in the province of Alberta. This work has brought her in contact with many of the issues in this book as she works closely with a broad range of children's services in the community. Rena has been a program developer and evaluator for a range of programs for new Canadian families, in addition to her work as the dean of Health and Human Services and the dean of Applied Research at a college that is known for its commitment to diversity, serving students from every corner of the world. We hope that our experience in these realms brings life to the issues discussed in this book. It is our students from whom we learn the most. As we continue to teach about families, we learn more and more about families from the stories our students tell us about their own lives, and about the lives of the families with whom they work.

part

Understanding Families

1

Part 1 provides a framework for understanding families. Chapter 1 discusses the concept of family and the ways family is described and defined. Chapter 2 studies changes that are occurring in the roles of family members, and Chapter 3 discusses developmental transitions for children, parents, and the family unit.

These chapters will enhance readers' understanding of families. Most people understand families based on their own experiences. They sometimes see differences as undesirable or somehow wrong. However, everyone has different experiences and expectations about families and how they should function. It is our intention that early childhood educators read through these three chapters, reflect on their own families and experiences, and become aware of how these have affected their lives as adults. We also hope that educators will reflect on the diversity that exists within and among families. In the end, early childhood educators should come away with an increased awareness, understanding, and appreciation of the children and families with whom they work.

Defining and Describing Families

chapter 1

Objectives

- **To discuss the concept of family.**
- **To highlight the diversity in today's families.**
- **To discuss the relevance of the study of family for professionals who work with children.**

> At a grade 12 graduation ceremony, a five-member rock group provided musical entertainment. After an enthusiastic round of applause, the leader of the group bowed and said to the audience, "Now I'd like to introduce you to my family." His parents, who were in the audience, were about to stand up proudly, but the young man proceeded to introduce his fellow band members as his family. Proud as they were of their son, his parents still looked a trifle disappointed.

Why Study the Family?

Each of us comes from a family of some sort, and many of us have or will go on to create our own families. Because of our experiences, the word *family* brings forth certain mental pictures and associations, some that we share with many other people and some that are unique to us. Families are being defined and redefined continually, both by those who study people and society (such as psychologists and sociologists) and by those who influence laws and policies that affect families (such as lawmakers who determine spousal and child benefits and maternity and paternity leave policies). Some kinds of families are so new that research has not yet provided us with needed information. For example, little is known about the socio-emotional development of children who have been conceived by in vitro fertilization or surrogacy, although preliminary studies indicate positive or neutral outcomes for both groups of children (Golombok et al., 2002; Shelton et al., 2009; Ulrich et al., 2004). As societies evolve, they continually challenge more traditional notions of the concept of family as they try new kinds of emotional, financial, and living arrangements. Social scientists, policy makers, and legal experts are being called upon to expand definitions of the family (Holtzman, 2006), while at the same time some are being called upon to return to more traditional definitions (such as that of the Institute of Marriage and Family Canada).

Professionals who work with young children also work with their families, whether directly or indirectly. Just as children in child care are affected by their families and have an influence on the dynamics of the child-care program, so too, do those children return home from child care to influence and affect the dynamics of their families. More than three decades of research have pointed to the importance of family involvement in early childhood education (Harvard Family Research Project, 2006; Lopez, 2010). When good relationships exist between the families of the children in early childhood settings and the educators who work directly with those children, there is increased satisfaction both at home and at the centre. Parents can be outspoken and effective advocates for child care, and in many ways they can provide as much support to the centre as the early childhood educators provide to the families. The children also benefit from positive relations between staff and parents. The more we learn about families, the more effective we will be at developing and maintaining positive, supportive relationships with them.

Marisa, Age 4

Working effectively with children and families requires an understanding and appreciation of families in all their diversity. In any class of preschool children, there is likely to be at least one child whose family is undergoing a divorce, in the process of becoming a blended family, or experiencing the hardships of unemployment or poverty. In some cases, early childhood educators will have children who have witnessed or directly experienced violence and abuse. Professionals working with children must therefore understand how these phenomena affect the child, the parents, and the family unit. A first step in developing rapport with families is the ability to empathize—to be able to imagine what it feels like to be in another person's situation. Only with this understanding and empathy will early childhood educators be able to support children and their families.

We live in a multicultural society. Each cultural group brings with it its own traditions, beliefs, and values regarding child-rearing and, either consciously or unconsciously, its own definition of the family. We can learn much from other cultures and thereby add to our understanding of children (and ourselves). We must be sensitive to cultural norms and rules if we want to ensure that children's experiences at child care or nursery school are not contrary to the beliefs and norms of their families. Yet, it is vital that we avoid stereotyping cultural groups and that we recognize the diversity that exists among families within the same cultural group. We must realize that culture and religion are often interpreted and reflected differently by each family and by each family member. One way to avoid making stereotypical assumptions is to ask people directly about their beliefs, customs, and traditions. We have done this, and throughout the book we provide examples describing the perspectives of people from different countries and cultures and with different religious orientations. They do not speak as representatives of their ethnic group or culture, but rather as individuals whose ideas about families have been strongly (but not exclusively) influenced by their cultural heritage.

One of the hallmarks of an effective early childhood educator is self-awareness. Over and over, we learn that before we can be effective in helping others, we must have a good understanding of our personal beliefs, our values, and our attitudes (Portrie & Hill, 2005). At the root of understanding ourselves is understanding the families we came from. Therefore, any study of the family has to involve some reflection on the way that this new knowledge "fits" with our own experience of family. We should gain a deeper understanding of what affected our own families as we were growing up, and this should help clarify our own values regarding family. It is hoped that this process will contribute to our personal and professional development.

Perspectives

Alemu Ayallel is a 40-year-old man from Ethiopia. He describes himself as an Orthodox Christian.

"I arrived in Canada from Ethiopia in 1988. I am married and have one daughter, aged 7. I was unable to return to my country due to the political climate there. I had nowhere else to go; I either had to stay in a refugee camp in Sudan or come to a place where I could be accepted on a humanitarian basis. Fortunately, I had a cousin in Canada who could sponsor me. Because of the civil war in Ethiopia, my extended family was dispersed, and I don't even know where many of them are today, or if they are alive.

"I came from an old country with old traditions. In that culture, the mother's role is to nurture her children and stay at home. The father is the breadwinner;

he is the guardian of the family, and the brother is socialized to become the father figure later on. He is given responsibility in the family.

"Grandparents are treated with a great deal of respect. If someone rejects or disrespects their grandparents, they are considered an outsider by their community. Grandparents have the power and control in family decisions. The paternal grandparents have more influence than the maternal grandparents. While many marriages are arranged, not all are. However, the wife needs to be accepted by the husband's parents and extended family. Marriage in our country is not only a relationship between husband and wife, but a relationship between two sets of extended families. These relationships have a great influence on the married couple. Therefore, it is extremely important that the extended families accept each other.

"The traditional family life that I have described does not relate to all parts of my country. In many urban areas, the lifestyle is very different.

"The roles in my family here have changed somewhat. I now contribute to household chores, and my wife works outside the home, so there are two breadwinners. Decision making is mutual. I don't have a son, but if I did, I would try to treat him more on an equal basis than what has been traditional.

"I am quite comfortable with these changing values. I would expect more discipline and respect for parents than is common today. I am uncomfortable with violence and open sexuality in the media. I feel that these things are disrespectful to the family. I believe that we are still far away from full acceptance and integration of people of colour in Canadian society, and I want to instill in my daughter a sense of pride in her roots and her heritage."

Personal Perceptions of Family

Our own definition of family is usually rooted in our own experience and is affected less by the latest sociological, psychological, and legal definitions. As professionals, however, it is important that we be aware of current definitions and debates about what constitutes a family. This knowledge, combined with an awareness of our own beliefs and feelings about family, will enhance our ability to understand and work with families.

Definitions of Family

While probably few people in North America would disagree that a married couple living together with their biological children is a family, there is less consensus about other family constellations. Consider, for example, the following situations:

- If a couple has cohabited, had a child together, and then separated, are the parents and child still considered a family?
- Is a cohabiting but unmarried heterosexual couple a family?
- Is a gay couple who lives with the biological child of one of the partners a family?
- Is a child who was never formally adopted but has grown up with a couple and their biological children a member of that family?

The answer to some of these questions will be "It depends." It depends on whether one is considering the concept of family as it relates to the emotional bonds between members (e.g., the rock group who considered its members a family) or whether one is considering legal aspects of the definition (as they apply, for example, to benefits, parental leave policies, and other matters). The answer to these questions will in turn depend on the time and place they are asked. For example, as of 2010 gay couples can be legally married across Canada, as it is a national jurisdiction (Woodford, 2010). Although gay couples are gradually becoming more accepted in North American society, they still meet with much opposition, especially in the political-legal sphere of the United States but throughout much of Canada as well. Cohabiting couples were not legally accepted as families until 2000, when the Canadian parliament extended benefits and obligations to common-law couples, be they of opposite or the same sex (Ambert, 2005).

Government Definition of Family

Government definitions of family typically differ from sociological ones since the purpose of these definitions varies. Governments require strict definitions for the purposes of collecting census data and of planning and determining benefits. Government definitions tend to see families as small groups based on an affiliation or legal bonds, not on feelings, roles, or responsibilities. As of 2006, Statistics Canada has defined family as a "married couple and the children, if any, of either or both spouses; a couple living common law and the children, if any, of either or both partners; or, a lone parent of any marital status with at least one child living in the same dwelling and that child or those children" (Statistics Canada, 2006). The Vanier Institute of the Family also includes a couple in its definition of family (Ambert, 2005).

An Inclusive Definition of Family

While similarities do exist in the way the family has been described, it is clear that there is no one "right" way of defining families and little probability that scholars will ever come to a consensus on the topic (Holtzman, 2006). However, it is important to have a working definition of the family that reflects the realities of life in North America rather than one particular group's ideal.

The Vanier Institute of the Family's Working Definition of Family

Any combination of two or more persons who are bound together by ties of mutual consent, birth, and/or adoption/placement, and who, together, assume responsibilities for variant combinations of some of the following:

- Physical maintenance and care of group members
- Addition of new members through procreation or adoption
- Socialization of children
- Social control of members
- Production, consumption, and distribution of goods and services
- Affective nurturance—love

Source: Vanier Institute of the Family, 2011.

As early childhood educators, we need to remember that it's important to be accepting, respectful, and understanding of the challenges faced by the wide variety of families. It may be interesting to compare your views on defining families with those of other Canadians. According to a national study (Bibby, 2006), almost all Canadians see a married man and woman with at least one child as a family. Six out of 10 Canadians see a single parent with a child as a family, and 5 out of 10 Canadians see same-sex parents with a child as a family. Only 3 out of 10 Canadians see cohabiting couples with no children as a family, and only 2 out of 5 Canadians see gay couples as a family. However, there are very significant differences in these opinions among different age groups. For example, 68% of Canadians between the ages of 18 and 34 see two people of the same sex with at least one child as a family, whereas only 24% of Canadians over the age of 55 share that view. The trend seems to be that the younger generation, many of whom have grown up in non-traditional families, are setting the stage for a more inclusive definition of family.

Characteristics of Healthy Families

So far, we have addressed the question "What is a family?" through different perspectives. We have avoided making value judgments about what a "good family" is because this is a tricky question and because the answer we give is greatly influenced by our own beliefs and values, and is certainly affected by our cultural background. But tricky as the question may be, all professionals who work with families must ask themselves what they believe the components of a healthy family are, and they must combine their personal knowledge and beliefs with their professional knowledge about that subject. Below, we consider some characteristics of a "healthy family," as derived from Western psychology and sociology. We must consider these ideas in light of ideas about healthy families in other cultures. Note that healthy families are described in terms of what happens within the family rather than in terms of the structure of the family. That is, regardless of whether the family has a traditional structure (a married couple with children) or a nontraditional one (the rock-group family described earlier), these characteristics could apply.

Characteristics of Healthy Families

1. *Commitment.* Family members are committed to promoting each other's welfare and to investing time and energy in the family group.
2. *Appreciation.* Family members appreciate, support, and encourage each other.
3. *Effective communication patterns.* Family members spend time talking with each other and listening to each other. They solve problems effectively, and feel free to express ideas and emotions with each other.
4. *Spending time together.* Efforts are made to ensure that joint family times happen (meals, recreation, chores). Time together is spent in "active interaction" (rather than in passive activities, such as watching television).
5. *Shared value system.* Family members share and base their actions on the same value system. This system could be based on religion, but that is not always the case.
6. *Coping with stress.* Families have to cope with stress. This includes being aware of the stressors that develop and working together to cope with such stressors.

---

7. *Balancing of needs.* A healthy family finds ways to balance the needs of the family as a group with the individual needs of its members. For example, while parents spend much time meeting the needs of their children, they also realize that they need to spend time together as a couple and to find time to develop their own interests as individuals. Also, parents understand that developing children need to spend time with their peers in order to make and have friends beyond the family.

This list is not definitive; we provide it simply as a framework for discussion. Questions you may want to ask include the following:

- Does this list, or parts of it, relate to "real" or "ideal" families?
- Does this list, or parts of it, relate to all families, or is it culture biased?
- What would you add to this list, and why?
- What would you remove from this list, and why?
- Think of two or three families you know. Does the list apply to them?

Diversity in North American Families

As you work out your own definition of family, consider the following scenario, in which a 22-year-old social work student tries to come to grips with what the word *family* has meant in her life.

Scenario

Who Is Family?

"When I was a little girl, my parents took in two foster children for three years. The children then returned to their biological parents, but we remained very close. When we finished high school we got together again, and we've been sharing an apartment now for four years. We truly are a family.

"Last month I got engaged. My fiancé immigrated to Canada a few years ago, and most of his extended family still live in Greece. At our engagement party, I looked around the room at his wonderful family, with whom I couldn't communicate because I don't speak their language, and whose way of life seems so different from mine. These people, after the marriage, would become my family. Then I looked at my former foster sisters who have shared so much of my life and so many of my most intimate thoughts. It's amazing that these people are not really considered family."

This is a touching example of how formal definitions of family often don't capture the feelings and relationships that are connected with the concept of family.

The following scenario is a remarkable example of the diversity in structures that we see today.

Expect the Unexpected

A 4-year-old at a child-care centre was enthusiastically telling his early childhood educator that he was going to Vancouver to visit his uncle. The educator asked the child what they were going to do when they got there. "Oh," said the child, "I'm going to take him for a walk in his stroller." The educator smiled and said, "You mean you're going to take your *cousin* for a walk in the stroller?" "No, he's my uncle," said the child as he strutted off to play. When the mother arrived to pick up her son, the educator related the conversation to her and said that perhaps the child was confused about the meaning of the words *uncle* and *cousin*. The mother laughed and told her an enlightening story. "My mother died four years ago, and my 75-year-old father soon after remarried a woman much younger than him, and they had a baby." This $1\frac{1}{2}$-year-old baby was indeed the uncle of her 4-year-old son!

Clearly, in this scenario, the early childhood educator's perception of family had led her to assume that uncles are adults and cousins are children.

Examine Your Attitudes

When you answer the following questions, think about what influenced your answer. What have you learned about your own personal definition of family?

- A divorced mother and her daughter live together in an apartment. The biological father lives in another neighbourhood. Do the three of them constitute a family?
- A household consists of a married couple, their biological son, and two teenagers who have been living with them in an informal fostering arrangement for several years. Are they a family?
- A cohabiting couple have been together for one year. Are they a family? Are they a family after 5 or 10 years of cohabiting?
- A young man and woman began to cohabit last week. Are they a family?
- Would the same couple be a family if the female was pregnant and the man was the biological father?
- Would the same couple be a family if the man was not the biological father?

At the conclusion of this chapter, there are exercises that will help you reflect on how your own family has affected your perception of how families are defined. As early childhood educators, however, we must understand families not only from our personal perspectives, but also from a more theoretical point of view. We need to become educated about different kinds of families as a means of ensuring that our relationships with families are not hindered by stigmatization or prejudice.

Did you know that of the 8.9 million families in Canada:

- 54.3% are married or common-law couples with children.
- 29% are married or common-law couples without children.
- 6.3% are common-law couples with children.
- 7.5% are common-law couples without children.
- 15% are lone parents (81% of these are female).

Source: Statistics Canada, 2006 Census.

Models for Understanding Families

Many different theories about families have been formulated, each with its own particular view of how families work. Two approaches or models considered in this book are the family systems approach and the ecological approach. Both of these are highly relevant to working with families. Family systems theory has become the theoretical framework used in psychology and social work to guide the practice of family counselling and therapy. The ecological approach, which can be seen as a systems theory as well, forms the theoretical foundation for most early childhood educators.

A Systems Approach to the Family

Most would agree that when a group of people are connected together by family ties, what happens to one member of the family usually affects other members. Parents often bring home stresses from their work environment, and children pick up and often act out that tension. A situation as common as a child with a cold or ear infection often affects the entire family dynamic. If parents are up with a sick child several nights in a row, their exhaustion may well influence their relations with each other and with other children in the family, as well as the siblings' relations with each other. Because family members function as a unit composed of interacting members, psychologists began to think of families as "systems."

Family systems theory provides us with a way of looking at individuals, families, and groups to get a better understanding of how each of these units function both separately and as a whole. While family systems theory is used mostly in family counselling and therapy, it is highly relevant to early childhood settings (Garris-Christian, 2006). The main concept in family systems theory is that the family includes interconnected members, each member influencing the others in predictable and recurring ways (Van Velsor & Cox, 2000). This theory focuses on family behaviour, and considers communication patterns, separateness, connectedness, loyalty, and dependence, as well as how families adapt to stress (Garris-Christian, 2006). A major contribution of this theory is the ability to see the family both as a whole and as a series of interconnected parts. Just as people who are concerned about the environment talk about an ecosystem, in which what happens to one part (e.g., using chemicals for weed control) eventually affects other parts (the water supply), professionals who advocate a systems approach to family therapy see the members of a family as forming an interconnected whole.

While this interconnectedness seems obvious, considering the family as a system has not traditionally been part of working with families. It is still quite common for a child with behavioural problems to be seen by a therapist who has little or no contact with the parents. Teachers will sometimes have a conference with parents and expect them to carry out certain tasks with their children (such as homework) without attempting to gain an understanding of the bigger picture of how that family functions as a system.

Scenario

The Bigger Picture

The mother of a 5-year-old developmentally delayed little boy was asked to carry out a "simple" behavioural program at home. The mother was to make sure that her son always made an attempt to communicate verbally before being given what he wanted. This seemed simple enough, and the early childhood educator wondered why the mother seemed reluctant to do it. She was unaware that the mother had two younger children, that she helped with her husband's business, and that she tried to care for her aged, chronically ill mother, all in addition to working part-time. This simple request was not as simple as it had seemed.

Families, like all other systems, can be open or closed. An open family system is thought to be more flexible and adaptable to change, and a family system that is closed is considered less adaptable to change. Open family systems can react to and cope with changes—both positive and negative—more readily than closed family systems.

Understanding this concept can make early childhood educators' interactions with different families a little easier. For example, closed families may be less likely to discuss their problems or concerns or to look for outside sources of support. Families that are more open tend to discuss their concerns and to use outside supports. The degree to which a family is open or closed will often be a prime consideration in determining how the early childhood educator will interact with the family.

Moreover, the degree to which a family is open or closed may be affected by factors outside the family, such as prejudice or preconceived ideas, as well as by internal factors. Culture also plays a role. Garris-Christian (2006) observes that educators in the past may have worked from the assumption that openness is equated with "better"; however, they should recognize that differences in openness do not equate with differences in quality of parenting.

Family Balance (Homeostasis)

All systems strive to maintain some kind of a balance, called *homeostasis*. The human body, for example, is a system that maintains a steady temperature. When the outside temperature is exceedingly hot, various mechanisms in this system work toward maintaining a steady temperature (e.g., perspiration).

Likewise, a family system finds ways to maintain its balance. One analogy to the preceding example is the way various families "let off steam" to maintain balance when tension arises. Taking a vacation, with or without the children, could be seen as an attempt to maintain balance. Similarly, many families develop ways of discussing and solving problems as a method of maintaining balance. However, sometimes less positive measures are employed to maintain family balance, and many of these are not even conscious. Family therapists often relate anecdotes of how children become ill when tension develops between parents.

A System Out of Kilter

One therapist tells of a family in which the youngest son had a severe stutter. The parents had been experiencing serious marital problems but decided to put their own problems aside in an effort to help their son. Due to the parents' efforts, the child received treatment and support and soon his symptoms almost disappeared. However, it seemed that as the son got better, the tension and conflict between the parents worsened. As the stress in the home increased, the boy's stuttering returned.

This scenario is not atypical. In some families, a child may function as a "stress barometer." As the stress rises, so too, does the incidence of behaviours such as stuttering, bed wetting, and nail biting.

Balance and consistency in families are important for providing children with a secure environment. Rituals and customs help keep families together during times of change and stress. Early childhood educators can assist families in establishing and maintaining equilibrium through providing as much consistency as possible when the family is undergoing change and stress, and providing families with information about routines and rituals that can give children a sense of balance while the family is going through change (Garris-Christian, 2006).

Climate

Climate is about two things: the emotional and physical environment a child grows up in, and the emotional quality in the family. Climate is not necessarily caused by economic status or educational level. It is more about how family members relate to each other. Garris-Christian (2006) explains that the climate of a family system can be assessed by asking, "What it would feel like to be a child in this family—would she feel safe, secure, loved, encouraged, and supported or scared, fearful, or angry?"

Family Subsystems

Another important aspect of systems is that they can be divided into subsystems. In the case of families, these consist of smaller groupings of members within the family. The parents form both a marital and a parental subsystem, and the siblings form a subsystem as well. Sometimes other subsystems form, such as a mother–child or a father–child subsystem. It is important to understand how the subsystems interact with one another, but we should keep in mind that they may interact differently from family to family. The following is a short overview of basic subsystems.

The interaction between husband and wife or between partners is referred to as the *marital subsystem*. Having a child or children affects partners' relationship and their marital subsystem. Some parents may find their marital relationship constricted when children come along, while others may find children or the role of parenting to be a source of conflict. The parental subsystem consists of interactions between the parents and the children. This relationship will grow and change over time as the child grows and as parents develop parenting abilities. Again, these interactions will be influenced by many factors. Parents' interactions with children are impacted by cultural norms, life circumstances such as employment, and their own personal histories. Siblings often have a profound impact on each other. They often spend a great deal of time with each other and will develop unique ways of interacting. Siblings can support one another or be in conflict. Recent research has highlighted the significant effect of siblings on each other

(Bibby, 2006; Rocca et al., 2010). In spite of myths about the proverbial mother-in-law, extended family relationships can make a major contribution to the quality of life in many families. Research in Canada has shown that in times of stress or tragedy, extended family members are often the major sources of support (Fuller-Thomson, 2005), especially in immigrant and Aboriginal families (O'Donnell, 2008). Today, as discussed in the next chapter, grandparents are emerging as the heroes in many families, often taking an active role in nurturing the children of working or single parents. The nature of extended family relations will depend on many factors, including geography, health, family history, and the personalities involved.

Boundaries

Families vary tremendously in the kinds of boundaries that exist between the subsystems. For example, in some families, the house is arranged in terms of "children spaces" and "adult spaces"; in others, toys are found in all areas, including the living room. Some couples want to maintain distance from their own parents as part of their need to become independent. For other couples, parents are included in the decisions they face. There is no right or wrong way to establish boundaries between family subsystems, but it is generally considered healthy to have clearly identified (though not necessarily rigid) boundaries between them (Hull & Mather, 2006).

The relationships between, and boundaries surrounding, family subsystems may be influenced by culture. In some cultures there are very clear expectations for how to maintain relationships and boundaries with parents, siblings, grandparents, and other extended family members, whereas in others there are fewer distinct rules and expectations.

Family Roles, Rules, and Hierarchies

While the family unit functions as a system, each member of that system has "official" and "unofficial" roles: mother, father, son, daughter, and grandparents, to name the most common. With each role comes expected, permitted, and forbidden behaviour. The role expectations come from societal norms and are affected by age, gender, and personality, and can change over time (Hull & Mather, 2006). In most families, individuals have roles, although they are often never spoken about. For example, there is usually a peacemaker, a clown, a rescuer, a victim, a problem solver, or a problem maker. These roles often carry over to other contexts, such as the child-care setting, the school, and work (Garris-Christian, 2006). The next chapter takes a more in-depth look at the roles of mothers, fathers, grandparents, and siblings, and at how these roles are changing.

Hierarchy is related to who has the power and control in the family. In some families, the parents share family responsibilities, with a different parent perhaps taking more responsibility for decisions related to specific matters. Some families attempt to be as democratic as possible, including the children in all major decisions. Hierarchy often has a cultural basis; for example, in some families the oldest member is the authority on most decisions (Garris-Christian, 2006).

Rules govern all systems, including the family. Some of these rules are clear and some are not so clear. Some families, for example, may clearly state that the family will eat supper together or that the children are to tidy their rooms before watching television. Other rules may not be as clear, though they may be evident to an astute observer of families. A discussion that took place among early childhood students yielded some interesting examples of family rules:

- Boys play hockey; girls play quietly.
- Daughters clear the table after meals; sons do their homework.
- We don't want to know if you had a bad day.
- Complaining gets you nowhere.
- Crying helps you get your way.

Nobody talks about these informal rules in the family, but everyone seems to know them. Children's behaviour is certainly influenced by these rules. The first indication of this is often when the 4- or 5-year-old begins to play with other children in their homes and sees different things happening. Young children will often bring these examples home and make comparisons with their own family. For example, they might remark, "At Lindsay's house, her dad cooks," or "Jill and her brother take baths together." When families experience conflict, a family counsellor or therapist might try to help the family understand how these "unstated rules" are affecting relationships.

Early childhood educators working with families need to be sensitive to family rules, even though some may not be congruent with the professional's ideas about raising children. For example, in some families there is a clear division of sibling roles based on gender, and boys do not participate in activities such as housekeeping and playing with dolls. Child-care centres can and should distinguish between home and centre rules, being sensitive and respectful to the home environment. Early childhood educators can watch for unspoken rules, and ask for families' input and assistance when there is a discrepancy between home and centre rules (Garris-Christian, 2006).

Scenario

Not in Our Family

A father came to pick up his 4-year-old son from child care. When he arrived, Jonathan was in the housekeeping corner dressed in a long yellow gown, a floppy hat, and high heels. The staff explained that Jonathan loved to pretend that he was a princess. Jonathan's father was extremely embarrassed. He reprimanded his son and the staff openly, saying that in his family men didn't dress like women and he did not want his son playing there again.

The family-systems approach is broad and complex, and our purpose has been to familiarize early childhood educators with some key concepts, especially as they relate to professionals' work with children and families. Although early childhood educators do not engage in family therapy, understanding some of these concepts will heighten their awareness of how they may inadvertently or purposefully affect the family as a whole (Garris-Christian, 2006).

An Ecological Approach to the Family

Just as a child is affected by the entire family system, so too, are families affected by other systems with which they interact. These include the neighbourhood in which they live, the parents' workplace, and the nature and scope of available support services. These aspects of family life are affected, in turn, by the social policies and ideologies prevalent in our society. An ecological approach recognizes that interrelated factors ultimately affect the way in which each child develops. An understanding of the ecological model can help early childhood educators empathize with families and better understand their role in supporting and helping families.

The conceptual foundation of the ecological model stems from the work of Urie Bronfenbrenner (1979, 1990), who outlined four basic structures—microsystem, mesosystem, exosystem, and macrosystem—in which relationships and interactions that affect human development take place (Berk, 2000). Today, 30 years after Bronfenbrenner developed this theory, it remains a foundational concept in early childhood education. The first of the four basic structures within the ecological approach is the microsystem. This consists of settings or environments with which the individual has direct, ongoing contact. The family, the school, and the peer group are examples of microsystems with which the child interacts to significantly affect development. The workplace, place of worship, bowling club, golf course, or community centre are examples of microsystems with which adults in the family may interact. Another aspect of the microsystem today is the virtual microsystem. Family life has been altered significantly by technology—television, the Internet, and cellphones (Devito et al., 2001; Little et al., 2009). We will likely learn more in future years about the influence of the virtual microsystem on families and children.

The second structure is the mesosystem. This consists of links and relationships between two or more of the microsystems with which the individual interacts. Examples include the relationship between a family and the child-care centre or a workplace and the child-care centre. These connections between microsystems can be weak or strong, positive or negative.

The third structure in the ecological approach is the exosystem. The exosystem consists of the many structures in a society that affect people's lives even though they may have no direct contact with them. These include institutional and government decisions and policies, societal norms, and laws.

The fourth and final component of the ecological approach is the macrosystem. The macrosystem encompasses the beliefs and values (i.e., the ideology) and lifestyles of the dominant culture and the subcultures within a society. Macrosystems are viewed as patterns or frameworks for exosystems, mesosystems, and microsystems (Berk, 2000). For example, policies made at the exosystem level (such as universal access to school) are based on shared assumptions and beliefs about the value of education in our society.

The ecological model describes the influence of different systems on each other as dynamic and reciprocal. This means that individuals or families can influence policies just as much as they are influenced by them. Consider the following example: a government decision (an exosystem) to reduce funding for services to children with special needs can affect many of the microsystems with which family members are involved. The schools (a microsystem) may have fewer resource teachers to help children with special needs, which may result in policies (an exosystem) that discourage the integration of children with special needs into the school system. These children will be in need of much family (microsystem) support. However, if the families of these children join forces with the schools (forming a mesosystem), they may be able to advocate effectively enough to force the government (the exosystem) to rethink its policy.

Applying the Ecological Model

How does the ecological model relate to early childhood educators? Its significance can be understood in a variety of ways. First, the model helps us see the child in a more holistic way, in the context of the environment that is affected by and, in turn, affects the child, both directly and indirectly. When we look at the importance of the micro- and mesosytem to the child's well-being, we gain a better understanding of the kinds of supports children need. Consider, for example, the families that must move frequently due to the parents' careers. With each change comes the need to forge new connections with child-care centres, schools, communities, places of worship, neighbours. Supporting the children and their families can be an important part of the early childhood professional's role. In addition, understanding families through the lens of the ecological model can help us become less judgmental toward parents.Parents are frequently blamed for not providing the best possible environment in which to care for and nurture their child. Often, however, the stressors (such as unemployment and poverty) that make positive parenting difficult stem from factors outside the family (in the exosystem or macrosystem).

Furthermore, the ecological model helps us see that what early childhood educators can offer to children often depends on factors beyond the doors of the centre, such as laws, policies, and cultural values. Lastly, the ecological model suggests to early childhood educators that promoting the well-being of children entails involvement on many levels: direct work with children, working with families and other microsystems with which a child is involved, influencing policies and legislation that affect children and families, and helping to define the value that society places on children. The challenge for early childhood educators is to identify, within the different systems, strategies for their work that are feasible and realistic, given the limits of their time and professional qualifications.

A Strength-Based Perspective for Working with Families

As you learn more about different kinds of families, the challenges they face, and strategies to provide them with support, it's important to consider what you learn through a lens that recognizes families' strengths. The main components of strength-based practice include the following:

- Every member of the family has strengths that can be developed, built on, and channelled in a direction that is positive for the family.
- Everyone has the potential for growth and change, within a supportive environment.
- Most parents want to be good parents.
- Hardships can be challenging for families, but can also be an opportunity for growth and positive change.

Conclusion

Today's families are undergoing rapid transformations: families are very different from what they were a generation or two ago (Mitchell, 2006). This causes some confusion and even alarm as researchers struggle to untangle the complexity and find ways of capturing the essence and meaning of these changes in the lives of adults and children. It is important to gain an understanding of families as they exist in society today. Although the nature of families varies in different eras and in different cultures, they have almost universally retained their prominence as a primary social unit. This chapter has outlined some of the theoretical definitions and concepts of families in order to provide a framework for the information contained in the rest of this book. By being aware of how our own experience of families has affected our views, and by being aware of the need to learn more about the many different kinds of families that exist today, we will become more competent as professionals who work with children and families.

Chapter Summary

- Perceptions of family are often rooted in personal experience.
- There is no one "right way" of defining families.

- The Vanier Institute of the Family defines family as any combination of two or more persons who are bound together over time by ties of mutual consent, birth, and/or adoption, who get together and assume responsibilities for some of the following: physical care of group members, addition of new members, socialization of children, social control of members, production, consumption, and distribution of goods and services, and affective nurturance or love.
- Western views of healthy families include commitment, appreciation, effective communication, shared values, coping mechanisms, and a balancing of needs.
- A systems approach to families sees the family as a system distinct from its environment, with a boundary that separates it from the environment, and with each part influenced by other parts.
- An ecological approach considers family in the context of the micro-, meso-, and exosystems.
- Early childhood programs that work effectively with families provide better support to children. Effective work with families requires an understanding and appreciation of families in all their diversity.

Recommended Websites

The Canadian Council on Social Development (CCSD) is one of Canada's most authoritative voices promoting better social and economic security for all Canadians:
www.ccsd.ca/factsheets

According to the CCSD, "The structure of the family and the character of relations within it make up the primary setting for child development":
www.ccsd.ca/pccy/2006/pdf/pccy_familylife.pdf

The CCSD's "Guiding Principles of Family Support":
www.frp.ca/_data/global/images/resources/guiding-e.pdf

Child & Family Canada:
www.cccf-fcsge.ca

National Association for the Education of Young Children:
www.naeyc.org

Statistics Canada:
www.statcan.ca

Vanier Institute of the Family:
www.vifamily.ca

Videos/Films

For Generations to Come. 1994. National Film Board of Canada. www.onf-nfb.gc.ca. Although this film was made in 1994, it remains relevant today. It comes with a pamphlet that includes discussion questions.

You might instead consider showing either *Growing Up Canadian: Family* (2003) or *Variations on a Familiar Theme* (1995). These films are also described on the National Film Board's website.

1. In this exercise, you will draw a family map. This will bring to light many factors that have had an impact on your own family, and will help you in identifying the range of factors that have influenced your concept of family.

   For this exercise, you will need a large sheet of paper and markers. Use symbols or pictures rather than words to illustrate some of the most influential factors in shaping who you are today. You may include family members, friends, places of worship (church, synagogue, mosque, temple), activities, interests, travel, and any other factors that occur to you. Try to draw the symbols in order of importance or in chronological order.

   After you have completed your family map, compare it with others' maps or reflect upon what you've drawn. Which factors were most prominent in your development?

   How are the factors in your diagram interrelated? For example, some students recall that happy family memories are associated with holidays, leisure activities, or religious festivities. Unhappy memories may be associated with events such as a divorce or a death in the family. A consideration of the family map leads to an awareness of how factors outside the home, such as the nature of the community, influence the family.

2. One simple but effective method for evoking thoughts about the family is simply to draw a picture of a festive family dinner. Include in the drawing empty chairs for family members who are not present. Notice the seating arrangements around the table. Who is sitting next to whom, and why? Who is not present, and why? Who is actively engaged in food preparation and distribution? A description of a family meal can sometimes tell us a great deal about a family's relationships and norms.

3. On a sheet of paper, make columns listing the following relationships in your life: parents, siblings, extended family, friends, classmates or co-workers, and strangers. Then ask the question, Whom would you tell about . . . ?

   The list of situations that complete this question should range from very personal (e.g., trouble in an intimate relationship) to quite superficial (e.g., a good book I've read). Compare your "whom would I tell about" chart with those of your fellow students, and note similarities and differences. What does this tell you about your own family's rules and boundaries?

4. Identify some of your family's unwritten "boundaries." Were these boundaries established by you, or "inherited" from parents or other family members? How have these boundaries affected your family relationships?

5. What were the spoken and unspoken rules in your family? How did you learn about the "unspoken" rules?

6. How do you think your views and experiences affect your work with families?

7. Describe a possible role of the early childhood educator that relates to the micro-, meso-, exo-, and macrosystem.

Family Members and Family Roles

chapter **2**

Objectives

- To review some of the most important roles of family members.

- To discuss the impact of social trends on family life.

- To consider how family roles are interconnected in family systems.

One day Timothy, who was 5 years old, came home from his preschool with tears in his eyes. Brian, his father, paused in his lunch preparation to find out what was wrong with his son. "They called me a sissy today," explained Timothy.

"Why do you think they did that?" asked Brian.

"Because I was pretend cooking."

"Who called you a sissy?" Brian continued to probe.

"Petey and Mark."

"Well," said Brian thoughtfully, "I cook—am I a sissy?"

"No, of course not, Daddy."

"And we're friends with both Mark's and Petey's parents, and both of their dads cook sometimes. Are they sissies?"

"Daddy! Of course not!"

"So do you think cooking makes you a sissy?"

"No—I guess not."

"So then, what will you say to them next time they call you that?"

"I'll say that my daddy cooks and he's not a sissy and he's bigger than your daddy and can beat him up."

Well, thought Brian to himself, *this is the 21st century and men's roles are changing. We're allowed to be in the kitchen as long as we can still beat other people up!*

Family Members and Roles

Commitment to children forms the very foundation of the early childhood profession. Our education and training prepare us to consider most circumstances from the child's perspective—that is, from the viewpoint of what is in the child's best interest. However, we are also aware that the child's well-being is inextricably connected to the well-being of the family as a unit and the subsystems within it. An understanding of the roles of some of the key players within the child's family system should help us interact with them in a sensitive and empathic manner. It should also help us broaden our understanding of the world of the child.

After completing the exercise on perceptions of family in the previous chapter, you probably realized that opinions regarding who is (and is not) considered a family member are quite diverse. A parent's partner, an aunt, uncle, cousin, friend, nanny, or caregiver may well be included in many families. As professionals working with young children, you may have the opportunity to interact with many people who are considered family, whether or not they conform to biological or legal definitions of family. Therefore, although the discussion in this chapter focuses on mothers, fathers, siblings, and grandparents, it's important to be aware of the significance and role that other members of the child's extended family may have.

Mothers

The Role of the Mother

Although many people consider mothering to be "instinctual and natural," the roles mothers play have changed over time and differ across cultures. The most central issue today concerning the role of mothers relates to employment. There have been significant changes in women's participation in the labour force, from 22% in the 1940s to 57% in the 1990s (Cleveland & Krashinsky, 1998). In 2006, 80% of married Canadian women worked (Statistics Canada, 2006).

Today, we hear vocal advocates both for mothers staying home and for mothers working. Both sides can find research to back up their claim that "stay-at-home moms" have happier families, or vice versa (Baydar & Brooks-Gunn, 1995; McDaniel, 2010; McDaniel & Tepperman, 2007). In fact, researchers were never able to provide definitive evidence to support the claim that one way is superior to the other, if only because too many factors come into play—such as the availability of quality child care, the existence of support networks, and the role the father plays in child-rearing and household tasks—all of which affect how a working or nonworking mother influences family life (McDaniel, 2010; McDaniel & Tepperman, 2009; Nayyar, 2006). Although strong feelings may still exist on both sides of the divide relating to working mothers, most families in Canada do depend on the mother's income to make ends meet. The focus should now move away from questioning whether mothers should work to the question of how working mothers can be supported by their employers in providing flexibility in schedules and "return to work" options (Benjamin et al., 2008; Nayyar, 2006), and to the provision of flexible, high-quality child-care support (McDaniel, 2010).

Our society today is undergoing a dramatic change in the traditional roles of parents and grandparents. Many fathers have been taking on much of the caring and nurturing roles traditionally associated with mothers, and many mothers have become breadwinners (Vanier Institute of the Family, 2010). For example, 2007 statistics indicate that 85% of Canadian families have two or more earners (Vanier Institute of the Family, 2010). Social changes like the prevalence of single-parent and dual-income families have resulted in a rediscovering of the potential of grandparents as nurturers and providers of care and support to the family (Lever & Wilson, 2005). For example, more than 50% of children aged 4–5 spend at least part of their week in care while parents are working or studying, and most commonly with relatives or neighbours (Statistics Canada, 2006).

Scenario

Supermom

"When I read some of the magazines, I get the impression that mothers are supposed to be these 'superbeings' who rise at dawn to exercise, jump into the shower, and run downstairs to prepare hot breakfasts for their families. Then they put on their business suits, successfully finalize two or three business deals at work, and pick up their children from child care and school. On the way home, they lead singalongs of 'The Wheels on the Bus' as they battle the traffic. After serving nutritious meals, engaging in quality time with their children, and then bathing and putting them to bed, these women miraculously transform themselves into loving and sexy wives before the evening ends."

For many women, the task of nurturing and rearing their children is the most fulfilling and rewarding experience they will ever have. Yet mothering in our society is not always easy, and the stress factors faced by mothers today affect the family as a unit as well as all the subsystems in the family.

One of the key stressors facing all family members, but mothers in particular, is the lack of time required to fulfill all the tasks and expectations. Terms like *time crunch, juggling,* and *second shift* reflect the growing sense of guilt and frustration about needing to "get it all done" and never having enough time for families and children (Milkie et al., 2009).

Daly accurately describes the woes of a hurried society:

> The demands of time are so paramount in families now that it is almost pure folly to think of families living without sophisticated scheduling tools. The family calendar usually maintained by mothers serves a critical and essential function in the family, ensuring a carefully orchestrated set of pick ups and drop offs. In the early morning hours, clock radios chime in unison throughout the household, calling both adults and children to their individual temporal routines outside of the home. Where once families were more likely to live and work together in the household, their daily routine is now more akin to a ritual of dispersion, with babies being called to the drop off time for day care, children to the schedules of school, and virtually all parents to the demands of their paid work. At the end of the day, families re-converge on the household only to face additional responsibilities that include meal preparation, homework, lessons, shopping, and scheduling for the next day. The cumulative impact of these bloated schedules is that time has become a more urgent preoccupation in managing the many demands of contemporary work and family life (Daly, 2000, p. 123).

Source: It Keeps Getting Faster: Changing Patterns of Time in Families by Kerry Daly, University of Guelph (2000) http://www.vifamily.ca/library/cft/faster.html.

It is important to note that the strain of the "second shift" or time crunch mothers face is increasingly faced by fathers as well (Harrington et al., 2010).

Attitudes Toward Mothers

A simple word-association exercise can be helpful in beginning the process of understanding the vast range of society's expectations of mothers (some positive and some negative). When our classes of early childhood students have been asked to write down quickly the first associations that come to mind when the word *mother* is mentioned, the whiteboard quickly fills up with a wide range of adjectives: *loving, caring, nurturing, steadfast, nagging, cranky, always there*, and *never there* are but a few examples. Some students have considered their mothers their closest friends, while others would not even think of having an intimate conversation with their mothers. Understanding that the assumptions we make about family are often based on our own experiences can help us avoid being judgmental about others.

Examine Your Attitudes

What do you think of mothers?

A. Complete the following sentences:
1. Mothers are _____.
2. Mothers should _____.
3. Mothers could _____.

B. Write the word *Mother* at the top of a blank sheet of paper, and then fill the page with other words this term suggests to you.

Consider the results of both exercises. Are your feelings about mothers predominantly positive? Are they negative? Or are they mixed? How strongly do you think your attitudes toward other mothers have been determined by your relationship with your own mother?

Preparation for Motherhood

In previous times and in many other cultures today, by the time a woman becomes a mother she has participated in the care and nurturing of either younger siblings or babies of neighbours or extended family members. For many women in North America, however, their own experience of childbirth is often the first time they have had contact with babies. This remains true even though childbirth is occurring at a later age for many women. Furthermore, there is a value conflict inherent in motherhood. More than 30 years ago, Sheila Kitzinger (1978) wrote a classic study of mothers that still rings true today. According to Kitzinger, the school system prepares young women to be successful members of society, which entails training them, from a very young age, to be task-oriented—to establish timelines and schedules, to be precise, and to work hard toward a successful finished product. These skills are not necessarily the same ones required of mothers. Today, ironically, these scheduling skills seem to be an absolute requirement for managing a household, and yet they do not meet the requirements of the essence of parenthood, which is about being open and responsive to children's ever-changing needs.

The Best-Laid Plans . . .

A 40-year-old woman who held a managerial position at a large institution had the first year of motherhood all planned out from two weeks after the baby was conceived. According to her plan, she would take a two-month maternity leave, after which the nanny (who had already been interviewed and hired) would begin. She had all her appointments scheduled for the next year based on her well-thought-out plan. Eight months after the birth of the baby, she met her friend in a park. "I thought you were going back to work!" the friend commented with surprise. The mother laughed and said, "I had everything all figured out, but I didn't consider for a moment that the baby wouldn't endorse my plans."

Motherhood doesn't neatly fit into a system of values that promotes high productivity and a fast pace. Mothers can't learn "perfect procedures" for child-rearing because the child is constantly changing and developing. In motherhood, there is no "finished product" by which mothers can measure their success as there is in academic or business settings.

Role Ambiguity

The role of mothers is changing and will continue to be influenced by social and economic factors beyond the control of the family. Personal and societal values are also reflected in attitudes toward mothers. In our diverse society, there should be many possible ways to mother children. But sometimes this ambiguity or freedom of choice is associated with stress and feelings of guilt that impede enjoyment and fulfillment of the task. So, as well as juggling work, family, and child-rearing, many mothers are struggling to sort out the mixed messages they receive about what society expects of them. The images of women in the media rarely reflect the value of motherhood (except in advertisements about products directly associated with child care). Women are now expected to be successful at full-time careers and to be available to their children and husbands at all times as well. Society also demands that they be well groomed and slim and trim while they are accomplishing all this.

Mixed Messages

"I stayed home with my first baby until she was 4 years old. Wherever I went, people would ask me what I did. 'I'm at home with my baby' was my reply. In so many words, the usual response was, 'Is that all you're doing?'

"When my second child was born, I went back to work after a six-month maternity leave and placed my child in a child-care centre. Now when people ask me what I do, I get a variety of responses that range from accusations of child neglect to pity for my child and me. Talk about mixed messages."

Early childhood educators can sometimes inadvertently add to the stress and guilt that mothers feel. A study of the relationship between early childhood educators and parents

(Shimoni, 1992a) indicated that some educators felt quite strongly that mothers should be at home with their children unless they absolutely had to work. Early childhood educators grew especially angry when mothers left their children at the centre at times when they weren't actually at work (to do shopping or simply to rest at home). Feelings such as these will likely be conveyed to the parents in one way or another. One mother (Shimoni, 1992a) reported that when she tried to discuss her son's problem behaviour, the early childhood educator stated outright that perhaps the solution would be to spend more time with her son. Unfortunately, there doesn't seem to be evidence of a reduction in these feelings of guilt in the two decades since that study was conducted, despite societal demands that often require women to work outside the home.

On the other hand, early childhood educators can be instrumental in providing support and understanding. The first step in this direction is developing the ability to empathize with the problems and challenges that mothers face as they raise their children in a rapidly changing society (Galinsky, 1981, 1987). This kind of awareness and sensitivity is, of course, important at all levels of education.

Mothers and Experts

Scenario

Who Knows Best?

"Before the birth of my first baby, I spent many hours talking with my grandmother, who had nursed her children until they could walk. The expression on her face as she talked about her babies said more than any advice book could. Two months after my baby was born I was visited by the community health nurse, who told me that I should begin the baby on solid foods. Reluctantly, I did as she said, and shortly after that my baby didn't want to nurse anymore. Two and a half years later, my second child was born. The same community health nurse visited, sat in the same chair as she had two years before, and with the same expert manner proceeded to tell me that solid food should not be introduced for several months, and that breastfeeding was by far the preferable method."

Historians of childhood have studied the extraordinary amount of advice from experts (Schaub, 2010). The difficulty is that experts don't seem to agree on many topics, and sorting out the contradictory messages can be confusing. Often mothers are unsure of what is the "best" advice to follow (this is commonly referred to as "analysis paralysis"). Consider how many different opinions there are today for how children should be treated at bedtime. Should they be allowed to cry in order to learn to cope with going to sleep alone? Or, should they be comforted until they fall asleep? The answer will depend on which expert opinion you're reading. In addition, parents today are bombarded with advertisements for books, toys, computer programs, and foods that will make their babies smarter and more successful. Parents who are on limited budgets and cannot afford many of these items are also at risk of feeling guilty and inadequate.

As educators in early childhood development, we have come to appreciate the scientific knowledge available to help guide our interactions with children. But the preceding examples should make us humble. Every few years, as research and theories develop, new ideas emerge on the subject of what is best for children. Some of the practices that seemed unquestionably right are re-examined and reconsidered in light of new knowledge.

"Expert advice," whether it be in the form of books, magazine articles, websites, or parenting classes, can sometimes undermine a mother's confidence and make her feel that she can never learn how to do things right. Expert advice can be highly important and helpful, of course. Professionals in a variety of fields, including medicine, psychology, social work, and education, have provided parents with an abundance of knowledge concerning health and development matters. Today, however, many authorities on parent education are acknowledging the importance of parents' own expertise, and of working with them in a way that is collaborative and empowering. Scholars on the topic of motherhood emphasize the continued need for empowering mothers (O'Reilly, 2006). This is especially important in a culturally diverse society where there are many different ways of interacting with children, and no one "right" way. We hope that the understanding gained from reading this book will help early childhood educators find ways to share this knowledge with parents in a manner that is respectful and empowering.

Fathers

The roles of and expectations for fathers have been changing drastically in our society (Harrington et al., 2010). Many of today's fathers are moving closer to the current ideal of women and men being equal partners in child-rearing (Wylie, 2000). However, the move from the traditional image of the father as provider and disciplinarian to the new image as equal partner in child-rearing has by no means been a smooth one. This changing role of fathers evokes strong emotions, as summarized by Dubeau (2002) in the following box.

Examine Your Attitudes

Examine Your Attitudes

Examine your attitudes by reflecting on how many of the following statements you could see yourself saying or agreeing with:

"Given the current economic situation, wanting to offer more services to fathers means we'll have to cut services we offer to mothers" (*a social service professional*).

"It's true that fathers play an important role and now, whenever I phone (a student's) home to discuss a problem, I'm careful not to ask to speak to the mother. But often it is the father himself who says, 'Just a minute, I'll put my wife on the phone'" (*a school psychologist*).

"I did everything around the house. Now that we're divorced, I'm told he does the wash, the cooking, and when he has the children, he reads them their bedtime story, gives them their baths, etc. Why didn't he do that when we were together? It isn't because I didn't ask him to, believe me" (*a divorced mother*).

"I'd like to do my share of the work, really. But according to her, it was never done right. It wasn't just a case of doing things—they had to be done as she liked. In the end, I gave up" (*the father of a four-year-old boy*).

"People keep saying that nowadays fathers are more involved than the fathers of the generation before. OK, but can we maybe agree that mothers often still do most of the work when it comes to the child's daily care and education?" (*a female university researcher*).

Source: Dubeau, D. Portraits of Fathers. Contemporary Family Trends, The Vanier Institute of Family, 2002.

Until just over a decade ago, most of the research about the effects of fathers on the development of children focused on the father's absence rather than his presence (Roer-Strier et al., 2005). That is, psychologists looked for (and found) negative effects on those children whose fathers were not a part of their lives. Today, these ideas are mirrored by media reports that link fatherless homes to crime, gangs, and drugs. Keep in mind that early studies of fathers' interactions with children were based on assumptions of parent–child interactions that were derived from the literature on mothers. Only recently have we learned that we need to understand fathers not as they compare with mothers but possibly as an entirely different phenomenon that is still relatively unstudied.

Historians have noted that before the Industrial Revolution, fathers played an important role in their children's lives (Couchman, 1994). Although mothers fed and cared for their infants and toddlers, fathers assumed responsibility for their moral education while the children were still quite young. Children (particularly sons) would work alongside their fathers in childhood and adolescence to learn their means of livelihood. As industrialization drew men out of the home and into the marketplace, father involvement with and influence on their children declined. While many men remained the disciplinarians, the hours spent away from the family resulted in emotional distance, and child-rearing became the almost exclusive domain of women.

With the rapid social changes that have occurred in the past three decades, the role of father as the "provider" for children has changed. Perhaps the most noticeable change is the number of fathers who don't live with their children. The concept of fathering is all the more complex in light of the statistics on divorce and remarriage. While most men begin their parenting career with their own biological child, today it is not unusual for some men to begin fathering as a stepfather. In his lifetime, a man might be the father of children who no longer live with him while being a stepfather to his new wife's children. Then, with his new wife, he might once again become a new father (Dubeau, 2002). A teacher from the ProsPère community program in Quebec, which promotes father involvement, gave a good example of the complexity of studying fathers. When she asked children about activities with fathers, she was surprised by their responses: "What father exactly? My real father or my new father?" and "I don't have a father." As well, the teacher noted one mother's response to her son's drawing of his father playing hockey with him: "He's never played hockey—he never sees him" (Dubeau, 2002, p. 6).

While there is a high number of fathers who do not live with their children, there has also been a significant increase in the percentage of fathers who are the primary caregivers of their children (Statistics Canada, 2007). For example, there has been a 57.5% increase in single-father single-parent households since 1981 (Statistics Canada, 2007). In addition, a Statistics Canada (2006) study found that 79.5% of adult men spent time caring for children aged 15 and below, compared with 86% of women. This suggests that the gap in how much caregiving men and women participate in is lessening.

Expectations of men have changed in recent years. Their participation in housework and child-rearing has increased significantly (Lamb, 2010; Marshall, 2006), as has the number of stay-at-home fathers. The proportion of fathers taking time off and receiving paid parental leave benefits has increased sharply, from 3% in 2000 to 20% in 2006 (Statistics Canada, 2006), due at least partly to changes in the Government of Canada's Parental Benefit Leave program, which allows for fathers to take optional time off when their child is born. In 2005 Quebec instituted the Quebec Parental Insurance Plan, which includes a five-week individual, nontransferable paternity leave. After instituting this program, fathers taking paid leave jumped from 32% in 2005 to 56% in 2006 (Statistics Canada, 2006). This highlights the importance of government policies that support fathers.

Many fathers are involved in child-rearing right from the beginning; they accompany their partners to childbirth preparation classes and participate in the birth experience. Psychologists have observed this trend of newly involved fathers, and have concluded that men indeed can, and do, engage in many of the activities of child-rearing with as much success as women. They can, for instance, soothe babies as capably as mothers can, and they react to babies' signals as appropriately as mothers do. Yet, psychological studies of father–child interaction point out that the way in which many fathers respond to and interact with their children is different from that of mothers. Play with fathers seems more intense and "rough and tumble" than mother-child play (Flanders et al., 2009). Fathers tend to read and play less quietly with their tots than mothers do; as well, fathers are less likely to sing and talk to their children quietly, or to play at routine care times such as during diapering and bathing. Fathers tend to interact verbally with their children less than mothers do. More recent writings have pointed out that conclusions drawn from such studies need to emphasize that these differences do not indicate parenting that is better or worse—just different.

Researchers have begun to study fatherhood independently of motherhood, as opposed to comparing fathers and mothers (Blewett & Lamb, 2008; Lamb, 2010; Waller, 2009). Pruett and Pruett (2011) have devoted a chapter to discussing the role of fathers—not as a deficiency but as representing important differences in the development of children. Fathers bring different perspectives and dimensions to the lives of children that are just as important as what mothers bring. Differences in holding, responding, playing, and communication are discussed (Pruett & Pruett, 2011). The point is made that fathers are not "substitute mothers" (p. 28) but rather play a valuable role in the development of the whole child.

Since there are no "recipes" for good fathering, families have to evolve their own patterns and norms. In some senses, society has had a hand in influencing the image of the good father, especially through the portraits conveyed by television, newspaper and magazine articles, and advertising. Some fathers complain that the image of a good dad really means that dad is a good "mom."

Many fathers claim that caring for their children is the most rewarding and enriching experience of their lives. Relating to their children on a deeply emotional level "liberates" men from the restraining stereotype of males. Indeed, many men who derive great pleasure from the cuddles, kisses, and diaper changing have no memories of physical contact with their own fathers other than a handshake.

Studies have attempted to highlight the factors that seem to be related with the amount and kind of involvement fathers have with their children. Personal traits, family traits, the father's work environment, and the kinds of services and supports available to fathers in the community all play a role. After reviewing these studies, Dubeau (2002) reminds us that we may be focusing too much on the quantitative aspect of father involvement. Do we know for sure that more is better? And, more importantly, we may conclude that professionals may not yet be certain what type of father involvement should be promoted—as most of the knowledge we have accumulated on parenting is derived from studies of mothers.

Supporting Fathers

In spite of the increasing number of manuals, advice books, and television shows about fathering, many men still feel that they are relatively unsupported. Some complain of "the mothering double standard"—although women complain that men do not participate enough in child-rearing, they themselves are hesitant to "let go" and allow men to take part. This is referred to as "gate-keeping" (Schoppe-Sullivan et al., 2008). Mothers learn at an early age that child-rearing is their domain, and feel obligated to train their partners to do it the "right" way. While we must be careful not to generalize and blame mothers for the lack of father involvement, this may be a factor in some families. In cases where this is so, mothers can be encouraged to give fathers more opportunities alone with the children, to acknowledge the differences in parenting styles, and to build fathers' confidence by repressing the urge to "check up on" or "correct" them.

Outside the immediate family, fathers can be supported by more public acknowledgment of their child-rearing role, and this could be reflected in paternal-leave policies and informal support at the workplace. Many fathers have admitted that they are ashamed to tell anyone that they're missing work for reasons associated with their children. There is a need to ensure that current legislation and official documents reflect the changing nature of fathers' involvement in child-rearing (Lamb, 2010; Lero et al., 2006).

Scenario

White Lies

"When my two children were young, I helped out quite a bit. I would chauffeur them to their ballet lessons, take them to the doctor, dentist, and orthodontist, and often stay home with them when they were sick. Looking back on that time now, I realize how many times I told 'white lies' to my boss and my coworker. Any excuse for absence was better than actually admitting that I was busy with my kids."

Early childhood educators can help by ensuring that they are addressing fathers as well as mothers in their efforts to work with parents. In addition, it might be appropriate to offer fathers special programs, where they will have the opportunity to mix with and learn from other fathers (Palm & Fagan, 2008).

Society's attitudes toward fathering are both inconsistent and changing (Lewis & Lamb, 2010). We all have different ideas concerning the role (real and ideal) of fathers, and we must not let our personal views interfere with our acceptance of the diverse nature of fathering styles that we come in contact with. Our own acceptance of the diversity in fathering styles and roles may help family members be more accepting of each other, if that is appropriate, or support each other as they try to alter their roles and lifestyles. More than 15 years ago, the Vanier Institute of the Family published a document with recommendations for supporting father involvement in families (Glossop & Theilheimeir, 1994). In 2009, the Public Health Agency of Canada published "The Father Toolkit" (see the Recommended Websites at the end of the chapter). This toolkit builds on many of the ideas the Vanier Institute described in the 1990s and may serve as a useful reference for encouraging father involvement. These ideas include the need for supportive policies, both in the workplace and in government. The need for education and promotion of active fathering is also emphasized. Interestingly, the fathering toolkit includes the need to value "women's work," since, as long as caring and caregiving are undervalued, it will be harder for men to engage in these activities.

Siblings

Almost 80% of Canadians have at least one sibling, so it is an important type of family relationship and one that outlasts the parent–child relationship (Ambert, 2006). Furthermore, recent research suggests that sibling relationships may have as much, or more, influence on the development of children than the parent–child relationship (Kluger, 2006; Tucker & Updegraff, 2009). During childhood, it is likely that siblings spend more time together than with their parents or with friends. Although conflicts are inevitable among siblings, sometimes the relationship is characterized by warmth, affection, and mutual support, while in other families jealousy and rivalry extend into the adult years.

Parents can play a vital role in fostering healthy sibling relationships; sometimes, however, we tend to simplistically blame the parents when siblings do not get along. In reality, many factors will affect how siblings relate to one another. The gender of the siblings, the spacing between them, the temperament and personalities of both parents and children, and external factors all come into play. Although sibling relations have been increasingly studied in recent years (Kowal et al., 2006; Lawson & Mace, 2010; (Tucker & Updegraff, 2009), there is still much that needs to be learned.

Older siblings have been shown to be role models, both negatively and positively (Ambert, 2006). This is becoming an important area of study as researchers (Craine et al., 2009) provide more examples of sibling effects on delinquent behaviour. But siblings can also have a positive effect on each other (Kramer & Conger, 2009).

How do the structure and dynamics of the family affect sibling relationships? Researchers (Dunn et al., 2005; Strow & Strow, 2008) studied differences in sibling relationships in different family types (nonstep, stepfather, stepmother, and single mother) as well as sibling type (full and half siblings). Dunn et al. (2005) and Deater-Deckard et al. (2002) suggest that negative relationships between siblings, such as more conflict and aggression, were more prevalent in single-mother homes. Strow and Strow (2008) found that children in families with half-siblings (i.e., biological children and stepchildren living together) had more behavioural problems and scored worse on reading achievement lists.

Not surprisingly, family dynamics have been shown to impact sibling relationships (Updegraff et al., 2005). When older and younger siblings experienced more warmth and involvement from parents, aggression among siblings was decreased, compared with conditions in which less warmth and involvement were provided. Less positive relationship experiences with mothers and fathers contribute to aggression between siblings. Conversely, the quality of sibling relationships can affect the outcome of family risk factors (Conger et al., 2009; East & Siek, 2005).

Parents' Role in Facilitating Healthy Sibling Relations

Unfortunately, there are no simple formulas to help parents foster good relations among siblings, despite the number of advice books available on the topic. Certainly, it is thought important to help older siblings adjust to the birth of a new baby in the family by ensuring that they feel important (e.g., by giving them tasks, or preparing a snack for the older child to eat when the mother is breastfeeding the baby). While these strategies can be significant, they are only a small factor in ongoing sibling relations.

Parents sometimes feel that they must treat all their children in the same way, but this is probably impossible to do when the children have sharply different personalities. One sibling, for example, might need a lot of support and coaching in school work, while another manages independently. Yet the latter may feel jealous of the attention received by the former. These problems are often exacerbated when one of the siblings has special needs.

Rather than attempting to treat each child in the same way, it might be more helpful to focus on family communication. Children who grow up in families in which they feel free to discuss their emotions, including the common feeling of being treated unfairly, may be less likely to suffer from the jealousy and rivalry that plague the relations of so many brothers and sisters. Although we still have much to learn about the ways brothers and sisters influence each other's lives, it is clear that the impact of growing up in a family with other children is very potent indeed, and that the family's sibling subsystem can be one of the few constants in a rapidly changing society.

Handling Sibling Rivalry

1. Keep in mind that most siblings fight a good deal of the time. It is quite normal behaviour.
2. Make a rule that they cannot call each other names or hurt each other physically. If you sense that they are about to do so, separate them.

3. Do not become their judge and jury; help them work it out. Try to keep in mind all the times that they play together nicely.

4. Try not to pay too much attention to fighting siblings, since this may result in even more fighting.

5. As a parent, perhaps your best and surest recipe for peace of mind is to expect considerable conflict between your children, appreciate its normalcy, and do what you can to manage it. But keep in mind that fighting and squabbling are a way of life for many children. They enjoy it. Even the very young child tends to have a strong sense of self-preservation. Most could avoid a major part of their fighting if they wanted to.

The advice to parents in this box reflects norms and expectations regarding conflict, sibling relations, and parent–child relations. Early childhood educators need to view this advice with caution and sensitivity. For example, does the advice take cultural differences into consideration? Early childhood educators are aware of the vital role played by adults in modelling desired behaviour for children and in mediating conflict situations when children don't have the skills required to do this on their own. The preceding suggestions do not reflect this aspect of adult–child relations. Finally, it is important to ask whether conflict and squabbling are normal or whether this idea is peculiar to our culture. Some parents may want to raise their children with values that encourage mutual respect, sharing, and compromise, and conflict may be considered "normal" only because it is deemed so by the predominant culture.

Birth Order, Family Size, and the "Only Child Syndrome"

It has often been said that the order in which children are born has a strong influence on their development. This belief is so strong among both psychologists and lay people that one often hears children being described as a "typical first-born" or of having a "middle-child syndrome." The first-born child is often thought of as a perfectionist and an ambitious high achiever (Booth & Kee, 2009). Since first-born children have no siblings acting as models, they have to look up to and learn from their parents. Parents have more time for their first child, so their influence on them is thought to be stronger than on subsequent children. The middle children are thought to be secretive and rebellious but more social than the first-born. They are considered to be more socially competent with peers than first-born children, and their success with peers is somehow connected to their need to make up for the lack of parental attention through companionship with other children. The last-born is often thought to be a charmer. By the time the third child is born, parents are thought to have relaxed their expectations, and to prefer to pamper rather than discipline (Harrigan, 1992).

The problem with birth-order theory is that children's development is influenced by so many different factors: gender, age spacing, peer and school experiences, accidents, illnesses, random events, and economic factors (Booth & Kee, 2009). The research on birth order is not at all conclusive and is sometimes contradictory. While some studies do show that first-borns seem to have higher IQs and achieve more in school and in careers (Booth & Kee, 2009; Haan, 2009), these statistical differences are quite small. Studies have shown that differences commonly attributed to birth order have more to do with the parents having less time for caregiving and decreased financial resources (due to the increase in family size) than personality or genetic differences (Gugl & Welling, 2010). In addition, there is a greater recognition that child temperament can explain differences in child development (Popkin, 2007; Turecki, 2000).

Today, researchers are giving more emphasis to children's relationships in different family contexts than to children's birth order (Ambert, 2006).

On a similar note, a much-studied topic in child development is the effect of family size on children. Studies have shown that children from large families tend to be less successful in school and careers than children from smaller families, which is usually attributed to the "dilution of parental resources" (Ambert, 2006; Gugl & Welling, 2010). As mentioned earlier, with each additional child, parents have less time and financial resources.

However, these studies failed to look at the possible benefits of growing up in large families. Zajonc and Mullally (1997) suggest that children from large families are more affectionate, good leaders, and less prone to depression, and may be less individualistic and more cooperative. Siblings act as role models and encourage and support each other (Åslund & Grönqvist, 2010).

On the other hand, the only child has earned a negative reputation in our folklore, and is often considered to be spoiled and inconsiderate, lacking in self-control, more dependent on parents, and more self-centred than are children with siblings. However, the research seems to indicate that, although only children may be like first-borns in IQ and achievement, in reality the negative traits mentioned are not necessarily associated with being an only child.

One small study does suggest that only children are less autonomous than first-born children. The authors suggest that this may be because the process of separating from parents involves aggression toward them. When there are no sibling relationships for "backup," children may fear this individuation process (Byrd et al., 1995). Another study contradicts this, however, by concluding that only children tend to be more autonomous than children who have siblings (Mellor, 1995). Since family size is decreasing and more parents are having only one child, researchers will have ample opportunity to devote more study to the nature of parent–child relationships in single-child families.

Perspectives

Jan is a 29-year-old college student and the mother of a 2-year-old daughter. She comes from St. Lucia, which she left at the age of 8. Jan's mother moved from St. Lucia to Toronto in 1968 with the hope of getting settled in Canada and then sending for her two daughters so that they could have a better life and education in their new home. From the age of 2 until the age of 8, Jan lived with her grandmother and sister in St. Lucia.

"My grandmother was very strict. We were brought up with the expectation of proper behaviour at all times, and especially that we would show respect to our elders. Because my sister was four years older than me, I was expected to respect her as well and do what she said. My older sister, as in many West Indian families, was expected to look after me when Gramma was busy. And I was expected to do as my sister said. Gramma was from the old school, a devout Catholic who stressed the importance of self-discipline and study.

"I don't remember my grandmother expressing affection readily. She seemed more concerned about raising us as proper young ladies. When I was 8, we moved to Canada to join my mother. The pattern of interaction between me and my sister stayed the same throughout my childhood. My mother was a single working mother who relied on my sister's help in raising me and maintaining the household. Even today, all these years later, when I talk about my parents I am really referring to my sister and my mother. Having lived in

Grandparents

For many people, the word *grandparent* evokes idyllic pictures of a little old lady with grey hair fixed in a bun and an apron, retrieving a baking tin full of cookies from the oven while her kindly husband works in the garden. For others, it evokes a picture of frail and elderly people dependent on a young family for assistance and support. The fact is, though, that fairy tale images rarely reflect the realities of our society, and these are no exception. There are many different meanings associated with grandparenting, and grandparents can take on many roles (Thiel & Whelan, 2006). Increased life expectancy, women's increased participation in the labour force, and the fact that Canadians are working longer mean that many grandparents fulfill work-related and other family roles (Kemp, 2003). Nevertheless, stereotyping of grandparents is still quite prevalent (Helmes, 2009).

In Canada today, 76% of adults over the age of 65 are grandparents, and the average grandparent has 4.7 grandchildren (Ambert, 2006; Rosenthal & Gladstone, 2007). Between 1991 and 2001, the number of Canadian children under 18 years of age who were living with grandparents without a parent at home increased by 20% (Fuller-Thomson, 2005). In 2006, 3.8% of all children aged 14 and under were living with their grandparents without a parent at home (Statistics Canada, 2009). Grandparents can be as young as in their thirties, or as elderly as in their nineties—and they can be totally committed to raising their grandchildren, or have totally separate lives. As older people's health and life expectancy have increased, grandparents are gradually becoming recognized as a vital force in the family system, a force that warrants much more consideration than it has received to date.

In one early childhood class about families, students were asked to identify the most constant relationship in their life. Many students named their grandparents, and talked about their appreciation of the love and support their parents' parents showed them, often in much more positive terms than they used when discussing their own parents.

Cheriline, a First Nations social work student, had the following to say about her grandmother:

Scenario

The Contribution of Elders

"On my reserve the grandmothers raise the children. I never would have been able to look after my kids without my mother's help. She didn't only look after my children, she brought up her sister's children, too. But, you know, life on the reserve is changing as well. Some of our elders are beginning to realize that they want their freedom too. Our traditions are changing, just like the rest of the world."

In the United States, researchers have highlighted the fact that during times of tremendous familial difficulties, grandmothers who themselves have low income, and may have impaired physical health, are assuming responsibility for their grandchildren (Bachman & Chase-Lansdale, 2005). In some cases, taking on the care of grandchildren is related to increased stress and depression (Edwards, 2003), health problems, and fatigue (Rosenthal & Gladstone, 2007), while in others it is associated with heightened well-being (Szinovacz & Davey, 2006). For example, some grandparents reported high satisfaction from the role related to the joys of children, the tasks of child-rearing, participating in the grandchildren's activities, and watching the child's accomplishments (Dunne & Kettler, 2008). Many grandparents show amazing strength and resilience as they overcome stressors and difficulties to provide loving and committed care to their grandchildren.

The grandparent's role, like all family roles, is affected by cultural norms and expectations. Some research from the United States indicates that grandparents in African-American, Asian-American, Italian-American, and Latino families are more involved with their grandchildren than are grandparents in other groups.

While culture seems to play an important role in determining the role of grandparents, there is likely almost as much diversity within each ethnic group as there is across ethnic groups. This is even apparent within families, as a Jewish student related.

Scenario

Differences Within Families

"My grandmother on my father's side came to Canada from Poland. She spoke Yiddish, was the best cook in the entire world, and fit practically all the stereo typed notions of the typical Jewish grandmother, or 'Bubby.' I loved going to her house for Sabbath and holiday meals; she and my grandfather kept Jewish tradition alive in my family. My mother's mother was a professional woman. She hardly ever cooked, and in her free time she played bridge, golfed, and read. She would take us out for dinner and even sometimes on trips. But there was nothing 'traditional' about this grandmother—she was a very modern woman."

Grandparents can affect the family system in a number of positive ways. And many factors will influence the relationship between grandparents and grandchildren: geography, personalities, and the nature of the relationship between the parents and the grandparents. Although grandparents can be heroes to their grandchildren, it is not uncommon for conflicts to arise between parents and grandparents. These conflicts may sometimes be related to the fact that child-rearing norms have changed considerably over the years, and what is now accepted as positive parenting may seem like "spoiling" to grandparents. On the other hand, grandparents often glean so much enjoyment from being with their grandchildren without having to worry about discipline that parents claim they're spoiling the children. Often, when grandparents are involved in the rearing of their grandchildren, roles and family boundaries may be confused. This might be especially problematic in single-parent families where the grandmother lives with her daughter and grandchildren, and where the mother has to balance the responsibilities of being a daughter and a mother at the same time.

It is clear that grandparents play a vital role in the lives of many families, and for many this is a positive experience. Early childhood educators may find that grandparents who play a key role in the lives and development of their grandchildren can benefit from advice and support. Grandparents may require information about child-rearing because much has changed since they were parents. They may need information about their right of access to their grandchildren, which is now an important issue (Henderson, 2005). As well, grandparents may need some encouragement and support in working out old conflicts with their own children so that they will be welcome to share in the joys and challenges of raising their children's children. Successful programs, as well as policies, have demonstrated that with appropriate support grandchildren fared better as educators became more informed about issues facing grandparents (Cox, 2010).

Conclusion

In this chapter we have provided a brief overview of some of the key family roles. North American society encompasses a considerable degree of diversity in the way mothers, fathers, siblings, and grandparents perform their roles. Some of this diversity is related to culture and ethnicity. Social, economic, and geographic factors also influence the way in which family members relate to each other, and their expectations of each other. Understanding and appreciating this diversity will help early childhood educators in their work with families. While other extended family members, such as aunts, uncles, and cousins, play a pivotal role in family life in many cultures, there is little research that can inform us of the impact of these roles on children. However, early childhood educators need to keep this in mind, and be open to invite key extended family members to activities where possible, and include this awareness in the day to day interactions with the children and parents.

Chapter Summary

- Understanding the roles of key players within the child's family system broadens an understanding and ability to provide a supportive environment.
- Attitudes toward mothers have historically been complex and have contributed to feelings of guilt. Expert advice can be confusing and can also inadvertently add to stress and guilt. One of the biggest challenges facing mothers today is the "time crunch."
- Canadian fathers are becoming more actively involved in domestic life and child-rearing.
- The influence of siblings on a child's development is profound and can affect social behaviour in both positive and negative ways.
- An increasing number of grandparents are caring for children. The role of grandparents is influenced by cultural norms and expectations, as well as by economic circumstances.

Recommended Websites

Voices of Canadians: Seeking Work–Life Balance document:
http://compassionfatigue.dreamhosters.com/wp-content/uploads/2012/06/voices-of-canadians.pdf

The University of Guelph's Centre for Families, Work and Well-Being provides information on a variety of work and family issues:
www.worklifecanada.ca

National Resource Center for Community-Based Child Abuse Prevention:
http://friendsnrc.org/about-us

The Father Toolkit, Public Health Agency of Canada:
www.phac-aspc.gc.ca/hp-ps/dca-dea/prog-ini/funding-financement/npf-fpn/father-papa/index-eng.php

Canadian Father Involvement Initiative:
www.cfii.ca

Fatherhood Institute:
www.fatherhoodinstitute.org/index.php?id=0&fID=4

Canadian Council of Social Development:
www.ccsd.ca

Public Health Agency of Canada:
www.publichealth.gc.ca

Child and Family Canada:
www.cfc-efc.ca

Harvard Family Research Project:
www.hfrp.org/hfrp/search?q=fathers&x=0&y=0

York University Centre for Research on Mothering:
www.yorku.ca/crm

Vanier Institute of the Family:
www.vifamily.ca/library/publications

Videos/Films

A Balancing Act: Work and Family in the 90s. 1992. 23 min. National Film Board of Canada. This film is old, but still relevant.

My Brand New Life: Only Child/Big Family. 2004. 23 min. National Film Board of Canada.

Life Without Father. 1995. 29 min. PBS.

Exercises

1. Think of some "expert advice" you have been given, or ask a new mother about any advice she has been given from professional sources. Discuss whether you (or the mother) took the advice, whether or not it was helpful, and how you or the mother would change the advice based on your/her experience.

2. Interview some mothers and fathers and ask them about the challenges and problems they face as parents raising children in today's society.

3. Compare the problems, joys, and challenges of parenting today with parenting a generation ago.

4. Discuss what you think you'll be like as a grandparent, and how similar or different this will be from your grandparents.

Family
Transitions

chapter 3

Objectives

- **To examine the stages of family development.**

- **To understand the stages of parenthood.**

- **To review the stages of psychosocial development.**

- **To examine the ways in which the development of individuals, parents, and the family interact.**

- **To understand the stressors and joys associated with transitions.**

- **To highlight the role of the early childhood educator in supporting families through transitions.**

A young teacher recounted her daughter's first morning at school. "Tammy and I were so excited about her first day. I was enthusiastic about the new possibilities for her learning, and for me, it represented a new stage in our relationship and in my parenting abilities. I could now help her to explore, to learn, and to interpret the new parts of her world just waiting to be discovered. We arrived to find many other parents and children, all suitably attired for their first day. Some children looked excited, others looked apprehensive, and some looked scared. After the introductions were complete and the children made their way to their new classrooms and new teachers, all the parents left. I was amazed at the number of parents outside in tears because the first day of school signified that their 'babies' had grown up and didn't need them any more. They certainly weren't feeling the enthusiasm and excitement that my daughter and I had felt on that morning."

Individuals, couples, and the family unit experience many changes in their lives and their relationships. Many of these transitions are developmental; that is, they are considered natural and somewhat predictable. Changes in marital relationships, changes in family composition such as the birth of a baby or the departure of a grown child, changes in children as they develop, and the concomitant changes in parenting and in the family itself are all inevitable over time (Couchenour & Chrisman, 2011).

Some transitions result in a change of roles. For example, the roles of husband and wife are modified when they become parents. This may, in turn, cause changes in interactional patterns. Many new parents will claim that there is little time to interact at all after the baby, and that the nature of their interactions changes dramatically. As the preceding scenario indicates, some parents may view these transitions as interesting, challenging, and exciting, while others may find them stressful. In fact, this scenario is a good illustration of how the same event may affect different people in completely different ways.

Much of this book looks at transitions that occur in families. A divorce, sudden death, escape from an abusive situation, relocation, or blending of families can all be seen as transitions (McDaniel, 2010; McDaniel & Tepperman, 2007). This chapter examines transitions that are associated not with exceptional circumstances but rather with normal development. We will discuss family life cycles, parent development, and child development separately, and then consider how the interactions among these transitions uniquely influence each family.

Family Development

Early childhood educators have a broad understanding of children's stages of development. Families change and grow over time, just as each individual member changes and grows. Some of these changes are predictable. Family life will change drastically, for instance, with the arrival of a new baby, and it will change again when children grow up and leave home. Other transitions are more subtle and are recognized only in retrospect or upon reflection.

The following scenario illustrates quite normal developmental changes in the child, along with the required adaptation in parenting abilities and the resulting changes in the marital subsystem and in the entire family unit.

Scenario

It's Hard to Keep Up

The mother of a teenage boy was having some difficulties with his behaviour. There was a growing feeling of tension in the family, and the parents noticed that they were quarrelling much more often, both with each other and with their son. As a result, they decided to attend a series of parenting seminars. After listening to hours of advice and reading volumes of material, the mother commented that parenting was hard work. "We just got the knack of being parents to a new baby and he turned into a toddler. By the time we figured out what to do with him at that stage, he turned into a sweet, lovable 3-year-old. Things changed again when he started having playmates and going to school, and my husband and I actually managed to remember that we had a relationship. It seems as if we just figure out what it is we should be doing and he changes again."

The concept of family life cycles, or stages of family development, gained recognition in the 1970s. Sociologists and psychologists began to study how families came together, developed, and adapted over time in relation to the changes occurring in their lives (e.g., marriage, children). The theories emphasized typical phases or stages, along with tasks and reactions common to each. Some parents, for example, remember their child's infancy as a time of joy and happiness, whereas others remember anxiety, exhaustion, and apprehension. For some parents the "empty nest" years are a time of loneliness, whereas other parents thrive on their newfound independence and opportunities for self-discovery.

Our theoretical understanding of family development has been primarily based on information from "traditional" families. As well, theorists have tended to give little consideration to cultural, ethnic, or religious influences. More recently, researchers have attempted to consider family development in different family structures, such as blended families and families undergoing a divorce (Carter & McGoldrick, 2005). Professionals have relied heavily on family development theories to aid their understanding of families and guide their practice. They have divided the "typical" family life cycle into seven stages:

- Beginnings (coming together as a couple)
- The arrival of children
- The family with young children
- The family with school-age children
- The family with adolescent children
- The family with older children (launching period)
- The family in later life

We will now consider each of these family life cycle stages in turn.

Beginnings

The description of family life cycles typically begins with courtship and the development of a relationship that subsequently leads to marriage (McGoldrick et al., 2010). Involvement with the new person and developing the relationship become top priorities in both partners' lives. This period is a time of exploration, discovery, excitement, and happiness. Sometimes, adjustments may have to be made to include the new spouse in family and friendships that already exist (McGoldrick et al., 2010). This integration can happen very easily if the new person is welcomed into the family and friendship circles, but in other cases, the introductions may be challenging and stressful. Another potential source of stress may be the difficulty of defining boundaries between the family of origin and the new family.

The Arrival of Children

For many people, the birth of the first child signifies the true beginning of the family (Shimoni et al., 2003). Becoming parents is considered one of the most significant transitions in the family life cycle (Hull & Mather, 2006). This social transition involves reorganization in many areas of the new parents' lives and creates both stresses and rewards (Ateah et al., 2009). Parents generally agree that children add affection, improve family ties, and give parents a sense of accomplishment (Ateah et al., 2009). Stress may stem from the multiple roles now required (e.g., wife and mother), from the demands of caring for a new baby, and from the financial burdens of parenthood (Ateah et al., 2009).

In addition to the roles of partners, the roles of mother and father must be negotiated and defined. This process may require some adjustments, and again relationships outside the new family may need to be changed. For example, when couples are part of a social circle that does not include children, they may lose some of their old friends and develop new friends with a common interest—children. New parents may seek more contact with family members as a means of support that may not have been desired previously.

The stage of becoming new parents requires change and adaptation in all aspects of life—in finances, in social lives, in sex lives, and in routines such as sleeping and eating (Bee et al., 2006). Sometimes there is a decline in marital satisfaction during the period when all these factors are changing. For example, joint activities no longer consist of dining out or going to the theatre; instead they are restricted to the home and to daily chores like cleaning and laundry. All leisure time is centred around the baby. Couples are making two adjustments—to the new baby and, once again, to each other (Brooks, 2010).

Parents are often physically exhausted and have less time for each other—for conversations, for sex, for simple affection, or even for doing things together. The following scenario portrays the stress felt by one mother as she experienced feelings of inadequacy with both her baby and her husband.

Scenario

The Most Stressful Period

An elementary school teacher finally became a mother after many years of trying to get pregnant. Years later, when asked to share her memories of being a new mother, she said, "I always considered myself an easygoing, competent person, but then this baby came along and shattered my image of myself. My baby cried all the time unless I held her. Some days I was lucky to get showered and dressed before my husband got home. Then he would look at me as if to say, 'Is that all you did today?' Our relationship seemed different because I don't think he liked this new woman who nagged and watched him all the time to make sure he got it right. All my friends remember their babies with such joy, but it really was the most stressful and most unhappy period in my life."

The Family with Young Children

During this stage of family life, the relationship between the couple often continues to change. In "traditional" families, the mother becomes preoccupied with the needs of the children and home, while the father becomes increasingly absorbed in work or in meeting his family's economic needs. Tension between the couple can result from misunderstanding each other's roles. For example, the mother might interpret her husband's preoccupation with work as lack of interest in the family, while the father may perceive the mother's total involvement with the children as lack of interest in his work and as undervaluing his contribution to the family. There is often little time for the couple to relate to each other or to focus on matters other than the children. This stage of development, when children are little, is a stressful and demanding period of time.

This stage is commonly referred to as the "pressure cooker" phase (Couchenour & Chrisman, 2011, p. 12), where families balance child care, household duties, financial pressures, and, more often, full-time employment. There are many factors that will influence how the new family adjusts to this phase. First, there is the division of labour in the family—the actual division of labour and the couple's perceptions of what the division of labour should be. If one partner feels that he or she has taken on a disproportionate amount of responsibility for the economic, household, or child-care work, the more likely he or she is to feel unsatisfied (Marshall, 2009). Research today is suggesting that in working families, fathers are taking a more active role in child-rearing (Daly, 2004; Harrington et al., 2010). Interestingly, the time mothers spend in child-rearing and household tasks has not declined (Statistics Canada, 2006).

Many of the stresses of child-rearing described in the past have been associated with families where the father is employed and the mother stays at home with the children. Today, the norm is families in which both parents work. Thus, many stressors are exacerbated by the "time crunch" phenomenon (Daly, 2000; Milkie et al., 2009) described in Chapter 2. The willingness of workplaces to support new parents and the availability and easy access to quality child care will influence parents' stress level as well (Lewis & Lamb, 2010). A high level of stress at work can leave parents feeling distant, inattentive, and emotionally unavailable to their children. In contrast, satisfying work has positive effects on the parent–child relationship and on children's developmental outcomes (Daly, 2004, 2006; Lewis & Lamb, 2010).

The Family with School-Age Children

The next stage of family development occurs when children grow old enough to attend school. In traditional families, some mothers may be pleased with this change since it leaves them more time for themselves. Full-time mothers may also feel less needed and will look to other means of gaining satisfaction, such as part-time work and school or volunteer activities. While this may enrich the mother's life, it sometimes leads to conflict with the father or is perceived by him as yet another way for the woman to distance herself from her marriage. At this stage, men have traditionally been very preoccupied with their career, trying to ensure that they can continue to meet their family's needs. This may be a time when some women choose to return

Tyler, Age 4.5

to work and refocus on their careers after being away from work while their children were at home. Child care becomes an issue for working parents when their children enter schools. Regular schools have shorter days and more holidays than child care has, and parents may find themselves juggling child-care needs even more.

The Family with Adolescent Children

The stage in which families have adolescent children is often described as a time when everyone seems to be very busy, with little opportunity to connect with each other. Teenagers are typically involved in their own lives and peer groups, fathers continue to work hard to establish themselves in their careers, and mothers have likely developed many interests outside the home or may be re-establishing themselves in their careers. This level of engagement outside the home can leave little time for communication. In addition, parents need to make adjustments in their relationship with their children to allow for their teenagers' newfound sense of independence (McGoldrick et al., 2010). Challenges facing families in this stage include shifting child–parent relationships to allow the child to move in and out of the family system, shifting the focus back to midlife marital and career issues, and beginning a shift toward concern for older generations in the extended family (Bateman, 2006). The stressors on families with adolescent children can be quite exacerbated in a blended family, where new step-parents are trying to develop bonds of closeness and intimacy at the same time as the adolescent wants freedom from the family. Many parents of adolescents are beginning to feel additional pressures at this time as their own parents are at an age where they may require more support and may be placing extra demands on them.

The Family with Older Children

The final two stages of the family life cycle involve families with older children. The first of these stages is the so-called launching period (McGoldrick et al., 2010), when children move on and the parents find themselves alone in their "empty nest." One of the most significant changes in modern society is the growing trend of much later launching. Adult children are leaving home at a much later age, although often returning home after they have left (Arnett, 2010; Arnett & Tanner, 2009; Daly, 2004). Thus, 57% of young men and women aged 20 to 24 were living with their parents in 2001, compared with only 41% in 1981. The rates were particularly high for Asian and Latin-American-born parents as compared with Canadian-born (Turcotte, 2008). The reasons for this are complex, but have to do with economics, changing expectations of young adolescents and young adults, and the breakup of partnerships in cohabiting and marriage relationships. Indeed, the period of adolescence has been extended by some researchers to the age of 30 (Arnett, 2010; Daly, 2004).

When the adult children are launched, the marital relationship can become a key focus. Older couples in this situation sometimes notice that without the day-to-day focus on the children, they have lost some of their compatibility. Generally, however, this time can be exciting and rejuvenating for the relationship. In addition, parents need to realign their relationships with their grown-up children, which may include additional relationships associated with grandchildren and in-laws if the children leave home and get married.

An interesting perspective about this life stage was shared by Kathy O'Connor, who works in a community college and has recently become a new grandmother. She was describing to her colleagues a rather difficult week she had experienced—helping her son and his wife, caring for her grandson, and making arrangements for looking after her father, who had recently taken ill—when someone in the office quipped about her being part of the sandwich generation. Kathy remarked, "I'm not a sandwich, I'm a club sandwich, caring for three generations and working full-time!"

The Family in Later Life

The last stage in the family life cycle is later life, when parents attempt to maintain relationships with their children and their children's new families. As well, parents are dealing with their own issues associated with getting older and all its concomitant changes, health issues, and the loss of significant roles.

Family Development in Nontraditional Families

If we look at the families around us today, it may seem that few of them fit exactly into the preceding description of family life stages. Couples who are not married have children, and many families now are headed by a single parent. Blended families may be a union of people at different stages of individual and family development. In addition, many more families today include women who, through choice or necessity, work while their children are young. As we have described, the challenges faced by a family in which both parents work usually differ considerably from those in a family where one parent stays home. Certainly, changing economic and social forces influence family development. Some middle-aged men are not coping with career ladders and job stress, if only because unemployment has deprived them of any career at all. Many families postpone child-bearing for many years so that their careers, finances, and personal relationships are solidified before children arrive. Children born to more mature parents tend to be advantaged in our society, while it has been noted that parenting later in life is associated with having only one child, thus precluding the possibility of sibling relationships (Daly, 2004).

When life doesn't unfold in the expected order or pattern, individual family members may experience stress and uncertainty.

Scenario

An Abbreviated Visit

Remeiko and her husband, Frank, were visiting friends with their 16-month-old daughter, Masami. Their friends, who didn't have children, had a house full of beautiful but fragile objects. It seemed as if every two minutes one of them would have to jump up and rescue a china figurine, cup, or saucer from the coffee table. To have even the shortest conversation without being constantly disrupted was impossible. After a very short visit, Remeiko apologized to her friend and the young family departed. On their way home, the exasperated parents burst into laughter as Frank remarked, "I'm glad we had 10 years of conversation before Masami was born, because I don't think we'll ever finish a conversation again."

Scenario

Empty Nest or Revolving Door?

A 45-year-old woman remarked that she had read a lot about the empty nest syndrome as her children got older. "I wondered what life would be like without my two teenage children at home. Was I ever surprised to find out that the

> empty nest has turned into a revolving door. My son is 26 years old and has never left home. He's unemployed and can't afford to move out. My daughter's marriage broke up, so she and my 3-year-old granddaughter now live with me. My nest isn't empty at all—it's bulging at the seams!"

While it is difficult to think of Canada's armed forces as "nontraditional," participation in the military can lead to a very nontraditional family life. Today women are being deployed, and fathers are left at home to assume total responsibility for child care and household tasks. Both mothers and fathers whose spouse is deployed may feel many of the same stresses as a single parent, with the additional worry that their loved one may be facing injury or death any day. One student who had undergone this experience also talked about the stresses faced when the deployed spouse returns home. At best, a lot of re-adjustment of roles is required, and often this is accompanied by various degrees of post-traumatic stress (Auld, 2010) suffered by the returning military person. Research has shown (News-Medical.net, 2009) that children from families with a deployed parent face a number of emotional and behavioural challenges that can influence their psychological social and academic adjustment. Clearly, we need to explore this in more depth and translate this understanding into support for these families.

Family Development Theory: A Multicultural Perspective

A final reservation about family life development theory is its relevance across different cultures. Cultural norms, beliefs, and traditions all have an impact on the kinds of challenges posed by transitions during the family life cycle, as well as on the adjustments made to those transitions. Yehudit, a mature early childhood student, made the following observations after a class discussion on family development:

Scenario

Not Like in the Book

"I was married at the age of 17, immediately upon completion of high school. The marriage was arranged; I had not met my husband before our engagement was formally announced. Birth control is not practised in my culture, since the primary purpose of marriage is procreation. I had five beautiful children by the time I was 25. We didn't spend years discovering each other or defining and negotiating roles, as they are dictated by our religious beliefs. We did not consider children an adjustment—they were a blessing. We have a happy family life but not like the one in the book."

The Importance of Understanding Family Life Development

Family development theories suggest to us that many of the problems faced by families as they enter and emerge from transitional periods are normal. Many families derive comfort from this realization. If family members are aware of the potential stressors associated with impending transitions, they can prepare for them. For example, couples expecting a baby may discuss how they will share the responsibility, or how they may try to reserve some time to share together alone. A mother who has stayed home to rear her children can begin to think about and plan for the changes that will occur when her children grow up. She may consider retraining for employment or furthering her education, for example.

Every family passes through life's transitions in its own unique way. A stressful transition for one family can be a joyous one for another. The age and developmental stages of each family member, their inner and outer resources, and economic and cultural factors all play a role in family development. Family members often learn about transitions from older family members or from friends, and sharing these experiences can be extremely helpful. The theoretical knowledge available about family development is an additional source of information that can be useful to families and to professionals who work with them. As we study family development theories, we need to bear in mind that their emphasis has been on the problems and challenges of each stage. Our strength-based perspective, by contrast, guides us to highlight the joys in each transition. Some cultures mark these transitions with elaborate ceremonies. For example, Bee et al. (2006) describe a Hispanic custom called the *cuarenta*, which is a period of 40 days following the birth of a child during which fathers are expected to take on typically feminine tasks, such as housework, and extended family members are expected to help out. This has been shown to ease the adjustment to parenthood. In Jewish culture, the transition to adolescence is celebrated by the bar or bat mitzvah, where the community acknowledges the young person's participation in the responsibilities of adulthood in matters relating to faith and community. A look across cultures will provide many more examples of rituals that mark family life stages.

Transitions in Parenting

Parenting, as we have discussed, also involves transition and changes in every aspect of life—money, sex, sleep, meals, social life, and finances. These changes may occur easily and be welcomed by parents or may cause stress and conflict. The adjustment to parenthood will vary from family to family, and will be influenced by family structure (a new blended family or a first-time family; single or couple parenting), and also by factors such as economic situation and culture. However, there are some fairly predictable stages that many parents go through as they experience parenthood. Ellen Galinsky, a prominent authority in early childhood education, formulated a model for describing the stages of parenting. The concepts described in her book, *The Six Stages of Parenthood* (1981), are still widely used today as a framework for understanding the growth and development of parents.

The Six Stages of Parenthood

The first stage is the **Image-Making Stage**, which occurs during pregnancy. This is the time when parents think and form images about their new baby, what they will be like as parents, how the baby is going to affect their lives, and the changes they will have to make.

The second stage, the **Nurturing Stage**, starts at birth and lasts until the baby is 18 months to 2 years—the age when "no" is your baby's most important word. At this stage, parents compare their ideas of birth, of their child, and their parenting experiences with reality.

The third stage is the **Authority Stage**. It starts at about the baby's second birthday and lasts until the child is 4 or 5. In this stage, parents have to decide how strict or permissive to be, what kind of rules they need and how to set them, and what to do when the rules are broken.

The **Interpretive Stage** begins about the time the child enters preschool or school and ends with the start of adolescence—about age 11 or 12. In this stage, parents are concerned about how realistic they have been as parents and how they are helping their child develop positive self-concepts. They may worry about how to answer their child's questions and what kind of values, knowledge, and skills they want their child to have.

The **Independent Stage** is similar to the Authority Stage but covers the child's teenage years. Parents have the same questions about rules, strictness, and permissiveness, but now need different answers. As their child grows to adulthood, parents also need to start forming a different kind of relationship with their child.

The sixth and last stage is the **Departure Stage**—the time when the child leaves home. This is a stage of evaluation and, often, loss for parents. Parents judge how well they have done and how their image of their child fits the reality. In addition, parents have to change their lives to let go of the child, to let their child become an adult.

Source: Reprinted with permission from University of Maine Cooperative Extension, Parenting: Growing with your child, bulletin #4170. Orono, ME: University of Maine Cooperative Extension, 2000.

The stages of parenthood just described are subject to the same reservations as those mentioned in the previous section. Social, economic, and cultural factors, as well as individual differences and the degree and kind of support available, all play a role in the way parenthood is experienced. This model of parent development focuses on the challenges inherent in parenthood and is a reminder that child-rearing entails parent development as well as child development. The transitions noted here may be anticipated and subtle, or they may cause tension for the family members involved. An awareness of the stages and an understanding of the changes that accompany these transitions will be helpful to professionals whose work involves supporting families.

Scenario

Change Is Difficult

"When my children were growing up, we believed that as parents the best gift we could give them was an education. To that end, we made few demands on them at home, as long as they devoted their time to study. They were responsible for cleaning their own rooms, and we had a rotation system for the dishes. After my daughter graduated from college and got a job, I noticed that I was feeling some resentment toward her. After a moment of reflection, I realized that we were both women who worked full-time, but I was the one who still felt obligated to run the household and prepare the meals. Changing old patterns is not easy, but we now have a more equitable arrangement. My daughter still doesn't cook, but she does take me out for dinner once a week."

Theories of Individual Development

Early childhood educators are well aware of young children's milestones across all areas of development. Through their ongoing interactions with the children in their care, they watch each child's development unfold in a unique manner. At the same time, they see children learn about themselves and the world around them and develop skills in a predictable sequence. This knowledge of child development helps them understand and support children. In this section, we will consider psychosocial development across the age span as described by Erik Erikson. Following this will be a discussion of attachment in the early years. These descriptions of psychosocial development and the development of attachment will help illuminate the interconnection between individual and family development. Knowing how children may perceive and respond to situations affecting them will assist early childhood educators in helping young children cope. This understanding will be fundamental to the following chapters, where we consider numerous issues facing families and how children may perceive them.

Erik Erikson (1963), the theorist best known for his study of psychosocial development, identified eight major stages in life and the tasks that require resolution in each stage. While Erikson's theory is not free of culture and gender bias (Trawick-Smith, 2010), it is one of the cornerstones of human development theory.

Infancy—Trust vs. Mistrust

According to Erikson, an infant's first developmental task is to acquire a sense of trust. This trust is the foundation upon which further emotional development builds. Children's sense of trust in the world is fostered when their needs are promptly responded to. Crying is babies' primary method of communicating, and if their attempts to communicate are ignored, either consistently or randomly, they may find it more difficult to learn to trust the people around them.

Scenario

Like Mother, Like Son

Brian and Belinda were new parents. Taryn was a contented baby and cried very little. When she did cry, Belinda would pick her up and check that everything was all right. Taryn usually stopped crying as soon as Belinda picked her up. One day, when the baby was fussier than usual, Brian remarked, "See, you've already spoiled her by picking her up all the time. My mother let us cry for short periods during the day to make sure that none of us were spoiled, and we should do the same."

This is one specific example that shows how children's task of developing a sense of trust can become a contentious issue. Some people believe that babies must learn to settle themselves and learn to put themselves to sleep. Others believe that children must be responded to in order to foster their sense of trust and security. Balancing these two ideas can be difficult.

Toddlerhood—Autonomy vs. Shame or Doubt

The second stage of psychosocial development is autonomy or independence. Autonomy is often referred to as the "no, no," "mine," and "me do" stage typical of toddlers, who generally want to do some things on their own. Anyone who has witnessed the temper tantrum of a toddler in a shopping mall should be able to recognize this stage. Toddlers have a strong drive to be independent but don't have the language or social skills required to manage the task completely. In addition, they are extremely reluctant to accept help. They often get frustrated and are, in turn, often frustrating for their parents. Sometimes parents misunderstand the behaviour of their toddlers, thinking that they are just being stubborn or behaving in a certain way to get attention. Yet toddlers need their parents' understanding and support, along with their patience and good humour, to help them master their developmental tasks. If toddlers feel they can master important tasks, such as feeding themselves or making choices, they will develop feelings of autonomy. If they fail, on the other hand, they will feel shame and doubt, especially when their parents demonstrate frustration or disappointment (Boyd & Bee, 2009; Burrous et al., 2009).

Scenario

A Toddler's Behaviour

At an annual picnic hosted by a child-care centre, the children were playing on the grass with a variety of toys. One 20-month-old little boy, Teddy, was busily snatching toys from the other children, declaring "mine, mine." His mother was embarrassed by the behaviour and reprimanded him. The early childhood educator approached her, and the mother confided that being a single working mom was difficult. She had been promoted recently, and this left her even less time to interact with Teddy. "It sure shows in his behaviour," she said. The early childhood educator listened sensitively and then explained to the mother that Teddy's behaviour was normal for his age. "Toddlers," she said, "go through a stage of thinking that everything is theirs before they can learn to share." After she gave the mother a few tips for avoiding conflict with toddlers, the mother said, "This won't make him any easier to live with, but at least I can stop feeling guilty about my parenting."

This example demonstrates that normal behaviour for a particular stage of development can be misunderstood and can evoke strong emotions in the parents.

Preschool Age—Initiative vs. Guilt

As children develop independence and leave the toddlerhood period, they move to the stage referred to as initiative, which spans the remainder of the preschool years (Erikson, 1963). During this time, children want to create, discover, explore, and try everything at least once. Creating crafts with paper, glue, paints, and sparkles becomes a favourite pastime of preschoolers.

Children at this age begin to take the initiative and make decisions on their own, and they crave the company of other children so that they may share in their creative endeavours.

For many parents, preschool children seem easier than infants and toddlers as long as they are kept busy and active. Children need many opportunities to create and explore, and they want to know that their work is appreciated by adults.

Scenario

A Lasting Friendship

"My closest friendships developed when Sandra was in preschool. We were new in the neighbourhood and really didn't know anybody at all. Three or four times a week, Sandra would want to play with Julie after school. At first I would just drop her off, but gradually her mother and I started having coffee together while the children were playing. Then we got together on weekends and our husbands got acquainted as well. Our friendship grew and lasted many years."

Sandra's developmental need was to make friends with children of the same age. We see how this need inadvertently affected the whole family. When children are able to initiate new relationships, they will develop confidence in their abilities. If, however, children are discouraged or punished, they will not continue to display initiative and may experience feelings of guilt.

School-Age Children—Industry vs. Inferiority

This stage relates primarily to children's school functioning, but it is relevant to children within the family as well. During this stage, children are industrious. They want to be involved in projects and in creating, but unlike the previous stage, completion and the final product are important. Children at this stage want to be involved in meaningful, real-life tasks, such as learning to read or write or helping with household chores. When children are successful in developing ideas and following through to the end product, and are successful in mastering new skills, a sense of industry will prevail. When these attempts are marked by failure, however, children will develop a sense of inferiority, which may be generalized (e.g., "I'm no good at school") or specific (e.g., "I can't draw," "I am not an athlete").

Scenario

Failure

In an introductory early childhood education class, students were engaged in an assignment that required them to draw and be creative. When it was over and we were evaluating the activity, one student remarked, "I hated this. I can't draw. My teachers never displayed any of my artwork at school." The same sentiment was echoed by several of her classmates. Another student added, "It's just like me—I've hated music from the time I was in grade 4 and the choir teacher told me to just mouth the words."

From their comments, it was clear that these students' failures in school had led to feelings of incompetence or inferiority in certain areas that lasted long beyond their school years. The family plays a role in providing successful learning opportunities and also in supporting children in their school experiences.

Adolescence—Identity vs. Role Confusion

The next stage is associated with adolescence. During this time, adolescents are attempting to determine who they are, what they stand for, and where they are heading. They review their history and then try out new possibilities and new roles in preparation for adult life. Through the course of development in this stage, adolescents need to establish a strong sense of identity. In order to do this, they often feel the need to break away from the traditions and expectations of the family, and to "try on" new ways. This often results in conflicts with parents and other authority figures. Failure to resolve the crises associated with the formulation of an identity results in role confusion—a sense of uncertainty about "who am I?" Other related issues and concerns, such as sexuality and peer influences, can also affect families.

Perspectives

Mark, a 32-year-old social work student at a community college, comes from a blended family. His father was a black American who immigrated to Canada as a child, and his biological mother was from the Cree nation in Manitoba. Mark, his two brothers, and his stepsister and stepbrother were raised by his Danish stepmother and his father. Mark described his transition to adolescence and his later development in the following words:

"When I was about 13, we had a family reunion with my stepmother's family in another province. I asked if I could stay at home with friends. In a way I wanted to test my parents to see whether they really wanted me to be part of this family. They let me stay, and I interpreted this as quite a devastating rejection. I really didn't feel part of the family anymore, and I remember quite desperately seeking out a group with whom I could identify and feel as if I belonged. The group I felt comfortable with at that time was basically a bunch of kids in trouble. Drinking, smoking, drugs, and vandalism were the norms for this group. This rebellious stage lasted for two years. I still lived at my family's house, but I didn't feel or act as part of the family. Although my parents didn't understand (and I never told them) why I had emotionally 'left' the family, they put up with me. My father tried to influence my behaviour (for example, we had arguments about my smoking), but he was unsuccessful.

"After two years (at the age of 15), I left home and continued to get into trouble until about the age of 17. I lived with friends, on the street, or with anyone who would take me in. At age 17, I sought out my biological mother. She was very happy to have me, although I was not very easy to like at the time. I blamed her for a lot of my problems and acted as if she owed me a great deal. I found out that my mother had left me as a baby because of a serious and chronic problem with alcohol. When we were reunited, I had an addiction problem with drugs, and she still was an alcoholic. We lived together for a couple of chaotic years.

"My addiction led me to trouble with the law, armed robbery, and a three-year jail sentence. The only support I had through that period was my mother, since my father and I terminated our contact while I was with my mother. At the age of 21 I was released from jail, still with an addiction problem, and still on a path to self-destruction. My father died when I was 23. I became suicidal, and blamed it on my mother. This situation continued for about three years. When I was 25, my stepmother died of an accidental overdose. Finally, I realized that I badly needed help.

"I entered a recovery program. A crucial part of my recovery was realizing the need for reconnecting with my Native roots and culture. At the age of 30, I entered the social work program. I'm still very involved with the Native community. The transition from childhood to adulthood and the development of a strong sense of self was a long process for me. The most important learning for me during those stormy transition years was that each person needs to make his own choices in life."

Young Adulthood—Intimacy vs. Isolation

Once young adults have developed a clear sense of identity, they are ready to enter into an intimate relationship with another person. Intimacy involves commitment and closeness to another person, and may be more easily achieved when both people have a developed sense of self—of who they are and what they want. When intimacy does not develop, isolation and loneliness may result.

Middle Adulthood—Generativity vs. Stagnation

Adulthood is marked by the striving to reach social and professional acceptance (Boyd & Bee, 2009). Adults need to feel that they have contributed to the world either by raising children or by having successful careers. Often, they direct considerable energy toward maintaining the sense that they have contributed to the next generation, that they will leave someone or something behind them when they die. When the adult is not involved in such activities, there is a tendency toward stagnation, which may in turn lead to living in the past, when the person was more successful.

As parents pass through the stage of middle adulthood, their parenting skills will probably be affected. Ongoing parenting and career development will both occur during this period. Parents will likely be heavily involved and invested in these activities as a means of increasing their generativity.

Later Adulthood—Ego Integrity vs. Despair

The last stage is the culmination of all the previous stages. Adults in this stage attempt to make sense of their lives and to see their lives as meaningful in some way. As adults review their lives, they may feel satisfied and prepared to meet the challenges of growing old and dealing with the prospect of death, or they may feel despair, helplessness, and a fear of dying. Families will certainly be affected as older family members go through this stage.

We need to remember that there have been tremendous societal changes since Erikson developed this theory. We have seen news reports that describe women becoming mothers well after menopause—a process now possible with the aid of modern medical technology. Becoming a new mother past the age of 50 would certainly impact the developmental tasks of middle age. People are living longer, and adults stay in their nuclear family home much longer. We are only beginning to understand these new social phenomena and certainly don't yet have new theoretical approaches that accommodate them.

Given these changes and the questions raised earlier about the cultural differences that may impact how these stages are experienced, we need to remember to use developmental knowledge as an aid to our understanding rather than as a mantra that "this is how people should be." We also need to remember that the tasks described above in each stage are never completely accomplished and may carry over to later stages. People whose early childhood experiences have not been conducive to establishing trust may have difficulty with trust later in life. But positive experiences with relationships later in life can often compensate for earlier experiences. Similarly, positive experiences early in life cannot completely immunize people from the effects of persistent stressors and crises later on.

Development is a complex phenomenon, and any attempt to predict its course with accuracy is open to pitfalls. However, understanding the challenges typical of different life stages can enhance our ability to consider people's behaviour in a positive light, to empathize, and to offer support. For example, we can help parents understand that the toddler is not trying to frustrate the mother—he is exercising his independence—or that the young adolescent's perceived negativism toward her family is often temporary and an expression of her need to find out who she is, separate and apart from her parents. Understanding aspects of the development of the individual child may help parents understand why their child behaves in certain ways. In turn, this knowledge may lead to less stress and more effective parenting. Early childhood educators can play a major role in providing parents with information related to all areas of development.

This review has focused exclusively on psychosocial development to illustrate how development, across the lifespan, may influence the child or family. We must remember, however, that development occurs across all areas simultaneously—physically, emotionally, and in language, cognition, and so forth.

Development in the Early Years

Developmental research over the years has provided us with many insights into how children grow and change, and how they may view and interpret the events of their lives. Recent research on brain development has given us new insights into the development of emotional and relationship abilities. We will now consider how attachment and emotional development may be impacted by conditions within the family in the early years. This brief review will help adults understand how children may interpret the world around them and how caregivers may support them.

Attachment

Attachment (Ainsworth & Witting, 1969; Bowlby, 1951, 1969) is the process of developing a trusting bond and relationship with a significant other over the first three years of life. Secure attachments are formed when primary caregivers are emotionally available and responsive to infants, when they are attuned to babies' cues, and when they respond appropriately (Bee et al., 2006). New research is focusing on children's ability to form multiple attachments that involve the significant others in their lives (e.g., family members, caregivers). Secure attachments are enhanced when children live in a predictable, nurturing environment where their needs are met. Having a secure attachment is thought to be one of the best indicators of competence, friendliness, and positive self-image (Trawick-Smith, 2010). A secure attachment also provides children with the knowledge and confidence to explore the world and to develop the ability to soothe themselves.

Healthy attachment can be harmed, however, when children's needs are not met consistently by a warm and nurturing person or when infants' cues are not read and responded to in a timely manner (Gonzalez-Mena, 2002; Minnis et al., 2009). Because this relationship serves as the foundation for future intimate relationships, it may be relevant throughout people's lives. Conditions that may put children at risk include neglect, abuse, sudden separation, or severe and prolonged depression of the primary caregiver (Bee et al., 2006; Minnis et al., 2009). When any one of these conditions exist, children's ability to form a trusting bond may be hampered. Babies with insecure attachment may be more aggressive and hostile in later years, may have difficulties in exploration and in peer relationships, and are more likely to have social and emotional problems. As well, it is now generally accepted that the early years are critical to brain development.

Family Role Theories

Role theory explores the expectations people have of their own social positionality, and how this relates to their self-identity (Raffel, 1999). A key concept in role theory is role-conflict theory. Role-conflict theory explains how one's expectations and requirements of his or her different roles can come into conflict with each other. This can be resolved when a person chooses which role to fulfill and how that role will be fulfilled. This may apply, for example, to grandparents, when they are expected to play the role of both primary grandparents and primary caregivers (Poehlmann, 2003). Life-course theory is described as an analysis of how individuals change over time and how transitions and trajectories are linked across family members. This theory emerged in the 1960s out of criticism of lifespan development, which Elder (1998) considered not comprehensive enough (Lerner, 2003). "Human lives are socially embedded in specific historical times and places that shape their content, path, and direction. As experiments of nature or design, types of historical change are experienced differently by people of different ages and roles. The change itself affects the developmental trajectory of individuals altering their life course" (Elder, 1998, p. 969).

Life-course theorists see development as a lifelong process that includes both individual and social experiences (Bengston & Allen, 2004). Unlike earlier theories of development, such as Erikson's psychosocial lifespan development theory, the life-course theory is an interdisciplinary study of personal actions and social institutions in a collective context, focusing on changes in human lives over time across a large series of cohorts and life domains (Mayer, 2009). Because the "intergenerational family can be best understood as a relational process" (Lowenstein, 1999, p. 401), applying life-course theory involves examining the connections and relationships that shape people and their social roles.

The Interaction of Developmental Cycles

The development of the child, of parenting skills, and of the family does not occur in isolation. Parents are learning about children and their own parenting abilities "on the job" as changes and transitions occur. At the same time that parents may be adjusting to the birth of a child, they may also be dealing with their own developmental tasks, such as establishing themselves in a career. While they are trying to strengthen and develop the intimate bond between themselves, the attachment needs of their first child may seem to interfere.

As a family progresses through the different stages in the life cycle, there may be times when the developmental needs of the family unit, the parents, and the children seem to fit together well. For example, a couple who are settled in their careers and have a firmly established relationship may be able to respond with more ease to the demands of a developing toddler. On the other hand, if young parents are struggling with their own identity issues, meeting the demands of their own relationship and those of parenting may be more difficult.

The two following examples highlight the interaction between different developmental patterns and the needs associated with each.

Example 1

A single teenage mother with a newborn baby moves back home with her mother.

Family Life Cycle Tasks

Teen Mom

- unattached young adult   - develop peer relations
                                  - differentiate self from family
- arrival of children   - assume parenting role
                                    - realign relationships to include parenting and her mother's grandparenting

Teen's Mom
- family with adolescents   - shift parent–child relationship to permit more independence

Parenting Tasks

Teen Mom
- nurturing   - deal with challenge of attachment
                                    - deal with demands of infant
                                    - deal with changing relationship among family members

Teen's Mom
- interdependent   - address authority and communication issues
                                    - develop new relationship with child
                                    - acquire increased independence
                                    - assess own identity as a parent

Developmental Tasks

Baby
- trust vs. mistrust   - require stable, consistent, and nurturing environment
                                    - depend totally on caregivers

Teen Mom
- identity vs. role confusion   - sort out her identity
                                    - deal with peer influence

Teen's Mom
- generativity vs. stagnation   - contribute to the next generation
                                    - pursue generativity at work

As we consider the different developmental stages of each family member, potential sources of stress become clear. The teen is dealing with issues of independence, while her situation calls for increased dependence on her family. As she is sorting out her own identity, how have the physical changes associated with pregnancy affected her? How will her new role of mother interact with her other roles? Likewise, her mother may be at a stage when she wants to devote her energies to her career, and is now faced with a long-term commitment to her daughter and grandchild. The baby's key needs are for stability and consistency. How will these needs be met, given the multiple transitions that all the family members are experiencing?

Today we are seeing a growing trend to delay parenthood, often until parents are close to, or in, their forties. While it is known that there are increasing developmental risks to the newborn related to conception later in life (Tarin et al., 1998)—and that these risks are related to the father's age as well as the mother's (Benzies, 2008; Tang et al., 2006)—these risks are somewhat mitigated by social and economic factors. For example, higher income and education will result in enhanced prenatal assessment and care. As the following example illustrates, later parenthood comes with different kinds of challenges—adults who have been used to autonomy and control over their lives may now have a very small but powerful addition to the family who will dictate many changes, including how many hours of sleep they will have at night!

Example 2

A working couple in their early forties have a 4-year-old and new baby. The husband's parents are elderly and will probably need nursing care in the near future.

Family Life Cycle Tasks

Parents
- family with young children
  - adjust marital relationship to make room for children
  - assume parenting roles
  - realign relationships to include parenting and grandparenting roles

Grandparents
- family in later life
  - maintain functioning in face of deterioration
  - deal with losses
  - prepare for death
  - make room for emerging role of middle generation

Parenting Tasks

Parents
- authority
  - establish rules, authority
  - learn to communicate with their children and with each other about their children
  - begin to form self-concepts

Grandparents
- departure and individuality
  - adapt to and accept child's separateness
  - examine successes and failures
  - redefine identity as a couple

Developmental Tasks

Toddler
- autonomy vs. shame
  - exert need for independence and decision making
  - resist accepting help

Four-year-old
- initiative vs. guilt
  - wants to do, to create
  - seek peer relations

Parents
- generativity vs. stagnation
  - want to contribute to the next generation and career work
  - strive for acceptance

Grandparents
- ego integrity vs. despair
  - make sense of own lives
  - cope with changes due to aging and impending death

Again, we see family members dealing with multiple transitions in their lives. The parents need to allow the older child to take initiative, while at the same time ensuring that the toddler is safe and understands that the same opportunities are not available to him or her at this age. The parents are simultaneously struggling to meet the needs of their new family and their marriage and to cope with the needs of their aging parents. Without considering any other factors, the multiple transitions occurring here may contribute significantly to family stress.

Conclusion

This chapter has focused on the transitions that are common within a family over its lifespan. As children grow and develop, so too, do parents in terms of their parenting skills. Families develop and change over time, and many factors affect the way in which families experience these transitions. Early childhood educators who are aware of the nature of transitions may be better able to provide resources and support families as necessary.

Chapter Summary

- Family development theories guide the practice of professionals.
- Family life cycles can be seen as stages, beginning with the arrival of children, followed in succession by families with young children, adolescent children, and older children, and concluding with the family in later life.
- Stages in parenthood have been described as image making, nurturing, authority forming, interpretation, independence, and departure.
- Erikson's theory of psychosocial development remains a foundation for professionals: trust vs. mistrust; autonomy vs. shame and doubt; initiative vs. guilt.

- Developmental patterns of the individual family, the parents, and the family unit interact, and these sometimes conflicting developmental needs can be a source of stress.
- Early childhood educators who understand these developmental challenges will be better able to provide support.

Recommended Websites

Center for Parent Education and Family Support:
www.cpe.unt.edu/roper/module2/theory.php?

Prepare Tomorrow's Parents:
www.parentingproject.org

Child Development Institute of Toronto:
www.childdevelop.ca

Videos/Films

Baby I'm Yours. 2003. Wendy Ettinger and Donna Wick. A feature-length documentary portraying three first-time mothers as they experience pregnancy to early motherhood. To contact the filmmakers, write or call Teri Kane Public Relations: 212-570-5144 (office) or 917-692-1076 (cell). Terikane@nyc.rr.com.

Exercises

1. Interview a couple with young children. Ask them how their relationship changed and grew when children came along. Take notes and write a brief report after the interview.
2. Interview a single parent of a young child. Ask how his or her life has changed in response to the growing and developing child. Write a brief report afterward.
3. Interview your own parents. Question them about how your own family developed, and ask them how they changed as parents over the years. List the ideas or concepts relevant to your family history.
4. Compare the responses in the three brief reports you have written. Write a final report summarizing your findings and answering the following questions:
   - How did the family life cycle differ for the three parent groups you interviewed?
   - What similarities did you note in these three families?
   - What can you conclude about the family life cycle after considering these similarities and differences?
5. Find three articles related to the risks and benefits of postponing parenthood After reading these, write your own reflections on the ideal time in one's life to become a parent.

Facing Family Challenges

In most child-care centres today, you will find children whose families are facing particular challenges. Research suggests that some high-risk children may develop difficulties due to living in these environments; however, many become competent, healthy adults. In the past, the approach of professionals was to deal with the problems associated with adversity. Our focus will be on *understanding* these difficulties—the causes or correlated factors and the effects on children, on parents, and on the family as a system. Early childhood professionals are not trained to provide counselling or therapy. However, understanding the issues will lead to empathy and support, as well as an ability to utilize appropriate resources in order to help families.

Part 2 will examine the various issues that families may face, although not all families will face every one of them or be affected by them in the same way. Each chapter will explore a different issue in detail, outlining the adult's and child's views of the situation and closing with practical ideas that caregivers may use to support the child, the parent, and the family as a whole. Early childhood educators must become aware of the potential risks families may face so that they will be better prepared to support families as needed. We emphasize that these are *risks*; they may not affect some families at all, or they may not affect families in the same way. Topics include divorce, blended families, death in the family, poverty, single parenting, teen parenting, violence and abuse in families, the child with special needs, the parent with special needs, adoption, same-sex parenting, and immigrant families. We hope that, as caregivers learn more about these issues, they will develop an understanding of the challenges faced by children and their parents. This understanding should in turn form the foundation of support offered in a nonjudgmental and empathetic manner.

Part 2 will also review some of the factors important in developing an understanding of how children may comprehend their world and particular situations in their lives so that we, as professionals, may foster resilience.

chapter 4

Resilience

Objectives

- To gain an understanding of the crucial role of resilience in children and families.
- To gain an understanding of the role of caregivers in promoting resilience in children.
- To gain an understanding of the role caregivers play in helping families develop strategies for resilience.

Jorge grew up in a family with two siblings and his parents. His father was an alcoholic until all three children were in their teens. They dealt with periods of poverty, unemployment, fighting, and arguing as they grew up. Jorge reflected on this as an adult and talked about how these experiences helped to make him stronger—he learned to be more inde-pendent, to know whom to approach to get his needs met, and where he could go to escape the chaos in his house. But, he said, his older brother never seemed to be able to cope. "He was always having trouble at school, which caused more fighting and arguing at home. He has had trouble in relationships, and his marriage is falling apart. His last coun-sellor told him it was partly because of his mother and parenting when he was little," said Jorge. However, Jorge thought, "I had the same mother and father and lived in the same house with the same issues and I'm okay." He ended by saying, "I think this is what resilience is and what resilience looks like."

The concept of resilience provides a useful starting point for understanding the educator's role in helping children cope with difficult situations. Resilience has existed as a concept for many years, and there have been many programs to promote resilience in children. Understanding resilience and the characteristics associated with it may help educators support the children in their care, especially when the child or family is dealing with challenges. However, it should be noted that promoting resilience is not reserved only for times when children are experiencing challenges; promoting resilience in every practice can help children cope with difficult situations better, whatever the situation may be.

The term *resilience* has been defined as the ability to bounce back or cope in the face of adversity. Although it varies in different contexts, it is marked by the ability to persevere and adapt when things don't go as expected. Resilience includes the capacity to cope with adversity or risk. It is not static but changes over time.

Resilience helps people deal with stress and challenges in their everyday lives. We cannot prevent stress or challenges for the children we work with, but we can help them deal with it in more positive ways. Research suggests that resilient people are healthier, more successful at school and work, and generally happier and less prone to depression (Pearson & Kordich Hall, 2006).

Continuing research serves to further clarify what resilience is and how it may be developed. For the purposes of this text, we have focused on the definition and concepts currently used by the Reaching IN . . . Reaching OUT (RIRO) program (www.reachinginreachingout. com/aboutresilience.htm). This organization has provided an abundance of information specific to young children and their educators.

Understanding Resilience

Resilience is often conceptualized as a balance of risk factors and protective factors. *Protective factors* are those qualities or situations that help to deal with expected negative outcomes. Resiliency can be promoted by providing and nurturing these qualities or by providing these types of situations. *Risk factors* are those that have the potential to cause difficulty, either short term or long term. These can be cultural, economic, disabling, or health conditions that limit opportunities for optimal development. These factors can be thought of from the perspective of the child, the family, or the community.

Protective Factors
Child

Protective factors can be *intrinsic* (i.e., existing within the child) or *extrinsic* (i.e., existing in the child's environment). Intrinsic factors tend to include personality, temperamental traits, and abilities. While it is possible to change and develop abilities (e.g., communication skills, problem solving), changing inborn temperament or personality may be more difficult, although individuals can come to understand these better and so better cope. Individual protective factors include the following:

- Sense of being loved
- Sense of belonging
- Self-esteem
- Empathy
- Sense of control
- Cognitive and reasoning skills
- Social skills
- Good communication skills

Family

- Trusting relationships
- Supportive relationships
- Parental monitoring
- Financial security

Community

- Access to supportive caring communities—child care and schools
- Positive child-care and school experiences
- Educators as caring role models
- Availability of social activities with caring adults
- Positive peer influences

Resilience research indicates that during the early childhood years, it is important for children to have good-quality care—including opportunities for learning, adequate nutrition, and community support for families—in order to facilitate positive development of cognitive, social, and self-regulation skills. In early childhood, it is particularly important that children have the protections afforded by attachment bonds with competent and loving caregivers, the stimulation and nutrition required for healthy brain development, opportunities to learn and experience the pleasure of mastering new skills, and the limit-setting or structure needed to develop self-control (Masten & Gewirtz, 2006).

Risk Factors

Risk factors are those that may cause difficulties or put the child at higher risk. Risk factors may exist within the child, the family, or the community, and include the following:

Child

- Poor nutrition
- Poor physical health
- Low self-esteem
- Developmental delays

Family

- Unstable family relationships
- Poor attachment
- Lack of support from mothers or fathers
- Poverty
- Mental health issues

Community

- Lack of access to health care
- Social isolation
- Lack of access to resources
- Lack of available green spaces

Maria had a friend, Rose, who lived in California. They were roommates at school and kept in close contact after they graduated and had families. Rose came to visit in the middle of winter. The weather was extremely cold and miserable, and Maria told her friend that her children were grumpy and restless because it had been too cold to go outside all week. Rose asked if there were higher rates of child abuse here. Maria was surprised by the question and asked Rose why she would think this. Rose replied: "Well, at home, if the children are getting overly rambunctious or grouchy, they just go outside and blow off some steam and I have a bit of break. How do you or the children get that kind of break here?" Maria realized that the environment may impact how we interact with children.

Resilience involves the balancing of stressful life events or risk factors with protective factors (Gonzalez-Mena, 2002). To reduce risk factors, early childhood educators need to first understand the risks that exist with a particular child or family and then to try, as much as possible, to help alleviate these. This may be as simple as helping parents find child care after hours, or it may involve accessing community support services for parents and families. Early learning educators may not be able to solve some of the difficulties or resolve all of the risks, of course, but they may be able to provide parents with resources so that they may better cope with the stresses they may be experiencing. Sometimes, it may be sufficient for educators to simply understand the situation and provide a little support or understanding (e.g., if a parent forgets something, or a child is late). Early learning educators can also play a role by knowing the community resources that are available and advocating for community supports for children and families.

The other factor in resilience is enhancing protective factors (Drummond et al., 1998). As stated earlier, protective factors may be developed within the individual (e.g., by promoting health, self-esteem, self-efficacy, a feeling of control, social competence), within families (e.g., by developing communication and effective parenting, providing supports or coping strategies), and within communities (e.g., by developing a sense of community, increasing access to services). Resilience can be enhanced by helping to develop protective factors while attempting to control or decrease existing risk factors.

We will review characteristics associated with resilience in more detail so that educators may feel more comfortable in developing and promoting these protective factors.

Characteristics of Resilience

Researchers have identified several key factors associated with resilience:

- Availability of someone special in a trusting relationship
- Temperamental or personality characteristics of the child
- Ability of the child to seek out someone to help
- Children who tend to view experiences positively and constructively
- Children who have been needed by others
- Warm, secure family relationships

- Supportive, predictable environments
- Development of coping strategies
- Individuals who listen
- Children who have a sense of control over their own lives and are provided some degree of control

As you can see, there are a number of traits or characteristics associated with resilience. Some are personality or temperamental characteristics, and some are abilities or skills that educators can help to develop. We will focus on those abilities and traits. However, it is important to remember that one key factor discussed over and over is the availability of someone special who has a special relationship with the child. This may be a parent, a sibling, an extended family member, a teacher, a coach, or an educator. You may be the special person in a child's life who provides the foundation for resilience—what a privilege and what a responsibility! In your everyday interaction with children, this is important to remember so that you'll always be mindful of what children need and will be prepared to provide it to them.

The key abilities associated with resilience that may be enhanced or promoted include the following:

- *Emotional regulation* is the ability to manage children's emotions so that they can remain calm and in control. The expression of emotions, both positive and negative, is important. Emotional regulation does not mean that children keep negative emotions bottled up. It means that they learn how to express emotions, especially negative ones, in an appropriate and responsible way. Children begin to learn to calm and soothe themselves at an early age by sucking their thumb or by seeking out their blanket. As children grow and develop, they begin to understand more about their feelings and begin to express themselves in more ways (e.g., more than just crying). They need to learn that some ways of expressing themselves are not acceptable even though the feeling may be very real. Children need to understand the feelings they experience (e.g., anger), but they also need to know the limits for expressing those feelings (e.g., it is not okay to throw the toy or hit someone). Educators and parents play a huge role in helping children develop emotional control.

  Impulse control is related to emotional regulation (when a child doesn't get what he or she wants, strong emotions often follow). Impulse control is associated with delaying gratification. Children need to learn to wait for something that they want or see. Young children will see an object or food item and want it immediately (e.g., a candy bar in a grocery store), but they must learn to wait. This can be very difficult—just ask the parent of a toddler! Educators can help children to control their impulses and desires and to choose a better way to express themselves.

- *Problem solving* is the way in which children work through the challenges in their lives. It includes a number of skills and takes a long time to develop. Children must learn to analyze problems and determine what the cause is so that they can take action. Children will need to learn a wide range of social and communication skills in order to solve problems effectively. Educators and parents can assist by helping children first understand problem situations and then find reasonable ways to solve them. This can include acknowledging the child's feelings, accepting the feelings but putting limits on the actions, defining the problem clearly for the child, and helping the child determine possible solutions and then try it out. Educators are often quick to stop behaviours from escalating by taking a toy away or by separating children when they are in conflict. Sometimes, stepping in and using the opportunity to teach problem solving can be very beneficial. However, caregivers will likely agree that there aren't enough hours in the day to do this every time a problem or difficulty arises. While this may be true, it is still important for educators and parents to capitalize on these moments as often as possible.

- *Self-confidence* involves children having a strong but realistic belief in themselves and their abilities. It includes feeling valued and loved, a sense of belonging and acceptance, and self-efficacy or the belief that what we do matters (Pearson & Kordich Hall, 2006). This begins early when we give children choices so that they learn they have control over what they do. When the child succeeds at making good choices, his or her confidence grows. This is only one example of how self-confidence is developed; educators and parents foster a self of self-confidence in multiple ways throughout the child's life. Self-confidence is important because it facilitates coping with challenges and maintaining a positive view of the world.

  A sense of optimism has also been associated with resilience (Pearson & Kordich Hall, 2006). Optimism is the ability to maintain a positive outlook and believing that you can make the best out of a situation. This develops when children have self-confidence and believe that they can make choices, control their behaviour, and solve problems effectively.

- *Empathy* involves understanding the feelings or needs of others. Adults often think that children are not capable of empathy since they are egocentric and think they are the centre of the universe. While it is true that young children are egocentric, they do learn to see other perspectives and are better able to understand that others have feelings and needs that may be different from their own. Adults can promote the development of empathy by helping children to identify and express emotions in themselves and others and by modelling empathy. When children see adults responding to and comforting other children, they are learning empathy.

- *Seeking support.* One last characteristic associated with resilience is the child's ability to seek support when she or he needs it. Children need to learn to reach out for new opportunities and to take risks. When children are able to seize these opportunities, it will become easier for them to seek support and guidance when they are struggling. Although this sounds easy, it requires skill to understand how much one can cope with and be willing to ask for help. In addition, children need to learn to ask in appropriate ways. For example, adults often have a low tolerance for children who whine, but these children may have real concerns and difficulties, and may need to learn how to express their needs to better access support.

The Role of the Early Childhood Educator

Recently, the role of good-quality child care has been discussed as one potential solution to serving children at risk. This new trend involving the role of child care in healthy development must be taken seriously by caregivers, since good-quality child care can bring long-lasting benefits to children and families.

Educators are in a key position to support the development of resilience, not only in children but also in families, as we discuss in the following section. Educators aren't limited to these ideas, of course. It is hoped that this chapter will help you think about your role in building resilience in children and families so that as you progress through the chapters you may focus on developing resilience in your practice. In addition, it should be noted that building resilience is part of developing many other skills you're involved in during the day, including promoting communication or social skills, working through problems in friendships, and building attachments.

Caregivers are in a unique position to promote resilience. Since children's relationships are key to their developing a range of social skills (e.g., interpersonal communication, regulating emotions, empathy), your relationship may serve as a protective factor for a child experiencing adverse conditions (e.g., poverty, neglect).The following guidelines may be helpful in fostering resilience:

- **Learn to identify risk factors and protective factors.** Caregivers may become aware of and try to alleviate risk factors in children or families and promote protective factors, for example by focusing on and enhancing children's social competence, by noticing and listening to them, by acknowledging their feelings, and by structuring activities for cooperation rather than competition.

- **Model coping behaviours.** Remember the impact of modelling—children develop resiliency and associated skills by watching how adults in their world cope with problems/adversity. Adults can talk about their thoughts and feelings (e.g., "OW! I shut my finger in the cupboard door and it hurts! I'm angry!"). Then adults can model how to calm themselves down (e.g., taking a deep breath, taking care of the problem, finding a way to settle down).

- **Teach social skills to make connections and gain support.** Helping children express their feelings and emotions begins with children understanding their own emotions and putting labels to them. It continues when children learn to understand how those feelings feel and then learn ways to cope with them (hopefully appropriate ways).

- **Help children differentiate between reality and fantasy as they become developmentally ready to understand.** Use short but accurate explanations. Art, stories and books, and dramatic play can be used to promote discussion with children about complex and emotionally laden issues.

- **Become a special, caring person in the life of a young child.** Non-family members, such as teachers, coaches, and counsellors, can often cushion a child from the adverse effects of a disturbing family situation. The presence of an adult who provides sensitive caregiving has been linked with adaptive functioning later in life.

- **Practise responsive caregiving.** Provide opportunities for children to develop confidence in the support others provide, to develop confidence in themselves, to view themselves as worthy, and to experience a sense of mastery of their world. You can enhance the development of self-esteem by encouraging children to try and reinforcing their accomplishments (e.g., "I see that you shared the sand toys with Billie, and you both played so well together!"). The importance of this position cannot be overstated.

- **Give children responsibilities.** Give children chores or have them help care for younger children, plants, or animals (Gonzalez-Mena, 2002).

Children need to experience mastery in their world. You can facilitate this by giving them choices, guiding them to make their own appropriate choices, and highlighting successes.

- **Help children develop problem-solving skills in daily interactions.** For example, use everyday situations to teach children to solve interpersonal problems when they come up. Although it's very tempting to take the toy away or separate children when they're not getting along, these are perfect occasions to teach children how to solve the problem themselves. It does take time (which educators don't always have), but being aware of the opportunities and capturing these teachable moments will have far-reaching benefits.

- **Be a good source of information for the child.** Caregivers may be in a unique situation to provide information (e.g., why some mommies give their children up for adoption) in a clear and less emotional way, and to provide the child with support (e.g., suggesting a better way of dealing with the hurt than hitting or acting out).

Use stories and puppets to help children understand and develop some of these concepts. Providing different ways of experiencing and understanding these complex concepts will enhance learning.

- **Support parents.** Caregivers can be instrumental in helping parents understand the child's view and providing support at home (e.g., helping the parent understand that the preschooler will ask over and over in an attempt to comprehend something, not because the child doesn't grasp it or because he or she is trying to drive the parent crazy, but because that's the stage the child is at). Caregivers will need to work together with parents as situations arise to ensure that the child comes to understand and learns to cope.

- **Engage in professional development.** Be prepared to deal with difficult situations, such as substance abuse in the family or your possible discomfort with homosexual parents.

- **Get support from friends, family, and professionals.** Dealing with difficult situations that may be encountered, or witnessing children in distress, takes an emotional toll on caregivers. You must protect yourself from overinvolvement and/or burnout by getting support for yourself.

Research (Pearson & Kordich Hall, 2006) has demonstrated that when early learning educators understand resilience and plan their program around its concepts, they too derive benefits. A pilot study in which early childhood educators learned evidence-based resilience skills to use with young children found that these educators felt their approach and language changed after the training. Educators first focused on asking children about their feelings, and later asked them about their thinking; these educators were able to help children change their thinking about situations and find workable solutions. As mentioned earlier in the chapter, Reaching IN . . . Reaching OUT (RIRO) has developed these strategies for working with young children and is an excellent resource for educators to use to enhance their own skill development.

Fostering Resilience in Families

As early learning educators, understanding resilience can be of assistance in helping parents foster it in their children. Educators can promote resilience by supporting attachment between the parent and the child on a daily basis. For example, educators may find ways to ensure that families are represented in the program or to promote ways of communicating during the day or afterward. Parents too will learn by modelling the ways educators interact with children. For example, respectful approaches to encouraging children to cooperate will help to support attachment between the parent and the child (especially on those days when everything has gone wrong). Early learning educators can also provide parents with resources to develop resilience. RIRO provides an extensive list of children's books focused on resilience. These could be used in the child-care program or referred to parents for use in particular situations, for example, new siblings, moving, separation, or divorce. Educators need to know when it's appropriate to use these in the child-care centre as part of a group story time, when to use them one on one, or when to suggest that the parent read the book to the child. Sometimes starting a difficult conversation with a storybook can work very well.

The RIRO project is now looking at developing resources specifically geared toward parents. Educators can investigate national resources (Invest in Kids had excellent resources for parents that will be distributed to organizations across Canada) and local resources. For example, the Alberta Mental Health Board developed a series of resources for parents called *The Bounce Back Book: Building Resiliency Skills*. One book was developed for parents of infants and toddlers, one for preschoolers, and one for the early school years. The books provide readily understandable information about resilience and a series of ideas that parents can use in their daily interactions with children, primarily in the home environment. Parents and educators have found many excellent ideas in these books.

Early learning educators can also play a role in reducing risk factors. This may be accomplished by knowing what community resources and supports are offered and by making this information available for parents. Many of the ideas discussed in Chapter 16, "Understanding Parent Involvement," will also provide opportunities for families to develop the skills associated with resilience.

Conclusion

Resilience, as a concept, has been around for quite some time. More recently, practitioners have considered how resilience can be incorporated into programs for young children, since research has shown that resilience can be fostered. This has led to the development of strength-based approaches in working with children and families and has provided further ideas for working with families.

Chapter Summary

- Resilience is the ability to cope or bounce back.
- Resilience involves the balancing of protective factors and risk factors.
- Protective factors may be intrinsic (e.g., personality, abilities) or extrinsic (e.g., in the environment, the community).

- Many of the skills associated with resilience can be fostered in children or individuals, families, and communities.
- As part of good child-care practices, educators may help promote a number of key capabilities associated with resilience in young children. Educators may help foster resilience in times of stress as well.
- Early learning educators may also foster resilience in families and parents by supporting them in minimizing risk factors (e.g., by providing a stable environment) or increasing protective factors (e.g., by modelling good child-care practices).

Recommended Websites

Resilience Research Centre:
www.resilienceproject.org

Encyclopedia on Early Childhood Development:
www.child-encyclopedia.com/en-ca/child-resilience/perspectives.html?RId=CA

Reaching IN . . . Reaching OUT (RIRO):
www.reachinginreachingout.com

Exercises

1. Check the RIRO website for checklists focused on resilience. Complete one of the checklists on yourself to better understand how you cope. Share this with a classmate or colleague.

2. Consider all the ways in which you promote resilience during a typical day. How do you foster protective factors? How do you decrease risk factors for the children in your care?

3. Check community resources that might help families to (a) reduce risk factors (e.g., clothing or toy swaps, babysitting co-ops), and (b) improve protective factors (e.g., free recreational activities so that families can spend time together; equipment swaps so that children can be involved in sports).

chapter 5

Divorce

Objectives

- **To understand the prevalence of divorce.**
- **To understand the potential impact of divorce on the child and family.**
- **To understand the factors that influence adjustment to divorce.**
- **To examine attitudes toward divorce.**
- **To discuss ways that the early childhood educator can support children and families who have experienced a divorce.**

> When Karen's mother brought her to child care one Friday morning, the woman was clutching an infant car seat and an overnight bag in her arms. "We just finalized our separation arrangement," she said matter-of-factly. "Please make sure that her dad remembers the car seat. He doesn't have one for his car and he'll need it." Gabriella, the early childhood educator, sighed and thought to herself, "I knew that something was going on at home because Karen hasn't been her usual happy self, but I had no idea this is what it was."

Estimates of the prevalence of divorce in Canada over the past decade vary slightly, but it is reasonable to assume that "the number of Canadian marriages that end before the 30th anniversary is just over one-third" (Clark & Cromton, 2006; McDaniel, 2010). It is important to note that divorce statistics do not include the breakup of common-law partnerships, and that the number of these partnerships has been increasing. In the mid-nineties, 20% of babies in Canada were born into cohabiting unions (Juby et al., 2005), with 14% of families (in 2001) living in these unions (Milan, 2003). And when these unions end, as over 50% do, there is no record of divorce (Ambert, 2009), although from the children's perspective, the impact of these breakups would differ little from that of divorce.

Bearing these statistics in mind, we will discuss the various aspects of divorce, how it affects the young child's perceptions and feelings, and how it affects the relationship between the children and their parents. Finally, we will discuss how the early childhood educator might provide support to children and families who are experiencing a divorce.

Marisa, Age 4 (I love mom)

A Multi-Faceted Life Event

Even though divorce and separation are much more prevalent today than in the past, children and adults alike often consider it to be a major crisis that greatly disrupts their lives (Ambert, 2009; Wallerstein, 2005). Divorce is a multi-level crisis that children and adults may experience emotionally, socially, and financially, and that can have a devastating effect on the parent-child relationship (Dunn, 2004). Initially, there are a series of immediate and significant transitional changes. All parties should realize from the start that periods of crisis and stress will occur and, in fact, will likely reoccur over long periods of time. In fact, relationships that are fairly quiet can often become more conflicted as divorce occurs, with some evidence showing that women are at a higher risk of being assaulted or killed by their partner during this transition period (Fleury et al., 2000; Morash et al., 2008).

Attitudes toward divorce are becoming more tolerant, and there seems to be a realization and acceptance that relationships are inherently fragile (Gubernskaya, 2010; Hughes et al., 2009). Most people believe that divorce is the best solution when marital difficulties cannot be overcome, and that divorce is an alternative to an unhappy marriage rather than a personal failure. More people are questioning the link between marriage and parenting, and the institution of marriage is undoubtedly changing (Hull & Mather, 2006). However, we must remember that there is also a growing body of organizations that claim that divorce and "family breakdown" is costly to individuals and society, and that the institution of marriage must be maintained as much as possible (Walberg & Mrozek, 2009). This viewpoint, usually held by conservative or traditional organizations, runs counter to the philosophy of this book and of many (if not most) early childhood educators, which is to support families regardless of the circumstance.

Divorce is a process that begins and ends at different times for parents and children (Lansford, 2009; Wallerstein, 2005). For example, the parents may have accepted the idea that their marriage is over and may have made plans to separate long before they inform the children, so the parents may be near the end of the process while it is just beginning for the children. On the other hand, when parents have been arguing and fighting over long periods of time, the children may have been wishing for the fighting to stop or for a separation to occur. When the announcement is finally made, the children are more than prepared. In this case, the children may be at the end of the cycle while the parents might be at the beginning. In families undergoing divorce, children do often exhibit well-documented problems before the parental separation (Dunn, 2004; Li, 2007). Early childhood educators could remind parents of this, if, for example, the parents don't understand why their preschooler is not yet sleeping through the night or is showing signs of anger many months after the divorce.

Divorce is a disorganizing process that extends over years, with lasting effects (Amato, 2010; Wallerstein, 2005). Many adults may recover after two or three years. However, two or three years in the life of a young child may have much more of an impact on that child's development. In the eyes of preschool children, the world consists almost entirely of the family, and divorce means that the family ceases to exist. Such children must adapt to living with one parent rather than two and may experience a sense of abandonment by the parent who is not living at home. There may also be tensions associated with building a relationship with a "weekend parent." This visiting relationship will usually be an unfamiliar experience for both the parent and the children. Because of the frequent disruptions—the repeated need to say goodbye to each other just when they are renewing their relationship—hostility may develop on both sides. Also, there will likely be a substantial decline in the children's standard of living (Ambert, 2009), as we will discuss later in this chapter. All of these factors will prove to be of major significance to child development.

Effects of Divorce on Children

Research on divorce is highly varied, and depends on the time of the study, the subgroup studied, and the angle from which it is looked at. Often there are two extreme positions. The first is that long-term effects of divorce have a significant negative effect on children's mental health, academic achievement, relationships, and more (Lansford, 2009). The second, at the other end of the spectrum, is that divorce does not significantly affect children (Lansford, 2009).

During the mid-eighties and nineties, as North American society was seeing rapid increases in divorce rates, several studies focused on the impact of divorce on children (Furstenberg & Teitler, 1994; Skolnick, 1992; Wallerstein, 1991). Some of these studies have been criticized for being too "one-dimensional," and today the focus has changed to look at broader structural issues and their impact on children. While there are negative effects that repeatedly emerge (Amato, 2010), many researchers are suggesting that these negative effects are not "as bad" as originally thought (Hetherington, 2005). For example, a study that looked at data from a survey of 5004 Canadian children concluded that divorce is unrelated to changes in parenting behaviour (Strohschein, 2007). This study showed that there are more similarities than differences between married and divorced parenting (Strohschein, 2007). Divorce has been associated with poor academic achievement, behavioural difficulty, poor self-esteem, aggression, and depressive behaviours (Ambert, 2009; Bee & Boyd, 2007). Researchers have recently noted that lower academic achievement has to do with the lower well-being of the child and general family functioning prior to divorce, rather than the divorce itself (Li, 2007; Potter, 2010). The magnitude of the effects appear to be related to children's temperaments and personalities, the quality of the parental relationships prior to the divorce, the adjustment by the custodial parent, and the parents' post-separation relationship (Ambert, 2009). It has therefore been suggested that early childhood educators (as well as researchers and parents) should look at divorce not in terms of specific outcomes, but with the expectation that children of divorced parents will experience certain adversities (Ambert, 2009).

Finally, it is important to consider that many of the negative effects of divorce have more to do with the effects of poverty than divorce itself, as we will review later in this chapter (Ambert, 2009; Li, 2007). Comparisons with European countries, which have a wide social safety net for families, show that support and policies can mitigate the negative effects of divorce (Ambert, 2009).

There is great diversity in children's reactions to divorce (Dunn et al., 2005; Hetherington, 2003). Sometimes divorce will remove children from stressful relationships, thereby enhancing their competence (Ambert, 2009). Children who generally adapt to new situations with ease will likely have an easier time adjusting to the divorce than those who seem to need regularity and consistency, and who have trouble adapting to new situations. Children who have witnessed severe conflict between parents over a brief period prior to the divorce may experience divorce quite differently from children whose parents gradually grew apart and agreed to terminate the marriage. Similarly, children whose parents continue to demonstrate their love, commitment, and involvement with their children, and who relate to each other respectfully, will experience divorce differently from those children whose parents are involved in bitter post-divorce conflict (Ambert, 2009; Wallerstein, 2005). While environment plays a major role, research indicates that a certain gene, coupled with the environment of divorce, explains why some children are resilient and others are more vulnerable (Amato, 2010).

Factors Affecting Adjustment to Divorce

Several factors have been identified as possibly affecting both adults' and children's understanding of and adjustment to divorce. Not all children will react in precisely the same way following a divorce. Throughout the divorce process, both adults and children experience emotional highs and lows that often resurface and intensify when a new crisis or transition occurs. Divorce is multifaceted, and children and families may be affected by a number of divorce-related factors, such as conflict, poverty, disruption of routine, or change of neighbourhoods (Bee & Boyd, 2007).

The length of time that situations like this one continue, and the intensity of the related mood swings, will vary from person to person. But early childhood educators need to be aware that strain does manifest itself long after the actual decision to separate or divorce is made, and may intensify rather than diminish over time.

Factors Affecting Children's Adjustment to Divorce

- Amount of parental conflict
- Number of changes after the divorce
- Economic factors
- Absence of father or mother
- Availability of both parents
- Extra responsibilities placed on the child
- Custody arrangements.

Missing the Father

Marcy had been divorced for two years. She had a well-paying job and had managed relatively well with her two children, aged 4 and 6. By the second summer after the divorce, she felt that she was ready to take her children on a vacation. In a holiday mood, they drove to their favourite campsite and began to set up camp. As she unpacked their camping equipment, she suddenly realized that the task of setting up the tent was all hers. As she tried to ready herself for this task, her 6-year-old noticed the look of despair on her face. "Daddy always did this part, didn't he?"

The Amount of Conflict

The amount of conflict that exists in the marriage is one factor to consider when gauging children's emotional adjustments (Ambert, 2009; Wallerstein, 2005). Conflict may exist before and/or after the separation. Evidence shows that low-conflict marriages that end in divorce can actually have more negative impact on children, whereas divorce for couples living with enhanced conflict can sometimes be beneficial for children (Ambert, 2006; McDaniel & Tepperman, 2007). When children have been living in an environment with a high degree of conflict and much fighting, they may be better off living with one stable parent rather than with two parents who are constantly embroiled in conflict (Parke, 2006).

Circumstances may also exist where conflict escalates only after the separation or during the divorce process, as the parents attempt to divide their belongings and decide on custodial arrangements. The children then become central to the conflict, whereas previously the parents tried not to involve them in their problems. The chances of an easy adjustment are greatly hindered when the children become the focal point of the conflict, such as in a custody battle. This scenario works against the best interests of the children involved (McDaniel & Tepperman, 2007).

Changes in Relationships After Divorce

It is rare that separation and divorce result in the change of only one relationship, that which exists between the parent and child. For example, the loss of the father often leads to changes in the standard of living (Ambert, 2009). A stay-at-home mother may need to go back to work, leading to the need for child care, thus leaving the mother with less time for the child. Other relationship changes within the family may also occur. For example, the child may not continue to live with his or her siblings, and contact with grandparents, aunts, uncles, and cousins may lessen. If the divorce necessitates a change of residence, then friends, child care, school, and lifestyle may also change. The child may lose a pet with a change of residence. The more changes children encounter, and the more new factors they must learn to cope with, the more disorganizing the entire process is likely to be (Amato, 2010).

In addition, during the process of separation and divorce, children may feel estranged from one or both parents and from other people (e.g., not seeing or interacting with grandparents). It is common that few people outside the family may know about the situation, which may also cause stress for the children.

In recent years, there has been a growing trend to counter some of these negative developments by divorced parents seeking joint custody of children. There is evidence showing that this arrangement leads to better adjustment of children following divorce (Rutkin, 2010). Sharing custody improves the long-term relationship between separated parents and their children (Juby et al., 2005; Rutkin, 2010).

Economic Factors

The most problematic and enduring change for mothers and their children is the decline in economic conditions (Ambert, 2009), which will often last for an extended period, particularly if the mother remains a lone parent. One likely reason is the difficulty for mothers with children, especially preschool children, to find and maintain employment. This problem may be compounded by the fact that women earn lower wages than men in most occupations and by irregular child support payments from fathers (Ambert, 2006). Withholding child support payments may be associated with the ongoing conflict between spouses and the frequency of visits from the non-custodial parent. The reality is that most families need two incomes to make ends meet. After the divorce, lone parents are faced with the same expenses for child care and (increasingly) with care for older family members. However, now the full burden is usually on them, and with only one income (Vanier Institute, 2010). Families living in poverty are more likely to divorce and to have difficulties adjusting, partly because they generally experience more stressful lives (Ambert, 2009).

From Father Absence to Father Involvement

Many studies have focused on the father's absence and the effects it has on children after a divorce. For example, it was thought in the past that children raised in father-absent homes experienced higher levels of school failure, delinquency, and promiscuity (Furstenberg & Teitler, 1994). However, more recent research has indicated that the father's presence is only one of a number of factors that change for the child when divorce occurs. As society shifts toward a view of the importance of fathers in their children's lives, the idea of "father absence" is being replaced with that of "father involvement." The biggest barriers to father involvement are the ongoing stereotypes of the fatherhood role, policies surrounding custody, and the mother–father relationship. As we will review, fathers are increasingly active in their children's lives following divorce.

In most divorce settlements in the past, mothers were granted custody and fathers became the non-custodial parent (Furstenberg & Teitler, 1994). This arrangement required changing roles and functions for all concerned, which could be extremely difficult. For men, divorce may lead to a sense of loss and failure, both as husbands and as fathers. Over time, fathers may have a diminishing incentive to maintain a relationship and support. For example, both fathers and children may have to re-form their relationship on the basis of weekend visits. Thus, there may be continued stress in always having to say goodbye, and conflicts may increase if spouses disagree about the children's upbringing and parental visits. Fathers who were the decision makers within the marriage may experience a sense of loss of control over their children after divorce. Children may be confused by different rules and standards, different ways of interacting, new people who become involved in relationships with either parent, etc. All of these factors may have negative implications for the parents' relationship with the child (Umberson & Williams, 1993).

Custody Arrangements

Until the middle of the 19th century, fathers were automatically awarded custody of children after a divorce because children were considered the property of their fathers (Jaffe, 1991). Later, mothers were generally awarded custody because people believed that they were more nurturing;

fathers were given custody only when they were able to prove that the mothers were somehow unfit (Jaffe, 1991). There are now a variety of options or trends associated with custody arrangements (Juby et al., 2005; Rutkin, 2010). Until recently, it was still more likely in North America culture that the mother will get custody of the children, although amendments to the Divorce Act in Canada in 2006 have made it easier for men to gain custody (McDaniel & Tepperman, 2007). Baker (1997) argues that the practice of awarding custody and child support remains closely tied to traditional gender roles and labour-force gender inequality. Increasingly, fathers are opposing this practice because they want to continue their parental role and spend more time with their children. Indeed, joint custody is steadily increasing as an outcome of divorce (Juby et al., 2005). However, the most popular arrangement is still the one where the mother maintains custody during the week and children spend alternating weekends with fathers. This arrangement often presents difficulties. The father may be perceived as having the "easier" role, since he does not need to place any demands on the children over the weekend, and their time can be spent having fun. Mothers, on the other hand, find it difficult to spend quality time with their children during the busy weekdays when other chores and responsibilities vie for their attention.

Joint child custody (shared parenting) is becoming the most common arrangement for children of divorce. A recent U.S. study (Bauserman, 2012) found that children from divorced families are better adjusted when they live with both parents in different homes, or when they spend significant time with both parents (referred to as *joint physical custody*), as compared with children who interact only with one parent (*sole physical custody*). The study suggested that children in joint custody arrangements had fewer behavioural and emotional problems, higher self-esteem, and better family relationships compared with those in sole custody arrangements. In fact, in terms of their developmental outcomes, "joint custody children" were no different from children living in an intact family situation.

Nonetheless, it should be remembered that, especially for young children, it can be very difficult to understand and make the necessary adjustments to living in two homes. The children will have to contend with two different homes and with two different sets of rules, expectations, and routines. Just as they become accustomed to one, it will be time to change to another. Moreover, if parents live in different neighbourhoods, children lose a sense of continuity with their friends and neighbourhood activities. The day-to-day problems of keeping track of their belongings and other aspects of their lives lead most children to think of one place as home, as their permanent residence (McDaniel & Tepperman, 2007; Skolnick, 1992). Indeed, some people believe that dual residence arrangements penalize children.

Bauserman's study emphasizes that the influential factor in custody is not where the child lives, but rather the amount of time the child spends with each parent. Children from divorced families who either live with both parents at different times or spend certain amounts of time with each parent fare better than children who live and interact with just one parent. Decisions about living arrangements in child custody arrangements should depend on the particular needs of the child—and these needs will change as the child grows and develops. For younger children who alternate between two homes in this manner, the child-care centre might be the most consistent environment in their lives.

Given the difficulties inherent in divorce and in finding a solution that will work best for all parties involved, the most common basis for determining custody arrangements has been called "the best interest of the child" principle (Lansford, 2009). This process includes consideration of the parents' wishes, the expressed wishes of the child, the child's relationship with both parents, the length of time in residential custody with the one parent, the child's adjustment during the separation period, and both the financial and emotional ability of either parent to provide for the child's needs (Skolnick, 1992). Any past history of neglect, abuse, or addiction may also be relevant in determining custodial arrangements. Needless to say, custodial arrangements are by their very nature controversial. The bottom line is that long-term legal battles full of conflict are ultimately not in the best interest of the child. In Canada, there are now many programs for divorcing parents that focus on the interests of children.

In summary, many factors influence children's eventual adjustment to divorce. Children must cope with the accumulation and interaction of many stressors at the same time (Bee & Boyd, 2007). When there are a greater number of stressors, poor coping mechanisms, and few resources, children are more at risk for serious adjustment difficulties (Olson et al., 1983). There is a growing body of research showing that most children from divorced families end up fine (Hetherington, 2003; Rutter, 2009). Others argue that effects are neutral (Li, 2007). "Most researchers have come to the conclusion that divorce has some negative effects on children's adjustment but that these effects may be small in magnitude and not universal" (Lansford, 2009, p. 140). Recent research argues that we shouldn't ask whether or not divorce affects children, but how and under what circumstances it affects children either positively or negatively (Amato, 2010). Factors like the parents' relationship, socioeconomic status of the family pre- and post-divorce, marital quality prior to divorce, and the quality of parenting have more of an effect on children's experience with divorce than the act of "divorcing" itself (Lansford, 2009). Technologies like Skype can be helpful for divorced families as children can have the opportunity to see and talk to a parent who may be living elsewhere.

In addition, the growing body of research that highlights both risk factors and factors that promote protection and resilience in children has led to improved interventions aimed at helping children of divorce (Kelly & Emery, 2003). Such interventions often employ a systems approach by addressing families as well as broader social and legal systems. This approach attempts to contain parental conflict, to promote closer relationships between children and both parents, to (when possible) include children in post-divorce arrangements, and to enhance economic stability (Kelly & Emery, 2003). In societies (such as Sweden) that have highly liberal policies for nontraditional families, and that support divorced parents, divorce produces fewer stress-related outcomes (McDaniel & Tepperman, 2007). This shows that the effects of divorce can be mitigated by supportive government policies and other social supports.

Children's Perceptions of Divorce

Young children know more about divorce than is commonly assumed (Ebling et al., 2009). Infants or toddlers may not react to a separation or divorce itself simply because of their level of cognitive development (Ambert, 2009). That is, infants will not comprehend the changes that have occurred. Infants or toddlers may, however, react to any change in the quality of caregiving from the mother. For example, since the mother is preoccupied with her own stresses related to the divorce, she may be less attentive to her children's needs. Babies may cry more, want more cuddling, or change eating and sleeping patterns as a consequence of this change in the mother. Children's attachment to the departing parent may be at risk. In situations where the father is the non-residential parent, it is he who frequently feels excluded and, as a result, decreases contact over time (Ebling et al, 2009). Divorce also impacts children's definition of family. Children affected by divorce at a young age often have vague, confused definitions of both "family" and "divorce" (Ebling et al., 2009).

Toddlers may be just as affected as infants by the change in caregiving from a distressed or resentful parent. Toddlers may not yet have the time concepts to realize that Daddy has been gone for a long time; thus, their reactions will be similar to those of younger children. However, since toddlers are moving from the developmental stage of acquiring trust or security to independence, this transition may be threatened as they experience a loss of security in their world (Ebling et al., 2009). Achieving autonomy and independence may be much more difficult for such children under these circumstances.

Preschool-age children have developed fairly clear ideas of their own families, and divorce is disruptive because it destroys those concepts. Divorce is a devastating event for young children because they do not yet have the cognitive or language capacity to fully understand this kind of change. For example, such children may ask, "How long will Daddy be gone?" or "What do you mean Daddy is gone?" Regressions to earlier forms of behaviour are common (Ebling et al., 2009) and may include crying, clinging, separation anxiety, bedwetting, or needing a soother, bottle, or blanket again. Preschool children, who see the world from their own perspective and have difficulty separating reality from their own thoughts, can experience guilt, confusion, and self-blame (Amato, 2010). For example, a little girl may tell herself, "If I'm a good girl, Mommy will come back." It is common for young children to have fantasies of their parents or families reuniting (Ebling et al., 2009). When divorce occurs, classic childhood fears may become more pronounced because the home base is no longer secure (Johnston et al., 2009). Fear of abandonment by adults, leading to clinging, is common in young children (Johnston et al., 2009). While acknowledging the confusion that preschool children experience, Hetherington (2003) suggests that their cognitive immaturity may actually be beneficial over time, since they tend to forget the conflict and their own feelings about it rather quickly.

Children aged between 5 and 7 are considered to be more vulnerable (Wallerstein, 2005) because they understand more about the implications of divorce but do not yet have ways to cope or a means of arranging activities that give them some relief. Children at this age may feel sad, deprived, angry, and lonely; they may be more demanding or disobedient; and they may often experience fears (Johnston et al., 2009), including the fear of abandonment or loss of love. For example, children at this age may reason that "Mommy loved Daddy and Mommy loved me. Now Mommy doesn't love Daddy, so maybe Mommy doesn't love me either." Although adults may not understand this fear, it can be very real for children.

Preschool and school-age children are likely to view divorce from their egocentric point of view (Amato, 2010) and, therefore, believe that they are to blame (e.g., "I should have cleaned my room better" or "If I didn't fight with my brother, this wouldn't have happened"). In addition, since children are often not provided with all the details or given all the information about the divorce, they try to make up their own understanding of it by piecing together bits of information. Adults are sometimes puzzled by children's understanding or conceptualization of the situation, but it is important to remember the child's developmental stage and reasoning abilities. Helping children to understand and cope with divorce requires seeing the situation from their perspective, bearing in mind how children think and feel at different developmental stages, and providing them with age-appropriate information.

Grieving the Loss

Adjusting to a divorce may be similar to the grief process experienced after a death (Ambert, 2009). Children may deny that the parent is gone forever and may maintain that the separation is temporary. They may experience anger at one or both parents and then may attempt to bargain to get the parents back together. As well, children may exhibit sadness or depression followed by adjustment (Ambert, 2009). Not all children will react in the same way, and often many of these emotions do not last for long periods of time (e.g., they're sad until they need a peanut-butter sandwich). Parents and early childhood educators should recognize the importance of these emotions, however, and should not minimize them merely because the emotions are short-lived. On the other hand, children may feel a recurring sense of loss because the "departed" parent still comes by. In summary, children may experience one emotion or a range of emotions that may last for a long time or be short-lived. No matter how long they last, though, these feelings have a powerful impact on children.

The Impact of Divorce on Parenting

Divorce is considered to be a crisis or tragedy in the lives of many adults (Ambert, 2009). Generally, the mental and physical health of divorced adults is at greater risk than that of their single, widowed, or married peers. Men tend to exhibit more symptoms of distress (Ambert, 2009; DeGarmo et al., 2008). Divorced fathers generally have less social support, are more anxious and angry, show less affection to their children, communicate less, and punish more. It is clear that emotions can interfere with parenting (Amato, 2010; DeGarmo et al., 2008).

Because parents are enmeshed in their own problems and need for support, the needs of their children are sometimes forgotten, and it becomes increasingly more difficult to provide a consistent environment for them. Due to the crisis, parents may be unable to respond to the emotional needs of their children. Several studies have noted that the quality of the mother-child relationship is more likely to suffer because of her personal emotional needs at the time, her anxieties associated with being single, and her self-involvement (Hetherington, 2003). All of these effects on the adult have corresponding effects on children, as well as on parenting.

Often, as both parents become immersed in their own situations and the wide range of emotions involved, the first and most significant result is that the amount and quality of communication between parents and children declines (Amato, 2010). This effect is due partly to the parents' inability to verbalize their feelings and thoughts to their children in a way that they will understand. How do you explain love, infidelity, or a change of heart in terms that children will understand when these things are difficult even for adults to grasp? This feeling of helplessness often leads to less and less communication, because parents automatically assume that young children won't understand, or because they feel it's crucial to protect their children from the crueler aspects of life.

However, young children usually do know that something is going on, and they often think that since no one will talk about it, it must be *really* bad. If we also consider children's way of thinking (i.e., the egocentric thinking, the self-blame, and the guilt) and the disproportionate fears they often have, we realize that children may perceive the situation to be much worse than it actually is.

In the period of transition after a divorce, parents of preschool children are often much less effective and consistent in their discipline, communicate less (and less effectively), and hold changing expectations for their children's behaviour (Hetherington, 2005). When the parents feel able to cope, they are attentive to the needs of their children (e.g., "It's time to take a bath" or "Tidy up your toys" or "Eat all your supper"). When parents are in a period of emotional upheaval, these day-to-day activities may not be completed. It is also common for the remaining parent to spend extended periods of time alone or on the telephone, and for the children to be left to fend for themselves or shuffled from babysitter to babysitter.

As parents experience a range of emotions, they may respond to their children in inconsistent ways. There may be times when they make few demands for appropriate behaviour, while at other times their expectations are very high. These conditions may alternate without their children understanding the cues that govern the particular situation. For example, one request for a bottle may be met with a quick response while the next is met with reprimands (e.g., "You're too old for a bottle" or "Stop acting like a baby" or "Daddy doesn't like babies"). Children begin to fear that there will be a negative reaction every time they approach the parent, and communication again is diminished. Although these things do happen in all families, it is likely that they happen more frequently when a family is experiencing high levels of stress, as in a divorce.

The last factor to consider is that, under the demands of the situation, parents may actually lose the ability to listen to their children. This failure is partly the result of parents' self-preoccupation, but it also stems partly from their children's cognitive representation of the situation. Children ask the same question over and over (e.g., "When will Daddy come home?") in an attempt to increase their understanding of the situation ("Never is a long time; it's more than one sleep"). Children also put together pieces of information in ways that seem incomprehensible to adults, which further reinforces the parents' belief that their children cannot grasp even the least complex aspects of the situation. Children may express strange ideas (e.g., "You were angry and yelled at Daddy and he had to leave, so if you get angry with me, I'll have to leave, too") or may begin to play out the happenings at home (e.g., the fights, the threats, the separation). Sometimes, children direct their anger at the custodial parent ("I hate you" or "You can't make hamburgers like Mom" or "I like Dad's stories better"). The parents may think their children's coping mechanisms are inappropriate or indicate a lack of acceptance, rather than trying to understand how children think and express themselves.

Supporting Families

We will now consider how early childhood educators can deal with the children in their care whose parents are divorced, and how they may help the parents understand their children's point of view. Despite the controversy regarding the long-term impact of divorce on children (Amato, 2010; Ambert, 2009; Wallerstein, 2005), there is little disagreement that the process of divorce is traumatic and will certainly greatly affect children who are in child care. Early childhood educators can provide a great deal of direct support to affected children, and provide either direct or indirect support to the parent.

Examine Your Attitudes

- Do you think children are better off with one parent than with two who fight?
- Is divorce always traumatic for children?
- In your opinion, can children ever get over the divorce of their parents?
- Can divorcing parents keep the interests of their children in focus?
- Should custody always be awarded to mothers?
- Can divorce have positive effects for children and families?
- Do you believe that parents should sacrifice their personal happiness and gratification to keep the family together?

As early childhood educators whose primary concern is for the well-being of the children in our care, we sometimes find it difficult not to feel angry when we see children deeply distressed because their parents have decided to divorce. These feelings may be exacerbated if the divorce brings forth associations from our own lives, rekindling memories we find painful. If, for example, your father abandoned your family for another relationship, there may be some carry-over of personal resentment to the present situation. On the other hand, your parents' divorce may have been a relief for you. If this sort of memory interferes, you may not be as aware of the impact of divorce on the children in your care.

Scenario

Personal Experiences Can Affect Our Sensitivity

Dianne was an early childhood educator in a playroom of 5-year-olds. Her earliest memories were of her mother and father fighting constantly. Often, her mother was physically abused. When her mother decided to leave, the fighting and beatings stopped. Dianne felt a sense of relief and thought that divorce was a good thing. So when 5-year-old Jessica was sad because her daddy had left, Dianne tried to explain that this was good and that her life would be much better now. Jessica felt otherwise and stopped talking about her feelings about the divorce. Because the circumstances were entirely different, Dianne's personal experience interfered with her ability to respond with sensitivity to the child.

Sometimes religious or cultural values prohibit divorce. And sometimes, even when we have the most liberal views, seeing children suffer can encourage us to view the parents as selfish.

Scenario

An Early Childhood Educator's Perspective

Shauna, an early childhood educator at a child-care centre, admitted she had negative feelings for Bernice's parents. Bernice was a well-behaved, happy child until her parents separated. They arrived at a joint-custody agreement that meant Bernice spent one week at Mom's and then one week at Dad's. Both parents felt that this was the best possible arrangement for all concerned. Shauna saw Bernice every day of the week and had a different impression. On Mondays and Tuesdays, Bernice was unsettled and cried at transitions and any change in plans for the day. Wednesdays and Thursdays, she was more settled and calm, but by Friday she was anxious, clingy, and unsettled again. Perhaps the weekends were fine for the parents, but Shauna indicated that she was lucky to have one or two good days a week with Bernice.

While there is no easy way to overcome these feelings, it is important to recognize and be aware of them, show empathy for parents, and offer practical advice when appropriate. Some reminders may be helpful:

1. Remember that there are two sides to every story and that you may not be hearing the whole story. The family is a complex system and many factors may lead to divorce. Although painful, the divorce may very well be in the best interest of the whole family.

2. Never take sides. You may have heard one partner's version, but this may differ substantially from the other partner's version. As a professional, you must remain concerned about the child's best interest without becoming involved in the parents' conflict.

3. When appropriate, provide information to parents that may help them support the child, for example, the development of a parenting plan that both parents agree on and that allows a child to have as much stability as possible in both homes, taking into account the child's friends, siblings, afternoon activities, and religious events, and the agreement to be flexible to allow a child to remain at one home for special events.

4. Provide lists of websites that provide information to parents on helping children cope with divorce and custody arrangements.

5. Examine your own beliefs and attitudes toward divorce and how these will translate into interactions with the young children and families with whom you work. Try to remember that divorce can have positive effects, especially for families in which divorce may represent an escape from an abusive situation or an opportunity for a second chance.

Lea is a 44-year-old divorced mother of two children, Rebecca, aged 9, and Grant, aged 5. Lea was recently talking about her divorce with several of her colleagues.

"I grew up in a small town in Saskatchewan in a strict Catholic home. I went to convent schools for all my education, and our family was very religious at home. I left for Saskatoon to continue with university. I worked very hard at my studies and then later at my teaching career. Consequently, I didn't marry until later in life. I met Pascal, who was also a teacher and a devout Catholic, at a church fundraiser. We were both actively involved in the church, and our love grew from there. We married when I was 33 and he was 37.

"I think we both realized that our marriage was in trouble when I was expecting our second child. I was having a difficult pregnancy, and Pascal wasn't as supportive as he'd been when our daughter was born. We had a major argument the day I arrived home with Grant, and I remember thinking, 'What am I going to do?' Divorce was just not something we could consider—the church forbids it, and my parents have been married 44 years and Pascal's parents were married 46 years before his father died.

"I stuck it out—I think we both stuck it out because we felt that we had no options. I tried seeing a counsellor, who suggested joint sessions, but Pascal figured that I had the problem, not him, so I didn't continue.

"Last year, things became unbearable. I knew that Pascal was seeing another woman, although he denied it. I finally broke down and issued him an ultimatum—either me or her. To my utter surprise, he chose her and left.

"I can't say that I'm proud of my behaviour over this last year. I've been mean, vindictive, have used the kids to get at him, and have blamed all our problems on him. Needless to say, he also blamed all our problems on me. Now that the air has had time to clear, I know why I did what I did. First, I was hurt and I wanted him to be hurt, too. But I also realize that my Catholic upbringing played a role. Divorce wasn't allowed, so I couldn't let the problems be my fault—if the breakup was his fault, then it was his sin and I wouldn't need to feel guilt. I did feel guilt, and some of my behaviour was a result of it, too, I guess. I blamed him for everything, everything was his fault, he was always the bad guy so that I could carry on with a clear conscience. I realize that much of my behaviour was influenced by my traditional religious and family beliefs."

Working with the Child

Children of divorce often understand far more than adults in their lives think they do (Ebling et al., 2009). While young children are aware of the changes going on in their family, they may express frustration at either or both parents and at others (Ebling et al., 2009). It is important that early childhood educators are aware of this and are prepared to help and support children as best as possible during this time.

Lack of stability typifies the lives of children whose parents are in the process of divorce. Therefore, the early childhood educator must try to maintain as stable an environment as possible. If circumstances permit, it may prove beneficial to have a primary early childhood educator assigned to such children to ensure this constancy. It is important to maintain consistent expectations for these children, to maintain firm yet reasonable limits, and to try not to overprotect or to indulge them. Although it's true that children may need more attention and affection, consistent limits will usually be helpful. For example, children cannot come to believe that it is okay to hit or act out frustration, or to expect extra privileges because of what is happening at home. Nevertheless, these feelings of anger and frustration must still be acknowledged and validated. There are a number of helpful Internet resources for supporting children of divorce and their families.

Children need to be listened to in an honest and nonjudgmental way. They may need to say that they hate their mom without fear of reprisal. In such cases, reflecting children's feelings may be helpful (www.helpguide.org/mental/children_divorce.htm). When a child asserts, "I hate Mom," the responsive early childhood educator can say, "You're feeling pretty angry at your mom, right?" Listening to the child can provide the early childhood educator with some insight into what might be happening at home so that further support can be offered. Listening in this way includes observing what the child does in interactions with other children, with adults, and with toys.

It may be possible to help children of divorced parents gain an understanding of their situation both cognitively and emotionally (www.helpguide.org/mental/coparenting_shared_parenting_divorce.htm). Give these children information through discussion, by reading stories, or by sharing information—other children may have had similar experiences. Recognize that children may experience a variety of emotions and may need to grieve the loss of a parent or of their family. Provide them with opportunities to work through their feelings. This means allowing each child some time to spend alone, providing them with a variety of activities like art, playdough, physical activity, or dramatic play to work through their feelings (www.helpguide.org/mental/coparenting_shared_parenting_divorce.htm).

Minimizing the Risks of Divorce for Children

There is much that the early childhood educator can do to minimize risk factors and promote protective factors when a family is experiencing a crisis such as divorce. However, every family will differ greatly in the kind of help it wants or is able to receive. Timing may be a critical factor. If parents, for example, are experiencing intense emotional turmoil, this may not be the most appropriate time to supply information about how to talk to their children. Although parents may find it helpful to be informed about their children's possible reactions, they will also find information difficult to digest or use under conditions of duress. It may be best to pass along this information at another time, but soon enough to prepare the residential parent for the child's "I hate you" screams when they come.

Bearing in mind the vast individual differences among parents in their need for and ability to act upon information, the following suggestions are cautiously offered. At the minimum, this may consist of ensuring that the parents feel confident that their child's needs will continue to be met at the child-care centre or day home. Sometimes just acknowledging the possibility of positive parent–early childhood educator communication will smooth the way for such communication to occur. There may be times when the early childhood educator is certain that something is happening at home but will not actually be told anything until much later, usually when raising a concern about the child's behaviour (see this chapter's opening vignette). All parents are different; some are open and willing to divulge all information, while others believe that divorce is a private issue. These feelings must be respected and deferred to in future communications. Early childhood educators must convey to parents that their place is not to judge but to offer support.

As well, early childhood educators need to be sure that clear boundaries are established when working with families experiencing a divorce. While early childhood educators possess a firm foundation of knowledge concerning children and some knowledge about families and family dynamics, they must also be prepared to acknowledge the limits of their expertise. Early childhood educators are not marriage counsellors and must be careful about which aspects of the divorce they discuss with parents. They need to understand these boundaries and know when to refer the parent to appropriate community resources.

The following scenario demonstrates how one early childhood educator offered support within the context of appropriate professional boundaries.

Scenario

Dealing with a Distraught Parent

Mrs. Kortright approached Guadelupe, the early childhood educator, at the end of the day. She had tears in her eyes and seemed to be on the verge of sobbing. "Everything seems to be falling apart," she said. "My ex-husband disappeared two weeks after the divorce." Shanda, her 3-year-old daughter, was wettting her bed every night and then couldn't get back to sleep. Steven, her 9-year-old son, had been called to the principal's office three times that week for fighting with the other children. "I feel like I'm going to collapse," Mrs. Kortright said.

The educator responded with empathy, acknowledging that there were a seemingly endless number of pressures Mrs. Kortright had to face. "Perhaps I can offer some ideas that may help you and Shanda through this difficult time. It's often helpful in times of crisis to have contact with a trained counsellor who specializes in helping families cope with divorce. I know that things may seem overwhelming now. Would you like me to give you the names and phone numbers of some counsellors? Their services are offered on a sliding fee scale, so cost shouldn't be a concern. Also, I know that a counsellor will be available immediately. We'll continue to do all we can here at the centre to help Shanda through this difficult period."

Note that the early childhood educator responded with nonjudgmental support and empathy, outlined clearly the boundaries of her professional expertise (i.e., the preschool child), and referred the mother to more appropriate resources that she had checked out ahead of time. She also reassured the mother that her child would continue to be cared for at the centre.

Early childhood educators must be very careful not to take sides with one parent against the other. Parents embroiled in custody disputes may try to put the early childhood educator in a difficult position by using comments made against the other parent in court. Early childhood educators must recognize this possibility and try to remain neutral.

A very moving report by Leon (University of Missouri, 2004; www.helpguide.org/mental/children_divorce.htm) represents the voice of a child as a way to illustrate how divorcing parents can reassure their children of their love and commitment. The focus of these requests is a desire on the child's part that each parent respect the other, and not fight about the child, because children often feel that they are to blame. The child pleads with the parents to communicate directly with each other and not to ask the child to take sides. The child needs to know that both parents will continue to be a part of the child's life, and help out with life's problems. She urges her parents to actively engage in frequent communication by visits, phone calls, and questions. This would be very important information to share with parents, and the way it is presented on the website makes it hard to ignore the child's plea.

Early childhood educators should keep their director or supervisor updated about families going through divorce so that an informed neutral person is available if needed. Educators may also want to discuss potential situations, such as the scenarios provided earlier, to ensure that they'll know in advance how to deal with future situations.

Early childhood educators should have the expertise to explain to parents how their children may be perceiving the divorce and to prepare them for reactions or behaviours their children may exhibit. Such behaviour may include, for example, more crying, increased need for cuddling, more resistance, strange explanations, and constant questioning. Children may also play out the divorce. Assure parents that their children need to be listened to, and suggest trying to talk about what is happening in their family and home. It may also be helpful to encourage parents to talk openly to their children to reassure them that the divorce is not their fault and that both parents still love them. The early childhood educator may help the parents by suggesting they use simple words or explanations that children may understand, by providing them with books or videos to promote discussion, and by providing concrete activities that may enhance planning (e.g., "You'll see Daddy in four sleeps"). Make sure that the parents understand that children also need to grieve and to express their anger. Children may ask the same questions over and over ("When is Daddy coming back?"), and although this may be difficult, parents need to provide answers and reassurance ("Daddy still loves you"). Children need to feel safe, and for this reason they need time to adjust to the situation emotionally.

Children's need for stability becomes apparent when transitions occur from one situation to another. Both parents and early childhood educators may have to be more aware of the need to warn children in advance. Although it seems odd, early childhood educators may want to let the children know when they're about to move to another group of children, or to make a transition to a new playroom at the end of the year, so that the children don't come to think that everyone leaves them.

Resources may be useful for both children and parents going through a divorce. Books such as *Two Homes* (Masurel & Denton, 2001) and *Standing on My Own Two Feet* (Schmidt, 2008), among others, can be instrumental in helping parents promote discussion with their children, or in helping children realize that divorce is a normal experience for many families. A simple Internet search or visit to the local public library shows that there are countless books, DVDs, and other resources designed for both parents and children to help them cope with divorce. In addition, parents can be referred to local social agencies that may provide emotional support for them or for their children. Awareness of the resources available in your community will be most helpful to families in this time of need.

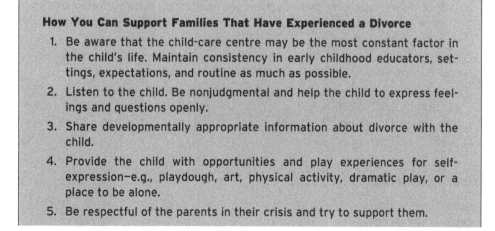

How You Can Support Families That Have Experienced a Divorce

1. Be aware that the child-care centre may be the most constant factor in the child's life. Maintain consistency in early childhood educators, settings, expectations, and routine as much as possible.

2. Listen to the child. Be nonjudgmental and help the child to express feelings and questions openly.

3. Share developmentally appropriate information about divorce with the child.

4. Provide the child with opportunities and play experiences for self-expression—e.g., playdough, art, physical activity, dramatic play, or a place to be alone.

5. Be respectful of the parents in their crisis and try to support them.

6. Establish clear boundaries with parents.

7. Provide resources and referrals for families as requested.

8. Encourage the parents' understanding of their child's reactions. Encourage parents to talk openly with the child about divorce, to discuss feelings and impending changes or plans.

Conclusion

For some families, divorce can proceed smoothly, but for others, it is a time of crisis for adults and children. Parents may be experiencing their own loss and associated pain, while the children are suffering the loss of the familiar family structure and secure home base (Amato, 2010). This change may include the permanent loss of one parent and, at least temporarily, a lessening of the availability of the remaining parent. Communication can easily break down because parents become involved in their own concerns, but also because they may think that their children are incapable of understanding or that they need to be protected from the harsher realities of life. Early childhood educators can play a key role by maintaining a safe and stable environment for the child, one where it is okay to talk and express feelings. They can also help by providing parents with the support and information they may be ready to hear (Amato, 2010). Empathetic and knowledgeable professionals can offer stability and support during this difficult time for both the child and parent.

Chapter Summary

- Over one-third of Canadian marriages end in divorce before their 30th anniversary. This figure does not include the breakup of common-law marriages.
- The impact of divorce can be seen as a disorganizing process for children and adults, which can endure over years and have lasting effects.
- There is great diversity in the way children react to divorce, including poor academic achievement, poor self-esteem, aggression, and depressive behaviours.
- Factors that affect a child's reaction to divorce include the amount of parental conflict, the number of changes after the divorce, economic factors, the presence or absence and availability of both parents, the amount of extra responsibilities placed on the child, and the custody arrangements.
- Early childhood educators can support children by listening with empathy, maintaining a stable environment for children, and maintaining consistent expectations.
- Early childhood educators can support families by finding the appropriate time to provide parents with helpful information on the child's needs, assuring the parents that the child's needs are being met while at the centre, and referring parents to community resources when appropriate.

Recommended Websites

Single Spouse: A Community for Single Parents:
www.singlespouse.com

Children and Divorce:

http://helpguide.org/mental/children_divorce.htm

www.divorceinfo.com/childrenpreschool.htm

http://parents.berkeley.edu/advice/family/divorce.html

http://kidshealth.org/parent/positive/talk/divorce.html

Four Everyday Tips from a Child of Divorce:

www.radicalparenting.com/2008/03/09/4-everyday-tips-from-a-child-of-divorce

Joint Child Custody:

http://singleparents.about.com/od/jointcustody/a/joint-child-custody-disadvantages.htm

http://fatherhood.about.com/od/managingcustody

Videos/Films

One Divided By Two: Kids and Divorce. 1998. 24 min. National Film Board of Canada. www.nfb.ca/collection/films/fiche/?id=33641

Exercises

1. Role-play or consider your responses to the following situations. (Early childhood educators may not be confronted with any or all of these, but a thoughtful response to any unexpected situation may cause less stress and conflict than making an inappropriate response on the spot.)

   a) One parent asks you for information about the other parent.

   b) The custodial parent puts you in the position of telling the noncustodial parent that the weekend visit has been cancelled.

   c) The parent wants to tell you everything about the divorce.

   d) The child refuses to go home with Mom. He says he hates her because she made Daddy go away.

   e) The father is attacking the quality of care at the child-care centre. You find out that if Dad has custody, the child will stay at home with a full-time nanny. If Mom has custody, full-time child care will be required.

   f) The mother lies to the child and says, "Daddy isn't here because he didn't want to see you this weekend."

   g) The parent tells you that what happens at home is none of your business.

2. Check community resources for those that deal with divorce-support groups for parents and programs for children. These will vary from community to community, so it may be useful to know in advance what is available.

3. Check your local library and bookstore for books about divorce. Are there any you would want to recommend for parents? Are there any that would help parents understand divorce better from the child's perspective? Is there a book that might stimulate conversations about divorce with the child? Would this book be appropriate for parents to share with their children?

chapter 6

Blended Families

Objectives

- **To consider the challenges involved when new families are formed.**

- **To discuss children's feelings about becoming part of a blended family.**

- **To discuss parents' reactions to their children during the blending process.**

- **To discuss the role of the early childhood educator in supporting parents and children.**

Frank, a 50-year-old man who had been divorced for 15 years and whose children were grown up, made the following comment shortly after his marriage to Margaret, a 42-year-old woman who had a 5-year-old son. Margaret and Jordan had moved into Frank's condominium while they were all waiting to buy a new house. "When I came home from work the other day, I tripped over Jordan's toys as I entered the front door. Jordan heard the beginning of a string of profanities, which I controlled as soon as I realized that I was not alone in the house! I guess there are a lot of things that I'm going to have to get used to, not the least of which is having to share my living room with a 5-year-old and his toys!"

Remarriage has become much more common today. In Canada (excluding Quebec), approximately 58% of divorced women and 70% of divorced men remarry (Ambert, 2009). Nevertheless, the view still exists that stepfamilies are incomplete or inferior, a view that is reinforced by negative stereotypes, myths, and media representations. The adjustment to a parent's remarriage is a complex process that plays out differently in different families (Dupuis, 2007). This adjustment is often complicated by the fact that, as a society, we do not yet have norms or realistic expectations for how this type of family should operate or for how the new roles and relationships should be defined (Dupuis, 2007). Step-parents themselves may be oversensitive to family problems due to the stigma related to stepfamilies. People often assume that stepfamilies are more susceptible to problems than two-parent biological families. Researchers have noted that there is a lack of quality assistance available for remarriage and stepfamily preparation. Traditionally, few family professionals have been trained to work with stepfamilies, although this is changing (Dupuis, 2007). The tendency to consider stepfamilies as nontraditional, atypical, or pathological, however, has been decreasing in recent years (Dupuis, 2007).

Many terms are used to describe what results when previously distinct families come together. Examples include *reconstituted, blended,* or *stepfamilies,* as well as *The Brady Bunch* or *Yours, Mine and Ours.* Some of these terms seem to carry with them negative implications. *Step-parents* may bring forth images of Cinderella's wicked stepmother, and the myth that stepmothers are evil has significant consequences for both the self-esteem of the stepmother and the relationships she has with family members (Fanning, 2008; Planitz & Feeny, 2009). The term *blended families* has to a large extent replaced the term *stepfamilies.* Dr. Margorie Engel, president and CEO of the Stepfamily Association of America, opposes this change. She claims that the term *blended* is misleading, and that "couples with 'blended' as their objective tend to have the most problematic households because some or all of the members won't buy into the blended concept" (Engel, 2002). Whatever they are called, the myths are still very much with us. What we will see in this chapter, though, is that the "blending" is different for each family, and in some cases there may not be much blending at all after a remarriage.

There is great variability in the makeup and structure of "blended" families. In some of these families, both spouses will have children from previous marriages; in others, only one spouse will have children. As well, new children may be added after the remarriage, or the new couple may have no children together. In some cases, one of the spouses has never been married before and thus has no experience with young children, or, if there is an age difference between the couple, a new stepmother who has had no experience raising adolescent children may have difficulty stepping into a parental role (Hull & Mather, 2006). Thus, the experiences of stepfamilies may be very different because of the great variation in structure that exists among them.

When two families join together to form a new family, the end result is often a positive one. Remarriage can offer each spouse emotional and financial security (Ambert, 2006), and it can result in having another adult to share parenting duties, intimacy and sexual satisfaction, and the happiness that comes from having a successful relationship. For all these reasons, the task of parenting itself may seem easier, partly because step-parents may enrich the child's life and provide an extra measure of emotional security. After divorce or single parenthood, parents may perceive this as a welcome relief. However, most step-parents will attest to periods of friction and doubt with their stepchildren. They will also point out the need for patience and support from within the family, as well as for external support. In this chapter, we will consider the challenges facing blended families, both from the adults' and the children's perspectives, and the role of early childhood educators in supporting families in this major transition period.

Challenges for Stepfamilies

Stepfamilies face many challenges in the context of the couple relationship, in the new parent–child relationship, and in extended family systems. Other challenges may be related to previous family histories. We will explore these various challenges in more detail.

Myths About Step-Parents

One of the co-authors of this book tells the following story about her daughter.

The Evil Stepmother

"One day I was driving with my 4-year-old daughter. She repeatedly asked to have the window wipers turned on, even though it wasn't raining. After I refused her request for the third time, she said that if I didn't turn on the wipers, I would be a stepmother. My daughter has never met a stepmother and doesn't understand what one is, but she obviously has her own idea of what a stepmother must be like."

We can assume that the daughter's perceptions have been shaped by stories or television, and that if she were to become part of a blended family, that perception would have an impact on the development of her relationship with a new stepmother.

Children can develop myths about their step-parents—either positive or negative. On the one hand, they may have unrealistic expectations that the new step-parent will "fix everything" and may be quite disappointed when this does not happen. On the other hand, the new step-parent is often blamed for causing all the changes that the child faces. The child may have to move to a different neighbourhood, change schools, and possibly lose friends. In these circumstances, it is common for children to feel hostility and resentment (Hull & Mather, 2006). Several authors (Claxton-Oldfield et al., 2002; Ward, 2006) have described additional myths about stepfamilies. The first is that "step is less" (Wald, 1981). This myth entails the belief that a nonbiological or step-parent can never love a child as much as a biological parent does. On the other hand, some people believe in the myth that blended families will replace the biological parent, thus re-creating the two-parent family (De Angelis, 2005). This may create an expectation of "instant love," which may be exceedingly difficult to live up to. Finally, as cited above, sometimes there is the belief that the new parent will "fix everything." For the child who has had an absent father, or for the child who has experienced parental conflict prior to divorce, the hope is often that the new step-parent will be the "rescuer" who will undo the damage done in prior relationships. Obviously, this is an unrealistic expectation.

Roles and Expectations

While it is hoped that we are moving away from the concept of "the wicked stepmother," we still lack a clear idea of the new roles parents take on in a blended family situation. Sometimes step-parents are seen as "mature friends" for the children of their spouses, who play with the children but do not participate in discipline or in making major decisions. However, in a shared household (as in the scenario at the beginning of the chapter), this role may be difficult to maintain. Is the new parent to become a partial replacement for a noncustodial parent? If so, in what aspects of parenthood should the step-parent engage—financial commitment, discipline, or recreational activities?

Often one or both step-parents wonder who is responsible for managing money, and who will discipline whom. Stepmothers may face the challenge of a societal expectation that they will take on the major responsibility for raising the children, and this can be very difficult, especially if they are not readily accepted by their stepchildren.

One of the factors that can contribute to or impair healthy family development in a newly blended family is the relationship with the ex-spouse (Ambert, 2006). Often there is animosity, and the ex-spouse may have serious concerns about the way the new spouse relates to his or her children. The biological parent and the step-parent may share in the care of the child, but may not share approaches to discipline and child-rearing. When the ex- and current spouse have shared the same partner, it is likely that boundary issues could be quite complex. As pointed out by Ambert, we have little research to date on these factors, but plenty of anecdotal stories exist in movies, magazine articles, and conversations between people who are in these situations. Former in-laws can complicate matters, as can unresolved past issues that may interfere with a partner's ability to trust the new spouse (Coleman & Ganong, 2004). We also know little about how extended family members impact the new blended family—they can either be supportive or an added stressor.

Complexity of the Family Structure

We do not have well-established norms for depicting the many kinds of relationships that evolve when a marriage dissolves and a new one is formed. This results in "role ambiguity" (Carroll et al., 2007). Examples of this ambiguity could relate to the "grandparents" (parents of the step-parent), to the relationship between the siblings and step-siblings, as well as between the ex-spouses and the new spouses, who may need to relate to each other over matters of child care. Children have been known to ask "Which dad?" when an adult asks them a question about their father.

Scenario

When Stepchildren Are Treated Differently

Sam and Marina married when Marina's two daughters were aged 14 and 16. A year after their marriage, they had a son, Steven. When Steven was 2, Sam's mother invited the family to a Christmas dinner. As the gifts were opened, Steven gasped with delight when he opened his generous gift from his grandmother. The step-granddaughters tried to hide their hurt feelings when they opened their token gifts. In discussing this later with a family counsellor, the two girls were embarrassed about their reactions. "We know she's not our 'real' grandmother," said the 19-year-old, "and it's very childish of me to feel hurt. But it's kind of hard being 'family' but not really part of the family."

In a further complication, blended families often have different values and traditions, and even when core values are the same, those values may be played out quite differently in different households (Davis, 2000; Henry & McCue, 2009). Little things, such as how birthdays are celebrated or which holidays will now be celebrated when two cultures join, may cause confusion. Families may be at very different stages in the life cycle. One parent may have adolescent children and may be dealing with the associated concerns and parenting issues, while the other spouse brings an infant or toddler into the remarriage, introducing a completely different life cycle into the blend. All of these factors add complexity and perhaps play a role in the adjustment of all family members. Blended families may also struggle with complicated financial arrangements as well as conflicting practices and priorities (Gold, 2009).

The Couple Subsystem

A new intimate relationship is usually a source of joy to both partners. As they begin to explore the physical and emotional aspects of their new relationship, they can be hampered by the presence of young children. Generally when newlyweds begin their life together, they have time to adjust to their changing roles in this union before they become parents. With stepchildren, they have to adjust to parenting roles at the same time (Ambert, 2006). Again, there are few guidelines for blended families regarding boundaries between children and parents and for prioritizing the couple relationship. On the one hand, if the new spouses take the time to be on their own to enhance their relationship, the supervision and support of children may falter. At the other extreme, the couple relationship could suffer if the children are always the top priority and if guilty feelings about the remarriage distort the parents' perceptions about reasonable expectations of the child.

Scenario

Adjusting to the Presence of Young Children in a Remarriage

A single mother with a 4-year-old daughter had been involved with a young man for a few months when they decided to marry. He had not been previously married, and had become very fond of the young girl. When they decided that the three of them would go on a honeymoon together, it did at times seem strange to the young man to hear his future stepdaughter discuss her honeymoon plans with her friends.

Sometimes step-parents may feel that their needs come second to the needs of their partner's biological children. On the other hand, the relationship between the couple is legally binding, as in any marriage, but there is no such binding relationship between the step-parent and stepchildren. A remarriage does not require that the new partner take any financial or social responsibility for the stepchildren.

Planning the blending process by taking into account these potential difficulties might help to reduce their intensity. For example, steps can be taken to foster the development of the relationship between the step-parent and children before the marriage, and agreements regarding household task-sharing can be discussed during this preliminary stage. The development of new boundaries between subsystems in the new family will be one challenge that will require some thought (Sweeney, 2010).

One newly remarried parent confided the following: "I read all the books, and I knew all the 'recipes' for successful blending. Then I did everything practically the opposite of what I had planned to do." Experts often forget that emotions do sometimes interfere with the implementation of their advice or that advice may not be available until it is too late. When conflicts appear, parents may encounter feelings of guilt, self-blame, helplessness, or confusion. Children's reactions to the new situation, which we will discuss in the next section, can increase these feelings, thereby putting further stress on the marriage and on the task of parenting.

Children's Reactions

The results of research on the effects of remarriage on children are ambiguous. It is difficult to separate the effects of the "blending" from other factors that will have impacted children's lives. Earlier studies indicated that both divorce and remarriage put children at risk for developing social, psychological, behavioural, and school problems (Hetherington, 2005). Children in blended families were more likely to be described as aggressive and noncompliant, to display acting-out behaviour, to be disruptive in social relationships, and to have adjustment difficulties. Behavioural problems were more prominent in the early months after the remarriage, when the family was consolidating. The educational achievement of children from blended families seems to be lower than in children of two-parent families (Case et al., 2000).

On the other hand, some writers suggest that behavioural problems, common after remarriage, may result from reduced involvement with the noncustodial parent and may not be a result of the remarriage per se (Hetherington, 2005; Sweeney, 2010). In addition, some authors argue that behavioural problems and educational differences may be the result of previous marriage dissolution and the experience of single parenthood prior to remarriage, as opposed to remarriage itself (Sweeney, 2010).

Ambert's (2006) review of the research reveals that boys may adjust better than girls, although the research is not definitive. The age of children at the time of remarriage seems to have an impact, with younger children adjusting on the whole more readily.

DeAngelis (2005) describes a study that looks at different kinds of stepfamilies and their relative success with the children. The most successful were what he called "neotraditional" families, where parents formed a solid committed partnership so that they could nurture their marriage and the children, and didn't get stuck on notions of what an ideal family should be like. A second category of stepfamilies is referred to as "matriarchal," where the mother marries for her own companionship and does not expect her new husband to take on a significant role in child-rearing. This seemed to work as long as the new husband did not want to play a greater role. The most divorce-prone families were those who had romantic notions and unrealistic expectations, and wanted to create a "perfect" family atmosphere.

Children's reactions to this transition, as with other major life changes, will be related to their own developmental level and their ability to comprehend. Their responses will be influenced by the way in which they are prepared for the event, by their experiences prior to the blending of families, and by the number of changes that accompany the remarriage. Besides adjusting to a new parent, children have to adjust to new rules, new traditions, new extended families, new siblings, and a new way of life. We also know that the relationship between the biological parents impacts the relationship quality and contact between the step-parent and child. If there is conflict between the biological parents, the stepfather–child relationship has been shown to suffer (DeGarmo et al., 2008). Furthermore, the degree to which stepchildren are monitored will influence the outcome for the child. The research suggests that children may be monitored more closely in homes with two biological parents. Thus, higher levels of monitoring of children in step-parenting households will likely lead to better outcomes for children. Also, influences like friends, neighbours, and schools can be very helpful for children throughout this transition (DeAngelis, 2005).

A stepfamily typically comes together after a loss, such as divorce (Ambert, 2006). Children need to grieve this loss and to bid goodbye to the dreams they carried about their first family, which can take up to two years or longer (Favazza & Munson, 2010). Remarriage may shatter children's fantasies that their original family will reunite or that their parents will reconcile (Goldenberg & Goldenberg, 2008). Children may lose their status as the oldest child, the baby, or the only child when other children enter the stepfamily. They may also lose a valued role with their biological parent. For example, a mother and daughter may have had a close relationship in which they confided in each other about everything, which may be lost within the new stepfamily. Similarly, children who have been raised in single-parent families may feel that they are losing a unique relationship with their parent, and may feel that they are losing some of their independence and autonomy.

The early stage in stepfamilies involves coping with the loss of the old family. During this time, a new co-parenting style must emerge while all family members need to accept the new family dynamics and feel comfortable in both houses. The middle stage represents a time of adjustment and rebuilding. An understanding and appreciation of the new family, and the way each parent behaves, develops during this period. The later stage involves the continued reorganization of rules and boundaries as all family members, particularly children, grow and develop.

Long-term adjustment is related to the personality of the child, the number of new stresses encountered by the child, the quality of the new blended family's home environment, and the resources available to support the child (Hetherington, 2003).

Obstacles in Step-Parent–Child Relations

The establishment of the step-parent–child relationship can be challenging, and several obstacles appear to be common.

Discipline and Child-Rearing Issues

As described previously, even when the new couple shares basic values they may not share the same ideas about daily living. It would be quite miraculous if the two families that came together had exactly the same practices for guidance and discipline. Children may react strongly to a change in expectations of their behaviour, and may respond with strong statements, such as "I hate him!" In a family with two biological parents, the reaction of parents might be something like, "I know you're angry at Daddy now, but I'm sure you'll get used to the new rule." In a new blended family, the reaction is more likely to be one of stress, guilt, and concern about the future of the relationship.

When the new parent undertakes the role of disciplining and guiding the children, it is sometimes a matter of trial and error. While all parents make "mistakes," a step-parent does not have the long-standing bond of unconditional love that forms over the years between parents and children. While the biological mother may overreact to a cup of spilled milk and speak harshly to her daughter, an apology and a cuddle might set things straight. However, if the step-parent overreacts to the same incident, it is harder afterward to resolve the hurt feelings (Hetherington, 2003).

Divided Loyalties

In many cases, new step-parents, usually stepfathers, will have children of their own who live with their ex-spouse. It is not uncommon in such a case for guilty feelings toward the biological children to interfere with the development of positive relations with the stepchildren. In families where the children of both marriages reside together, jealousy and rivalries between the stepchildren are not uncommon. A new stepmother who tries to establish a bond with her stepchildren may feel disloyal to her own children. A stepfather may need to decrease involvement with his biological children in order to make his new marriage and stepfamily work. Stepmothers often feel caught between their love for their husbands and guilt for remarrying against their children's wishes (Hart-Byers, 2009). Not surprisingly, women seem to be more deeply upset about stepfamily problems than men are (Hart-Byers, 2009). It is not uncommon for all the members of newly reconstituted families to feel pulled in many different directions.

Just as the parents may feel torn between bonds of loyalty toward various members of the new family, children, too, often experience this dilemma (Goldenberg & Goldenberg, 2008). Attachment to the step-parent may cause the children to feel disloyal to their biological parent. A simple issue such as what to call the new father can be a source of major concern and trigger many emotions. When the new step-parent assumes a role in discipline and guidance, children may feel that compliance involves disloyalty to their biological parent. It is difficult for children to ascertain where their loyalties should lie or how to divide those loyalties among all the players.

Sexuality

This man's anxiety was well founded. There is a higher incidence of sexual abuse in stepfamilies than in biological families (Ambert, 2006). While most step-parents are not abusers, fears surrounding this sensitive, seldom-discussed issue can impede the development of affectionate relations. Certainly it is also true that, as children grow older, stepsiblings can be attracted to each other and will need guidance and protection in this regard. Stepfamilies that include adolescents may need to consider this issue before moving in together (Hetherington, 2003).

Finances

Although the blending of families often results in improved living conditions (Gold, 2009; Hetherington, 2003), money can become a source of conflict in some cases (Gold, 2009). Some studies have suggested that financial strains are more frequent in remarried couples (Lebow & Newcomb-Rekart, 2007). Typically, financial matters are more complicated, with issues to be resolved such as support payments to children. And since there are no norms regarding the obligation of step-parents to offer financial support to stepchildren, problems often arise regarding decisions as to who pays for what. These problems are more likely to occur when the children get older and questions such as who will pay for college education arise. However, there are many expenses involved in the rearing of young children, and issues of financial responsibility need to be carefully worked out.

Idealized Images

Children often idealize the parent who no longer lives with them. Although this is more likely to occur after the death of a parent, it does happen after divorce as well. When the shadow of an "ideal" real parent looms large, it is difficult for children to form an attachment to their step-parent. "Mommy would never get mad at me for doing that" or "My real daddy always played with me after supper" are difficult ideals for the new step-parent to live up to.

As well, children may become jealous of their parent's affection for the new partner and new stepsiblings. Children may view the new adult as a threat to their established parent–child relationship (Hetherington, 2003). This may be more pronounced for the only child of a formerly single parent, who may not be used to sharing parental attention with anyone, and who may have had a special relationship with that parent (e.g., "You used to tell me everything; now you only ever talk to him"). When we bear in mind that the parents may be very involved in their own relationship, it is understandable that the child may feel left out and jealous.

Supporting Blended Families

Sometimes children who are in the process of blending into a new family are undergoing so many changes in their lives that the child-care setting or preschool becomes a secure haven for them. There is currently much more recognition that appropriate intervention, parent education, and counselling can be highly significant in preventing divorce in blended families (Higginbotham & Adler-Baeder, 2008; Higginbotham & Myler, 2010; Higginbotham et al., 2010; Hull & Mather, 2006; Sobon, 2005). Providing stability for the child and support for families may be the most important way early childhood educators can help blended families. Structured, predictable environments may offer much-needed stability at a time of major changes at home. It may be especially beneficial to provide the child with a primary early childhood educator, if possible. The constant reassurance of having a caring and trusted adult with whom the child feels secure can play a strong role in providing that extra bit of support that the child may require at this time of transition.

Empathizing with the tensions that the family may experience is an essential component of supporting families. Our attitudes and beliefs about step-parenting will affect our ability to empathize and offer the necessary support. One of the most helpful things an early childhood educator can do, if the step-parents are open to having this discussion, is to encourage work with a therapist who has expertise in working with stepfamilies, and possibly to help them in accessing information about where such therapists may be found. Early childhood educators can universalize the experience by sharing their knowledge about the challenges faced by all or most blended families, which can relieve some of the guilt and stress that parents may feel.

Check the following "Examine Your Attitudes" box to see whether any of the myths about blended families mentioned earlier in this chapter influence your thinking. It would also be a useful exercise to think of how you would address the step-parent in a letter or in a face-to-face exchange. In this way, you may be better able to empathize with any feelings of awkwardness the stepchild is experiencing.

Examine Your Attitudes

- Do you view the step-parent as the "wicked stepmother (father)" or as a "white knight" who rescues the stepchildren from an uncomfortable situation?
- Do you think that mothering comes naturally to women and that there will be "instant love" between a stepmother and her stepchildren?
- Is a stepfamily something less than a "real family" in your view?
- Do you believe that a stepfamily is automatically a better situation for children than a single-parent family?
- Do you think blending is an easy process that just naturally happens when people love each other?

Sharing Information with Parents

Bearing in mind our hesitations about giving advice, we still believe that there are times when providing parents with information can be helpful. The three major issues most likely to be raised in a blended family are (a) establishing discipline and parental authority for children, (b) forming a strong marital relationship, and (c) developing ongoing arrangements with the noncustodial parent. Early childhood educators may be able to provide this type of support and information. It is important that the information shared not be interpreted as criticism of the parents or as an expectation that they will implement the advice. We must also bear in mind that the advice we have to give is tentative, since we too have much to learn about what works and what does not. In addition, we must remember that blended families form a diverse population; therefore, not all suggestions will be appropriate to all families.

New Territory

A review of the challenges and problems involved in the blending of families should not be interpreted as a warning against remarriage. In fact, second marriages tend to last. The age of couples at their first and second marriage is a factor, with greater success for older couples than for younger ones (Statistics Canada, 2006). As well, social support seems to be a decisive factor in the success of second marriages (Statistics Canada, 2006). We have a lot to learn about how different kinds of reconstituted families work out ways to face their challenges and become familiar with ways that may be quite different from the biological nuclear family.

Scenario

Different Family Backgrounds

Charlene and Lauren were talking in the back seat of the car. Lauren was explaining that she was going to spend part of the summer with her real mom and Bill, her new stepfather. She would see her old stepfather and stepbrother for a week, then spend the rest of the summer with her real dad and her stepmother and her children. Charlene had trouble following the conversation and tried to understand by describing her family with her one dad and one mom. Lauren sat for a minute and then remarked, "That means you only get one birthday present from your mom and dad. Wow, that's too bad."

This conversation between children from very different families shows that children often accept their lives as being normal or typical once they grow accustomed to them. Lauren was shocked by the news that her friend would only get one present because she had only one set of parents. By helping children to recognize and appreciate the differences in routines, expectations, roles, and other aspects of family life, early childhood educators can help children adjust to blending.

Hetherington (2003) suggests that stepfamilies need to give up the fantasy image of the happy, nuclear family in order to adjust. When they let go of this ideal, they will become more flexible, more realistic, and better able to cope. They may need to establish more flexible boundaries with the many people involved with the blended family, including the non-custodial parents, rather than closing in like the nuclear family.

Time

Some step-parents might appreciate being reminded that, just as they are exploring the new territory of a remarriage and blended family, so too, is society at large only beginning to learn about this increasingly common phenomenon. Stepfamilies may need encouragement to give the adjustment period more time, and may require professional help in establishing new norms and boundaries for the family (Hull & Mather, 2006).

Sometimes step-parents feel pressured to "make it work," and they become frustrated when the bond between them and their stepchildren does not develop as well or as rapidly as they had hoped. They may find it helpful to be reassured that these relationships often take time. Emotional attachments between the step-parent and child may take longer to develop because this relationship is not as binding as the marriage is and because integration into a family can take time (Goldenberg & Goldenberg, 2008). Children may need some time to adjust to all the changes and to the new parent. Step-parents cannot be expected to like or love their stepchildren automatically, and, likewise, demands cannot be placed on children to accept or love their new parent (Hetherington, 2003). They will gradually learn what works for them and what doesn't and then be able to establish their own expectations.

In the early stages, stepfamilies are typically made up of two subsystems—the "absorbing" or "veteran" family members and the "newcomer(s)" (Hull & Mather, 2006, p. 264). Eventually, the subsystems become less distinct, but this does take time.

There is another time factor involved in the relationship of the parents. It is important for a newly married couple with children to have time alone together. Early childhood educators can help alleviate parental guilt by demonstrating an understanding of their need to be alone and by helping them explain this to their children.

Permission

We described earlier the problem of divided loyalties that many children experience during the transition to a new family structure. Children may not be comfortable calling the new parent "Mom" or "Dad," but they may be more comfortable with first names or an original title. One early childhood educator told her class that she was called "Mom Number Two" for many years after she became a step-parent. Another said that she was called "New Mom."

It may in fact be easier for children to adjust to the new situation if the adults in their lives give them explicit verbal "permission" to maintain their loyalty to their biological parent. Communication between early childhood educators and parents can ensure that children's decisions about how they refer to their biological and step-parents are reinforced both at home and in the centre.

Communication

Studies have indicated that major improvements take place in behaviour, child adjustment, and self-esteem when communication occurs between step-parents and the children (Braithwaite et al., 2004; Halford et al., 2007). This includes open and frequent communication about family roles, boundaries, shared identity, adjustments to the family, and diverse expectations, conflicts, and feelings. Communication seems to be the key to adjustment for a step-family (Braithwaite et al., 2004; Golish, 2003; Halford et al., 2007). Sometimes early childhood educators can help parents formulate these role clarifications in simple language, at the child's level of comprehension. "When Mommy isn't home, John will give you supper. If you don't want to finish all your food, you don't have to. You can have a snack later when Mommy gets home. When Mommy's away, John will be in charge."

Activities

With all the new arrangements and attempts to blend, families sometimes lose sight of the joy of being together. Joint fun activities can go a long way in helping the development of positive relationships. Early childhood educators may be able to suggest child-care activities or community events for families. Sometimes a gentle reminder and permission to let go and laugh can be very helpful.

Adjusting Expectations

A child in nursery school was having a difficult time getting used to living with his new father. His mother had remarried four months previously, and his new dad had never been married or had children. One of the first activities they participated in as a family was a picnic at the nursery school. Afterward the parents remarked that the event had been special because it was the first they had enjoyed as a family and because the father was finally able to see what other 3- and 4-year-old children were like. He could now readjust his expectations for his stepson's behaviour.

New Family Traditions

Family traditions and rituals can be seen as binding agents that help hold families together (Hutchinson et al., 2007). Newly reconstituted families can be encouraged to develop new family traditions to replace the ones that the members may have left behind, or to adapt rituals and traditions from the previous household. These could be as simple as the stepfather making a pancake breakfast each Sunday or the family watching a video or DVD every Saturday evening. New traditions could also involve more elaborate events like celebrating the anniversary of the family's move to their new home. Establishing such traditions can add to children's sense of security and identification with the new family.

Sometimes, newly remarried parents suffer from "super parent" syndrome. They may feel that the world (and their children's teachers) are judging them, and that it is important to demonstrate that all is well. An empathetic early childhood educator somehow gets the message across that parents will not be judged and that the door is open to discuss issues that concern their child. If parents express concerns that go beyond the professional boundaries of the early childhood educator, they should be referred to community resources such as support groups for stepfamilies or family-counselling agencies. Early childhood educators may also be able to suggest books for children or adults that may be helpful. When parents understand that early childhood educators can be counted on to listen and, if necessary, to provide resources, then both children and parents can adjust much more easily to their newly blended family.

Conclusion

Each stepfamily is different from every other one, and each faces many challenges. Families may include different people from various extended families, each with his or her own histories. There may also be complicating factors, such as the need to deal with noncustodial parents. Stepfamilies are still subject to societal pressure, as is evident in the many myths that still exist about stepfamilies and in the common belief that the most successful stepfamilies are those that most closely resemble the nuclear family. The mere fact that these myths are so commonplace puts an enormous amount of stress on the blended family. However, the literature suggests that, over time, children do adjust and that stepfamilies do integrate successfully (Hetherington, 2003). When families understand the problems they may have to deal with and know about the support systems available, successful adjustment is more likely. Early childhood educators can play an important role in promoting resilience and adjustment in children and parents of blended families.

Chapter Summary

- Over 50% of divorced Canadian women and 70% of divorced men remarry; thus, blended families are a growing reality in our society.
- Challenges for blended families include societal myths, unclear role expectations, and the complexity of the new family system.
- The effects of living in a blended household are difficult to extract from effects of other life events that the child has undergone, such as divorce, but seem to be linked to lowered academic success, increases in noncompliant and aggressive behaviour, and disruption in social relationships.
- Positive and frequent communication about changes, boundaries, and feelings seems to be a key ingredient for success.
- Early childhood educators can offer support, encourage blended families to enter into counselling or therapy, and provide the child with a secure and stable environment.

Recommended Websites

National Stepfamily Resource Center:
www.stepfamilies.info

The Step and Blended Family Institute:
www.stepinstitute.ca/index.php

The Stepfamily Foundation:
www.stepfamily.org

Blended Family Focus and Resource Network:
www.blendedfamilyfocus.com

Videos/Films

For Generations to Come. 1994. 82 min. Ward/Weaver/Allen/De Young Family. National Film Board of Canada.

Exercises

1. List some of the challenges a new blended family might face. Discuss strategies that might help the family overcome these challenges.
2. What beliefs do you hold about blended families? Try to identify how you might have acquired those beliefs. How might your particular beliefs hinder you in providing appropriate care for the children of blended families?
3. How would you explain blended families to a group of young children, all of whom come from nuclear families?
4. Check out community resources and support groups that relate to blended families. Which would you feel comfortable recommending to parents? Under which circumstances?
5. Check your library for books pertaining to blended families. Make a list of those that would be appropriate for children and those that would be beneficial for their parents.
6. Review the books in your centre. How many of these show blended families to be as normal as two-parent nuclear families?
7. Consider ways in which noncustodial parents may stay involved in a child's life. Is this possible? Desirable? Discuss.

chapter 7

Single Parents

Objectives

- To understand the nature and prevalence of single parents in Canada.
- To clarify attitudes toward single-parent families.
- To discuss the implications of single parenting for adults and children.
- To consider the role of the early childhood educator in supporting single-parent families.

A young single father made every attempt to attend preschool events with his 4-year-old son, Rahim. He regularly acted as a classroom volunteer and never missed a parent function. At the final windup party, the preschool teacher kept telling the children to show their moms this, or get their moms to help them with that. Jokingly, the single father would yell out each time, "And dad!" The last straw came when the teacher gave each child a year scrapbook and said, "Show this to your mom!" When she presented Rahim's book, he threw it down and began to wail for his mother. "Why can't she be here, I hate her!" he cried. At this point, the early childhood educator realized what she had done, but it was too late. A very upset father gathered his son and his belongings and left.

Profile of Single-Parent Families

Single parents, sometimes called lone parents or one-parent families, are often referred to as a particular group in society, but in fact they are very diverse. In earlier days, most one-parent families were created when a spouse died—whereas today the majority are created through divorce (Ambert, 2009). One-parent families form when a couple separates and one of the ex-partners has custody of the children, when a woman gives birth to a child and does not live with the child's father or any other partner, when a father or mother is widowed, and when a single person adopts (Ambert, 2006). As well, there is a relatively small number of single women who have a child using in vitro fertilization who would also be included in this category, which will be addressed in more detail in the "single mothers by choice" section in Chapter 9. The vast majority (85%) of one-parent families are headed by females (http://family. jrank.org/pages/1574/Single-Parent-Families-Demographic-Trends.html), although there has been a 57.5% increase in single-father single parent households since 1981 (Statistics Canada, 2007a). Most one-parent families result from divorce, and about a quarter of one-parent families are a result of nonmarital birth. Only a tiny proportion of single fathers have never been married—they usually become single fathers following a marriage breakup (Beaupre et al., 2010). It is now estimated that close to 50% of children live in single-parent families for at least a brief period in their childhood (Ambert, 2009).

The financial and social circumstances of single-parent families vary as well. Many single parents are women who are struggling to make ends meet financially and who are stuck in low-paying jobs that grant little satisfaction. In fact, the vast majority of single mothers suffer from economic disadvantage (Walberg & Mrozek, 2009). Single fathers seem to be at less risk of economic disadvantage than single mothers are (Beaupre et al., 2010). Some single parents live with and receive emotional support from their extended families, while others live alone with their children and feel socially isolated. Some children of lone parents have ongoing positive contact with the nonresidential parent. In other cases, especially where there is continued animosity between the parents, children have little or no contact with their noncustodial parent. Some single parents may be living with partners who are actively involved with the children, and some may live alone. All of these differences, in addition to family background, personality, and coping styles, will have an impact on how single-parent families function and how the children in those families develop.

Effects on Children

As described above, there is so much diversity in the population of single parents that it is difficult to lump all the children of single parents together when considering the effects of single parenthood on children. Overall, however, most researchers agree that children in one-parent female-headed homes do not fare as well as their counterparts from two-parent homes. It is difficult to determine what effects living with a single parent may have on children, since any effects may be complicated by the factors of separation, divorce, and the absence of the noncustodial parent, all of which may have a cumulative effect on children. The existence of the single-parent family presents a different reality for children and may impact them in a variety of ways. In addition, families who are headed by a single parent due to death face different issues than families headed by a single parent by choice, divorce, or military service. Different issues are involved if remarriage is pending. In fact, most of the literature is based on studies from father-absent homes, where the interaction of a number of variables may not have been fully considered. As well, difficulties associated with increased stress, a lower standard of living, and fewer social resources may complicate our understanding of the effects of growing up in a single-parent family. Children from single-parent homes have been characterized as more dependent, less compliant, more anti-social, and more likely to experience difficulties at school. They also raise more behavioural and psychological concerns (Ward, 2006) and are more at risk of becoming young offenders (Anderson, 2002).

When considering these rather discouraging findings, it is vital to remember that the worrisome outcomes for children of one-parent families are almost identical to findings from studies on the impact of poverty on children (see Chapter 13). Children of one-parent affluent families do not show the same difficulties. Furthermore, the outcomes for siblings differ even when raised in similar circumstances (Dunn, 2004; Lansford, 2009), suggesting that genetics, child temperament, and personality may play a role as well. Thus, the outcome for children of lone parents seems to depend mostly on the economic circumstances, but also on the mother's characteristics, education, mental health, and social support. Also important are the quality of the parenting, the child's characteristics, and the characteristics of, contribution of, and relationship with the nonresidential parent (usually the father) (Ambert, 2009).

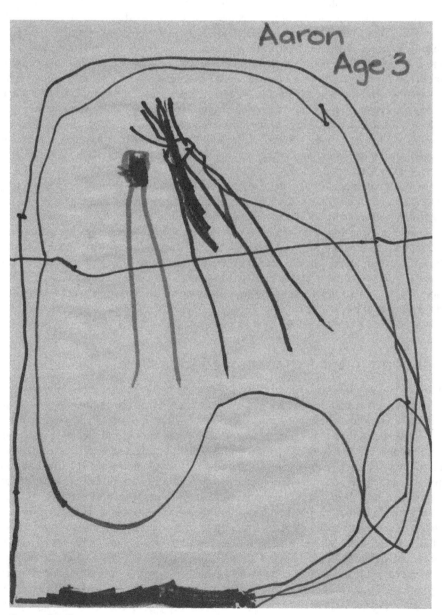

Aaron, Age 3

Attitudes Toward Single Parents

Single parents have often found themselves socially stigmatized. Even today, cultural values of most societies dictate that children be raised by two parents who are married, or at the very least, cohabiting (Amato, 2010; Ambert, 2009).

This stigma may still hold in parts of society today. Not too long ago, terms such as *illegitimate children* and *children from broken homes* were used in reference to children being raised by single parents. Families in which the mother and father did not live together were referred to as *broken*, implying that they were in need of fixing (Ward, 2006). There appears to be a difference in the acceptance of single parenthood for men and women, and one study has shown that single fathers generally face less approval in society, and experience more role ambiguity than do single mothers (DeGarmo et al., 2008; Goldscheider & Kaufman, 2006). There is still very little research available on single fathers, and the little that exists does not point to any dramatic differences between single fathers and mothers in regard to their contribution to their children's development. The research does suggest, however, that despite the increasing numbers of single fathers, they may experience more difficulty with regard to work–family balance, and as a result experience more stress (Janzen & Kelly, 2012). In addition, there still seem to be fewer support services available to single fathers than to single mothers, and perhaps a greater reluctance on the part of fathers to access the supports that may be available (Janzen & Kelly, 2012).

Generally, there are indications that attitudes are gradually shifting, and that younger people (many of whom grew up in single-parent families) are more accepting of the phenomenon (Cherlin, 2009; Goldscheider & Kaufman, 2006). Previously, the only kind of lone parents that seemed to escape moral judgment were widows and widowers. In spite of statistics that indicate that single parenthood is a prevalent family structure, many single parents feel that although their families may be different in structure from society's concept of a "normal" family, they are still just as intact and functional, and should thus be equally acceptable. However, society clings to old concepts despite the decreasing gap between the number of single parents and the number of two-parent families.

Abandoning Our Preconceived Ideas

While we cannot ignore the evidence that links single parenthood to economic disadvantage and the stress that results, we can and must overcome moral judgments that may interfere with developing a supportive professional relationship with single parents. We live in a society today that sends mixed messages. Divorce and sexual activity among non-married people are no longer condemned, but the resulting single parenthood is still somewhat stigmatized. We also need to remember that most single parents are highly committed to providing the best possible environment for their children, in spite of the obstacles and barriers described. And, finally, we should remind ourselves that most of the research has been conducted from a "deficit model" that outlines the challenges and concerns. We have seen few or no studies that look at the strengths of single-parent families, nor have we seen studies that focus on children who have been raised in one-parent families. For all these reasons, early childhood educators might be better advised to shift the focus from asking which form of family is better to understanding the facts at hand. Early childhood educators can play an important supportive role with single-parent families, as with any other kind of family, if they develop an understanding of some of the challenges faced by single-parent families today.

The Challenges of Single Parenthood

While the diversity among the single-parent population makes it difficult to generalize, there do seem to be some specific challenges associated with single parenthood that are worth considering for the early childhood educator. Care must be taken not to make assumptions, while at the same time early childhood educators must be sensitive to some of the areas in which support and understanding might be welcome. Although many parents indicate that single parenting presents no special problems, many others report that they do indeed face a considerable number of challenges.

The Economics of Single Parenting

The economics of one-parent families have been described briefly above. Canadian and American statistics on poverty lead to the inescapable conclusion that single parenthood and poverty often go hand in hand. A Statistics Canada report (2006) indicates that lone-parent families headed by women have, by far, the lowest incomes of all family types. (We examine poverty and its impact on Canadian families in Chapter 13.) As a result, we should be aware of and sensitive to the financial burdens that complicate the lives of many single parents.

Barriers to Employment

Working becomes a necessity in single-parent families; however, many single mothers with preschool-age children are not able to work because of the needs of their children. There are multiple barriers to employment of single parents, particularly single mothers, including issues of self-esteem and job readiness following a divorce, ambivalent social attitudes about women's roles in the labour force, and sexual harassment in the workplace (Chan et al., 2008). Research has shown that the majority of single mothers would work if quality, accessible child care were available. Working mothers with school-age children are constrained by school hours and school holidays. The choices of child-care facilities may be limited by income, and such a large portion of the single parent's income may be used for child care that there is little left over for anything other than the most basic necessities.

Job opportunities may be restricted for single mothers due to limited, inflexible hours and single mothers' inability to work overtime. Even lone parents with good incomes will experience more economic strife than their married counterparts, who are either in a two-income household or not burdened by child-care costs because one parent is at home. Because of employment and child-care conditions, the only alternative for many single mothers is social assistance, the benefits of which typically do not provide an adequate standard of living and which come with a stigma attached.

Stress

Being a single parent can present many challenges. In Chapter 2, "Family Members and Family Roles," we looked at the "supermom" syndrome—that is, the pressure that many women feel to have successful careers while at the same time being excellent homemakers and child-rearers. However, single parents have to assume the roles of both mother and father, which require patience and flexibility and may lead to role overload. As one single mother noted, "It's as if there is this obligation upon me to be a better mother than a mother in a two-parent family, since I'm also expected to be the father. I'm the breadwinner, I do the nurturing, I'm in charge of the household and finances, and I do a lot of the kinds of things that are normally associated with fathers, like sports and special outings."

Although the majority of single parents are still women, more men are assuming the role of single father. Approximately 8%, or 33 800, of single-parent families in Canada are now headed by single fathers (Beaupre et al., 2010), and the number is increasing as more fathers seek custody of their children after divorce. Many of the concerns and challenges faced by single fathers are similar to those faced by single mothers. Although single-father families are much less likely to live in poverty (since the fathers tend to be better educated and better employed), many single fathers feel more social stigma attached to them than to women in similar circumstances. Single fathers report that they feel they are able to provide the daily care and affection required to "mother" and that they feel close to their children, although parenting styles can differ (Beaupre et al., 2010; Goldscheider & Kaufman, 2006; Lamb, 2010).

Perspectives

Ron is a 24-year-old single father. He recently attended a parent night at his children's child-care centre and discussed his experiences as a single dad.

"I come from a military family. My father was a commander in the Canadian Armed Forces, and he raised me and my two brothers in the 'army ways'—lots of discipline and a firm hand. My mother died when I was 11 years old, and it was really hard for all of us, especially my dad, who wasn't really good at talking about things that were bothering him. He never changed at home; he was still the boss, the disciplinarian, the commander.

"I joined the army as soon as I finished high school, just like my two brothers. It wasn't something we thought about; we just did it; it was expected. I got married and we had two children; Amy was 13 months old when Andrew was born. I was a father just like my father—I set out the rules and was the commander at home. When the children got older, I decided to quit the army because it was too hard to balance work with my family life—the army is kind of like that. I quit and became a firefighter, which gave me more time at home. I don't really know what happened, but six months after that major change in my life, my wife decided that this was not the life for her and left me with a 3-year-old and a 2-year-old. I have never felt so scared and so alone in my whole life, and I had nobody that I could talk to about being a father. My dad and brothers didn't understand, my guy friends weren't used to sharing stories about bedtime routines and sick children, and single mothers were a bit unsure about this single father. I thought I knew what being a father was all about—I'd done it for three years and had a strong role model in my own father—but I had no idea how to be a mother.

"One of the first things I did was to quit my job, since it's hard to be a single parent on shift work. I found a job in an office—not what I want to do forever, but at least it's easier to manage a home life. I had to put the children into child care.

"When we started at the child-care centre, I was very quiet and very cautious. I really felt that I had to do it all. I didn't tell them very much and tried to pretend that our lives were normal. When the staff would ask questions or offer suggestions, I would get really bent out of shape. I remember once coming to pick Amy up at the end of the day. She was excited because her early childhood educator had French-braided her hair with ribbons. I was so angry because I saw this as a slap in the face—you can't do this, so we will. I blew up at Sally, the educator. She was shocked at my reaction and explained that all the staff try to spend individual time with each child. Amy had gotten up early from nap that day, and they'd had lots of time to spend together and play with her hair. It took me a long time, and other incidents like this, to realize that I couldn't do it all, and that I needed other people to help. Their mom wasn't coming back, finding a new mom wasn't not a solution, and Sally was just trying to give Amy the things she needed, things I didn't have time for.

"Things are getting easier. Being a single parent will always be hard, but at least now I have some people I can count on, and I don't feel so alone and so scared—that's enough for now."

Social Support

As alluded to in a previous chapter, we are living in a hurried culture. With a dramatically accelerated pace of change, most families experience "time crunches," where responsibilities for work and family cause anxiety and stress. Lone parents who work suffer from too many responsibilities with too little time to carry out those responsibilities (Daly, 2006). The responsibilities of work and child-rearing can make it very difficult for the single parent to find time to meet her own needs—for socializing and for support.

A primary concern for many single parents is the lack of emotional support. Emotional and social isolation are still cited as having a significant impact on the well-being of children and their single parents (Copeland, 2010; Copeland & Harbaugh, 2005). When single parents have good informal social networks for emotional support, child care, and financial assistance, their adaptation and experiences as single parents are more positive (Ambert, 2006). Some single parents become very dependent on these informal supports, however, and then may have to deal with constant interference from family and friends. In addition, lone parents also report that they have difficulty depending on these supports for long-term arrangements. In such circumstances, feelings of isolation or loneliness are increased to the point where single parents need to reach out for support from social agencies.

Single fathers report that even less social support may be available to them, as the following scenario suggests.

Scenario

No Support for Single Fathers

Jack is a single father of two children—Jillian is 3 years old and James is 18 months. Jack tells two stories that exemplify his experiences as a single father.

Whenever Jack is out with his children and they're upset, crying, or dirty, people repeatedly remark, "Where's their mom?" or "Your mommy will take care of you." He says that this happens so often that it clearly demonstrates society's views of fathers in general and single fathers in particular.

Soon after Jack's wife left, he knew that he needed help and someone to talk to about parenting. He did manage to find a local support group for single parents, but when he walked into the first meeting, all the single mothers stopped talking. He joined the group, but said, "I felt so uncomfortable, and it was so obvious that they were all uncomfortable that I left at the break." Next, he tried a men's support group, but his concerns about parenting were a foreign issue to this group. "The bottom line," he said, "was that I just didn't fit anywhere and I am truly on my own."

Time

Many parents talk about the need for having time for themselves. Although this is a yearned-for luxury among most parents, those who live without partners often find it even more difficult to get some time away from their children. One Canadian study shows that lone parents have less free time than any other group of adults 25–69 years old (Ambert, 2006). A more recent report by Vanier Institute further drives home the time crunch felt by lone-parent families: "Not surprisingly, those working the longest hours (10.9 hours of paid and unpaid work per day averaged over a 7-day week) are female lone parents aged 25-44 with full-time employment" (Sauve, 2010). "I can't call a babysitter if I just want to go for a walk for 15 minutes, and the extra cost of babysitters makes going out for an evening or weekend something I very rarely do," said one single mother.

Child-Rearing

It used to be that single-parent families were characterized by lack of discipline or consistent control (Brooks, 2010). Many studies suggested that single mothers were less effective in discipline, more negative in their comments, gave more commands, and were more hostile and dominating than mothers in two-parent families (Bank et al., 1993). Poor single-parent families seemed more likely to experience violence and abuse within the home (Bank et al., 1993; Jaffe, 1991). Conservative viewpoints continue to highlight the negative aspects of single-parent families (Walberg & Mrozek, 2009), but recent studies have considered how ineffective discipline may result not from single parenting on its own but from the increased level of stress that is common in single-parent homes, combined with social and financial pressures (Amato, 2010; Lansford, 2009). Moreover, recent studies suggest that the parenting abilities and attitudes of single parents may not differ from those of married parents to the extent that was previously believed (Amato, 2010; Lansford, 2009). The biggest differences in parenting are attributed to lack of time compared with two-parent families, and the added economic strain that so often accompanies single parenthood (Amato, 2010). Single parents who have social and emotional support find it easier to deal with authority issues in a consistent manner.

Different-Gender Role Models

Earlier studies that focused on children's developmental need for role models of both genders are being challenged today, as gender roles are becoming blurred. As women engage in career activities that formerly fell within the exclusive domain of men, many men are taking on traditional female roles associated with nurturing and homemaking. Nonetheless, there are still gender differences in how women and men parent. Dubeau (2002) summarizes these differences as follows: Mothers are more repetitive and ask questions more, while fathers verbalize less and more frequently use the imperative form. Fathers apparently promote the child's integration in settings outside the home and are less tolerant of children's dependent behaviours. Fathers tend to play rough-and-tumble games with children more often and use unconventional behaviours (such as putting blocks on heads), which may help the child develop self-control. Dubeau concludes that it is important to remember that there isn't necessarily one type of interaction that is better than the others—and that both parents contribute to the child's development by providing different types of learning experiences. In addition, while mothers and fathers do parent differently, the gender role model may be less significant than was previously assumed (Biblarz et al., 2010). Recent research has highlighted the fact that differences in how men and women "rear children" are relatively minor and have little impact on children's development (Biblarz et al., 2010).

Regardless of gender, in a family where two parents are present, children have the opportunity to observe different ways of communicating, solving problems, and resolving conflicts. They might also be exposed to a more diverse range of interests and talents than when in a single-parent household. Therefore, some single parents do wish that their children had other close adults in their life, as models and support. The feeling that the responsibilities of parenting are easier if shared by two was succinctly expressed over two decades ago by Clarke-Stewart (1988, p. 71), and there is little reason to believe that this has changed: "One parent can model only one gender role, give only so many hugs, offer so much discipline, and earn so much money."

The Role of the Early Childhood Educator
Clarifying Attitudes and Values

Perhaps the first step in providing support is to maintain a nonjudgmental approach. The way you answer the questions in the following box should reveal how you, as an early childhood educator, interact with single parents and their children.

Examine Your Attitudes

- Do you think a single mother or father can do an adequate job of parenting?
- Do you feel the child of single parents is missing something?
- Does the language you use reflect your knowledge of single-parent families? (For example, the teacher in the vignette at the beginning of the chapter did not demonstrate an awareness of single-father families.)
- What social stigma, if any, do you attach to single parents?

Supporting Families

Providing support to single parents and their children should not be very different from supporting any other family. Early childhood educators must remember, though, that single-parent families may be facing the challenges of parenting in conjunction with additional stresses brought on by the absence of one parent. Three dimensions appear to be important for single-parent family adjustment (Garanzini, 1995). The first is the presence of resources within the family, including the parents' abilities, along with the presence of authority and communication. Environmental stress is the second dimension of single-parent family adjustment. This might include pressures outside the family (e.g., illness, transitions). The last dimension is the availability of social networks to the family. Such networks may include child care, role models, and economic help. Single parents facing economic pressure will appreciate sensitivity on the part of early childhood educators when they ask for extra fees for special events or for special equipment for the children. All parents who find the task of juggling jobs and family life difficult will appreciate being understood by educators. No family likes to feel that their parenting is being scrutinized and criticized by educators, but single parents who are sensitive about being socially stigmatized may react a little more defensively. Staff members need to bear this in mind and take care not to offend, either in words or in actions.

Any efforts to eliminate the stigma associated with single parents by seeing them as competent and their children as typical will go a long way in supporting lone-parent families. Recognizing that additional stresses may be present and that extra support may be needed is an important step in this process, but single parents should not feel they are being singled out or pitied. Ensuring that the information and support provided by the centre is addressed to single fathers as well as single mothers is very important. Whenever possible, accommodating single-parent families' complex schedules by arranging flexible hours or by organizing parent-involvement activities can help ensure that these parents are not excluded. Sometimes referring single parents to professionals can help link them to formal and informal community networks, such as support groups or short-stay relief homes.

Supporting Children

Scenario

Choose Your Words Carefully

An early childhood educator gave her group of 5-year-old children instructions for making Father's Day gifts. At one table, the children asked Amanda who she was making her gift for because her father lived far away. Amanda did not participate in the activity. At another table, Lisa declared that she was making her gift for her grandfather, because he took care of her when her mother worked at night. Her peers told her that she couldn't do this, because this craft was just for fathers.

In this scenario, the feelings of specific children could have been protected, and the understanding of all children enhanced, if the early childhood educator had been more careful with the words she used with the children. Explaining that the craft was for a special person would have helped include all the children in the activity.

Single parents and their children appreciate efforts to treat their family structure as normal. This normalization occurs when toys, books, and stories in the child-care centre reflect single-parent families as intact and typical. When early childhood educators read stories in which only traditional nuclear families appear, they can use the moment to explain that families are different, and then they can encourage discussion, if this is warranted. Sensitive educators should think carefully about events that are likely to make the child of a single parent feel left out. Mother's Day and Father's Day are just two examples.

Supporting children may also involve helping them understand the various types of families, and providing a range of experiences for them to think about. For example, the early childhood educator could provide books about different types of families or stories that feature male role models. Showing sensitivity in day-to-day activities may be the best starting point for developing a base of support.

Conclusion

Single-parent families are becoming more and more common in today's society. Nevertheless, they still face many challenges, some of which may come from the stigma attached to them by society, from increased stress, or from poor economic conditions. All single-parent families are different—they have each taken their own path and encountered different combinations of difficulties and challenges. Single-parent families need to be recognized as "normal" and as having the potential to raise healthy and well-adjusted children. Like all families, they may at times require support. The early childhood educator can play a supportive role by being aware of their strengths and difficulties and by maintaining a nonjudgmental attitude.

Chapter Summary

- Single parents, sometimes referred to as lone parents or one-parent families, are diverse. One-parent families are created when a couple separates and one of the ex-partners has custody of the children, when a woman gives birth to a child and does not live with the child's father or any other partner, when a father or mother is widowed, or when a single person adopts (Ambert, 2006).

- In 2006 there were more than 1.4 million one-parent families in Canada (16% of all families), the majority of which are headed by females and are economically disadvantaged.

- Children from one-parent families seem to fare less well than their peers from two-parent families on a number of measures, including academic achievement, incidence of behaviour problems, and health. These outcomes may be linked more to low income than to the fact of having one parent, as children from affluent one-parent families seem quite similar to those from two-parent families.

- Single parents still experience stigma today, as the perception that children should have two parents is still very prevalent in our society.

- Factors that single parents face include barriers to employment, lack of social support, and lack of time for themselves.

- Flexible hours, quality child care, and normalization of the single-parent family experience are ways that the early childhood educator can support single parents.

Recommended Websites

Single Parent Canada:
www.singleparent.ca

Single Parents Network:
http://singleparentsnetwork.com

Parents without Partners, Toronto Chapter:
www.pwptoronto.com

Videos/Films

Life with Dad. 2002. 43 min. National Film Board of Canada. **www.nfb.ca/collection/films/fiche/?v=h&lg=en&id=51093**

For Generations to Come. National Film Board. **www.onf-nfb.gc.ca**

Exercises

1. Interview three single fathers and three single mothers. Ask them about the joys and the challenges of being a single parent and about the support networks available to them. Record their responses, and then compare them. Were there significant differences in the responses you received? To what do you attribute these differences?

2. Review the books in your child-care centre. How many of these reflect the single-parent family as "normal" compared with the images presented of two-parent families?

3. Check local community resources for support groups that may be available to single-parent families. Will the needs of single fathers be accommodated in these groups?

4. Are the policies and activities in your centre sensitive to the needs of single-parent families?

chapter 8

Teenage Parents

Objectives

- **To examine the social factors related to teen parents.**

- **To examine attitudes toward teen parents.**

- **To discuss the risks to the teen parent and child.**

- **To discuss the role of professionals in supporting teen parents.**

> "I resent being singled out as a bad mother. I had my first baby before I turned 16 and my second child two years later. My children have always been well cared for, and they are just as well-adjusted as any of the other children I see around me!"
>
> (An early childhood student who was a teen mom.)

This comment came from a student who had sat quietly through a lecture on the sociology of teen parents. She felt that the lecturer had dealt with the subject in a judgmental fashion, particularly when he outlined the risks faced by the babies of teen mothers. In fact, many early childhood students have commented on the negative tone associated with the study of teen parents, claiming that they have teenage friends who are marvellous parents. Many young mothers do, in fact, respond to the challenge of rearing their children with commitment, courage, and determination, and they have positive relationships with their children. They face many of the same risks and challenges that all parents face. Yet, as we discuss in this chapter, teen parents do face a number of challenges, and research indicates that the children of teen parents face a number of very real risks (Ambert, 2006). As we learn about these risks, we must keep in mind that, despite common challenges, teenage mothers exhibit a broad range of parenting behaviours and abilities (Ambert, 2006).

As early childhood educators who work with families, we should be aware of the special challenges and risks facing any particular population. Perhaps our first concern should be to determine what risks to the baby are associated with teenage pregnancy, and how these risks can be reduced. Since we know that the well-being of the family and the child are inextricably connected, we should also be concerned with the potential risks faced by the mother. Will she be able to complete her schooling or participate in job training, or is she likely to be on welfare? Does becoming pregnant as a teen affect one's chances for a stable marriage? What is the likelihood of a second pregnancy? How does having a baby affect the young mother's own personal development?

In the following discussion of teen parents, we will bring to light some of the difficulties that young families face. Our main objective will be to enhance our ability to provide appropriate support when needed rather than to single out anyone for judgment. Our contention is that early childhood educators may be better able to anticipate and support the needs of teen parents if they are aware and informed. It is important to use this information sensitively and not stereotype or jump to conclusions. This chapter begins with a review of the prevalence, risks, and challenges of teen parenthood, and then looks at the role of the early childhood educator in supporting these families. We avoid stereotyping by reminding ourselves that whatever we have learned from research only informs us of general probabilities. It does not predict anything for a single individual.

The Prevalence of Teen Pregnancies

According to Statistics Canada data, the percentage of Canadian teens having babies has dropped by one-third since 1994 (Statistics Canada, 2008). Ambert (2006) reports that in 1998 there were nearly 20 000 births to women aged 15 to 19 in Canada. This translates to about 15.1 births in every 1000 women in that age group. By 2003, there were 14 800 births to teen mothers, which is 14.4 per thousand women (Statistics Canada, 2006). The proportion of Canadian pregnancies by teenage girls is 8% (Statistics Canada, 2008). Teen pregnancies in Canada may be declining, but, interestingly they are on the rise in the United States (Martin et al., 2009). In fact, research suggests that in the United States as many as one in six women will become teen mothers (Savio Beers et al., 2009). The differences between Canadian and American teen pregnancy rates may be attributed to better access to sexual education, birth control, and abortion in Canada, which is far more limited in the United States. Not surprisingly, policies legalizing abortion, as well as affordability and availability of abortion, decrease the amount of teen pregnancies (Medoff, 2010).

Factors Associated with Teen Pregnancy

Why do teens become pregnant? First and foremost, many teens in Canada are sexually active and do not use contraceptives effectively. As a society, Canada does not actively discourage sexual activity among young people. While most young people are aware of the need to use contraception and knowledgeable about its availability, many do not use it, especially when sex is unplanned. Alcohol and being "in the moment" are key factors that diminish the likelihood of contraceptive use (Brown et al., 2010). In addition, there is an irrefutable link between teen parents and poverty. The lower the socioeconomic group, with the accompanying higher incidence of poverty, the more teenage pregnancies occur (Savio Beers et al., 2009). Similarly, there is a significant link between low levels of education, low parent education, early sexual activity, decreased contraceptive use, substance abuse, and teen pregnancy (Savio Beers et al., 2009). Ambert (2006) relates this to the assumption that disadvantaged adolescents who hold low educational and vocational expectations may feel that they have little to lose by engaging in unprotected sex that leads to pregnancies.

Research suggests that there are certain interpersonal and environmental factors associated with teen pregnancy, including "decreased child–parent connectedness, decreased parental monitoring, more permissive parental attitudes regarding adolescent sexual activity, community and family disorganization and disruption, parental characteristics, absence of positive peer norms, and low partner support for contraceptive use" (Savio Beers et al., 2009, p. 217). Other factors include the prevalence of a family member with a drinking problem, physical assault by a family member, early age of first drunkenness, early age of first wanted sexual experience, and a culture of excessive sexualization and a lack of sex education (McDaniel & Tepperman, 2007). In addition, Ambert (2006) and Savio Beers et al. (2009) provide evidence that in families where there are sexually active siblings, the rates of teen pregnancy increase. In families where the mothers are openly sexually active with a variety of men and where there is little parental supervision, the incidence is also likely to increase (Ambert, 2006; Savio Beers et al., 2009). A smaller but significant number of teenagers become pregnant through coerced sex: At least 20% of teen mothers have experienced involuntary intercourse (Ambert, 2006).

The Risks of Teen Pregnancy

Risks Associated with Teen Pregnancies
- Teen parents are often poor.
- Teen parents often do not complete their education.
- Teen parents are likely to be single parents or have marital difficulties.
- Teen parents have limited knowledge about child-rearing.

Even teen parents who have some support face serious socio-demographic challenges, and their immediate physical, psychological, and emotional health is threatened by their situation (Birkeland et al., 2005; McDaniel & Tepperman, 2007). Teen parents are more likely to be poor when they become pregnant and to remain economically disadvantaged (Ambert, 2006; McDaniel & Tepperman, 2007). Teen mothers are more likely to experience school failure and require government support (Savio Beers et al., 2009). Those who continue their schooling or return to school have to depend on the goodwill of their families and friends for babysitting and the provision of other resources (Ambert, 2006; McDaniel & Tepperman, 2007). Teens who do not finish school are much more likely to remain in poverty. However, they face many barriers to completing school—resistance to school, the demands of parenthood, and concerns about money, safety, and child care—all of which increase the likelihood that their circumstances will remain unchanged.

Looking at the lives of many adolescent mothers, researchers have noted a higher accumulation of adverse life events. These could include a child dying or being taken away, a life-threatening accident or injury, abuse, addictions, and higher risks of depression (McDaniel & Tepperman, 2007). Adolescent fathers are also at risk for lower employment and financial opportunities.

Physical Risks Associated with Teen Pregnancy

Many of the risks associated with teen mothers and their children are related to the fact that they typically do not access prenatal care early enough or frequently enough (Resource Manual, 2000). A higher proportion of teenagers report physical and sexual abuse during their pregnancy in comparison with their nonpregnant peers. Children of teen mothers are more likely to suffer from health risks associated with low birth weight and/or prematurity, mainly due to the high rate of cigarette smoking among teenage mothers: Over 45% of teenage mothers smoke (Canadian Perinatal Health Report, 2003) in spite of the well-known dire effects of smoking on mother, fetus, and child. Teen mothers tend to be less healthy than older mothers, with higher incidents of illnesses, such as high blood pressure, urinary tract infection, and anemia. There is also a higher death rate for infants of teen mothers.

Related to the above health risks of the mother are higher rates of disability and lower intelligence quotient among children of teen mothers. The outcomes for children are discussed later on in the chapter. The birth problems associated with teen parents can stem from a number of factors. Sometimes teen parents do not know or don't admit to being pregnant until the pregnancy is very visible—in other words, well into the second trimester. It is well known that the development of the fetus during the first three months can easily be affected by poor nutrition, smoking, and drug or alcohol abuse (Resource Manual, 2000). Because many teens are already involved with substance abuse, the problems associated with it are more commonly found in teen pregnancies than in those among the population at large. Many teen mothers are unaware of these risks, and so substance abuse, as well as other dangerous behaviour, continues during pregnancy. Some pregnant teens will continue drug and alcohol abuse even when they are aware of the risks to their baby.

Added to this, maternal stress is thought to have an effect on the unborn child. Teens will not only experience the normal stress associated with pregnancy but may also experience tension with their parents, boyfriends, and peers, in addition to having to make difficult decisions for their future. All of these factors suggest that teen pregnancy presents serious risks for both teen parents and their children. Teenage mothers face a significant risk for depression, specifically post-partum, which may be related to a lack of social support and poor partner relations (Savio Beers et al., 2009).

The Teen Mother

When considering how the birth of a child might affect a 13-, 14-, or 15-year-old adolescent, it is helpful to consider the adolescent from a developmental perspective, and to think about the nature of the changes taking place in that period of life. The first is the crisis of identity versus role diffusion (Erikson, 1963). At the same time puberty, the second crisis, is taking place, complicated by pregnancy. The third crisis is caused by the physical, emotional, and temporal demands of the new maternal role. Let us consider each of these crises in more detail.

Adolescence in North America is usually a time when young people try to establish their individual identity. This process is referred to as identity versus role confusion or diffusion , as discussed in Chapter 3 (Erikson, 1963). Teens reflect on their own past, on who they are in the present, and on who they may turn out to be in the future. A sense of identity involves, first of all, a sense of independence from parents. Adolescents attempt to inform parents, in many different ways, that they are grown up and autonomous, an assertion that often puts teens in conflict with their parents. In the quest for independence, adolescents tend to be very responsive to their social environments. Peers are probably more important and more influential during the teenage years than in any other stage of life. Teens' emotional and psychological immaturity can also lead to a lack of understanding of the real nature of parenthood.

During pregnancy, teens are also dealing with issues associated with puberty, including hormonal changes, body changes, and the formulation of a sexual identity. Many parents joke about the hours that teenage girls spend gazing at themselves in the mirror. This preoccupation with the body and body image is part of the growing-up process. Teen mothers have the added burden of dealing with changes to their bodies and with body image as well as the hormonal changes associated with pregnancy.

Bearing in mind the developmental tasks facing adolescents, how might a pregnancy affect a teen's development? Becoming a parent will likely make the quest for individual identity exceedingly difficult, since the teen's world is changing so rapidly, and plans for the future are at least temporarily interrupted. Just at the point when the teen is attempting to become independent, the pregnancy can put her in a position where she is forced to depend on her parents for increased financial and emotional support. The physical changes that occur throughout the pregnancy can also be quite difficult for teenage mothers, since they complicate their attempts to define their sexual identity and sense of self.

Demands of the Maternal Role on the Teen Parent

Becoming a parent can result in alienation from one's peer group, and we have already stressed the importance of peers in this developmental stage. A teen mother's needs and life are so different from those of her old friends that they no longer associate with her. When the baby is born, child-care duties, time demands, and limited finances can interfere with her social life and lead to feelings of isolation. Finding a new peer group is not always easy.

The very nature of adolescence, combined with the physical, social, and economic stressors associated with pregnancy and childbirth, is thought to pose a risk to the parenting abilities of teens. Although many teen parents are characterized as caring, they are typically not competent as parents (Savio Beers et al., 2009). Teen parents may have less patience, be less sensitive to the child's needs, and be less emotionally involved than more mature adult parents. On the one hand, they may expect some skills to emerge earlier than they do; for example, they may be impatient for the baby to begin walking, self-feeding, and toileting. On the other hand, they are often unaware of the need for language or cognitive stimulation, for close attachment to the mother, and for praise and encouragement. The teen mother may not provide the stimulation required for all areas of development or may not realize the child's need for a close attachment, thus demanding independence earlier. Teen parents are also less likely than more mature parents to be aware of the baby's nutritional requirements (Ambert, 2006).

Scenario

Misreading the Baby's Needs

Fifteen-year-old Jenny frequently took her 12-week-old son Dylan to a McDonald's restaurant with her friends, and reported that Dylan loved McRib sandwiches. When the child-care staff questioned her, she pointed out that the ribs were big enough that he wouldn't choke on them, and hard enough that they wouldn't break into pieces. From her perspective, she had considered the baby's needs. Early childhood educators at Dylan's child-care centre were having a difficult time convincing Jenny that the baby was not ready for spicy barbecue sauce. When the baby turned up his nose at infant cereal, Jenny felt her choice of food was reinforced. "See," she said, "he likes barbecue sauce!"

What About Teen Fathers?

So far we have discussed teenage mothers and their babies and have not referred to the young fathers of these infants. The truth is that only recently has the role of the teenage father been given much consideration. Like teenage mothers, teenage fathers often have unrealistic expectations about support, and this is one reason that males are likely to give up involvement with the baby soon after birth. Moreover, only about 30% to 50% of children born to teenage mothers have an acknowledged teenage father (Mollborn et al., 2010). More teen women have children with adult men, whereas few teenage men have children with adult women (Mollborn et al., 2010). It is common for teenage males to be shut out of the decision in the case of abortion or adoption. Recent studies indicate that teen fathers are involved in a variety of relationships with the mothers of their children, but only a few of them result in marriage or long-term cohabitation.

Although only about half of teen fathers lived with the mother, compared with 9 out of 10 adult fathers, reported involvement (playing with and caring for their children) was similar to that reported by adult fathers (Mollborn et al., 2010). In addition, "adolescent fathers reported feeling more attached to their child than adult fathers did in terms of both talking and thinking about the child" (Mollborn et al., 2010, p. 16). A recent study found that despite usually lower socioeconomic statuses, a significantly lower rate of marriage, and lower residency with their children, there were few differences between father–child relationships of teen and adult fathers (Mollborn et al., 2010). Not surprisingly, teenage fathers typically come from more disadvantaged groups than adult fathers. While teenage fathers pay significantly less in child support than adult fathers, studies have found no significant difference in other monetary help (i.e., toys, health care) between the two groups, as teenage fathers pay "surprisingly high levels of informal, irregular financial support" (Mollborn et al., 2010, p. 15).

Studies of intervention programs involving adolescent first-time fathers indicate that participation in a support network (such as parenting classes or meetings with social workers) can have a positive effect. These support groups are becoming increasingly popular and are an effective way of engaging fathers.

Perspectives

Carlos is a social worker in his early fifties. He came to Canada as a refugee from El Salvador in 1984 with his wife, Rosa, two sons aged 11 and 12, and a daughter aged 7. Both Carlos and Rosa were teachers in El Salvador. Once they settled in Canada, Carlos felt that he could be more effective helping immigrants, so he retrained and has been a social worker for several years.

"When we left our home and came to Canada, my main goal was that my children complete their education and be healthy, happy, contributing members of society, while at the same time maintaining a strong sense of identification with their Spanish culture. Religion doesn't play a big role in our lives, but the beliefs are there in the background. My children all attended a Catholic school.

"When my son was 19 and a student at college, he fell in love with a 16-year-old girl from El Salvador. Although we'd hoped he would concentrate fully on his studies, we noticed that he seemed sad and withdrawn and seemed to be avoiding us. One day, my daughter heard from some friends that he was planning to get married. We were absolutely shocked, because he hadn't said a word about this to us. Normally, we talked a lot; we had a good relationship with lots of communication between us. Shortly after that he came to us and said, 'Dad, Mom, I need to talk to you. You'll be very angry with me. My girlfriend is pregnant.' Our first responses were 'We're here to help you' and 'Are you planning to get married?' and 'What about finances?' At that time he said he didn't think they should get married because neither of them had any money.

"We decided to speak with his girlfriend's mother, and we all came to the conclusion that it was probably best for them not to marry, and for the girl to live with her mother until they finished school. We would help them financially, if necessary, and of course my son wanted to be involved with the baby. But marriage just didn't seem feasible. However, the next time we saw each other, my son told me that they had decided to marry. We think his girlfriend's mother was desperate to see her daughter settled and officially part of our family, as she herself hadn't really integrated into Canadian life and hoped to return to El Salvador, confident that we would take care of her daughter. Part of me felt that I was losing my son, and not to the best of circumstances. It was quite sad.

"We held a family meeting. I said that we needed, as parents, to support our children. We didn't want our grandchild to suffer. The young couple was very emotional, and many tears were shed.

"They got married, with my son still in college and my new daughter-in-law at a high school for pregnant teens. Our biggest concern was that he stay in school. After all we'd been through, the thought of our son ending up uneducated and employed in some menial job was hard to bear. With some social assistance and a summer job, they managed to get an apartment in a municipal housing project, and six months after their marriage Juan Carlos was born.

"My wife gave up her part-time job to look after the baby while my daughter-in-law finished high school and my son attended college. Maybe it's a cultural bias, but we feel that babies should be looked after by loving family members. We both love the baby dearly, but Rosa at times felt burdened by the responsibility. My daughter-in-law loves her baby, but we worried that at times she seemed a bit careless about food and other matters. You can understand that—she's a young girl; she wants to go to parties and be like her friends. It must be quite a conflict for her. I think she regrets being in this situation, having such a big commitment. I believe that my son is a caring and responsible father and very proud of his little boy. He's working and studying full-time but tries to spend as much time as possible with the baby. He is still very connected to us. He calls or visits almost every day. Their marriage seems to be okay—they seem to love each other. I sometimes suspect that my son is being manipulated a bit, but that might be a biased perspective.

"Two years have passed now; my son has almost finished his education, and my daughter-in-law has completed high school. We feel now that it's time to pull back a bit. Rosa wants to have some time to herself again. I hope that soon my son will get a good job. We've been giving them financial support up to now, and that has been a bit of a strain. We've worked hard for many years and want to be able to think about our retirement. We also hope to return to El Salvador for a while so that I can spend some time with my own parents before they die. I think it will be a bit hard for them—finding care for the baby, and so forth.

"My son and daughter-in-law's unplanned pregnancy changed all our lives. It hasn't been an easy time for us. But always our first thought has been 'We must do what's best for the child.' We must support our children so that they can be good parents."

The Role of the Grandparent

As most adolescent mothers live with their parents following their child's birth, it is not surprising that grandparents play an important role in the lives of teen parents (Savio Beers et al., 2009). Mothers of adolescent mothers, for example, often provide housing, food, educational support, and parenting support, in addition to continuing to parent their adolescent children (Savio Beers et al., 2009). While research has shown that adolescent mothers gain more ability and confidence in their parenting through a positive relationship with their own mothers, these grandparents often face high levels of stress and decreased marital satisfaction (Savio Beers et al., 2009). In addition, grandparents run the risk of becoming so involved in their new role that the teen parent does not experience all aspects of parenting. For example, if grandparents are "built-in babysitters," the teen never has to worry about child care. When grandparents pay expenses for the teen and the baby, the teen may not come to understand financial responsibility. Often, the extended family needs to walk a very fine line between being supportive and letting the teen parent take responsibility and experience parenthood fully.

Compared with the relationship between maternal grandmothers and their adolescent daughters, researchers found far greater variability in relationships between maternal grandmothers and teen fathers (Savio Beers et al., 2009). For example, grandmothers may demonstrate "gate-keeping behaviour" and limit a father's access to his child (Savio Beers et al., 2009). When the teen mother and baby live with the maternal grandmother, father involvement tends to decrease (Savio Beers et al., 2009). However, paternal grandparents can play an important role in mitigating this. When the teen father is encouraged to stay involved and is supported by his own parents, his involvement may increase (Mollborn et al., 2010).

Supporting Teen Parents and Their Families

To work effectively with young parents, as with the members of any population, early childhood educators must consider their own beliefs and responses. On a professional level, they must make an effort to avoid being judgmental and to determine the areas where they can provide support. Moral convictions about premarital sex and other religious and culturally based beliefs make it difficult for some of us to accept teen parents in an objective fashion. In addition, there seems to be a general tendency to view teenagers as irresponsible, rowdy, and generally quite disagreeable. High school and college students commonly report incidents where they were wrongly accused of shoplifting or of other misdemeanours simply, they think, because they were young.

What Are Your Feelings About Teen Mothers?

After seeing a film about a 14-year-old new mother who was having trouble keeping her patience with a cranky baby, students were asked to jot down some of their feelings. Some said they felt sorry for the young mother and her baby; others were honest enough to admit that they felt quite angry. Why didn't she use birth control in the first place? Didn't she know that having a baby wasn't going to be like playing with a doll? Another student, a teen mother herself, said that she remembered feeling the frustration expressed by the mother in the film, but reminded the class that any mother, regardless of age, might feel frustrated with a baby who cries incessantly.

People often assume that children born to teen parents are unwanted and are largely the result of a mistake or promiscuous sexual behaviour. "Really? How could she? How could she not know to take precautions? How stupid!"—these are comments commonly made about the teen mother. This lack of understanding of teen parents and their particular situation can lead to the teen's feeling isolated, as if she were an outcast. Sometimes these feelings result in teens making unfortunate decisions about their babies.

A Mother's Defensiveness

Because of the increasing prevalence of child abuse, hospital emergency staff and medical staff in clinics have been trained to look for and investigate any signs of abuse. A teen mother was told by the child-care staff that her 8-month-old daughter had a slight temperature that should be monitored, and that the baby should be taken to the emergency clinic if her fever worsened. The young mother avoided going to the clinic for two days. When she returned to the child care with her baby on the third day, the baby was very ill. The early childhood educator asked the mother why she hadn't followed the staff's advice and gone to the clinic. The mother finally admitted that she hated going to emergency clinics because the staff there always assumed that she wasn't a good mother and that whatever was wrong with her baby was her fault. The educator realized how difficult it must have been for this young mother to deal with such a situation, so she accompanied her to the clinic to provide support.

This scenario shows that, despite the professionals' positive intentions, their attitudes and response to the mother made her feel angry and defensive. She had likely been exposed to these negative attitudes and statements before, and the latest instance served only as yet another affirmation that she was a bad mother.

Examine Your Attitudes

- Do you lose your temper when you see a teen mother failing to control her child? Or do you think, "Any mom would have her hands full with a baby like that!"?
- Do you tend to think you could do a better job of parenting than the teen mothers you know?
- If you are religious, does your religion emphasize that it is morally wrong to have premarital sex and children out of marriage? How does this affect your feelings toward teen mothers?
- Do you get along with teens in general, or do you find them too rowdy and irresponsible?
- Do you think the babies of teen parents are most often the result of (a) an accident, (b) simple ignorance, or (c) deliberate planning? Would your answer be different if you were asked the same question about adult parents?
- Consider the situation in which a baby is born to a 15-year-old girl who is poor and has dropped out of high school. Do you think the baby would be better off being put up for adoption and raised by relatively affluent parents? Or should the child remain with its natural mother, with support from the community?

Methods of Support

Despite the stereotype suggesting the opposite, the "consequences" of childbearing in the teen years may not be as set in stone as once believed (Savio Beers et al., 2009). Teen parents can be and often are very successful parents, especially if they have appropriate support from the child's father, both families, and the community (Savio Beers et al., 2009). In fact, researchers are now suggesting that teens who are also parents are not significantly different from peers of the same socioeconomic status.

Supporting teen parents can best be viewed from the ecological perspective (see Chapter 1). Although early childhood educators work primarily and directly with the teen mother and her child, other systems, such as the extended family, peer group, schools, and employers, all need to be considered in supporting the teen. After examining their personal beliefs about teens and teen parents, early childhood educators should become knowledgeable about the stressors and risks facing these families, and support them in a nonjudgmental fashion. This means not making any assumptions and recognizing the strength and potential in young mothers as well as the difficulties they may face. It is particularly important to ensure that the young parent does not sense any disapproval on the part of the professional.

Providing the babies of teen parents with nurturing, responsible, and stimulating care while the young mother completes her schooling can enhance the life chances of both the baby and the mother. A teen mother who can complete her education stands a much better chance of achieving economic stability and a reduction in all the adverse effects of poverty (Ambert, 2006). Early childhood educators can give demonstrations of appropriate care and invite young parents to spend time at the centre in order to observe and learn. Extra care needs to be taken to help young parents feel at ease and to reassure them that they are not being constantly observed and judged. Young parents may benefit from information about development, discipline, health, and nutrition, as long as the information is not transmitted in a threatening manner that may elicit defensiveness and possible resistance to accepting advice and information.

Many programs are currently available in Canada to assist teen parents, teaching them how to be effective parents and giving them an opportunity to continue their education (see Recommended Websites at the end of this chapter). Successful programs combine social, psychological, and educational support for the teen mother, her baby, the teen father, and the extended family. This support may include on-site child care, flexible hours and requirements, child-care classes, child-development classes, prenatal care, social workers, counsellors, and so on. All professionals in such programs work together with the teen. These comprehensive programs are thought to be effective in promoting the well-being of both the young mother and the baby (Artz & Nicholsen, 2009; Artz et al., 2007; Nicholson & Artz, 2006) and even in decreasing the likelihood of another pregnancy during the teenage years. Professionals committed to the well-being of children might wish to lobby for the establishment of such programs in their community. Finally, early childhood educators should be aware of online forums, virtual support groups, and websites that teen parents can use for support and education (Kauppi et al., 2008).

Supporting the Child

Attendance at a high-quality child-care centre could offset some of the risks for children whose young parents need time to develop their parenting skills. A good child-care centre can ensure adequate nutrition and can also monitor the health and development of the children in its care. A child's ongoing interaction with early childhood educators in the context of a secure and responsive environment can facilitate the cognitive, language, motor, emotional, and social development of the child. Such care is important for all children; however, if the young age of the parent and accompanying social conditions have a negative impact on parenting, the importance of having the highest quality of care is accentuated.

Conclusion

In essence, the needs of teen parents for information, support, and guidance are not very different from those of other parents. However, young mothers face a daunting challenge in needing to simultaneously integrate different life roles in an accelerated fashion. These include their life roles as adolescent/teenager, daughter, student, partner, and mother. It is, therefore, vital for the early childhood educator to understand these additional challenges faced by teen mothers, who must deal not only with new motherhood but also with the developmental tasks of adolescence. Professionals should offer support and assistance in an accepting, nonjudgmental, and nonthreatening fashion.

Chapter Summary

- The prevalence of teen mothers in Canada has decreased in the past decade. However, approximately 14 out of every 1000 women between the ages of 15 and 19 become pregnant, and approximately 8% of babies born in Canada are born to teen mothers. While many risks are associated with teen mothers and their infants, there are many individual differences between mothers. Many teen mothers are devoted and committed to their children in spite of the obstacles.

- Teen parents by and large come from poor families. Teenage pregnancies are associated with lower levels of parental supervision, sibling promiscuity, and coerced sex.
- Becoming a teen mother is associated with ongoing economic difficulties and accumulated negative life circumstances, such as abuse, drugs, and depression.
- Infants of teen mothers have higher rates of low birth weight, higher rates of handicap, lower intelligence, and delinquent behaviours.
- The majority of teen fathers do not remain involved, but this can be influenced by family support, professional help, and an expectation of inclusion.
- Excellent child-care programs that support and encourage a teen mother's return to school and school completion can significantly reduce the risks to the teenage mother and the child.

Recommended Websites

Active Parenting Publishers:
www.activeparentingcanada.com

Public Health Agency of Canada: Community Action Program for Children:
www.phac-aspc.gc.ca/dca-dea/programs-mes/capc-fs-1n1_e.html

Teen Parents:
www.teenparents.ca

Videos/Films

Too Young to Be a Dad. 2002. 120 min. Lifetime Television.

Exercises

1. Reflect on your own level of maturity at the ages of 13, 15, and 18. In what ways would you have been ready to become a parent, and in what ways would your level of development have hindered your ability to parent? How typical do you think you were at those ages?

2. Draw up a list of your preconceived ideas about teenage parents. After you have done so, ask yourself if these ideas could also apply to the following: new parents, parents over the age of 40, parents who are poor, or parents who are experiencing family problems. Can you identify a pattern of stereotyping in your attitudes toward parents?

3. Check community resources to find those that may be used to support teen parents and their children.

4. Check your local library and bookstore to find out which books might be helpful to teen parents in raising their children.

chapter 9

Culturally Diverse Families

Objectives

- To understand and appreciate the cultural diversity that exists in Canada.
- To understand the experiences of immigrants and refugees as they transition to life in Canada.
- To understand the experience and beliefs of First Nations, Métis, and Inuit families.
- To discuss ways in which the early childhood educator can support new Canadian families.
- To put into practice principles of respecting and supporting Aboriginal culture in Early Childhood settings.

Ilana is the mother of a 5-year-old girl who comes to a drop-in centre. Her husband was killed at the beginning of a war in their country, and the family spent almost four years as refugees, sharing a small apartment with extended family members.

"It was a time of poverty, loneliness, and sadness. Grief and loneliness seemed to be the only things I could feel. During our times as refugees, my daughter became extremely anxious when we were separated. She would cry at all times when I was out of sight. When we arrived in Canada, I wanted to look for work, or go to English classes, and tried to put my daughter in a child-care centre. Every morning, as we approached the centre, my daughter started to feel ill, cried, and refused to stay. I was becoming so frustrated, and feeling a bit angry with my daughter.

"The staff at the centre helped me understand that my daughter had severe separation anxiety as a result of the life we had led as refugees. My daughter never really had the opportunity to play, and we were always so tense. They helped me understand how important it was for me to let my daughter play, with me nearby. After a long time, she was okay if I left for a while. I can't believe that now I can leave for several hours, and my little girl lets me go. Sometimes she still fusses again, but I see other Canadian children behaving the same way. I am thankful for the help we received."

The cultural map of Canada has been changing considerably over the past few years. People immigrate to this country for many reasons. For some, it is the opportunity to participate in, contribute to, and enjoy the economic and social opportunities that life in Canada affords. For others, it is an opportunity to reunite with family and loved ones who have immigrated here in the past. For others still, Canada provides an escape and safe haven from war and other situations that are simply unimaginable to many Canadians. In this chapter we will discuss the demography of immigration and the impact of immigration on children and families. Then we will consider the ways in which the early childhood educator can provide support to new Canadian families.

Immigrating to Canada

Vast demographic changes are taking place throughout Canada. As of 2008, approximately 20% of Canadians were immigrants (Statistics Canada, 2008). Since 2005, about 250 000 immigrants have come to this country each year. Furthermore, it is estimated that, owing to an aging population, by 2030 Canada's only source of growth will be through immigration (Statistics Canada, 2010). A walk through any large city, many small towns, or just about any college or university campus reinforces the fact that Canada is largely a collection of many different cultures (Devito et al., 2007). Many cultural groups have been successful in preserving their uniqueness and special traditions while contributing to Canadian society as a whole. Accordingly, over the past decade, much emphasis has been placed on diversity in early childhood education. Twenty years ago, many articles, workshops, and chapters in books were entitled "Tolerating Diversity"; however, public awareness of the possible negative connotations of that phrase led to a reconsideration. We then began to talk about "celebrating diversity," which better reflects the idea that Canadians are proud of their multicultural society. Canadian identity is considered a multicultural mosaic, with different cultures and groups within the mosaic influencing each other in a number of ways.

Canada's multitude of ethnically diverse groups is constantly changing. For example, between 2001 and 2006, approximately 60% of new Canadians were from Asia (Statistics Canada, 2007) whereas, in the 1960s, Asians accounted for only about 6% of immigrants (Statistics Canada, 2007). In 2001–2006, only 16% of new Canadians were from Europe, compared with close to 75% in the 1960s (Statistics Canada, 2007). These examples indicate the ongoing shift in demographics, changes that will affect many aspects of society in the future.

While the terms *embracing diversity* and *celebrating diversity* appear in many textbooks, many Canadians feel some of the ambivalence that societal change often brings. It may be easier to celebrate difference when those who are different are in the minority than when there is a concern that the traditional ways of mainstream Canadians may be challenged. Nonetheless, we have to be careful not to automatically assume people are racist or prejudiced if they question how the changing landscape of Canada may affect their lives. Successful adaptation to change requires a strong commitment to mutual understanding and much dialogue. It is very important that, as professionals, we move beyond such slogans as "Celebrating and Embracing Diversity" and encourage these dialogues to occur. A first step for educators is to learn about the culture of others and about the range of behaviours and values that reflect these cultures. Second, and perhaps more important, is to understand our own culture. Third, we need to understand the challenges faced by many new Canadians who undergo the transition from country to country, some of whom have fled from circumstances that we can only begin to imagine.

It is often difficult to imagine the experiences of new Canadians as they build their lives in this country. For example, gender roles can change, and immigrant fathers often do experience a shift in roles and responsibilities upon immigrating to Canada (Este & Tachble, 2009; Roer-Strier, 1999; Roer-Strier et al., 2005). If a woman's earning potential is greater than her husband's, a woman's role may shift from a primarily domestic one to that of primary bread-winner, forcing men to take on more "traditional" mothering roles (Kim-Goh & Baello, 2008; Remennick, 2007). This is just one example of the many changes that may occur upon moving to Canada. Even under the best of circumstances, moving to a new location, communicating in a new language, and encountering a profusion of new sensations, experiences, and people can be simply overwhelming. Roer-Strier et al. (2005) have described a number of risk factors faced by immigrant families. Some of these are the same risk factors that apply to many Canadian families, and some are unique to immigrants and refugees.

Risk Factors Faced by Immigrant Families

- *Underemployment or unemployment.* Due to a number of factors, such as language barriers, different demand levels for occupations in various countries, and different qualification criteria, many immigrants do not find work in their own fields, despite arriving in Canada with education, experience, and professional qualifications (Este & Tachble, 2009; Schellenberg & Maheux, 2007; Statistics Canada, 2006).

- *Role reversal.* Often when new Canadians seek employment, women find jobs (often in child care or domestic realms) more easily than their husbands, and the father becomes their children's primary caregiver (Deaux & Bikmen, 2010; Shimoni et al., 2003). Some families find this role reversal very difficult, as fathers have not had the socialization or training to be the primary caregiver and nurturer of children (Williams & Vashi, 2007).

- *Generational differences in immigrant families.* Generational differences between older immigrants and their children or grandchildren may also alter traditional family roles (Este & Tachble, 2009; Roer-Strier et al., 2005). For example, adult immigrants may have arrived from a culture where daughters were expected to stay at home and help with domestic tasks, but their daughters, having grown up in Canada, may refuse this domestic role. Conflicts can and often do arise as immigrant families battle with "Canadian" values.

- *Social isolation.* Feelings of isolation often intensify the social, psychological, and economic pressures that immigrants face. Immigrants of diverse religious and cultural backgrounds can feel excluded from mainstream social events, and sometimes experience discrimination and exclusion (Ambert, 2006).

- *Barriers to helping services.* Barriers may prevent new Canadians from fully utilizing community and health services that offer support to individuals and families. These barriers can include difficulty communicating in English, lack of knowledge and information about services, perceptions that help is unavailable or that professionals won't be able to help, fear of stigmatization and deportation, and lack of child care. Health professionals have suggested additional barriers, such as fear of hospitals and clinics, professionals' lack of understanding of immigrants' cultural background, and agencies' inability to provide translators or workers who speak immigrants' first languages.

- *English/French as a second language.* Clearly, competence in the English or French language is necessary for success in Canada, and many efforts are made to help new Canadians focus on teaching and learning English. However, as Chud and Fahlman (1995) point out, people who required language training became labelled "ESL," much the same way that children were labelled "special needs." The skills, talents, and potential of the adult and child are often overlooked when the label "ESL" is applied.

- *Loss, grief, and depression.* Many immigrants to Canada are grateful for the opportunity to live in this country and appreciate all the advantages that Canada offers. However, even if they are here by choice, it is normal to grieve the loss of family, friends, and a way of life that has been left behind. Depression has been noted as one of the common problems among immigrants. This has a major impact on the child-rearing capacity of immigrant parents, who, for extended periods of time, may be emotionally unavailable to their children. In addition, studies on immigrants report that many cases of depression go undetected due to cultural barriers and inappropriate services.

- *Trauma induced by war or enforced refugee status.* It is well known that refugees and other immigrants who have been affected by traumatic events require special intervention and attention. Adults who have suffered these kinds of trauma appear to need to move through several stages as they seek to restore mental health after being uprooted and displaced. Post-traumatic stress disorder is fairly common and can deeply impact a family's life. This will be discussed further in the following section.

Effects of Refugee Experiences on Children

Young children who have experienced the trauma and horrors of war are often in need of extensive treatment and care. Imagine the impact of witnessing the torture or beating of a sibling, parent, or relative; of being moved from place to place to hide; and going for days without shelter or food. These experiences, followed by a trying journey to a new and unfamiliar country, are overwhelming for children. Parents, who usually provide support for children in stressful situations, may be so overwhelmed by their own reactions to trauma and grief that they are unable to provide emotional support and security to their children. It is no wonder, then, that refugee children commonly display signs of chronic sadness. They may seem excessively fearful or shy, and many develop symptoms of school phobia. This chapter's opening scenario portrayed a very common occurrence—a heightened degree of separation anxiety that under normal circumstances would be considered inappropriate for the child's age. Regressive behaviour, learning disabilities, and poor school performance are often seen in refugee children. Hyper-alertness or hyper-aggressive behaviour are other common symptoms.

Immigrant children who are not refugees will likely have experienced less severe trauma. But they will have experienced the uncertainty, fear, and sadness associated with moving from their familiar setting to a new and strange country. As they grow up, many immigrant children experience conflict between the norms and values of their peers and teachers and those of their parents, who maintain the beliefs and values of their country of origin. This is especially notable in the adolescent years.

In recent years, researchers have also focused on the trauma of terrorism and how this affects children and families (Danieli, 2005). Symptoms are often described as similar to those of post-traumatic stress disorder, and include many of the same issues as listed above (Danieli, 2005). One can assume that research into the impacts of global tragedies on children will surface more in the years to come (Cohen et al., 2010; Danieli, 2005).

New kinds of "play therapy" are helping children and families who have experienced trauma through war, civil unrest, or terrorism (Cohen et al., 2010). For example, programs run by the Israel Centre for the Treatment of Psychotrauma are helping children and their parents work through trauma using play therapy integrated with a number of themes such as independence, strengthening the parent–child bond, self-esteem, playfulness, reflection, and expression of feelings (Cohen et al., 2010). In addition, numerous publications, books, websites, and other resources provide information and support to parents and early childhood educators who are caring for children who have experienced trauma (Astor et al., 2010; Brom et al., 2008).

Coping Strategies of Immigrant and Refugee Parents

The previous description of the risk factors that apply to immigrant and refugee families may lead readers to the mistaken conclusion that the odds are high against successful immigration. The truth, however, is just the opposite. After an almost inevitably difficult beginning, most immigrant families acculturate and become successful Canadian citizens. As with many of the issues facing families with young children that have been described in this text, the appropriate support at the appropriate time can make a tremendous difference. For this reason, it is important to understand the risks facing immigrant families. It is equally important to understand some of the differences in child-rearing approaches and strategies so that we do not approach these families from an assumption of deficit. Effective support usually builds on the family's strengths.

Shimoni et al. (2003) describe the various coping methods used by immigrant and refugee families. These families will have different approaches to professionals—for example, some may be worried that professionals will interfere with their way of life, and some may feel disempowered as parents due to their own adjustment difficulties and may even go as far as abdicating responsibility for decision making to such professionals as teachers and nurses.

Scenario

Different Strokes

Lee was doing his practicum in a family resource program in two locations in the city—one with predominantly young single mothers living in impoverished settings, the other with new immigrant families. One of his tasks was to plan play experiences for drop-in time in both locations. For the young mothers' group, he planned open-ended activities that children typically worked on while their mothers interacted or attended support meetings. In the other location, the play experiences were totally different. Parents often stayed with their children and directed them in completing the tasks "right" for the "teachers." Parents often asked for models, sought clarification, and insisted that children complete their projects correctly. They joined circle time to ensure that their children paid attention and participated. Lee commented on the difference in his planning and how difficult this was for him, since he didn't really favour highly structured activities. However, he said that this was obviously important to those parents and that he would plan accordingly.

When immigrants move from one culture to another, they can either preserve the image of a successful adult from their home country or abandon it in favour of the image of the successful adult in their new country. In fact, it is never quite this clear-cut. Following immigration, many interrelated factors affect which image parents hold. But in each case, immigrant families have to find ways to cope with the different norms, expectations, and values regarding children that are prevalent in the new country. These can surface when they interact with professionals at preschool and school, and with health and social services.

Becoming Culturally Competent: Suggestions for Early Childhood Educators

Understand the need for time. Have patience for resolving difficult situations, and take time to develop quality relationships with parents.

Make sure that you understand how your own cultural point of view might be impacting your interactions and ability to develop positive relationships.

Avoid being judgmental—don't rush to draw conclusions based on assumptions you may have.

Use every opportunity to enhance your intercultural competence in order to understand the culture of the children in your care and their families. Look for opportunities to celebrate together. Share your intercultural understanding with other early childhood educators when talking about your experiences.

Source: Adapted from Durand, T. (2010). Celebrating Diversity in early child care and education settings: moving beyond the margins. Early child development and care, 7, pp. 835-848.

Sadhana, Age 4

Reconciling Parental Styles with Professionals' Perceptions

Almost without exception, parents want their children to grow and develop to be successful adults. Parents who have immigrated to Canada may have very different ideas of what a successful adult is, and therefore will have different child-rearing approaches and strategies. When they arrive in Canada and begin to interface with educational and other frameworks, they will develop strategies to cope with these differences. Some will hold dearly to the norms of their countries of origin, some will encourage their children to abandon these in favour of quickly becoming "Canadian," and others may attempt to help their children live successfully in both worlds (Roer-Strier et al., 2005). Usually these strategies are not evident in the extreme, but as general tendencies. There is no right or wrong way of making this adjustment to life in Canada. But if professionals understand these differences, they will be better able to understand parents. The mother who doesn't come to parent meetings because she feels she has little to offer and the teacher knows best anyway is not acting out of lack of concern for her child. She may well believe that her non-involvement is in the best interest of her child. Similarly, the parent who adamantly insists that his child should maintain customs and appearances that belong to the culture of the family's home country is generally doing this in the belief that it is in the best interest of his child. Therefore, rather than judging the behaviour of the parents and their approach to child-rearing, early childhood educators must appreciate that there are differences they need to respect and understand.

When early childhood educators work with families of different cultures, questions inevitably arise regarding value differences. Struggling with these value differences is sometimes difficult for educators, and can be a barrier to providing new Canadian families with empathy and support. Bradley and Kibera (2006) give two examples. The first relates to privacy. In some families in their study, mothers did not feel comfortable sharing information about the family, yet the early childhood educator felt that without this knowledge, she couldn't do her job properly. The second example relates to families' perceptions of disability. Cultural beliefs may have a significant impact on parents' expectation about their child's ability. Some may believe that "this is the way he was born and we just have to live with it" rather than accepting support to help the child reach his full potential. There are no simple solutions to the question of how to deal with these differences, but we can offer some advice.

Learning about other cultures sometimes helps put these value differences in a context to help us appreciate them. Citizenship and Immigration Canada has created a website that provides cultural profiles for close to 100 countries. (See "Recommended Websites" at the end of this chapter.)

Early childhood educators should work to actively develop cultural competence (defined as valuing diversity, becoming culturally self-aware, understanding cultural interactions, and adapting to diversity) and to create diversity-positive environments by planning activities to support and promote diversity (Brown et al., 2009; Perlman et al., 2010). As one researcher noted, "Becoming cross-culturally competent does not require us to become an expert on every discernible category of diversity . . . rather, becoming comfortable and supportive of diversity requires a certain mindset, a certain point of view, a certain process of sensitivity that becomes almost automotic when we deal with children and families"[†] (Durand, 2010, p. 837). It is helpful if staff have open discussions regarding which adaptations are possible for them to make and which are not (e.g., "We do treat boys and girls the same at the centre, and that shouldn't change, but we can appreciate that in homes this may not be the same"). Most children can sort out these inconsistencies. Bradley and Kibera (2006) stress that staff must recognize the benefits families can gain from connecting to the strengths of their cultures and accessing the sources of their cultural communities. Of course, there is no question that any parental behaviour that would be classified as physical or emotional abuse and/or neglect goes beyond (and is rarely related to) a cultural difference.

Source: Durand, T. (2010). Celebrating Diversity in early child care and education settings: moving beyond the margins. Early child development and care, 7, pp 835–848 (p. 837)

Shibana's parents immigrated to Canada before she was born. In some ways they adapted to Canadian customs, but in other ways they held onto their cultural beliefs. When Shibana finished ECCE at college, her parents felt it was time that she married, and they began the search for a husband. Shibana felt caught but did agree to meet the many eligible suitors. After several years, she decided to marry a man who lived in the same city and who was chosen by her parents. Prior to her marriage, her colleagues at the child-care centre threw a "traditional" bridal shower/stagette, where many "marital aid" items were given as gifts. Shibana received these gifts good-naturedly, but remarked that she wasn't sure what to do with them since, as was expected, they would be living with her future husband's parents.

Aboriginal Families

The term *Aboriginal* refers to "a person who reports that he or she identifies with, or is a member of, an organic political or cultural entity that stems historically from the original persons of North America. The term includes the Indian, Inuit and Métis peoples of Canada" (Statistics Canada, 2010). There are more than 500 distinct nations in North America, each with its own set of values, languages, dialects, and child-rearing patterns, as well as geographical differences, cultural differences, and differences between urban and rural peoples. However, we should bear in mind that many Aboriginal people share common values and world views, and it is the commonalities that we will explore while remembering the cultural diversity that exists and the need to learn more from local elders and resource centres.

There have been significant and rapid changes in North American society, all of which have had effects on the family—families have become more isolated, women are active members of the workforce outside of the home, children spend large blocks of time in and out of home care, people are busy, and stresses have increased. These changes also exist for Aboriginal families but have been compounded by the loss of traditional lifestyles, interventions in lifestyle, and the disruption of family life.

Historical Perspective

Before Europeans landed, First Nations societies were well developed, highly organized, and stable (Dickason & McNabb, 2009; Mandell & Duffy, 2000). The basic social unit was the family (Ambert, 2006), which existed primarily as the extended family and was communal in nature. Accordingly, reciprocity, cooperation, and sharing were basic values.

Europeans found this culture different and unfamiliar and considered it a barrier to their goals of colonization. They forced changes on First Nations people that eroded their culture and livelihoods and resulted in changes to family life as well. For example, some nations had matrilineal descent patterns, while Europeans were largely patrilineal.

One significant influence has been the Indian Act—which was established by Europeans who settled in Canada and which ensured that government maintained power over First Nations people by regulating every aspect of their lives. For example, the Act detailed who qualified as "Indian" and restricted activities that promoted First Nations culture (e.g., powwows) (Dickason & McNab, 2009). These laws stayed in effect until the 1980s.

In addition, religious and government authorities deemed it necessary to assimilate First Nations peoples into the "dominant English Christian ways," including language, culture, and religion (Steckley & Cummins, 2008). Churches established residential schools as part of their missionary experiences in Canada prior to Confederation (Steckley & Cummins, 2008). The Government of Canada assisted in the administration of these schools from 1874 to the last closing in 1996 to meet its obligation under the Indian Act to integrate First Nations people into Canadian culture. In an attempt to break all cultural ties with their culture and language, children were removed from their families and communities to be taught "Canadian" ways and culture. The short-term effects of residential schools included running away, acting out, depression, and alcohol abuse. Recently we have learned of large numbers of Aboriginal children who died while escaping from residential schools. The long-term effects are still being experienced by many First Nations people today. Residential schools disrupted or destroyed the First Nations family (Ambert, 2006). When children were raised in an institution, their parents lost the opportunity to develop parenting skills (Ambert, 2006). Children removed from family life were unfamiliar with family relationships when it came time to raise their own children (Ambert, 2006). It was assumed that First Nations people did not possess the skills required to parent because their cultural ways were misinterpreted. For example, First Nations cultures generally hold strong beliefs that children deserve full respect, since they believe that children are developed humans (Steckley & Cummins, 2008). Accordingly, First Nations children are not forced to do things they don't want to do, nor are they disciplined. Similarly, when parents encourage their children to participate in traditional cultural events that may interfere with school, the parents are sometimes seen as incompetent.

This tendency to "blame the victim" is often apparent with regard to First Nations communities. High rates of alcohol abuse, drug abuse, and physical illness have always been used to demonstrate that First Nations people are unfit, rather than considering the contributing roles of poverty, marginalization, and discrimination. This prevailing attitude has in turn led to more self-destructive behaviours, such as drug and alcohol abuse and suicide. Statistics on living conditions in First Nations communities have consistently noted the prevalence of fetal alcohol syndrome, drug addiction, poverty, teen pregnancy, low levels of education, and suicide (Statistics Canada, 2006).

Clearly, the history of First Nations in North America sheds light on the root of issues and concerns that exist today. First Nations children and youth have been estranged from their culture: They speak a different language; they have lost the traditional ways; and they have adopted the ways of modern society (e.g., based on television, movies, and popular culture). Many First Nations families are now speaking openly about residential schools—the abuse they suffered there and the lasting impact on their culture and family life. There has been a focus on community healing, for example, through the use of healing circles, to help break the silence and move forward. The consequences of colonization for family life and culture have had major effects on First Nations people that they continue to struggle with today.

Beliefs

To begin to understand First Nations families, it is helpful to understand their beliefs, particularly since First Nations values, beliefs, and communication styles differ from those of the dominant western culture society in ways that have caused confusion. One prominent example is the concept of time. North American society is dictated by time; our lives are run by watches and schedules. In First Nations culture, however, time is measured by natural events and not by a clock (Steckley & Cummins, 2008). The need to be on time, to rush, has little meaning in many First Nations cultures, which stress patience as a sign of respect. In another example, avoiding eye contact is also a sign of respect and humility in many First Nations cultures, whereas in North American society, eye contact is a prerequisite for learning, a sign that you are focused and ready to learn. As well, people from First Nations cultures are often careful about what they say, whereas North American culture values talking and asking questions. These different world views often lead to misinterpretation and judgments. The following table, developed as part of the Aboriginal Child and Youth Program at Mount Royal University, compares some traditional First Nations values with Western values (Dokis, n.d.).

Traditional First Nations Values	Western Values
1. Live in harmony with nature	1. Mastery over nature
2. Present-time orientation	2. Future-time orientation
3. Explain natural phenomenon through mythology	3. Scientific explanation: Everything happens according to natural law
4. Aspiration is to learn and follow the ways of elders	4. Climb the ladder of success—child expected to achieve a higher level than his or her father
5. Cooperation	5. Competition
6. Anonymity	6. Individuality
7. Submissiveness	7. Aggressiveness/assertiveness is socially acceptable
8. Work to satisfy present needs	8. Work to get ahead
9. Share	9. Save for the future
10. Time is always with us (Indian time)	10. Time lost can never be regained
11. Humility	11. Win at all costs

Source: Printed with permission of Doug Dokis.

Concepts of Family, Children, and Child-Rearing

It is essential to understand the very meaning of the term *family*, as well as basic beliefs about the role of family members, in traditional Aboriginal culture. According to LaBoucane-Benson (2005), the concept of family for early or traditional Aboriginal peoples in Canada included a complex combination of biological ties, extended family members, clan membership bonds, adoptions, and economic partnerships (i.e., hunting partnerships between communities): "The effect of these diverse, overlapping bonds was to create a dense network of relationships within which sharing and obligations of mutual aid ensured that an effective safety net was in place." Families mediated between the individual and society, which included members related biologically or by kin.

Kinship models varied between different communities (Family, Kinship and Organization, Multicultural Canada Encyclopedia), but they generally included members with biological and/or communal kin relationships, which were guided by strict rules and defined roles. These rules guided how individuals, families, and communities worked together, interacted, and ensured the survival of their people (LaBoucane-Benson, 2005). Rules always ensured that the children would be taken care of, and adults in the community formed mentoring, protective relationships with children. A powerful system existed to ensure that children would develop a strong sense of self-worth and grow up to be contributing members of society. A very useful description of relationship kinships in First Nations, Inuit, and Métis communities can be found in a video narrated by the elder Leonard Bastien (listed at the end of this chapter).

The fact that Canadian officials did not recognize the strength of the extended family and its role in supporting children contributed to the removal of so many children from their families. Aboriginal families were deemed inappropriate due to impoverished living conditions, to the fact that children were often cared for by grandparents who were seen as too old to care for children (Fournier & Crey, 1998), or to a perception of neglect of children. The nuclear model of the family was forced upon Aboriginal families through Family Services actions, even though it did not fit within the paradigm of the Aboriginal extended family (Fournier & Crey, 1998). The enormous price paid for this misunderstanding is only beginning to be understood today.

A comparison of some of the commonly held views of Aboriginal and western society concerning children and childrearing has been suggested by Dokis, (n.d.). This does not necessarily represent the diversity of beliefs in each group, but can be used as a focus for discussion.

Traditional	Western
1. Children are unique, whole individuals.	1. Children must be moulded and directed in becoming adults.
2. Children learn by observation and experience.	2. Children learn through formal education and planned activities.
3. Children are the responsibility of the extended family and community.	3. Children are the responsibility of parents or government.
4. Adults explain and model responsibility of society.	4. Parents discipline and teach the rules of society.
5. Children make mistakes many times until they learn.	5. Mistakes are made once; parents teach by consequences.
6. Children are children for life.	6. Children are adults (reach maturity) at age 18.

Source: Printed with permission of Doug Dokis.

In addition to these Aboriginal values and beliefs, there are many traditional child-rearing practices. For example, ceremonies are important to Aboriginal children and their families. The naming ceremony, for example, helps children establish their identity within the community. Names are considered an integral connection to family and are often passed down through generations, along with the stories that accompany them. Nurturing children is critical to child-rearing: The use of cradle boards allowed children to be close to their mothers with little separation. No one person assumes full responsibility for raising children—often responsibility is shared by family members such as grandparents, aunts, uncles, and cousins. Children are respected and understood. Children are valued by adults, as can be seen in children's involvement in all social activities and in the gentle styles of discipline used (Steckley & Cummins, 2008).

Children's education is largely intuitive, based on modelling older generations and expressed through daily activities (e.g., arts and crafts). Core values and beliefs are passed down through legends, traditional songs, dance, and prayer. Through stories and legends, children learn about relationships with other people and the environment. Children are taught to be good listeners and observers. Land and nature is considered the first teacher.

This brief overview has focused on Aboriginal families and children. It has not taken into account the myriad conditions affecting communities of Aboriginal people, including economics, finances, governance, laws, and funding. However, we hope that early childhood educators might begin to understand the unique and distinctive nature of Aboriginal culture and family life so that they can better care for Aboriginal children and provide support for their families.

The Role of Early Childhood Educators

Working effectively with people from cultures different from our own requires a willingness to examine our own values and biases. Much has been written about diversity education and the importance of increasing the awareness and competence of early childhood educators in multiculturalism (Durand, 2010). It may be helpful to explore experiences of oppression/ marginalization/racism that families have experienced. Early childhood educators should be aware of the child's family's cultural context. While we can only touch on some of these principles in this chapter, we highly recommend that readers refer to the work of Durand (2010) on developing cultural competence. There are also many articles on multiculturalism in early childhood journals, on websites, and in newsletters and other resources for educators. Answering the following questions might help you clarify some of the areas you need to explore further.

Examine Your Attitudes

- Is respecting parents more important than getting along with peers?
- Is it better to educate children in settings where boys and girls are together or separate?
- Is it more important to adapt to "Canadian ways" or to preserve your culture of origin?

There are no right or wrong answers here, although there would certainly be strong opinions that support one view or the other. If you do feel strongly about your response to any of these questions, it may be helpful to examine how your own cultural background influenced your opinion, and how and why a person from a different cultural background may have a different opinion.

Understanding and Empathizing

Providing support to children and families who are immigrants or refugees requires the ability to empathize with their difficulties. Try to imagine what young children who are refugees might feel like when:

- They witness the torture or killing of a loved one.
- They live in fear and hiding.
- They are hungry, exhausted, and confused.

Try to imagine the experiences of an immigrant child who:

- Experiences strange smells, new sounds, and a very different home.
- Doesn't see familiar people anymore, and doesn't understand why.
- Watches children behaving in very different ways from what he or she is used to.

Understanding the experiences of people who are victims of war is very difficult. You might want to think about watching films or reading books that capture the experiences of victims of war or trauma (there are many current films and books on war and terror).

Think about how might you feel as a new Canadian when:

- You feel that you have no right to complain, because you will be told, "If you don't like it, go back to your own country."

- You cannot work in your own profession, even though you have the appropriate education and experience.
- You cannot help your children with their homework because the subject matter or the language was different in your home country.
- You want your children to get along well in Canada, but see them forgetting about the things that were so important to your parents and grandparents.

Supporting Aboriginal children and families also begins by understanding. Imagine how you might feel as an Aboriginal child when:

- Expectations for interacting are very different from what you are taught at home.
- You are ignored or punished for acting the way you have been taught at home.
- People expect you to act in ways that are not valued in your home or community.

Imagine being a parent when:

- You are constantly worried that your ways, values, and beliefs are under scrutiny.
- You live with the constant fear that your children will be removed for no reason or little reason.

Providing Support to Parents

There are a number of ways you can provide support to parents who are immigrants and refugees:

- Provide them with easily accessible information about relevant resources. This would include information on preschools, child care, health services, and social support and recreational services.
- Provide information in first languages. Many immigrant-serving agencies translate brochures, posters, and handouts into a number of first languages. This is extremely helpful to parents who are struggling to learn English.
- Bring representatives of other agencies to the centre to meet with parents. The community nurse or social worker could make a short presentation at a parent evening. It may be easier for parents to make contact with new agencies after meeting these professionals at a familiar place.

Caregivers can help children who are new Canadians in a number of ways as well:

- Provide opportunities for staged entry into the program. As many immigrant and refugee children may feel insecure in a new setting, particularly if they do not speak English, they may need to spend a lot of time at the centre with their parents.
- Learn a few key words in the first language of the children. "Dolly," "lunch," "book," and a few phrases such as "good morning" may make a child feel at home.
- Find symbols that represent their home country and culture. Parents will be able to help you or perhaps bring something from home that will make new Canadian children feel that the centre is their home away from home.
- Ensure that you are familiar with, and respect, the dietary laws. If possible, provide food and snacks that the child might be familiar with.
- Be patient and work hard to develop a trusting relationship with the child. Children may be wary of new people in their lives, especially when they do not understand the language you speak. Try to be nearby, and watch for opportunities to provide support or to show the child something interesting. Gradually, a relationship will form.

Supporting children and families from Aboriginal communities may include the following:

- Begin by examining your own attitudes. There are many myths and stereotypical images of Aboriginal people in Canadian culture. What beliefs do you hold?

- Use everyday activities to introduce Aboriginal legends, stories, songs, and dances to daily activities so that all children can come to appreciate traditional ways. Include outdoor play and opportunities for contact with plants and animals so that children may strengthen their appreciation of the natural world.

- Aboriginal children and youth may feel disconnected from their community and ways of life. Find ways that they may connect both to traditional ways of life and to the community you are creating for them.

- Find Aboriginal people to guide you and your program to help ensure relevance and authenticity for both Aboriginal and non-Aboriginal children.

- Acknowledge and accommodate different learning styles. Provide opportunities for children to learn by watching and through trial and error; emphasize cooperation and group learning rather than competition.

Conclusion

Working with children from diverse cultures challenges us to understand the world view of others and to empathize with challenges faced by many families. Taking a journey to deepen our understanding of other cultures often reaps meaningful rewards, the least of which is a greater understanding of our own roots and culture.

Chapter Summary

- Vast demographic changes are taking place in Canada. In 2008, 5.5 million immigrants were living in in this country, representing approximately 20% of the total population.
- Immigrants to Canada face many challenges and stressors, even if immigration was by choice. These include role transitions, barriers to employment, and grieving the loss of what was left behind. Refugees will face additional problems related to recovering from the traumas caused by war or other extreme conditions.
- It is important to understand the current and historical context of Aboriginal people and culture.

Recommended Websites

Early Childhood Development Intercultural Partnerships:
www.ecdip.org/index.htm

Canadian Child Care Federation:
www.cccf-fcsge.ca

Citizenship and Immigration Canada:
www.cic.gc.ca/english/index-can.asp

Health Canada:
www.hc-sc.gc.ca/index_e.html

Parenting workshops and guides to support immigrant parents:
www.chestnutpublishing.com/books_CPW.html

Supporting immigrant and refugee fathers:
www.dadscan.ca/Module1.pdf

Instructor manual that accompanies *Stand Together or Fall Apart* (2012), by Judith Bernhard, about working with newcomers:
http://standtogetherorfallapart.com

Videos/Films

Walking Together: First Nations, Métis, and Inuit Perspectives in Curriculum. www.learnalberta.ca/content/aswt/#/kinship/observing_practice/a_relationship_model_of_kinship

In the Shadow of Gold Mountain. 2004. 43 min. Karen Cho, director. National Film Board of Canada. www.nfb.ca/playlists/bridging-cultures/viewing/in_the_shadow_of_gold_mountain

Speaking My Truth: Reflections on Reconciliation and Residential Schools. 2012. www.trc.ca

Exercises

1. Playrooms are often multicultural and include families from diverse cultural and religious backgrounds. How will you accommodate the different and sometimes conflicting perspectives and requests in your playroom (e.g., food requests, celebrations)?

2. Review the messages that a visitor to your centre would receive about culture. Look at toys, books, equipment and decorations, and information brochures and pamphlets on display. What cultures are represented? What would you change?

3. Consider different strategies you might use if children and/or their parents do not speak English or French.

4. What are some of the resources available to new Canadian families and Aboriginal families in your community? How will you communicate this information?

5. What resources (translation services, multicultural training, etc.) are available in your community to help staff work more effectively with new Canadians and with Aboriginal families?

6. What are the stereotypical images held about Aboriginal children and families? How do these images affect your relationships with Aboriginal children and families? Consider ways to address these images.

chapter 10
Modern Families

Objectives

- **To deepen our understanding of nontraditional families, including:**
  - **Adoptive families**
  - **Foster families**
  - **Same-sex parents**
  - **Single mothers by choice**
- **To discuss some of the challenges faced by nontraditional families**
- **To discuss how early childhood educators can support these families**

Nontraditional Families

Within the diversity that exists among Canadian families, there are families who are less accepted as *real* due to dominant societal perceptions and beliefs. These perceptions may be inaccurate, inappropriate, or based on myth. Many nontraditional families face unique challenges—some of which relate to being different or devalued. More often, the challenges result from a lack of knowledge or understanding by mainstream society. The nontraditional families reviewed in this chapter are those headed by same-sex couples, single mothers by choice, (i.e., mothers who chose to undergo medically assisted fertilization without a partner), and families who have adopted or fostered their children. While these subjects may seem unrelated, they share common elements. First, many of these families deal with negative societal views, lack of understanding, or discrimination. Second, the particular issues facing these families can become stressors that, like all stress factors, can impede positive child–parent relations and healthy child development. Third, in all three cases, the act of becoming parents involves considerable legal and/or medical procedures, or the involvement of social service agencies, generally not required for other kinds of families. If we work toward increasing understanding and eliminating stigma and prejudice, and if we provide appropriate support when and if required, children in these families can thrive.

Remember that families don't always fit into neat categories—a gay family may also be an immigrant family or part of a blended family system, and an adoptive family may also be undergoing a divorce. While we have divided the chapters in the book to highlight the unique needs of different kinds of families or the challenges facing families, there will often be overlap. It is equally important to remember that not all families described in this and other chapters necessarily require support. Many families survive and thrive despite the potential and actual stresses in their lives. However, when families are experiencing stress, as educators we may be able to support them or provide developmentally appropriate support to the child in our care.

Often the literature describes families as nontraditional when they are not headed by a heterosexual male and female married couple who are raising their biological children. However, as other chapters have indicated, few families in Canada today could be considered traditional families. There are many single-parent families, blended families, cohabiting heterosexual families, gay or lesbian families, and adoptive/foster families. In addition, a high degree of diversity exists within traditional families (and almost all families). There may be more similarities between a lesbian-headed family and two-parent-heterosexual-headed family than expected. So instead of seeing families as "traditional" or "nontraditional," early childhood educators should assume that all families are diverse and have unique needs and challenges.

Adoptive Families

Years ago, adoptive families were not always considered *real families*. Although this has changed somewhat, children and parents in adoptive families still face stigmatization that may cause extra pressure or stress in their lives.

Adoption is defined as the "legal establishment of a parent/child relationship between individuals who are usually not, with the exception of kinship adoption, related by birth" (Ryan & Whitelock, in Brown et al., 2009, p. 230). Adoption is a complex process and experience, involving at least three sets of participants: the birth family, the adoptive family, and the adoptees. Members of this adoption triangle may share some feelings and experiences, but they may also differ in how they experience adoption.

The past two decades have seen changes in the number of adoptions as well as in the dynamics of and process for adoption. During the 1980s, for example, domestic adoptions decreased by 47%. In 2002, the Vanier Institute reported that 57 000 of Canada's children have been adopted (Vanier Institute of the Family, 2003). Today, waiting lists for adoptions in many places range from 7 to 12 years. This situation is the result of several factors. Fewer infants are available for adoption because of the availability of abortion, young parents have more support services, and single or teen parenting carries less of a stigma. This is not to say that there is still not a high need for adoption, however. In fact, one Canadian agency cited that 22 000 children in Canada are currently awaiting adoption (www.canadaswaitingkids.ca). Adoption is a lengthy process, with many adoption cases in progress for months or even years. The waiting list for domestic adoptions has led to an increase in the number of families choosing international adoptions (Corbin-Dwyer & Gidluck, 2009). Citizenship and Immigration Canada estimates that there are currently 2000 international adoptions per year (Citizenship & Immigration Canada, 2010). International adoptions are most frequently from countries that are suffering from extreme poverty, and that are often in the aftermath of war or natural disaster.

People may assume that adoptions take place as a second choice when a couple has difficulty or is unable to conceive a child. Adoptive families are in a precarious situation because of this second-best idea. Many feel that they have failed in their ability to conceive their own children, and then have failed again because their adoptive family is only "second best."

Adoptive parents must often deal with complex feelings about their infertility, feelings complicated by the assumption that a biological tie is a prerequisite for bonding and attachment. Sometimes adoptees are expected to feel grateful because they have been adopted (Trawick-Smith, 2010). Because of these stereotypes, many adoptive families never feel truly comfortable in seeking assistance, and so for the most part deal with issues on their own. Yet although it is important to take these factors into account, they are not necessarily true for all adoptive families. It is also important to note that many families who adopt may already have their own children, or may have made the decision not to have their own children owing to their belief in and commitment to sharing their good fortune with children who are much less fortunate.

Until the 1970s, formal adoptions were almost always closed. Typically, the birth mother had "made a mistake" that brought shame to her family. She was instructed to give up the child because that was "best for the baby." The commonly held view was that if a birth mother received no information about the child and the adoption, she would be better able to get on with her life and forget about this "mistake." Adoptive parents were given little or no information about the child's history, and records were often sealed. Denial of the child's background was used as a strategy to encourage the development of a primary attachment between the child and the adoptive family. Adopted children were told that they were chosen and therefore special. Many were never told at all. They were thus expected to suffer no consequences.

In the past decades, professionals have learned that secrecy and anonymity actually create difficulties for all parties involved. For example, secrecy can disrupt the child's development of trust and capacity for intimate relationships. The result of this awareness has been a trend toward open adoptions. In an open adoption process, birth parents and adoptive parents meet, exchange information, and, potentially, carry on a relationship. The extent of "openness" within the adoption can range from minimal to a continuous, long-term relationship. Open adoption has been gaining popularity in Canada and the United States. Personal experiences with open adoption suggest that it can be very positive for all involved—the child, the biological parents, and the adoptive parents.

Impact of Adoption on Children

We know that children in adoptive families face some challenges in terms of their identity formation, and that their preoccupation with their biological family as they become adolescents may impact family dynamics (Trawick-Smith, 2010). Ambert (2005) reminds us that the need to search for biological parents, along with the feeling of incompleteness if this does not occur, is really a culturally imposed norm in Western society. This need, according to Ambert, coincides with pop psychology phrases such as "the need to find oneself." So, although it is a need that has been created by our culture, it is a need that exists and becomes an important issue for many adopted children.

Most studies of adopted children do not point to any significant differences between adopted and non-adopted children in terms of child outcomes. It has recently been suggested (Miall & March, 2005) that adopted children may face difficulties and require more professional support not because of parent–child interactions, but because peers and other adults often openly express their belief that adopted parents can't love their children as much as *real* parents do. In addition, some researchers have attributed any differences between adopted and non-adopted children to "adoption-coloured glasses," or to the fact that parents, teachers, and others often see issues as the fault of their adoption, as opposed to recognizing the normal diversity among children (Corbin-Dwyer & Gidluck, 2009). Recently, research has been addressing the possible effects of transnational adoption on child development, but again, most research attributes any major differences to the way adoptive families are treated by society at large (Dorow, 2006; Howell, 2007; Yngvesson, 2010). We are living in times when the adoption of children from war-torn or poverty-stricken countries, or from countries where natural disasters have struck, has gained considerable media attention. When high-profile entertainers conduct much of their family life in the public eye, it is hard for these children to grow up having normal lives. It is very likely that the excessive media attention, rather than the adoption per se, will be a significant factor in these children's lives. It is important to remember that children lack the ability to fully comprehend what is going on around them, so processing changes in their lives can be quite difficult.

Supporting Children Who Have Been Adopted

The most important thing a caregiver can do to support young children who are adopted is to help them, when necessary, accept the range of emotions they may express. All children occasionally feel angry, hurt, or rejected by their parents, but children who are adopted may need reassurance that it is natural to feel that way sometimes. Stories and dramatic play that include adopted children help normalize adoptive families. All children fantasize about wicked stepparents, abandonment by parents, and other themes that may be exacerbated for the child who is adopted. Being aware of this and providing assurance that they are special and loved by their adoptive parents can be very helpful to children.

Books recommended for preschool adopted children include *A Koala for Kate* by Jonathan London (1997), *Horace* by Holly Keller (1991), and *In My Heart* by Molly Bang (2006).

Some children may feel anger at their adoptive parents, believing that they are preventing them from being with their *real* parents. Children who are adopted later (i.e., not as infants) may have undergone traumatic experiences prior to the adoption, and care needs to be taken to help these children develop a sense of security, trust, and belonging.

The following recommendations have been suggested after several Canadian families adopted children who had lost their families in the 2010 earthquake in Haiti.

1. *Try to provide familiar surroundings.* This includes pictures, toys, and books. Provide a photo album or "adoption lifebook" that shows in pictures where the child is from.

2. *Be clear about rules and expectations.* The more clarity and consistency there is in expectations, the easier it will be for the child to adjust. Be careful to ensure that the expectations are age appropriate, and minimize the rules to a few at a time so that the child is not overwhelmed.

3. *Give the time needed to develop a relationship.* Remember that children who have experienced crises prior to adoption may be reluctant to receive affection. They may need to be asked permission to receive a hug.

4. *Children who have been adopted from countries after disaster or war may have habits that seem strange to us.* This may include hoarding food, being very vigilant, and being afraid to fall asleep. Show that you understand, and model ways of behaving.

5. *Give children time and space to grieve.* Understand that they may have lost more than most of us can imagine: family members, a home, a language, and a way of life. Remember that they are grieving for the life they lost.

Supporting Adoptive Parents

Understanding the stresses that families may have endured prior to the decision to adopt and demonstrating support when needed can make a remarkable difference. Making it easy to ask for advice and guidance, assuring parents that their parenting abilities are not being judged, and emphasizing that all parents struggle with parenting at times can also make a real difference. It is sometimes recommended that adoptive parents join support groups with other adoptive parents. However, it is important to respect the adoptive parent and child's right to privacy, and parents do not need to discuss the circumstances of the adoption with the school or centre if they choose not to.

Support groups have proved very helpful to some adoptive parents, as they provide a framework for validating their experiences, a social group with whom to celebrate the joys and share the concerns, and a mechanism for sharing resources and ideas. Most important, perhaps, is that such a group can reduce the feelings of isolation that are sometimes experienced by adoptive parents (www.adoption.ca).

Fostering

Foster families often face challenges similar to those faced by adoptive families, in that they struggle to be seen as a "legitimate" family. This is exacerbated by the headlines in the media following an incident of neglect, abuse, or both. There is a wide range of arrangements for foster care, from very short term to almost permanent. There is also a wide variety of approaches that foster families take to their foster care. For some, foster care becomes a substitute for the biological family. Others provide a warm, caring, supportive environment designed to be a support for the biological family in the hope that the child will be returned. But whatever the approach, the misconceptions and myths surrounding foster care can be a real barrier faced by children and foster parents alike.

In addition to the stereotypes and preconceived notions about foster families as "second choice" is the lack of permanency felt in many foster-care families. Foster care is often short term, and this can affect the parent–child relationship and level of attachment (Riggs et al., 2008). However, as for adoptive families described earlier, this is affected by how foster families are treated in comparison with biological families. Researchers have noted that foster parents feel "role ambiguity" within their parenting role, even in long-term (12 months or more) foster families (Riggs et al., 2008). Furthermore, foster families often struggle to claim a family identity (Riggs et al., 2008; Thomson et al., 2009). Finally, children placed in foster care are often from highly conflicted, disrupted homes. Many of the children entering foster care have faced multiple adversities, such as parental substance abuse, poverty, violence, abuse, and more.

Nonetheless, foster care families can provide a safe haven for children who have experienced adversities, giving them a chance to "start fresh" in a loving, caring family. Both foster mothers and foster fathers play an important role in caring for children (Riggs et al., 2010). For example, one study has shown that while foster mothers are expected to be the *nurturers,* foster fathers are often more nurturing or motherly than expected in traditional fathers (Riggs et al., 2010). In addition, foster fathers who model positive parenting and family behaviours can counter earlier abusive experiences in birth families, and help break negative parenting patterns experienced by children (Riggs et al., 2010). This could be because foster fathers are more likely to exhibit both authoritative, rough-and-tumble parenting (the traditional expectation of fathers) and nurturing behaviour.

There is considerable diversity in the way foster parents perceive their role. In some cases, they try to provide warm and protective care to children while keeping very much in mind that this is a temporary placement, and that their role is to help provide interim support until a child can be returned to his or her parents or a permanent placement is found. For others, fostering continues over years, and they see themselves as real parents.

Foster parents face many challenges. The biological children of foster parents often have struggles in adjusting to the changes in their home and family. Many foster parents feel that they do not receive the appreciation and support that is due to them. There is a chicken-and-egg situation whereby children who spend time in foster care are often very troubled, but then often it is the foster care that is blamed when these children get into trouble or are unsuccessful. For example, a recent article in the *Calgary Herald* found that out of 2000 homeless youth in Calgary, 52% had spent time in foster care. Although it is unfair to conclude that these youth are homeless because foster care was inadequate, that is the conclusion many people make. It is no wonder, then, that there is a current shortage of families willing to become foster families.

Efforts are currently being made to reduce the misunderstandings about foster care, about who can/should become foster parents, the financial aspects of foster care, and many other related issues. The Government of Alberta's website, caring4kids.ca, explains many of these misperceptions. In summary, they write:

> Some foster children have been mentally or physically abused. Others have been abandoned, or can no longer stay with their families because their natural parents don't have the skills to look after them. But almost always, these children are hurt, confused, angry, frightened, and in desperate need of care and stability.

Supporting Foster Families

Foster families can be supported both individually and systemically. Early childhood educators can help by showing their appreciation for the commitment foster families have to the children, and their empathy for the difficulties they face. Educators should provide these families with as much information about resources as possible (Riggs et al., 2008). In addition, early childhood educators should recognize foster families as legitimate families, and focus on using inclusionary language (Riggs et al., 2008). For example, ask the foster parents how they want to be addressed—by name? as the child's mom/dad or foster mom/dad? Early childhood professionals can also help by advocating that governments and community groups provide foster families with appropriate, high-quality education, training, and ongoing support (Caltabiano et al., 2007).

Supporting Children Who Are in Foster Care

Like most children who have experienced loss and trauma, many of the children in foster care will need extra support to build trust and to feel secure. Normal setbacks in toileting, eating, and sleeping habits can be expected, and need to be addressed with patience, understanding, and support.

The Jordan Institute of Families offers advice to caregivers of children in foster care whose parents have been incarcerated. This advice, which also applies to many of the circumstances that bring children into foster care, urges caregivers to understand their own feelings toward the parents whose children have been placed in their care. The guidelines also advise caregivers to consider that these children may be grieving, and to explain this to the child in an age-appropriate manner while stressing that the situation is not the child's fault. Consistent with other research on this topic, the importance of maintaining the connection between the child and biological parents, wherever possible, is emphasized (Jordan Institute for Families, 2002b).

Same-Sex Families

Same-sex parents have existed for many years, often in the context of, or following, heterosexual relationships (Mendez, 2009). However, statistics on the actual number of gay and lesbian parents have only recently been gathered. Canadian census data did not begin to officially capture statistics on gay and lesbian families until 2006, one year after gay marriage was legalized in Canada (Woodford, 2010). In total, the census counted 45 345 same-sex couples in Canada, of which 7465 (16.5%) were married couples (Statistics Canada, 2007a). The number of same-sex couples surged by 32.6% between 2001 and 2006, five times the pace of opposite-sex couples (Statistics Canada, 2007a). Approximately 9% of same-sex couples had children aged 24 years and under living in the home in 2006. This was more common for females (16.3%) than for males (2.9%) (Statistics Canada, 2007b). It is important to note that in both Canada and the United States, statistics on same-sex households are not accurate, as many same-sex families do not report their sexuality (Mendez, 2009). For example, some argue that the 2000 census in the United States underestimated same-sex households by 62% (Mendez, 2009).

Notably, over the past 10 years there has been a dramatic increase in the number of planned same-sex families through adoption or artificial insemination in both the United States and Canada (Mendez, 2009). However, the legal battle to allow same-sex couples to parent has been an ongoing challenge. Canada was only the fourth country in the world to recognize same-sex marriage (Woodford, 2010). Currently, same-sex marriage is legal in 11 countries around the world, a statistic that is rapidly changing. While legal recognition of same-sex marriage has been achieved, lesbian and gay women and men still fight for their right to parent. Same-sex-parent-headed families are often still not considered to be "real" families, and, like adoptive and foster families, often have to deal with stigmas and myths. Although there is great diversity among same-sex parents and their children, they often face homophobia, resulting in isolation, prejudice, discrimination, and invisibility in relation to society as a whole (Mandell & Duffy, 2005; Trawick-Smith, 2010). Homophobia faced by same-sex families is both systemic (i.e., policies discouraging adoption, legal recognition) and individual (i.e., interpersonal interactions) (Brown et al., 2009).

Challenges of Same-Sex Parents

Social support for lesbian and gay parents is slowly increasing. Canada's liberal same-sex legislation may suggest that Canadians are highly supportive of gay and lesbian parenting. However, a recent report highlights that close to 50% of the Canadian population does not believe gays and lesbians are capable of parenting effectively (Vanier Institute of the Family, 2010b). In addition, such institutions as schools and organizations within communities can be discriminatory toward same-sex-headed families (Brown et al., 2009) and many same-sex parents claim to face a general lack of acceptance (Brown et al., 2009).

A common critique that lesbian and gay families face is the perceived problematic nature of raising children without a male or female figure. Notably, this is faced more often by gay men, as many people struggle to accept men's capacity to parent without women (Vanier Institute of the Family, 2010b). Despite this criticism, studies have shown that gay and lesbian parents actively provide role models for their children who are of the opposite sex (Vanier Institute of the Family, 2010b). A well-known Canadian gay rights activist and scholar, Rachel Epstein, highlights the deeply gender-based notion of this critique, a notion that assumes women and men are homogeneous groups simply due to biology, while ignoring the diversity and degree of masculinity and femininity within categories of women and men (Vanier Institute of the Family, 2010b). Epstein argues that instead of worrying about the presence of male or female role models, we should be asking, "What do kids need and how can we best provide these things, regardless of biological sex?" (Vanier Institute of the Family, 2010b).

Lesbian and gay parents who overcome society's barriers tend to be highly motivated and committed parents. In planned lesbian families, children are treasured because the child-bearing is a conscious, and often very challenging, choice that requires considerable effort (Mendez, 2009). Likewise, a recent study shows that, unsurprisingly, gay foster fathers show a strong commitment to parenting, and are reworking the definition of what it means to father, as many gay fathers exhibit maternal properties.

Effects of Same-Sex Parents on Children

There are many myths about same-sex parents. Some include beliefs that children are more likely to turn out gay or lesbian, that children will not have a proper male or female role model (as discussed above), or, shockingly, that gay fathers are more likely to molest their children.

There is also a commonly held view that children of same-sex couples will be teased and ostracized by their peers, and that this will cause distress for the child and interfere with his or her ability to build and maintain friendships. Children may be impacted by the need for secrecy, the fear of exposure, and social isolation. Certainly, some children may experience this, but studies have suggested that no differences in friendships were evident. And while the experience of being teased or ostracized was significant, it may in fact build resilience and strength in children (Ambert, 2005; Mandell & Duffy, 2005).

Most of the common reactions against same-sex parents are continually disputed in research. So far, there is virtually no evidence that suggests parents play any role in children's sexual orientation (Mendez, 2009). Nor are there differences between gay and heterosexual adoptive families, or in children's behaviour (Averett et al., 2009). To date, there is no evidence showing that same-sex parents are less effective parents, that they organize their home and family differently, or that children develop differently (Averett et al., 2009).

There is, however, evidence that children are less confined to traditional notions of "boy" and "girl" roles, that children see women as independent human beings, and that, despite the homophobia experienced in society at large, gay and lesbian parents provide a strong, loyal family unit and an extended support network and community (Mendez, 2009). Gay and lesbian families are less confined to traditional gender norms and often use more innovative approaches to parenting (Dunne, 2001). In addition, there appears to be a more equal division of labour in lesbian and gay families than in heterosexual, two-parent-headed families (Patterson et al., 2004). Because of the lack of norms surrounding gay parenting, gay and lesbian headed families have the opportunity to renegotiate, redefine, and recreate roles and responsibilities (Dunne, 2001).

Scenario

The Risks of Being Open

Verna and Amira together form a gay couple who have lived together with Verna's daughter, Janne, for more than five years. As Janne began to approach her teen years, they were experiencing a fair bit of tension at home. Amira suggested that the three of them see a family counsellor. Verna replied that she was reluctant to do so, since it could be interpreted as an admission of failure. "I always feel as if we're on trial," she said, "and if anything goes wrong I may lose custody of my daughter."

The experience of being a gay father is not without challenges. Epstein and Duggan (2006) interviewed a number of gay men in Toronto and found that they were concerned with the extreme invisibility of gay fathers, especially in terms of programs and services and other formal elements of support. They also found that Canadian society is still largely disapproving of gay fathers, exhibiting negative stereotyping about gay men and parenting, and that homophobia, both systemic and individual, was a major issue gay parents face. Finally, it remains difficult for gay men to acquire children, owing to barriers in legislation and to an ongoing struggle for legitimacy as parents. For gay men to acquire children is often an emotional, time-consuming, and expensive process (Epstein & Duggan, 2006).

Supporting Same-Sex Families

Some theorists critique the uniform identity of gay and lesbian parents, since it discredits the diversity within gay families (Berkowitz, 2009). Instead, it should be recognized that, like heterosexual or one-parent families, there are considerable differences within gay families and no "one-size-fits-all" way to support these families (Berkowitz, 2009). It is important to recognize individual families and their unique needs, while also being aware of the large, systemic challenges facing same-sex families, including struggles with policies and access to system-wide support (Mendez, 2009). It is also important to recognize that same-sex families are likely to run into bias and discrimination, and to make very certain that gay and lesbian families are treated with respect and can participate in the welcoming environment of the child-care centre.

The Ontario Coalition for Better Child Care has published an excellent resource that provides important background information about gay, lesbian, and transgender families (Janmohamed, 2007). The manual provides many ideas for supporting both children and families and for ensuring that the centre is truly welcoming and accepting. Examples include displaying rainbow stickers and triangles to symbolize a welcoming environment; referring to "parents" rather than "mom and dad" in communications from the centre; integrating books with LGBTQ families into the reading corner; and acknowledging Pride Day as you would celebrations of any other minority group. Most important, child-care professionals should continually confirm that there are very many kinds of families, and that good families are based on loving and caring children and adults (Janmohamed, 2007).

Supporting Children of Same-Sex Parents

It is important to treat children of gay parents the same as all children, and to teach children from a very early age that there are many kinds of families. Prevailing myths should be countered with facts, showing that children of gay parents are known to be in warm, loving families (Johnson, 2010). Most children at one time or another are the brunt of negative interactions and teasing, and it is likely that children of gay parents will be no exception. The advice here is the same as for any other kind of negative interactions: We try to teach children to avoid hurtful behaviour, while at the same time reassure them that adults in their life will protect them should there be a need (Johnson, 2010).

Parents may also need reassurance of the commitment to diversity and inclusion at the child-care centre. It may be appropriate to occasionally remind all parents of this commitment, especially if there is a complaint of disrespectful behaviour toward a gay parent from another parent or staff member. It is possible to share your knowledge of research that indicates that children from secure loving families seem to thrive, regardless of the particular structure of the family (Johnson, 2010).

Single Mothers by Choice

A recent social phenomenon is the increase of single women, usually in the 30–45 age range, who plan to have children without a partner (Ambert, 2006). Termed *single mothers by choice,* these women are increasingly having planned births, through a known donor, an anonymous sperm donor, or adoption, and raising the children on their own.

Single mothers by choice are often women who would have wanted a traditional family, but career aspirations or other reasons meant that the traditional family did not happen (Hertz, 2006). Age (and women's "biological clock") is often the biggest factor in choosing single motherhood (Beck, 1986; Hertz, 2006).

This social trend began in the mid-1980s, as reproductive technologies made it possible for women to have children without having sexual intercourse with a male partner. Because this kind of single parenting is a relatively recent phenomenon, there are limited empirical studies describing the effects on children. The studies so far suggest that children raised by "choice" moms are secure and confident (Morrissette, 2008). Original "choice" children are now in their teens and early twenties, so one can assume that in the course of the next few years more formal research will be conducted on "single mothers by choice" families. Similarly, some of the long-term effects and ethical dilemmas around sperm banks—anonymous or non-anonymous sperm donors, international adoption, etc.—will likely begin to surface in the coming years (McDaniel & Tepperman, 2007).

Single mothers by choice often face a degree of criticism or skepticism from family and friends (Shechner et al., 2010). As is the case with "traditional" single parents, single mothers by choice are more likely to be stressed as a result of having fewer resources such as time and less parenting support (McDaniel & Tepperman, 2009; Shechner, 2010). In addition, the experience of becoming a single mother by choice can be emotionally and financially exhausting (McDaniel & Tepperman, 2007). Medically assisted procreation (such as in vitro fertilization) can be an emotional rollercoaster for women, as results are often unpredictable and it can take months or years to become pregnant (McDaniel & Tepperman, 2007). Finally, single mothers by choice can be lumped into the statistics and stereotypes about other single-parent homes that suggest these homes face more barriers and have negative outcomes for children (Morse, 2007). As we learned in Chapter 7, "Single Parents," single mothers often face financial difficulties and poverty, which in turn have negative outcomes for children. However, more of the single mothers by choice are fairly affluent, which may well mitigate some of the risks associated with single parenthood.

Supporting Single Mothers by Choice and Their Children

Today's reality is that nontraditional families continue to outnumber traditional families. Early childhood educators have a responsibility to support children and their families regardless of the circumstances. Supporting nontraditional families means being inclusive and accepting while avoiding negative stereotyping. It means that early childhood educators must forgo their own preconceived notions of what "family" means and whether there is a right or wrong way to parent. Instead, educators need to focus on the best ways to support individual children and their families.

Caregivers may wish to review the website www.singlemothersbychoice.com, which characterizes some aspects of single motherhood. This website is not designed by an advocacy group, but rather as a support site which provides information. The site highlights the fact that single mothers are women who have taken the initiative to become mothers, with all the entailed responsibility of raising a child on their own. Many of these women are well-off and college-educated, and can thus provide for their children without public help. The site offers support for single mothers as well as a peer support group for their children. A further aim of this site is to clarify issues and enhance public understanding for single motherhood by choice.

Effects on Child Development

It is difficult to make any conclusive statements about the developmental outcomes for children of single mothers by choice, as this has not been a widely researched topic. Here is an observation that is quite common: "The kids I have talked to tend to be very secure and confident. As most child experts and teachers will tell you, being able to devote individualized attention to a child has an enormous impact on self-esteem. The downside to that is the relationship between mother and child tends to be intense, making it important to find healthy ways of separating. Boys in particular need outlets with male role models. But in general, Choice Moms are resourceful, independent women who raise children to be the same as children in 'traditional' families" (Morrissette, 2008).

Conclusion

As the landscape of diverse families continues to shift, perhaps the *traditional* versus *nontraditional* terminology will eventually dissipate. The greatest challenge facing adoptive and foster parents, gay and lesbian parents, and single mothers by choice is being accepted by mainstream society—in line with the abundant research showing that such parents are perfectly capable of providing strong, nurturing, consistent care for their children.

As caregivers, it is most important that we suspend our own personal judgments about differing family types and remain committed to inclusiveness and the support of all children, regardless of their family circumstances. An awareness of the various stigmas and particularities of different family structures will makes us better able to provide the care, support, and access to resources that all children and families deserve.

Chapter Summary

- Modern families are very diverse in structure, role delineation, and the degree to which they are accepted by broader society. For some, the act of becoming parents may involve considerable legal and medical procedures, and involvement of social service agencies. These factors are often associated with higher levels of stress.

- There are an estimated 22 000 children in Canada awaiting adoption today, yet waiting lists for domestic adoptions may range from 7 to 12 years. This has led to an increase in international adoption, often from countries suffering from extreme poverty, natural disasters, or both. The psychological needs of these children need to be deeply understood. It is equally important to understand the psychological and social challenges faced by adoptive parents.

- Foster care is a temporary placement for children, although it can sometimes last for years. This is related to some feelings of role ambiguity among foster parents, and to difficulty in claiming a family identity. Foster parents vary in their perception of their role, from feeling like real parents to feeling like temporary caregivers. Many children have suffered trauma and abuse before entering foster care, and require consistent care and stability.

- The last decade has seen a dramatic increase in the number of same-sex families, planned through adoption or artificial insemination. However, gay and lesbian men and women are often still not considered as constituting real families, and may still face stigmatization. There is no evidence to show that children of same-sex couples may be disadvantaged in any way, and in fact some evidence indicates that children in gay households often grow up in a strong and loyal family unit with extended support networks and community.

- There has also been a recent increase in "single mothers by choice"—women who have planned births through a known donor, an anonymous sperm donor, or through adoption. There is little research to date that describes the outcomes for these children.

Recommended Websites

Adoption Canada:
www.adoption.ca

Canadian Foster Family Association:
www.canadianfosterfamilyassociation.ca

Gay Parent Magazine:
www.gayparentmag.com

Father Involvement Research Alliance, Gay/Bi/Queer Fathers:
www.fira.ca/page.php?id=20

Single Mothers by Choice:
www.singlemothersbychoice.com

Choosing Single Motherhood:
www.choosingsinglemotherhood.com

Videos/Films

The Kids Are All Right. 2010. 106 min. Lisa Cholodenko, director. Focus Features.

Exercises

1. Try to imagine how young children may have experienced the 2010 earthquake in Haiti, first losing their family, and then being transported to an eager and loving family in Canada. Try to describe what they may be feeling as they enter a Canadian home. Do you think there may be parts of this experience that could be extremely frightening? What might they be?

2. What are some strategies you could implement in your child-care centre to support these children and their new adoptive parents?

3. You have a new child in your centre who has recently been removed from his biological parent to a foster home. The child is having a difficult time at the centre, and is prone to hitting other children. What are some steps that you can take? What kind of conversation would you have with the foster parent?

4. Write a journal article reflecting on your feelings about some of the nontraditional or modern families described in this chapter. Try to reflect on your own background and socialization to examine what influenced these attitudes, whether positive or negative. Then, think about how your attitudes might affect your interactions with children and parents from such families.

Children with Special Needs

chapter 11

Objectives

- To understand the reactions of parents who discover that their child has special needs.

- To understand how parents' reactions affect their interactions with their child who has special needs.

- To understand how the family system and all its members are affected by the special needs of a family member.

- To understand the role of the early childhood educator in supporting families with a child who has special needs.

A support group for parents whose children had Down syndrome invited an early childhood educator to speak at an information session called "Choosing Quality Child Care." The speaker described all the important components of a high-quality centre. At the end of the session, one parent approached the speaker and remarked angrily, "You didn't even talk about children with Down syndrome." The speaker replied that certainly parents in this group would need to examine the additional aspects of a program related to the special needs of their children, but that it was important to remember that their children, like all children, required a caring and responsive social environment, a developmentally appropriate physical setting, and nutritious meals and snacks. "Sometimes," the speaker added, "we focus exclusively on meeting the 'special needs' and don't pay enough attention to the aspects of a program that are crucial to all the children."

Another parent was listening thoughtfully to the discussion. She commented, "A year ago I would have been just as angry, because I could see only how my child was different from all the other children. I know that Marcy will always have special needs, but I've learned that children with disabilities must be viewed first and foremost as children."

All expectant parents look forward to the birth of a normal and healthy baby. When a child's health or development is impaired, families often enter a period of intense crisis, which is followed by a lengthy and difficult process of adjustment. The scenario above describes two parents who are in different stages in the process of adjusting to the birth of a child with special needs.

The ecological perspective helps us understand how attitudes toward children with disabilities, legislation protecting their rights, and the extent and quality of both formal and informal support networks can either help or hinder the parents' ability to raise a child who has special needs. Early childhood educators can fulfill a vital role in facilitating the family's adjustment to the special needs of their child and can also help enhance the family's ability to provide for the child's optimal development. In order to do that, early childhood educators need to understand the profound effect that the special needs of a child can have on the family. They also need to be sensitive to the initial and ongoing reactions of parents during the process of adjustment, and they should be aware of the challenges faced by all families whose children have special needs.

Defining Special Needs

The term *special needs* is sometimes confusing, because every child has unique and special qualities that are often identified as needs. Some people prefer to use the terms *exceptional children, developmentally delayed, handicapped,* or *atypical.* Professionals debate both the advantages and disadvantages of using any label at all to describe children, as well as the pros and cons of each particular label.

We use the term *children with special needs* in this book for three reasons. First, this is the term most commonly used in the early childhood literature. Second, we know that some children require extra support so that they can develop their abilities to the maximum. The term *special needs* can apply to all children who need extra support, whether or not they are exceptional or have a particular disability. Third, we use the term as a reminder that we always need to consider the child first.

Special needs are usually described in terms of atypical development. For example, cognitive development may be delayed, or accelerated, as with gifted children. The special needs may relate to physical development, with atypical motor development (such as cerebral palsy), or sensory development (such as visual or hearing impairments). The special needs of some children relate to the social-emotional domain, for example, emotional or behavioural problems or disorders such as autism. Some children have special needs in the area of language, resulting in delayed speech or a stutter. Special needs may also be due to chronic conditions, such as epilepsy, diabetes, or severe allergies.

We will consider *special needs* in the broadest sense of the term—that is, as special needs relate to any child who presents specific concerns to his or her parents, and who requires extra support to integrate successfully into educational programs. Often, special needs are diagnosed at birth. Other kinds of special needs are identified only later in the child's development. In most settings, an official diagnosis (usually given by a medical doctor) is required in order to qualify for professional or financial assistance for the child and family.

There are many children, however, who, although not officially labelled as having "special needs," still warrant special consideration. For example, some children are extremely challenging for parents to raise due to a particular combination of temperamental traits. These children have been called many things, ranging from hyperactive children to children with behavioural problems to simply "difficult children."

The notion of the "difficult child" stems from the work of Thomas & Chess (1977), who describe a number of traits or characteristics that people seem to be born with and that remain fairly consistent over time. Examples of such traits are *activity level* (some people seem to need to be in constant motion; others are content to sit still), *adaptability* (some people adjust easily to new situations; others find change difficult), and *regularity* (some people have very regular sleeping and eating patterns, while others seem to thrive on an irregular schedule). For example, a child who is very active, who does not adapt easily to new situations, who does not establish eating and sleeping routines, and who gets fussy when exposed to different textures or sounds may pose difficulties for parents. This is particularly true if the parents' own temperaments differ greatly from their child's (Turecki & Tonner, 1989). Although these children are completely "normal," the fact that parents find them difficult to raise can put them and their families at risk.

Reactions of Parents

Parents' reaction to the news that their child has special needs has been compared to the grief cycle experienced after a death. This can also apply to families where a mental health diagnosis has been made (Kostouros, 2003). Parents struggle to cope with the loss of their "wished for" or normal child or with a symbolic loss—that is, the loss of hope and the perceived loss of potential (Kostouros, 2003).

Early childhood educators who have learned to accept and respect each child's uniqueness sometimes have difficulty understanding the intensity and duration of parents' responses. When educators are sensitive to the possibility that parents may be grieving, they are in a better position to offer support (Gray & Robinson, 2009). Each family's inner and outer resources and coping styles are unique. However, there is some commonality in the way families experience the grief cycle, and understanding this may help in appreciating the parents' point of view and in empathizing with their emotions. Early childhood educators must remember, however, that people do not generally progress through the following stages in this particular order.

Understanding the Grief Cycle

Shock

Often parents are completely unprepared for the birth of a child with special needs. Couples do not usually consider, mention, or discuss the possibility during the pregnancy, and childbirth preparation classes usually avoid the topic as well. When the birth of a child with special needs does occur, almost all parents react with shock (Penzo, 2008). The parents may experience such emotions as numbness (the inability to feel anything at all) and denial (thinking that the doctor cannot be right; there must be a mistake).

Guilt and Shame

Many myths about children and adults with special needs exist in society today. Although these myths have been proven untrue, they continue to influence people's views. For example, a belief stemming from the 1940s was that a child's disability was somehow the parents' fault. In the case of psychological or psychiatric disorders, there has been a tendency among professionals to blame mothers.

Some religions can reinforce parents' guilt or shame by teaching that a disability is a consequence of the "sins of the father." Although it has been demonstrated that these ideas are, for the most part, false, some people still harbour these beliefs. Thus, when parents receive the news of the disabling condition, they must question whether they hold these beliefs and attitudes themselves and learn to deal with their feelings of guilt and shame. The fact that some disabilities are linked to heredity or the parents' state of health at conception and during pregnancy can reinforce the sense of shame and guilt. Most societies expect that parents will love their children. When a child with special needs is born, the parent may experience negative emotions (e.g., rejection) and then experience guilt (Penzo, 2008).

A Period of Intense Emotions

Following the first stage of shock and denial, there is a period of intense emotions, including confusion, depression, loneliness, anxiety, guilt, and anger (Penzo, 2008). These emotions can be very strong and are often directed at a wide range of people (e.g., guilt can be directed at oneself; anger might be directed at the spouse, the doctor, or God). Parents often attempt to bargain with God or the doctor as their way of dealing with or denying the diagnosis.

These intense emotional responses can affect parents' ability to interact with the child. We know, for instance, that parents who are depressed will interact less with their children. In addition, the baby, due to his or her disability, may have a reduced ability to interact or to give parents positive feedback. Initial contact between baby and parents is sometimes limited because the baby is in an incubator, is attached to feeding tubes or other equipment, or simply does not respond well to cuddling. This lack of positive, rewarding interaction could hamper the bonding and attachment process. In addition, if the baby is ill, parents sometimes restrain themselves from becoming attached, fearing that the baby may not live. Given the importance of bonding and attachment to the social development of all children, the effects of these initial reactions can be significant in the long term.

While early childhood educators need to be sensitive to the intensity and potential risks involved in these initial phases of the grieving process, it is just as important to note that most parents do manage to move beyond these stages (usually with a few setbacks) to adjustment and acceptance. However, families may not come to closure after a period of time but, rather, may move back and forth between periods of emotion and adaptation. For example, families often move back to strong emotions as new milestones are missed (e.g., first day of school, graduation).

Adaptation and Reorganization

When the intense feelings begin to subside, the stage of adaptation begins; during this period, the parents usually feel better able to care for the child. This leads to the last stage, reorganization and acceptance (Penzo, 2008; Turnbull & Turnbull, 1990), when the parents reach a positive, long-term acceptance of their child's condition. This stage is marked by the parents' attempts to find suitable services and to organize their lives with their child's disability in mind. Penzo (2008) and Seligman (1991) talk about this stage as one of realistic acceptance in which parents love their children despite their disabilities but would still prefer, if they could choose, that the child not be disabled.

Parents vary in the intensity and duration of their grief as well as the order in which they experience their reactions. The emotions experienced may intensify or change over time. At the beginning, many parents relentlessly seek a cure for their child's problem. When it becomes apparent that there is no such "miracle" solution, parents often try to provide their child with a series of educational opportunities—they will teach this child everything he or she needs to know. When parents stop shopping for a cure or if they begin to think teaching is of little value, they often feel that they've lost control over their child's life—that they're powerless, without a plan. In time, families usually reach a stage where they no longer hope for miracles or can make the problem go away, but feel they can help the child develop to the best of his or her ability.

Factors That Affect the Grief Cycle

The parents' adjustment may depend on a number of factors, such as the presence or absence of support, the reaction from others, the severity of the child's needs, and often, the parents' religious and cultural beliefs.

Breaking the News

Adjustment may depend partly on when and how parents are told of the disability (McWilliam, 2010). The birth of a baby with a disability is often perceived as a "failure" for the parents and for the doctor as well (McWilliam, 2010). There seems to be an unwritten rule that if you do everything the doctor says, all will be well. When this is not the case, the medical profession is often at a loss. Sometimes medical professionals think they're helping by putting the new mother in a room by herself so that she can have extended visiting hours and time alone to deal with the situation. From the parents' point of view, though, this can lead to feelings of suspicion and isolation (Beattie, 2009).

Scenario

Ignored at the Hospital

A mother was in a private room with her newborn baby, who had been diagnosed as having Down syndrome. Due to concerns for their health, the mother and child stayed in hospital for four days. The mother reported that she was left pretty much to herself. She would wander the hallways and go in and out of the nursery, where she frequently heard nurses exclaim, "What a cute baby. Isn't he adorable?" She realized that no one had commented on her own baby until she was leaving, when the receptionist took notice and told her how sweet her new baby was. This lack of interaction with medical professionals was so noticeable that it had a significant effect on this new mother.

As the preceding scenario makes clear, the attitudes of the doctors, nurses, and other professionals involved can provide the parents with hope, or they can be subtly discouraging.

Sensitive professionals can assess a parent's need for support and information, and although they can't (and shouldn't try to) diminish the parents' sorrow, they can facilitate the adjustment process.

Delayed Diagnosis

Children may be diagnosed with difficulties immediately after birth or a traumatic event (e.g., head injury), or the diagnosis may be delayed (Gallo et al., 2010). When the diagnosis is not immediate, the parent is usually the first to notice that something is wrong with the baby's development. Anxiety often increases as parents read more books about development; as they attempt to compare their child with others of the same age; and as they discuss development with their family doctor. When this continues for a lengthy period of time, parents often report a feeling of relief upon hearing the diagnosis (Gallo et al., 2010). They feel that their concerns have finally been heard and their suspicions confirmed. This sense of relief is usually short-lived, though, as the parents adjust to the reality of the situation and as the quest for more information and services begins in earnest.

Religious and Cultural Beliefs

Earlier we suggested that some religious beliefs can reinforce a sense of guilt or blame. However, many parents have attested to the critical role their religious beliefs have played in helping them accept their child. The following scenario is an example of how one parent's religious beliefs helped her adjust to the birth of a child with special needs.

Scenario

Religious Beliefs as a Factor in Acceptance

Ann was raised as a Christian and was devoted to her religion. Her third son was born with severe developmental delays and major health problems. He was in intensive care for three months before he was physically well enough to go home. Ann seemed to deal with her son's condition extremely well. She did not appear shocked, did not deny the condition, exhibit anger, or blame others or herself. When questioned by the early intervention worker, Ann explained that in her religion, a handicapped child was considered a gift. She believed that God had chosen her and her husband as special parents because he felt that they were able to cope with the child. Her beliefs helped her and her family make the transition directly to acceptance.

Ongoing Adjustment Throughout the Life Cycle

As discussed earlier, the grief cycle may repeat itself at different developmental or family life-cycle stages. Although parents may have apparently adjusted to their newborn child's special needs diagnosis, they may re-experience strong feelings of grief or crisis at transition times. This may occur, for example, when the child reaches the age to begin school (Baxter & Read, 1999), or when other children become more independent and attend functions outside the home during their early school years. These transitions in development or family life cycles may either produce a mild reminder of their child's needs or launch the parents back into the emotional ups and downs of the grief cycle as they learn to cope with the difficulties and realities that each new stage will bring.

As the child grows older, the family once more realizes what a serious, long-term commitment they've made to daily care; they may have to renew their awareness of what social resources are available and the best ways to advocate for their child. Parents may be at a stage in their own lives when their friends are beginning to experience the freedom that comes with having older children; although the child with special needs may be the same age, he or she may not be able to get around without supervision or help. Again, the parents are likely to feel tied down and somehow restricted by their child's needs. Throughout the life cycle, parents are reminded of their child's disability, of their long-term commitment, and of the lack of support (e.g., respite care or babysitting) available to families with children like theirs.

The Impact on the Family System

As we have seen, parents of young children with special needs are confronted with many stresses and strains at a time that is likely to be emotional for everyone involved. The birth of a child with special needs can change families dramatically. Stresses, both long and short term, can affect the entire family, in what has been referred to as the ripple effect (Turecki & Tonner, 1989) or the domino effect. We must be aware that families who have a child with special needs are likely to deal with more stress than most families on an ongoing basis (Berns, 2010; McDaniel & Tepperman, 2007). Consequently, these families are likely to be at greater risk for marital difficulties, and the mothers are more likely to be subject to depression (McWilliam, 2010). There is a disproportionately high number of children with special needs living with neglect and emotional, verbal, and physical abuse, and with a greater sense of disruption in family life (McWilliam, 2010). Stress is also related to the severity of disability and whether the responsibility (or blame) is placed on a particular family member (McGuire et al., 2010). Parenting children with disabilities is more complex and can often cause increased levels of stress in parents, which may cause difficulties in all interactions within the family (Berns, 2010; McDaniel & Tepperman, 2007).

However, while recognizing these stressors, new research on families with children suggests that the experience of parenting a child with special needs isn't "as bad" as traditional disability research suggests (McDaniel & Tepperman, 2007). In the long term, the family has a generally positive experience, and successful coping with the disability is usually the case (Van Riper, 2007). Not surprisingly, this is affected by the type and amount of available support (Van Riper, 2007).

Let us now examine how the different subsystems in a family might be affected by the presence of a child with special needs or behavioural challenges.

The Parental Subsystem

We have described the intense emotional responses that parents of children with special needs experience and how the bonding and attachment process may be affected. In North American culture, where mothers still carry the major responsibility for raising children, they are also most often blamed when things go wrong. When a child throws a tantrum at the supermarket checkout counter, most people still think, "Why can't that mother control her child in public?" Many mothers believe that they should be able to raise and parent their children, and that they should love and like their children. And so when children exhibit difficult behaviour, the mother is left questioning her abilities, her intentions, and her effectiveness. It is not uncommon for mothers to feel such emotions as guilt, isolation, depression, embarrassment, or denial. A mother may overprotect her child or become over-involved as a means of ensuring that the child is successful.

Mothers often have difficulty interacting with the child consistently and effectively because they do not understand the child's behaviour and may inappropriately ascribe motives to it (e.g., "He's doing that to bug me; my child hates me") (McGuire et al., 2010).

Scenario

Misinterpreting Behaviour

At a preschool picnic, Monica was trying to get her $2\frac{1}{2}$-year-old son ready to leave. She had given several warnings that they were getting ready to go. When she finally called him to leave, he screamed and ran off in the other direction. She waited for several minutes, then called again. He looked at her and followed a group of children in the other direction. She called again and he screamed back "No!" The mother tried twice more before the caregiver approached. "See," she said, "he hates me."

Such failure to understand a child's behaviour may result in ineffective or inconsistent discipline. One day the mother may be restrictive; the next day she may be too tired to argue, and so will allow the child to run freely. She may then attempt to regain control by using harsher discipline techniques, which can make the behaviour worse. Punishment often seems to be immediately effective, which reinforces the parent's decision to use it; however, punishment is effective in the short term only because the child has not learned a better way to behave. This vicious cycle of control and behaviour leads to a lowering of self-esteem for both the child and the mother. Breaking out of this cycle can be a difficult process (McGuire et al., 2010).

In traditional families, the father may either present the solution for breaking out of the leniency/punishment cycle or contribute to its continuation. Dad may arrive home at the end of the day to provide Mom with a welcome respite and help re-establish her authority, or he may not understand why the child acts the way he or she does or why the mother reacts the way she does. His questioning of her actions may be interpreted as criticism or as a lack of confidence in her parenting techniques.

The father may be put unwillingly into the role of the disciplinarian or left out of the parenting process altogether because he does not agree with the mother. Researchers have noted that fathers of children with special needs are often estranged from the parent–child relationship (McDaniel & Tepperman, 2007). The mother may sense this lack of support or feel jealous because the father has a conflict-free relationship with the child. He, on the other hand, may feel that he's not permitted to be part of the parenting routine and may spend more time away from home to avoid further conflicts.

Although we have been speaking of the traditional family, we can see the same effects in all families. Two working parents, a single parent, or a noncustodial parent will experience this additional stress within their family unit as well. These parents may also find themselves without any supports to provide them with a much-needed respite or to restore balance within the household.

The Marital Subsystem

The stresses involved in raising a child with special needs can put a great deal of strain on the marriage. The husband may feel left out of the relationship with the child, and he may even feel left out of the marital relationship as well, since the mother may be too exhausted for intimacy with him. She may direct some of her intense and negative feelings—anger, anxiety, or resentment—toward her husband. The husband often responds by pulling away and decreasing his involvement in child care, which intensifies the mother's frustration and leads to an even wider rift between the parents. If the rift grows wide enough, it may lead to a breakdown of the marriage. However, while divorce continues to be disproportionately high in families with a child who has special needs, this is not always the case. In fact, some families report feelings of renewed closeness after the birth of a child with special needs (McGuire et al., 2010).

The Sibling Subsystem

Siblings may also be affected by the child with special needs (Kilmer et al., 2008). An example of the variation in effects on siblings can be seen in the work of Wolf et al. (1998). These researchers found that siblings of children with pervasive development disorders often feel that they are favoured by their parents over their special needs siblings, while siblings of children with Down syndrome may feel that their special needs sibling is preferred. One or both parents may have less time for their other children and may place higher expectations on them. These expectations may be in the form of day-to-day responsibilities or in expectations that they will achieve goals that their sibling with special needs is not able to attain. Siblings may find it difficult to talk about the situation or even to gain clarification about the disability (Berns, 2004; Kilmer et al., 2008). Later in life, siblings report either that the experience was positive and that it made them more accepting, tolerant, and understanding or that they experience feelings such as shame, guilt, resentment, and jealousy (Berns, 2010; Kilmer et al., 2008). This difference in feelings can be attributed to several factors, including attitudes of the parents, supports available to all family members, religion, culture, family cohesiveness, and severity of the disability.

Scenario

Doing Chores

Two students in a disability studies class were comparing their siblings, both of whom had special needs. Nina explained that her severely mentally challenged sister was always treated as a member of the family. She had her own chores to do, which were well within her capabilities—she set and cleared the table, and she loaded and unloaded the dishwasher daily. Even though she had special needs, there were expectations for her, just as for anyone else in the family. June responded that her asthmatic brother was treated very differently. Since no one was sure when he would have an attack, he was never expected to help out around the house, and his sisters did all his chores for him. Their mom woke him, prepared his meals, and protected him from the other children. As June and Nina talked, their lasting impressions of how their siblings affected them and their families became very clear. While Nina was quite accepting of her sister, June was resentful of her brother's needs and of the effect they had on her.

Siblings may also be affected by the presence of the child who is difficult to manage or who requires a lot of parental time and attention. Either or both parents may thus have less time to spend with the siblings, who may come to resent the difficult child, resulting in jealousy or competition. Siblings could decide that the only way to get attention is to be perfect or to get into trouble as well. These reactions can, of course, lead to further difficulties within the family.

Examples like these illustrate the domino or ripple effect, whereby one source of stress ends up affecting the entire family. The child with special needs presents a situation that entails different tasks, responsibilities, and emotions for each family member. The emotions felt by the primary caregiver in learning to cope may affect the interactions with the child with special needs, with the spouse, and eventually with other children in the family. Sometimes the ripple effects are even felt beyond the nuclear family, reaching the extended family and friendship networks as well (Turecki & Tonner, 1989). Again, however, despite the greater degree of stress associated with parenting an exceptional child, recent research suggests that many parents today show resilience in adjusting to the presence of a child with special needs in their family (Gerstein, 2009).

Challenges for Families Who Have a Child with Special Needs

In addition to coping with their own grief and with the stressors within the family unit, families who have a child with special needs often encounter difficulties in their interactions with "the outside world." These difficulties usually relate to common prejudices in our society about people with special needs. Sometimes parents are faced with negative and insensitive beliefs about people who have disabilities.

Scenario

Ignorant Remarks

The parents of Donny, a 5-year-old boy with severe mental and physical challenges, worked closely with the child-care staff in an attempt to get Donny ready for school. Since he was noticeably cross-eyed, staff recommended that the parents have his eyes examined. Donny's parents made an appointment but returned from it absolutely devastated. The optometrist had matter-of-factly declared that since correcting Donny's eyes would make no difference to "his condition," why would they want to spend the money?

Incidents such as these reflect a fairly widespread attitude, one that parents of children with special needs come up against all too often. In some cases, the negative attitudes may be less blatant, but parents still find themselves interacting with people who have very unclear expectations about the potential of children with disabilities.

These negative attitudes are usually based on ignorance, and the ignorance is usually a result of the fact that many people have limited interactions with those who have special needs. Therefore, they don't know what to expect or what potential a particular child may have in the future.

Scenario

Lack of Information Among Doctors

A young mother had just given birth, in a hospital, to a baby with Down syndrome. First the obstetrician came to deliver the news. This visit was followed by one from the family doctor and a pediatrician, who both described the child as someone who would grow physically to a normal size but would always have the mind of a 2-year-old.

Although this scenario occurred 20 years ago, it is not atypical of statements made today. In fact, researchers have noted that parents continue to express dissatisfaction with how medical staff communicate with them (Carbone et al., 2010). The kind of conversation illustrated above could be extremely frightening for parents who have had little contact with people who have special needs. Furthermore, it is often very difficult to ascertain at an early stage what the full potential of any child will be. Although professionals should not be unrealistically optimistic, nor should they err on the side of pessimism.

Interaction with Professionals

One of the most stressful factors reported by parents of children with special needs is the necessity for increased interaction with professionals (McWilliam, 2010). Parents who have had little contact with professionals may suddenly be required to deal with doctors, nurses, dietitians, physiotherapists, speech therapists, psychologists, and social workers. What makes these interactions so difficult is that the parent usually has a strong emotional reaction, while the professional normally does not.

Many parents interacting with medical professionals have reported that they feel a loss of control over their child's life and treatment (McWilliam, 2010) and that they feel disempowered by their constant struggle. This was even more common in the past, when families were made completely dependent on professionals (Gallagher, 1993). Parents may attempt to challenge a professional's authority, but this is a difficult task indeed. Parents and professionals, especially medical professionals, often operate at different status levels, which in itself commonly makes interaction and communication difficult. Parents may not understand the terminology or jargon or may receive conflicting messages from different professionals. And since each professional typically focuses primarily on a particular aspect of the child's development (e.g., the physiotherapist is concerned with physical abilities, the speech therapist with speech development), the "whole child" may sometimes be forgotten. Consequently, parents may be required to learn a new set of skills so that they can better obtain information and act as advocates on behalf of their child.

Scenario

Conflicting Advice from Professionals

Jan was the mother of Kaitlin, a 2-year-old girl with cerebral palsy who attended a hospital-based early intervention program. The program included a speech therapist, a physiotherapist, and a social worker, all of whom provided Jan with guidance and direction. The physiotherapist explained the absolute necessity of changing Kaitlin's position regularly and completing daily range-of-motion exercises. The speech therapist explained that Kaitlin was at the developmental stage when hearing speech and having many opportunities to communicate with her mother would be crucial to her development of language skills. The social worker closed by explaining that it was important for Jan to plan time off from her caretaking duties, and that she shouldn't become over-involved in Kaitlin's care. Needless to say, Jan felt a little confused by the end of the session.

This sort of confusion can be further complicated by the rapid turnover of professionals that sometimes occurs. One social worker may be replaced by another as the child grows older, or other professionals may be transferred or promoted. Each new professional represents another challenge for the parents and the child, and these continual changes can be extremely stressful.

Interaction with professionals often involves interaction with social agencies that provide specific care and assistance to children with special needs. Unlike systems for normally developing children (e.g., playschool or the public school system), a range of services are available for exceptional children, each with its own criteria for admittance and subsequent service. These criteria may be based on age, developmental level, severity of the disability, type of disability, proof of disability, and income. If parents wish to gain access to these services, they must acquaint themselves with what is available and with each service's particular set of rules. Whenever parents request something a little different for their child, such as inclusion in the neighbourhood school, their communication and advocacy skills are truly tested.

Traditionally, professionals and services have tried to deal with each and every concern or problem, but this approach has proven to be stressful for both the child and the family. Professionals need to recognize this fact and try to provide support based on the needs and desires of each individual family. Professionals should also try to remember that families with children who have special needs also have many other interests and concerns. For this reason, it is important to treat the family as a unit rather than singling out or focusing exclusively on the child with special needs (McWilliam, 2010).

Perspectives

Jody is now a single parent of two boys—12-year-old Ryan and 13-year-old Xenon. She works as a full-time college instructor.

Jody and her former husband, John, adopted Xenon who, at 3 weeks old, had major heart surgery to correct a congenital heart defect. At that time the doctor told them that children with this condition may develop on "both sides of normal," but that Xenon's progress was excellent thus far. In addition to the surgery, he was on Phenobarb for a period of time to control seizures, and had serious respiratory problems, with the possibility of cystic fibrosis. The list of medical conditions seemed to go on forever: auditory discrimination problems, memory problems, visual motor problems, mild myopia, poor tooth enamel, bowel and bladder problems, and asthma. If you were to meet Xenon, you would think he looks just like everyone else, but when all these "little" problems are added together, he has definite special needs. The frustrating part is that each problem is treated by a different doctor, specialist, or teacher, who doesn't know or think about the other problems. So one medication will treat one set of symptoms but cause an unpleasant interaction with another medication or affect Xenon's behaviour in some way that causes difficulties at school or in learning.

"As a parent, I always feel that I walk a fine line in what to tell to whom. On the one hand, I don't want Xenon singled out as the child with special needs, but I also don't want him to be labelled as lazy or having a bad attitude because people don't understand that, given his medical problems, his performance can't always be optimal.

"Xenon always has been, and still is, in a regular school with supports. So far, the schools and teachers have been great in meeting his particular needs, but sometimes they don't realize the impact that some of their statements, although likely quite innocent, have on Xenon or me. For example, one teacher explained to me that completing a certain assignment should be easy because 'even Xenon can do it.' I think I know what she meant, but Xenon was devastated by her comments and so was I, knowing how hard he tries to get things done. On one occasion, when Xenon was left behind on a class outing due to health concerns, he thought he wasn't allowed to go because he'd been bad. It took a lot of convincing by me and the teacher to reassure him that this wasn't true.

"Maybe my experiences have made me a little oversensitive, or maybe, because I know Xenon—a kind, gentle, caring, whole person—I'm a little more sensitive about what people say. Anyway, I hope that all the professionals and specialists who come into contact with Xenon see him for the person he is, not today's problem or symptom."

Unrealistic Expectations Placed on Parents

In the past two decades, professionals have made great strides in the treatment and education of children with special needs. They have learned through research and practice that therapy initiated in the early years is most effective in treating the disability as well as in preventing secondary problems that may result from the disability.

In addition, a number of earlier research studies led to the belief that the parent should be the child's primary teacher, and this became the cornerstone in many early intervention programs (Katz, 1980). Many intervention models were developed in which the professional would "teach" the parents to carry out a wide range of exercises and individualized programs with their child. Sometimes this put tremendous strain on families. Parents were instructed to teach their child at every possible moment, to have a wide assortment of professionals into their homes, and to always have the best interest of the child in mind. With such expectations placed on parents, some began to wonder when they would be able to relax and "just be a parent." When would they have time to cuddle and spoil their baby rather than always being the teacher and therapist? These expectations put additional pressures on the families of children with special needs. On top of all the other emotional stresses, the expectation that parents be available for constant teaching may have placed excessive demands on them.

In the past 30 years, however, things have changed, and now a more inclusive model, in which communities, educators, and families work together to support special-needs children, is largely the norm (Bruder, 2010).

Work and Parenting Children with Special Needs

Many parents face challenges trying to maintain employment and family responsibilities. When the family includes a child with special needs, there may be additional challenges in terms of extra expenses, changes in employment income, and stresses due to inadequate child care and supports in the community and workplace (Bruder, 2010).

In one report (Hope Irwin & Lero, 2004), researchers found that a significant number of parents were unemployed, underemployed, or worked fewer hours to meet the demands of their child with special needs. Typically, mothers' employment was affected. Unsurprisingly, these families felt that they experienced economic strains (e.g., extra expenses and loss of income in addition to increased stress). As well, 88% of parents said they felt tired and over-loaded, and 90% said they were stressed about balancing work and family obligations. A major cause of stress was the lack of access to appropriate, affordable, licensed child care along with workplace and social supports.

Supporting Families with a Special-Needs or Difficult Child

The presence of a supportive family will undoubtedly be a major influence in the life of the child with special needs. The child may require additional support from his or her family in daily routines and in developing new abilities. In addition, the child with special needs may be ridiculed and teased by other children in school and on the playground. A strong family unit provides the child with a solid foundation to face present and future challenges.

By attempting to understand and empathize with what families may be experiencing and feeling, early childhood educators may be better able to provide these families with assistance. The educators' role may be twofold. The first role lies in helping the family recognize that the child may have special needs. Through their studies of child development and their experience with groups of children in the early years, educators are often in a position to recognize a developmental or behavioural problem (McWilliam, 2010). In fact, early childhood educators who have basic developmental knowledge are often the first to notice delays or differences in development. But although this early identification is important, it can put educators in a precarious situation with parents, and so it may be helpful to have professionals (e.g., speech therapists, occupational therapists) who can support them in this. The second role is to offer support to the family members as they come to cope with this reality in their lives. Early childhood educators can help such families in their continual struggle to maximize opportunities for their special-needs children.

Changing times have altered the role of early childhood educators who work with parents of special-needs children. Professionals generally believed for many years that problems could be eliminated by direct and early intervention with the child (Gallagher, 1993). Thus, they thought that working with the child in a certain program would be sufficient to deal with that child's special needs. More recently it has become evident that families need to be considered as a unit, and that early childhood educators may play a valuable role in facilitating families' strength and in developing their support networks (Bruder, 2010; McWilliam, 2010). Family-focused programs serve to ensure that the child with the disability is not seen in isolation but as part of the family, and thus help to strengthen the entire family (Bruder, 2010). When early childhood educators are sensitive to a family's particular needs and provide appropriate support, the family develops a sense of control and empowerment over its world (Bruder, 2010).

Examine Your Attitudes

Negative attitudes—fear, prejudice, dislike—often influence people's reactions to the parents and siblings of children with special needs. After you ask yourself each of the following questions, consider it again for a person with one of the following challenges: cognitive, physical, visual, hearing, and mental health.

- Do you think people with special needs can't learn, or do they learn in different ways and at different rates than other people?
- Do you believe that people with special needs contribute to society, or are they unproductive members who sap medical and financial resources while contributing nothing themselves?
- Should people with special needs be educated together in special classrooms, or is it better to "mainstream" them?
- Is it true that parents are always directly responsible for their children's behaviour? Is bad behaviour the result of parents' failure to discipline their children?
- Have you found that parents of special-needs children are reluctant to work with professionals? If so, have you discovered a reason for this reluctance?
- Would you work with a staff person who had special needs in your child-care centre? Would you expect as much from him or her as from the other staff members?

Identifying Special Needs

When the early childhood educator suspects that a particular child may have special needs, the most difficult task will be in sharing this information with the parents (McWilliam, 2010). Many staff members feel anxious about facing parents in this situation.

Early childhood educators may first want to collect and document examples rather than making their suspicions known to parents with little supporting information. Discussing observations clearly and honestly, face to face, is often a better approach than discussing them over the telephone or using jargon that parents may not understand (McWilliam, 2010). Talking to parents can often be easier when information is shared; therefore, early childhood educators should be prepared to share ideas and resources. For instance, they can help parents decide what the next step will be, or they can provide a list of potential services to consider. Bearing in mind the stages of shock, denial, and intense feelings discussed earlier in the chapter, early childhood educators should also expect the parents to react intensely, sometimes with anger and vociferous denials, and be prepared to deal with such emotions (McWilliam, 2010).

FAS/FAE

Fetal Alcohol Syndrome (FAS) and Fetal Alcohol Effects (FAE) are two terms that are becoming more commonly known and better understood. Children with FAS and FAE have been variously labelled as having behaviour problems, emotional problems, learning disabilities, or attention deficit disorder. However, there is a constellation of difficulties associated with FAS and, to a lesser degree, FAE. These include developmental delays along with emotional and behavioural concerns, such as difficulty attending to tasks, difficulty in peer interactions, difficulty following directions, and difficulty following rules and routines. Children with FAS typically have particular facial features, which become more discernible with age, along with particular growth patterns.

Children with FAS and FAE can present challenges in the playroom, and so they require extra personnel and resources to help meet their special needs.

Often, families with children who have FAS also present particular challenges. Owing to the nature of the syndrome, it may be difficult for parents to come to terms with having a child with FAS; they may be unwilling to discuss concerns or deal with problems. Moreover, many children with FAS live in adoptive and foster care settings, which may itself present challenges to the child and family. Parents may experience negative emotions in dealing with the realization that this foster or adoptive child has lifelong difficulties. Other parents, however, are prepared to deal with the situation and readily work with early childhood educators to locate and access the appropriate resources.

Early childhood educators need to understand the difficulties associated with FAS or FAE along with the particular family dynamics that may result. FAS has become a focal area of study in many provinces and states; therefore, much more information on the syndrome and strategies for caring for children are becoming available to parents and early childhood educators alike. Educators may wish to search out potential information sources to ensure they're able to meet the challenges that children with FAS and their families may present in group care settings.

Providing Ongoing Support

Once the diagnosis has been made and the reality of the special needs or behavioural concern is evident, parents may require support on an ongoing basis. Early childhood educators may assist parents in many ways. First, they can share information regularly. This means not just describing what the child is doing, but also asking parents to share their own information, since they play an important role in creating a positive learning environment (Crowther, 2006). Parents know the child from a different perspective, one that early childhood educators rarely get to see. Make sure that, along with the not-so-pleasant details, parents hear positive things about their child. In the busy activity of the day, it is easy to overlook the positive aspects of the child's development and remember only the difficulties presented. Parents need to hear about both, and if they are having difficulty coping, it may be beneficial for them to hear more positive than negative statements.

Interpreting Information

The early childhood educator may also play a role in helping parents interpret information. For instance, parents may be unable to ask the specialist or therapist for an explanation of terms because these professionals are too busy or because the parents feel awkward admitting that they don't understand the terminology. In this case, providing information in understandable terms and in relation to this particular child may be of real benefit to the family. And even if the caregiver is unable to interpret the information, he or she can still play a valuable role in helping parents obtain information that's more readily understood (e.g., by giving them reading material or the number of another professional to call). This may be the first step in helping the family to build a support network.

Scenario

Difficult Terminology

Tony's mother was invited to a case conference with the speech therapist, physiotherapist, grade 1 teacher, and psychologist. She asked if Tony's caregiver from the child-care centre would come along because she felt intimidated by all these people. The conference began with each professional providing the most recent assessment results. The speech therapist talked about Tony's "inability to form fricatives and his lack of occlusion." The physiotherapist described his "poor motor control in the prone and supine position and total lack of balance and coordination." At this point, the mother left the room in tears. When the caregiver found her in the bathroom, she said she understood two things very clearly. First, her son wasn't capable of doing anything. Second, she was too stupid to understand what it was exactly that he couldn't do.

Caregivers may support the family by providing or interpreting information whenever possible. They may also escort the parents to meetings and help them listen and ask appropriate questions. Or, they may simply listen to the parents and act as a sounding board as they determine their course of action. When early childhood educators establish a good working relationship with parents, the particular course of action can be worked out together.

Sharing Coping Strategies

Early childhood educators can also play a role in making parents aware of ways to deal with difficult behaviour. Role-modelling effective strategies may be beneficial to parents. For example, the early childhood educator may help by intervening in and breaking the cycle of negative reactions with a temperamentally difficult child simply by giving the child time to settle down when the child and parent are embroiled in a conflict. Educators need to be cautious when they report their own "successes" with the child, since the parent may interpret this to mean that he or she is a failure in parenting. In addition, early childhood educators can suggest "computer-mediated support groups" as a way to share coping strategies (Bragadottir, 2008). There are numerous support groups and other resources on the Internet for parents, other family members, and early childhood educators, some of which are listed in the Recommended Websites at the end of this chapter.

Scenario

Establishing New Routines

A caregiver observed that when Shane arrived in the morning, his mother was usually in a rush. She would carry him in and help him remove his jacket, and then he would cry and cling. She would react with harsh words, and he would cling more. Whenever the early childhood educator attempted to intervene, both the mother and Shane would get upset. Finally, the educator realized that she needed to intercept the situation before it occurred. So the next morning she arranged with the other staff in the playroom that she would wait for Shane at the door. The moment Shane and his mother walked in, she greeted the two by saying, "Good morning! I know your mommy is in a hurry. I'll take you from here, so let's give her a big hug and kiss goodbye and say, 'Have a good day at work, Mom!'" There were hugs, kisses, and a cheery good-bye. The next day, the same procedure was repeated. By the third day, a new morning routine was in place.

Sharing Information

Scenario

Benefits of a Nonjudgmental Attitude

Ann, a 33-year-old mother of two boys, had returned to college to earn her diploma in early childhood education. In a class on working with families, the topic of temperamentally difficult children was being discussed. She remained quiet throughout the class, and when it was over, she approached the instructor to thank her. Ann's eldest son had many difficult traits, and this was the first time someone had ever said that his problems weren't her fault. She told the instructor that although not everyone openly accused her of being at the root of her son's behavioural problems, she could tell what people were think-ing by the way they said things or the advice they gave her.

Sharing information about the problems typical of children who are difficult or have special needs may be the first step in helping families cope. Often, it is not necessary for the child's behaviour to change; rather, everyone involved learns to deal with the behaviour. For example, if the child does not cope well when tired, every effort can be made to begin bedtime routines long before tiredness sets in. The child who does not adapt well to new settings may require more time and patience on the part of the parent and caregiver and will also appreciate warn-ings that activities are about to change. Changes in the parents' reactions may thus serve as a catalyst for the child's behaviour to improve.

Respecting the Family's Needs

Early childhood educators must remember that each family they deal with has a life extending beyond the child with special needs or difficult behaviour.

So much of the family's time and effort will be expended in caring for the child that other needs and perspectives may be neglected. Educators can easily fall into this trap themselves by urging parents to try a new idea or carry out a program at home.

If early childhood educators consider the entire family unit, they may be able to support the family in such a way as to benefit them as a whole. For example, providing information about accessible activities in the community may give the whole family the chance to do some-thing together. This may also help each family member feel as if they are part of a "normal" family and give them a chance to relax and enjoy recreational activities together.

Providing Emotional Support

Early childhood educators may also play a role in providing families with emotional support. Families will experience many different emotions and cope in many different ways. The educator may be able to provide different perspectives, approaches, or resources for families to consider. Sometimes parents simply need to have their feelings validated or be given permission to feel angry or disappointed. Providing emotional support requires understanding that each family will respond to circumstances in a unique way and will have different strengths and different needs.

Helping Families Access Resources

Parents of children who are difficult or who have special needs often benefit from support groups that consist of parents in similar circumstances (McGuire et al., 2010). Educators can play a fundamental role by offering leadership, support, and practical assistance. In this way, parents can share their fears and experiences and offer each other support and encouragement. They may need reassurance about parenting decisions they make or require specialized information and advocacy skills. These specialized needs can often be met effectively by other parents of children with special needs (McGuire et al., 2010).

Scenario

The Usefulness of Support Groups

A mother with a successful professional career had adopted two young children. The older child was 2 when the second baby arrived. It soon became apparent that the second child had severe special needs. The mother experienced a range of emotions, but felt that, since she was highly trained and skilled, she should be able to cope. When the child was 2, the child-care staff told the mother about a meeting whose topic of discussion was diet and nutrition for preschool children. Understanding her reluctance to seek support, the staff didn't emphasize that the presentation was for parents of children with special needs, nor did they coerce her into attending. The mother decided to go because her daughter experienced extreme feeding difficulties. After the meeting, she met other parents who had children with similar disabilities. They shared hopes, disappointments, and practical ideas. This was the first time this mother had been involved with other parents in similar situations, and she found it to be truly beneficial.

However, support groups may not be a good alternative for all parents. For example, a mother with a severely mentally and physically disabled baby was encouraged to join a local Moms and Tots program that met one morning a week. When she decided to attend, she was depressed to see how advanced the other babies were. The experience had been so depressing, she said, that she never returned and would never join another parent group. Parents are probably the best judges of how appropriate a support group may be for them. Early childhood educators can provide parents with information about support groups, and then leave the decision about whether to participate up to them.

Providing Advocacy and Education

The ecological approach reminds us that, for a child with special needs to develop optimally, factors beyond the child and the immediate family must be considered. These factors include attitudes in our society toward people with special needs, legislation that protects the rights of people with special needs, and the kinds of support services available to children and families. Research demonstrates that early childhood educators are critical in providing inclusive learning opportunities that promote development (Crowther, 2006).

Early childhood educators may find it necessary to teach others about children with special needs. This can happen in a number of ways. It may involve demonstrating to other children how to interact or play with the child who has special needs, and more broadly, establishing norms of acceptance and equity for all children within early childhood programs. Early childhood educators may also play a role in helping parents become effective advocates, or they may engage in direct advocacy themselves, which could include writing letters to the press or to politicians, making presentations, and providing information. Self-help groups should not be taken over by professionals. Instead, early childhood educators can assist by providing leadership and supporting autonomy. Educators need to consider how to empower parents, what supports may be useful, and how parents can help themselves and each other. Through advocacy and education, early childhood educators can contribute to the well-being of children with special needs by promoting their acceptance and inclusion in all aspects of society.

Conclusion

Early childhood educators need to be aware that although parents may be suffering their own type of grief even many years after the diagnosis, most parents' love for and commitment to their children help them overcome many obstacles. Extra understanding and appreciation of their struggles is always warranted.

Although the strategies for working with parents discussed in the final portion of this book will be just as relevant for these families, early childhood educators may have to search for resources, services, and information suitable to a particular child's and family's needs. It is important to remember that the child with special needs or behavioural concerns is part of a family and to consider and support that family whenever possible.

Chapter Summary

- Working with families that have a child who is difficult to raise, has a particular disability, or has chronic health problems will pose particular challenges for early childhood educators.
- Parents may experience a range of emotions when a child with special needs is born. Professionals need to understand their reactions and support families.
- All family members may be affected in some way. When early childhood educators use interaction and helping strategies, they need to take all family members into consideration.

Recommended Websites

Centre of Excellence for Children & Adolescents with Special Needs:
http://childrenandadolescents.lakeheadu.ca/the-centre-of-excellence-for-children-and-adolescents-with-special-needs

Centre of Knowledge on Healthy Child Development:
www.knowledge.offordcentre.com

SpeciaLink—The National Centre for Child Care Inclusion:
www.specialinkcanada.org

Supporting Children with Special Needs: Checklist for Early Childhood Educators:
www.naeyc.org/files/yc/file/200903/BTJWatson.pdf

Videos/Films

The Black Balloon. 2008. 97 min. The Australian Film Commission.

Exercises

1. Review the following case study, and discuss how you would present your information and concerns to the parent involved. Role-play this situation with a partner who can respond as a parent might. Have one person observe the role-playing to provide feedback about your role.

   Case Study

   Rhanda came to your centre at the age of 3 months. She was a very easygoing child who demanded little attention. As she grew older, she was quite content amusing herself with toys and activity centres and with watching the other children play. You noticed that she was usually the last child in the playgroup to achieve milestones, such as rolling over or sitting up, but she still did progress. Over time, more things became noticeable. At 16 months, she was just beginning to walk, relying far more on crawling. She seemed to be quieter and not playing with sounds and words as much as she used to. Sometimes, it seemed as if she didn't hear people calling her or was oblivious to noises in the room.

2. Check your community centres and local government offices to determine what types of resources exist for children with special needs and their families. Determine whether these resources are run by parents or by professionals (since parents may want a parent support group rather than adding more professionals to their list). Check to make sure that all the resources can provide support to children with special needs (e.g., a local Big Brother program might not accept children with special needs; a support group for difficult teens might not deal with children labelled as having behavioural problems). Keep your list updated so that you'll be prepared if a parent requests information.

3. Role-play the following situations or discuss them with a classmate or colleague. It might be helpful to write out a list of possible responses beforehand.

   a) You want to discuss a child's development with her parents because you believe that the child isn't progressing as are the other children in your group.

   b) A parent arrives after a case conference at the hospital and yells at you for not providing adequate information to her and adequate programming for her child.

   c) A physiotherapist has just asked you to develop and implement a program with one of the children in your care that will take "only" 45 minutes three times a day. The parent can't understand why this would be a problem.

4. You have just found out that, owing to funding cutbacks, support services for the integration of children with special needs in schools have been eliminated. Write a letter to the editor of the local newspaper explaining how these cuts may affect children and their families.

Parents with Special Needs

chapter 12

Objectives

- To gain an understanding of the effects on children when parents have mental or physical health conditions.

- To understand the impact of physical and mental health conditions on family well-being.

- To understand the role of the caregiver in supporting children whose parents have mental or physical health concerns.

- To understand the role of the caregiver in supporting families.

Maria greets Adele and her mom when they arrive in the child-care centre. Adele looks like she just woke up and has been crying. Her mother looks worse. She hands Adele over and leaves, something that has happened regularly over the last few months. But Adele's mother hasn't said anything about this to Maria, even though Maria has asked. Maria has been pleasant with Adele's mother, and Adele does seem to be fine once she has settled in. At the end of the day Maria shares her concerns with the director, who talks to Adele's mother the next day. The director reports back that Adele's mother has been going through a long diagnosis process and is now starting treatment. This helps explain what has been happening, and now Maria can try to support Adele and her mom.

Recent statistics made available through the Vanier Institute suggest that families are experiencing increased levels of stress (Vanier Institute of the Family, 2010). Approximately 23% of Canadians indicate that most days are stressful. Perceptions of stress peak for people between the ages of 35 and 44 and are generally higher for women. In addition, many Canadians are feeling overloaded by the demands of paid and unpaid work. If this is true for the average Canadian parent, imagine the extra struggles a family might have when a parent is afflicted with chronic mental or physical illness, or an addiction.

Not only do such afflictions increase the amount of stress families have to deal with, but the amount of stress families have to deal with can often lead to or contribute to such afflictions. And many parents whom early childhood educators interact with may be experiencing high levels of stress. This in turn can lead to health concerns (e.g., high blood pressure, heart disease) and, in some cases, to the use of drugs or alcohol to help cope.

A high level of stress among parents has an impact on their children, and it is therefore important for caregivers to be aware of these challenges. Furthermore, because of the stigma that is still unfortunately attached to these chronic health issues, parents are often reluctant to communicate to caregivers about them.

This chapter will explore the impact that a "special need" of a parent may have on the child in your care. In particular, we will explore:

- Parents with chronic health concerns
- Parents with addiction issues (e.g., drugs or alcohol)
- Parents with mental health concerns

Although these are quite distinct in their manifestations, they can all negatively affect the consistency of care and stability of routines in the home, and thereby be detrimental to a child's healthy development. For a variety of reasons, parents may be reluctant to discuss these matters with early childhood educators, but since they may influence the child's behaviour (e.g., routines and attendance), they may leave questions for the educators providing care.

The purpose of this chapter is not to diagnose or label parents, nor to counsel them. The purpose is to understand what may be happening in the life of the child at home and how caregivers may support both the children and their parents. An overview of these three conditions will provide some insight into how a child might be affected in his or her development. Increasing your understanding of illness, addictions, and mental health concerns will help you provide better support for the child and the family.

Effects on Children When Parents Have a Special Need

The emotional health of young children is closely related to the emotional characteristics of their environments, including parents, other family members, and child care. Children who grow up in homes where there are addictions, mental illness, or abuse face major threats to their emotional development, along with threats to development in general. Early childhood educators focus on developing intellectual, physical, language, and social skills. However, emotions play an integral role in the development of all skills, and, therefore, enhancing emotional development is crucial as well. There is still much more to learn about the dynamics of emotional development and resiliency and how these skills may be developed.

Recent brain research suggests that child development, specifically from birth to five years, sets the foundation for future development (National Scientific Council on the Developing Child, 2007). Brains begin to develop before birth and continue to develop into adulthood. Good early experiences lead to a sturdy, healthy foundation for development. Toxic stress, which includes chronic stress caused by poverty, abuse, or maternal depression (National Scientific Council on the Developing Child, 2010a), can be harmful to the brain and to brain development. Brains require supportive, interactive relationships in order to grow and develop, and young children need stable, caring relationships in order to ensure that healthy brain development can occur. Quality care, which includes warm, caring educators in child-care settings, is noted for influencing the development of social, cognitive, and behaviour skills in young children (National Scientific Council on the Developing Child, 2004). These relationships have been shown to influence both school adjustment and school achievement.

Recent research has also suggested that early exposure to situations that produce fear and chronic anxiety can affect children's development, including development of the brain (National Scientific Council on the Developing Child, 2010b). Although this is most common when the child is exposed to abuse, it has been shown that maltreatment occurs when there is excessive stress—addictions and mental health concerns included. When a person is faced with a threatening situation, stress systems are activated to cope with the threatening event. Exposure to stress and anxiety can trigger extreme prolonged activation of the stress response system. Very simply, when the stress system is activated for prolonged periods of time, the body responds in one of two ways. It anticipates everything as threatening, so the child responds to every event in his or her environment as potentially harmful. Or the body habituates so that the child comes to see nothing as threatening, and so responds inappropriately to danger.

It is well known that parents play a major role in the development of their children. Parents' personal histories, including how they themselves were parented and their patterns of attachment, will influence how they parent their children. Current psychological functioning will also influence their child's development. For example, if a parent is stressed, or going through the experience of a divorce, his or her parenting will reflect this. It is often thought that conditions affecting parents may affect children adversely. For example, there is a relationship between parental mental health and suspected child abuse (Invest in Kids, 2010). At least one family stressor or functioning issue was identified in 89% of emotional abuse investigations. This included substance abuse, personal history of abuse, and mental health issues. For this reason, it is important that early childhood educators understand these issues in parents or families so that they may be better able to support children and parents as necessary.

We know that young children are highly vulnerable to adverse conditions in the home, especially mental health issues and family violence. If the child's home environment is characterized by stress and chaos, the child may need a stable, interactive child-care environment to ensure that healthy brain development can continue. Furthermore, it has been documented that young children can benefit from forming secure relationships with multiple caregivers, including child-care educators, and that this will not interfere with the attachment to their parents.

Parents with Chronic Health Conditions

Although it may be uncommon for young parents to experience chronic health concerns, it does occur. In fact, it has been said that 24% of adults with cancer are parenting children under the age of 18 and that up to one-third of these are children under 6 (http://abcnews. go.com/Health/MindMoodNews/parents-cancer-million-parents-young-children-cancer-survivors/story?id=11013334).

Chronic health conditions are labelled as such when symptoms have lasted three months or more and/or there is persistent pain. Examples of chronic health conditions include diabetes, asthma, migraines, heart disease, and cancer. Along with symptoms of the illness, families often need to cope with difficulty accessing services, costs associated with treatment, and poor quality of care. Needless to say, this can be a very difficult and trying time for all family members.

Beyond the personal stress of their illness, parents with chronic illness are likely to be experiencing stress from worrying about how their condition is affecting their children. Parents with chronic or life-threatening illness are most likely actively trying to treat, manage, and cope with their health concern while they may be actively parenting young children. Their concerns can vary greatly, from how to tell their children to how to protect them and how to parent while being treated. Parents also may experience guilt about their decreased ability to parent effectively. In addition, they may feel they are receiving little or no support from their health care professionals in helping them deal with their young children. There are often additional costs associated with treatment that affects families, as well as stress on the healthy spouses who attempt to take on both parenting roles.

A common problem faced by people with chronic health problems is stigma. Some chronic conditions, such as arthritis, may be completely invisible to outsiders yet prevent that person from actively participating in many activities. They are often accused of being lazy, unhelpful, or simply unpleasant because others are not aware of the disabling condition. Furthermore, some conditions result in chronic pain or persistent feelings of unwellness. Under these conditions it is sometimes quite difficult to behave in a friendly and social manner, and this sometimes results in being labelled as unpleasant, "crabby," or simply not a nice person. All in all, coping with chronic health issues can be extremely stressful on parents.

Scenario

Parents Have Stress, Too

A new family brought their 4-year-old to a preschool program. At first there were no concerns with Aiden and his mother, but a few months later, drop-off and pick-up times became quite erratic. Aiden's mother was late or early and reluctant to let staff know her schedule. One day when she was particularly late, the director was on hand and decided to speak to her about her irregular schedule. Aiden's mother was visibly upset, and began the conversation by saying, "I guess *you'll* ask us to leave too? Aiden was asked to leave the preschool last year because I couldn't always be there on time to pick him up. They tried to put me on a contract so he could stay but that didn't work." She went on to explain that she struggled with Crohn's disease, which meant that some days were fine and she coped well, but other days could be a challenge. "Sometimes I'm ready to leave and everything is okay and then I run into problems. I really do try because I know Aiden loves it here and he needs to be in preschool, but some days I just can't control how things will work. It's really embarrassing to have to explain to people why I'm always late," she added.

Families with chronic health conditions have several features in common, since it affects the whole family. Often, family life revolves around the condition. Things happen on good days, and things don't happen on bad days. Children may arrive at the child-care centre early on good days and be late or absent on bad days. Life may be centred around medical needs and protocols—for example, doctor's appointments, treatments, and eating schedules around treatments. Routines and schedules may affect young children more when they are unable to influence the situation. Older children may be able to dress and get something together for lunch and even get to the bus stop or school, but this is very difficult for younger children.

Changes in the home environment will affect not only the stability of day-to-day routines, but also the psychological environment. For example, parents may not be able to be consistently attentive to their child's psychological and emotional needs. Young children may react to changes in the environment with regressions (e.g., need for a bottle at bedtime) or "acting out."

Parents often want to protect children, and so they may not provide information about their condition. In addition, it may be very hard to provide accurate information to young children without unduly scaring them. For example, young children may not understand what surgery or chemotherapy is. However, it is well documented that children cope much better when they understand (Rauch et al., 2002). It may be helpful to answer questions as simply as possible. If it's feasible, have the child visit the hospital or clinic where others may also be able to provide information. Supportive medical professionals view the patient in the context of family and may be able to offer helpful and appropriate information for the child. Explaining, for instance, that the parent may be in hospital for a few days and who will be taking care of them may help the child to cope.

When information is limited, children will attempt to create their own answers. Young children see the world from their own perspective, and may think that they created their parent's illness from their actions or thoughts (Rauch et al., 2002). When information is not forthcoming, children may assume that the illness is even worse than it is, and imagine many dreadful and often unrealistic scenarios. Children need to understand that they did not create the illness and that they will (likely) not get it. It is important that adults have these conversations so that children understand as much as possible and do not develop unnecessary fears.

The Role of the Early Childhood Educator

Early childhood educators may find themselves in difficult situations with regard to the child of a sick parent. There may be a period of time—for example, while waiting for a new diagnosis—when very little information is known about the parent's condition and anxiety is high. Treatment schedules and regimes may change, altering family life. Major transitions may occur—for example, a parent needing a wheelchair for the first time. It is not uncommon that information will not be shared with young children or with the child-care centre. However, changes in stress and anxiety levels in parents and children will be noticeable.

A child who has a family member with a chronic health condition will most likely need additional support while in your care. Consistent routines and schedules will be extremely important. While it is important to be understanding, educators want to be sure to maintain the same level of expectation for children. For example, it may be easy to explain the child's inappropriate behaviour based on the situation at home, but the child will need to learn ways to cope rather than ways to use the illness as an excuse for misbehaving. Young children may have difficulty expressing their feelings in words, and so you may see them expressing their feelings through play or inappropriate behaviour. Children may express frustration or anxiety in how they play with objects or other children. It is possible that children will play more aggressively or have more difficulty getting along with their peers. Educators will need to be aware that these changes in behaviour may be a result of the child's situation at home, and will need to assist him or her in finding coping strategies.

Communicating with children as much as possible will be helpful. This doesn't mean you will have answers or that parents will have information to pass along, but listening to the child—to his or her perspective and potential fears—is a good starting point. Educators may wish to warmly attend to a child's questions without having an answer immediately—"That's a good question. Let me think about that." It is always a good idea to check with parents, and you will need to respect their views even if they choose not to share information with the child. You may be able to support the parent in these conversations. Many support groups have books that may be suitable for younger children.

Parents with Addictions

Addiction is defined as an uncontrollable compulsion to repeat a behaviour regardless of its negative consequences. Alcohol, prescription or non-prescription drugs, and food are common addictions. Symptoms include an increased physiological tolerance for the substance, and in its absence, withdrawal—which can vary from mild cravings to severe illness, such as shaking, vomiting, and even death. Most addiction-forming substances initially result in a form of pleasure or a reduction in pain. For example, adults may begin to consume alcohol to experience a feeling of well-being, a common effect of alcohol. But drinking heavily over a long period of time can lead to such health problems as stomach ulcers, liver disease, and many kinds of cancer. Excessive drinking is often responsible for problems within families and with employment.

Most people are social drinkers; that is, they drink alcohol in a responsible ways. However, some people are problem drinkers in that they may be physically addicted to alcohol and not be able to function adequately without it. Other people are binge drinkers—they may not consume alcohol for long periods, but then consume large amounts. The risk of accidents, impaired driving, and health problems (e.g., seizures, stroke) increases with binge drinking.

In homes where there is alcohol abuse, there tend to be several unwritten rules that family members abide by (AADAC, 2010)—namely, that the issue of over-drinking is not to be discussed, and that feelings are not to be indulged in but instead suppressed. Families with alcohol addictions tend not to trust outside help. Living by these "rules" is harmful to everyone, especially children.

Drug abuse can include a wide range of drugs, both prescription and non-prescription. No one plans to become addicted to drugs. A person may start using drugs because he or she is curious, feels the need to fit in, or is trying to deal with physical or emotional pain. Drug use may continue for other reasons—for example, group pressure or dependence on the drug. Problems can occur quickly or gradually—when the person takes a drug too much, too often, over too long a period of time, or in combination with other drugs. Drug use is considered harmful when it causes physical, mental, social, or financial problems (AADAC, 2010). People are considered drug dependent if they experience discomfort when they try to stop using it. Drug abuse affects the user as well as his or her family and friends.

Recently, more attention has been paid to such addictive behaviours as a gambling addiction or an addiction to sex. These are every bit as problematic in terms of the risk to the addicted person and his or her family. For instance, although many people buy lottery or raffle tickets, go to the racetrack, or enjoy an evening of bingo, once the game is over they carry on with other non-gambling activities. But for others, gambling can become a problem. These problems can range from minor to very serious—from small, short-lived problems such as difficulty paying rent or bills to an ongoing negative impact on the person and his or her family. Signs that gambling may be becoming a problem include spending a lot of time gambling, placing bigger, more frequent bets, hoping for the big win, denying it is a problem, promising to cut back, and refusing to explain behaviour.

For many years, research has suggested that children living in a home where there is drug or alcohol abuse are at risk for emotional, behavioural, and cognitive problems (National Institute on Alcohol Abuse and Alcoholism, 1990). Children from these homes are more likely to need mental health, welfare, and special education programs. Many children have difficulties in school and display more behavioural problems. They often have more psychological difficulties, including depression, anxiety, and stress. They also tend to have more relationship problems and display more anti-social behaviour (National Institute on Alcohol Abuse and Alcoholism, 1990). Some behaviours (e.g., acting out) are noted as early as 2 years old. As

Dr. Bruce Perry points out, 90% of brain development occurs prior to the age of 3 (Perry, 2010). Early experiences shape the brain for a lifetime. Consistent, caring environments will lead to healthy brain development, whereas chaotic, neglectful, inconsistent environments will increase the likelihood of health problems, psychological problems, and substance abuse. In this way, homes that deal with addiction are similar to homes that deal with chronic illness in that they both create stress and disruption.

Scenario

Effects of Alcohol Abuse on Children

Sylvan was 5 years old and had been in the same child-care centre since he was a baby. Over the years, the staff who worked with him suspected that there may be issues at home. Sometimes he would be clean, cared for, and happy to be in the centre, but at other times he was tired, wore the same clothes over and over, and couldn't wait to eat. Repeated attempts to get information from his mother or father were met with silence. When Sylvan turned 5 his father left the home, and Sylvan began to talk about how his home life had changed—for example, "Now we eat supper every night" and "I sleep better now 'cause my mom and dad aren't fighting." Sylvan's mother did eventually tell the staff that his father had left due to alcohol abuse, and she described the effect it was having on her and Sylvan. This explained a lot to the educators who had worked with him over the years.

Parental drug addiction can affect children's development in two ways. The first is caused by the impact of the drug or alcohol abuse itself. Parenting may be inconsistent, routines sporadic, and care occurring irregularly. Children may be further impacted by an increased incidence of divorce, ongoing parental anxiety, and discord in the family. The second impact comes from what children are learning from adults. Children of drug- and alcohol-addicted parents learn different strategies for coping. As Jerry Mo points out (Mo, 2010), children who live with adults who cope by using drugs and alcohol may learn to cope using drugs and alcohol as well.

Resiliency has been studied in relation to children in homes impacted by addiction. Research has shown that these children can be quite resilient, and that more than 50% of children grow up without experiencing difficulties. Key factors associated with development include:

- Ability to get attention
- Having good communication skills
- Average intelligence
- Caring attitude
- Desire to achieve and do well
- Belief in helping oneself (www.alcoholism.about.com)

These factors are important in the role educators may play in the development of children impacted by addiction.

The Role of the Early Childhood Educator

It is important to understand that a person who suffers from a serious addiction may be unable to meet the needs of his or her children, since the need for the substance or behaviour is so strong that it overtakes any other thoughts or emotions. This can result in a serious decline in family income, quality of life, and even safety.

Early childhood educators may find themselves in a very awkward situation when working with families impacted by addiction. One possible scenario is the parent arriving at the child-care centre after using drugs or alcohol. Educators have an ethical and legal obligation to protect children, and so they may need to contact social services, which can provide immediate support to the child. Most child-care programs will have a policy outlining how to handle such a situation, which will assist caregivers to follow through. As difficult as this is, the primary focus on the safety of the child continues to be paramount.

In another possible scenario, children may tell you things about what is happening at home that you may question or be unsure of how to handle. In the presence of parents, you may have no concerns—they may seem attentive, caring, and interested in their children. But parents and family members may not realize that they have a problem or may not disclose this reality. As an educator and as a caring adult, you may wish to intervene and support the family as much as possible, but families may not always provide the opportunity. Young children have little or no choice but to adapt to the environment and the family they are part of. Although it may be difficult to provide support or to change the environment at home, it is important to support the child in your care. And of course if you suspect abuse or neglect, you have a duty to report this to social services.

Educators can support children in two ways. One is by engaging in good child-care practices that foster growth and development for all children. This includes:

- Developing and maintaining daily routines and schedules.
- Maintaining as much consistency in the environment as possible.
- Ensuring that the child has access to the necessities of life—adequate food and sleep.
- Ensuring that the environment is healthy and safe.
- Providing a caring, supportive environment where healthy brain development may continue to occur.

The second role for early childhood educators is to build programs and practices focused on resilience, as these are areas where educators may impact children in deliberate and thoughtful ways. For example, educators typically teach such communication skills as how to get attention in appropriate ways. Educators model caring or self-help and can assist in developing such skills as empathy and problem solving.

Parents with Mental Health Issues
Prevalence of Mental Illness in Canada

Here are some facts that may influence how you perceive mental illness:

- One in five Canadians will experience a mental illness during their lifetime.
- Three percent, or nearly 1 million Canadians, live with a severe and persistent mental illness.
- Mental illness is the second leading cause of hospital admission among those 20 to 44 years of age.

- The World Health Organization estimates that by 2020, depression will be the leading cause of disability in developed countries.
- Large numbers of people with mental illness are living on the streets. (Canadian Association of Mental Health, 2003)

Despite the prevalence of mental illness in our society, people with mental illness face so many kinds of stigmas that it seems preferable not to disclose to anyone. This, of course, makes it much more difficult to access treatment and support. Most mental illnesses today are treatable, some with medication and others with therapy, and often with a combination of both. Among the most common mental illnesses are mood disorders such as depression and bipolar disorder, schizophrenia, and anxiety disorders. The Canadian Association of Mental Health provides good information about these and other disorders. The symptoms and the severity of symptoms vary widely. It is important to keep in mind that most people with mental illness cannot control their symptoms on their own. When a person is depressed, for example, we often hear people saying things like "She just needs to pull up her socks, get busy, and stop feeling sorry for herself." This is both inaccurate and unhelpful.

Among the one in five Canadians who will develop a mental illness at some point in their lives (as listed above), 1% are likely to have a serious or continual mental illness. Mood (e.g., depression) and anxiety disorders are the most common conditions. Mental health issues are often associated with alcohol or drug use, especially prior to diagnosis as the person attempts to deal with his or her change in mood or anxiety with drugs or alcohol. It may take a long time for some people to be diagnosed as they come to understand that the reason for their feelings cannot be helped with drugs or alcohol. This realization may be preceded by a significant event (e.g., a breakdown) or prolonged difficulties that never seem to be resolved. Often, friends and family recognize that there may be a problem but are unsure of how to intervene. Early childhood educators may witness the same process.

As we discussed earlier, the early years are critical for development, especially brain development. Healthy brain development requires that the child be cared for, protected from illness, hazards, and excessive stress, and provided with predictable routines and schedules. Mental health problems in parents can be a source of fear and anxiety in children and can affect development (National Scientific Council on the Developing Child, 2010b). Parents may be less able to provide care; there may be neglect or abuse and exposure to other forms of stress that will have consequences on development.

Depression

Depression in mothers has been documented as one of the most problematic in terms of the effect on children (Center on the Developing Child at Harvard University, 2009). There are a number of symptoms of depression. They vary in intensity, duration, and the number of symptoms that apply to each person. Depression becomes an illness, or clinical depression, when the feelings described above are severe, last for several weeks, and begin to interfere with one's work and social life. Depressive illness can change the way a person thinks and behaves and how his or her body functions. These are some of the signs to look for:

- Feeling worthless, helpless, or hopeless
- Sleeping more or less than usual
- Eating more or less than usual
- Having difficulty concentrating or making decisions

- Loss of interest in taking part in activities
- Decreased sex drive
- Avoiding other people
- Overwhelming feelings of sadness or grief
- Feeling unreasonably guilty
- Loss of energy, feeling very tired
- Thoughts of death or suicide (CMHA, 2010)

It is not difficult to understand, then, how very difficult it is for someone who is depressed to be a responsive and attentive caregiver of a young child.

Depression can be short-lived or more chronic in nature. Owing to its prevalence, maternal depression is most commonly cited as a source of concern, with an estimated 10% to 20% of mothers depressed at some time. Depression is even more prevalent in families experiencing poverty, with one in four of these families affected. However, it remains common that only a small number of those experiencing depression will seek and obtain professional care. Depression will have a significant impact on children's development if it occurs during the prenatal environment or the first few years of life. The effects of paternal depression and mental illness has been studied much less, and the impact is less known.

The Role of the Early Childhood Educator

Scenario

Educator Support

Shino had her first son in the child-care program from the age of 19 months. When he was 5 Shino had a second child; she brought the baby in shortly after he was born and was quite excited. She began to bring her 5-year-old into the centre on a daily basis. Anika, the program director, didn't see Shino for a while, and when she did see her daily, Shino never stopped to say hello. The time Shino spent dropping off her son and picking him up got longer, and one day she popped into the office to ask whether babies really needed to have their diapers changed so often. She explained that her mother-in-law was here for an extended visit, and as Anika engaged her further in conversation, Shino divulged that she was being treated for postpartum depression during the evenings in a hospital setting but was at home during the day to bond with her baby. They were able to talk about places that offered support, and how the centre itself might provide support with Shino's older son. From that time onward, Anika watched a little closer and tried to engage Shino whenever she could.

This scenario may occur in any child-care centre at any time, which is why it is so important for educators and directors to observe and take the time to engage with parents. In this situation, an innocent question opened the door to a mother seeking help and the child-care director acting as another pillar in her support system.

Depression typically occurs in the context of other family issues. For example, mothers experiencing depression are often young, socially isolated, economically or educationally disadvantaged, and burdened by more family conflict and stressful life events than mothers who are not depressed. Mothers who experience deep or chronic depression are also more likely to have experienced intimate partner violence, to be in poor health, and to have problems with anxiety or substance abuse (Center on the Developing Child at Harvard University, 2009, p. 4). However, depression can and does affect people across social and economic groups.

Healthy development is based on interactions with the environment, in particular, caring adults. This interaction has been described as "serve and return" (Center on the Developing Child at Harvard University, 2009)—for example, when the baby smiles at the parent and the parent returns the smile or says a kind word back. Recent research has shown that these repeated interactions—involving words, gestures, touch, or attention—are critical to brain development. Children can be particularly at risk when their primary caregivers do not engage in these interactions. Parents can undermine the serve-and-return pattern in two ways. They may serve in ways that are difficult for the child to return—for example, when parents are intrusive or hostile. Or the child may serve and the parent doesn't return—for example, when the caregiver does not respond to the infant's cues consistently. Both of these possibilities arise when mothers experience mental health issues, especially depression.

Early intervention is critical. Hence, there has been a major focus on postpartum depression and dealing with the symptoms early. In addition to medical approaches (i.e., medication) and counselling, many programs have been developed that focus on parenting, especially on mother–child interactions. For example, many provincial and regional programs offer home visitation and support programs that focus on improving interactions. The promotion of positive parenting practices has been shown to have excellent results for children and families. Interventions that focus on reducing the mother's symptoms alone have not shown the same results in long-term outcomes for children or parents (Center on the Developing Child at Harvard University, 2009).

Mental illness continues to be highly stigmatized in North American society. The predominant coping strategy is secrecy or hiding the diagnosis (Hinshaw, 2005). Mental illness can be concealed, but this can lead to additional concerns—"Who do I tell? How do I let people know?" When parents are dealing with a mental health concern, having to also deal with the attached stigma may affect their parenting in that they may not be willing to seek support to cope as a family. Yet parental mental illness is a documented risk factor for mental health concerns in their children. This may result from the parent's lack of responsiveness, inconsistent parenting, or parental modelling (Hinshaw, 2005). Hopefully, as knowledge and understanding of mental illness and mental health increases, parents will come to understand the critical role they play in the early years.

Since the fear of stigma may be one of the main reasons that parents avoid sharing information about their physical or mental health conditions, it is important to find different ways to communicate to parents that staff are knowledgeable and unbiased. The Canadian Mental Health Association and other organizations offer materials about mental health and mental illness. Availability of brochures and posters about health issues at the centre will give parents this message. Taking a few extra minutes to ask a parent how he or she is feeling and responding with empathy and concern will provide parents with the opportunity to express a need for help or support. It is also important to have a good knowledge of resources for parents handy and available, including local associations and support groups for different conditions.

Repercussions of a Stigma

Joline, a 30-year-old student in a social work program, related the following story to her classmates after a lecture on bipolar disorder. Her story provides a moving example of how the stigma connected with mental illness can have devastating effects.

"I was an A student in high school, and had plans for preparing for architecture school. But on my 18th birthday, my life began to fall apart. My personality seemed to change drastically; I became aggressive, irresponsible, and even began to have paranoid delusions. Following that I fell into a deep depression that ended in a suicide attempt. I was so lucky to have the support of my family and good medical care, and managed to pick up the pieces and finish university. I got married, and am now the mother of two children. Two years ago my husband started drinking, and although he's never been physically abusive, he is emotionally abusive, and refuses to get help for his addiction or go to counselling. I want to leave him, I know that now, but I'm afraid that with my bipolar disorder diagnosis I may not get custody of the children, even though I've been well for many years now."

Examine Your Attitudes

- Do you think parents with mental health concerns are capable of parenting effectively?
- Do you think children should be protected from parents with addictions or mental health concerns?

Conclusion

New research in brain development tells us that the early years are even more important than previously known, and that responsive, reciprocal caregiving is the foundation for healthy brain development. Parents' mental and physical illnesses, as well as their addictions, negatively impact the child's development through the resulting inconsistency of care. Yet research also tells us that young children can cope with multiple caregivers without comprimisng their attachment to their parents. Therefore, the role of the early childhood educator in ensuring healthy development should be seen as critical in helping families face such issues.

The family situations we have discussed in this chapter all share one feature—parents may have less time and ability to provide the nurturing, interactive relationship that is so critical for development. Although the reasons for this vary, the child will need early childhood educators to provide rich, stimulating, nurturing, responsive environments. Educators may find themselves in situations where, for a variety of reasons, little information is forthcoming from families. Nonetheless, the role of the educator is to provide the child with an environment conducive to continued growth and development. In doing so, educators may help alleviate the stress and anxiety experienced by parents who feel that their parenting may be inadequate. This may be the best support you can offer to parents at this time. Providing information about community resources and supports may also be helpful, but all parents may need to feel ready or able to benefit from these.

Chapter Summary

- Parents living with a special need (health care, addiction, or mental health concerns) may affect children and development in a number of ways.
- Recent research suggests that the home environment is extremely important for early brain development, and that high levels of stress can be particularly detrimental. Young children need stable, interactive relationships to develop optimally.
- Each type of special need is associated with some type of stigma that may hinder or prevent the parent from seeking support and treatment. In addition, parents may be reluctant to share information with educators.
- It may be difficult to gather information to obtain a clear picture of what may be happening in the home. However, it is always critical that educators provide young children with a stable, caring environment filled with interactions so as to ensure that development continues.
- Supporting parents with special needs may be more difficult, but understanding and support will still be necessary.

Recommended Websites

Alberta Family Wellness Initiative:
www.albertafamilywellness.org

Canadian Mental Health Association:
www.cmha.ca

Center on the Developing Child at Harvard University:
http://developingchild.harvard.edu

National Institute on Alcohol Abuse and Alcoholism:
www.niaaa.nih.gov

Health Canada:
www.hc-sc.gc.ca/index-eng.php

Exercises

1. Search online for current information related to mental health agencies (e.g., the Canadian Mental Health Association or provincial organizations) for addiction support or health concerns.

2. Consider how stigmatization may affect people's behaviour. Talk with friends, family, and colleagues about their perceptions of parents who have addictions or mental health issues. In what ways will you be able to support families who are dealing with these perceptions?

3. Check community-based resources that support adults with addictions or mental health concerns. Are there community supports that a parent with a chronic health concern may be able to access (e.g., home nursing care)? Do these supports entail any associated costs?

4. Role-play the following situations. What might you watch for, and which actions might you take (now or after observations)?

   a) A father comes to pick up his child, and he appears to be "high."

   b) A child reports that Mommy sleeps all the time at home.

   c) A mother with a 2-year-old in your program decides to keep her in care after she has her second baby. After four weeks, the mother becomes quite unpredictable and less talkative.

   d) The parents of a 3-year-old have separated and take turns caring for him. During the father's week, the little boy is on time, well cared for, and settles in easily. But when it's the mother's week, the child's hours are chaotic, he arrives in the same clothes and is unclean, and his behaviour is less settled. You suspect the mother may be struggling, but you don't want to create more challenges for the couple.

Families and Poverty

chapter 13

Objectives

- **To describe the extent of poverty in Canada.**
- **To examine the factors associated with poverty.**
- **To examine the effects of poverty on families.**
- **To examine values and beliefs regarding poverty and the poor.**
- **To discuss the role of the early childhood educator in supporting children and families who are poor, including the homeless.**

"When my husband and I first split up, I talked to my kids about the changes that were going to occur. My older daughter would no longer be able to wear the same kind of jeans as some of her friends, and we probably wouldn't be able to afford many after-school activities. I wouldn't be able to chauffeur the kids, because I would no longer have a car. My younger daughter asked, 'Does that mean we're poor now?' I answered, 'Maybe, in a way, but it doesn't matter because we have each other.' That was four years ago. Now it's no longer a matter of doing without the extras—I can't even manage to buy the basic necessities. Now when my children ask me if we're poor, I say yes. But I can't say it doesn't matter anymore. It does matter. It matters a great deal."

Being poor affects every aspect of family life and every family member. It may mean getting food at a food bank, eating dog food to survive, or not having running water or heating. Being poor often means having only worn-out and inappropriate clothing. For many, being poor may result in homelessness and moving from shelter to shelter. Often poverty results in feelings of powerlessness, shame, isolation, helplessness, and hopelessness. Poverty is a fact of life for many Canadian families. It can have such an astounding effect on family life as a whole, and on the growth and development of children, that all professionals concerned about children's well-being must be committed to addressing the problems of poverty.

What Is Poverty?

The picture most Canadians have of poverty is of sickly children on the edge of starvation. In Canada, however, this scene is not typical. What prevails instead is deprivation in relation to others in society. People suffer deeply not because the necessities of life barely exist, but because unequal distribution of income blocks access to Canada's abundance. Poverty in this country is not a matter of starving, but rather of begging for food at food banks and shelters (Canadian Council of Social Development, 2007). A recent Conference Board of Canada report highlights that for the past two decades this country has earned a D grade on the poverty rate for working-age people and C grades on child poverty, income inequality, gender equity, and assaults. In short, Canada is not living up to its expectations or its potential (Conference Board of Canada, 2009).

Discussions of the poor often lead to heated debates about what constitutes poverty (Fremstad, 2010). We hear stories of times gone by when there was barely enough food on the table, clothing was mended and handed down from sibling to sibling and family to family, and brothers and sisters had to share a bed at night: "We all worked hard, didn't feel sorry for ourselves, and shared the little that we had. We didn't think about being poor."

Does *poor* simply mean not having enough money to meet survival needs (food, clothing, and shelter), or does it mean not having enough money left *after* meeting basic survival needs to participate in a lifestyle that is viewed as "average" or "normal" in our society? In fact, both are important measurements of poverty. Poverty has an *absolute* significance (i.e., there is not enough money for food) and a *relative* significance (i.e., there is not enough money to live as most North Americans do).

Statistics Canada's definition of a low-income cut-off (LICO) represents the number of Canadians who, compared with the average citizen, spend 20% more of their gross income on food, shelter, and clothing. A family is considered to be in "straitened circumstances" if they spend more than 55% of their income on the basic essentials for living (Fogden, 2006). While scholars and governments debate the exact definition of poverty, we are seeing an increase in the number of Canadians relying on foodbanks, an increase in homeless people, and an increase in the number of Canadians who live below the accepted LICO, especially after the 2008–2009 recession (Dearing, 2010).

When considering poverty in Canada, we must remember that the statistics typically used involve meeting the basics of food and shelter. Think about how many expenses families have that that go beyond food and shelter and seem so necessary for a reasonable life: Transportation and costs relating to health and child care are but a few examples.

Attitudes Toward the Poor

Scenario

Students' Attitudes

A class of early childhood students was asked whether they thought that people who lived on social assistance wasted taxpayers' money by drinking, playing bingo, and passing the days watching soap operas. The instructor expected the students to object to such obvious stereotyping, but to her surprise, at least half the class nodded their heads in agreement. She now starts every new class with the same question, and each time receives similar responses from the class. The instructor has realized that teaching facts about poverty is not enough. The assumptions and value judgments made about the poor have to be addressed as well.

Myths Surrounding Poverty

A number of myths are often associated with negative attitudes toward any group of people. A myth in this sense is a widely held belief that is accepted uncritically, even when much evidence to the contrary exists. The prevalence of myths about poverty has in fact interfered with government policy initiatives that have the potential to alleviate some of the problems of poverty.

For example, it is a common belief in our society that hard work pays off—and that if people work hard, they are likely to succeed in life. Perhaps because of these shared beliefs, many people who have never been poor feel at least a twinge of resentment toward poor people. "If they worked harder or wasted less money, they'd be able to make ends meet," some people say. This feeling is sometimes stronger among those who began their lives in poverty and through hard work have managed to overcome many obstacles to become successful. "If I did it, why can't they?" they wonder. When children arrive at the child-care centre or school without having had breakfast, all too often a bit of resentment toward the parents emerges. "Don't they care about their children? If they didn't waste all their money, the kids wouldn't have to come to school hungry."

Another offshoot of the belief in equal opportunity is the idea that people who are poor haven't tried hard enough and have only themselves to blame. The poor are often described as passive, unable to delay gratification, and as believing in luck rather than hard work. Yet today it is becoming evident that even among families with two wage earners, there are people who live in poverty. In fact, 8.2% of two-earner families are living below the poverty line (Walberg & Mrozek, 2009).

One of the myths surrounding poverty centres on what we might call the self-sufficient family. If we believe that "each family is on its own," then we have no responsibility to help others. Yet in our society, no family is completely independent, and families that lack the means to acquire their basic needs must rely on others for help. Another myth assumes that families that seek help are incompetent. Underlying this idea are stereotyped notions that the poor are lacking in motivation or are deficient in personal qualities or values. We think "There must be something wrong with those people" rather than considering that there may be something wrong with the economics or organization of our society. However, the causes of poverty are often not under the control of the individual. These causes include changes in economic forces, such as employment opportunities, rising costs of housing, sudden illness or death in the family, or unexpected medical needs. We must remember that a full-time job at minimum wage will not keep a family from poverty. This can be true even when there are two wage earners in the family (Beauschene, 2006).

A further prevailing myth is the belief that public assistance condones failure or takes away the will to be self-sufficient. We hear about "welfare bums" who would rather be on welfare than work. This generalization simply does not apply to many people who require financial assistance.

Many people are familiar with the concept referred to as "the welfare trap." People on welfare cannot receive continued assistance (such as medical coverage or child care) if they find work. Parents whose first goal is to protect and provide for their children often reluctantly choose to stay on welfare rather than become part of the unprotected group of working poor. The following scenario exemplifies this dilemma.

Retraining or Regressing?

A single mother with three children, aged 1, 3, and 5 years, had been receiving social assistance for a number of years. When she became aware that the assistance included a retraining program, she eagerly signed up for the early childhood education program at a community college. She graduated, got a job, but quit after three months. Her net income, taking into account her child-care expenses, clothing, and commuting costs, was about the same as what she had received on social assistance. More important to her, she was away from her own young children for most of the day, caring for other people's children and coming home extremely tired and stressed. The bottom line for this woman was that she and her children were better off on social assistance.

Early childhood educators will inevitably come into contact with children whose families are struggling with poverty. If educators have an attitude of resentment or blame toward poor people, they will have to overcome that before they can work effectively with these children and their families. The next step is to become educated about poverty in our society and understand the effects that poverty has on families and children. The third step is to learn more about the role of early childhood educators in working with families and children who are poor, and to advocate for policies that will result in a reduction of poverty.

Who Are the Poor?
Children

Over 20 years ago, the Canadian House of Commons unanimously resolved to "seek to achieve the goal of eliminating poverty among Canadian children by the year 2000." Yet more than 1 million children—one out of every nine in Canada—live in poverty (Jain, 2009). This is shocking for a country ranked among the wealthiest in the world. Canada ranks bronze on childhood poverty, with a rate almost six times that of Denmark's (Conference Board of Canada, 2009). Children make up the largest single group of poor people in Canada (Report Card on Child and Family Poverty in Canada, 2009). In the United States, 23% of children under the age of 3 are from poor families, while in Canada the rate is over 21% (Fogden, 2006).

Racial and Ethnic Groups

Poverty is disproportionately high among visible minority groups such as blacks and Aboriginals (Dwyer, 2010). When the rate of poverty is disproportionately high among members of a particular ethnic group, there may be a tendency to attribute this to characteristics of the minority groups themselves. The history of racism and discrimination faced by Aboriginal families plays a major factor in the poverty faced by many in those communities today. There are real barriers preventing these and other groups from acquiring adequate incomes (Canadian Council of Social Development, 2010).

A 2003 study by Beavon and Cook (referenced in Ambert, 2006) pointed out that although the United Nations Development Programme consistently ranks Canada as one of the best places to live in the world, "persons designated as 'status Indian' and living on reserves" would be ranked seventy-ninth. They have the lowest standard of living of any group in Canada. Infant mortality is significantly higher in First Nations families, and the rate of suicide among First Nations people is two to seven times that of the general population. Moreover, 40% of off-reserve First Nations children live in poverty (Ambert, 2006).

Gender and Poverty

The relationship between gender and poverty has been known for some time now. In the context of mothers in the workforce, if women were paid equitably, the poverty rate in Canada could be cut in half (Ambert, 2006). The economic disadvantages to women are exacerbated for single mothers.

Compared with approximately 20% of male single-parent households, 40% of women raising families alone are poor, and lone-parent families headed by women have by far the lowest incomes of all family types (Statistics Canada, 2006). Of the single, divorced, and widowed women over the age of 65, 45.6% are poor. The percentage of poverty among visible minority women, including Aboriginal and immigrant women, is significantly higher than for Canadian-born white women (Smith et al., 2008). Many women in Canadian society today face multiple disadvantages.

Effects of Poverty

Poverty is a complex, multidimensional phenomenon with a wide variety of effects. Bronfenbrenner's (1979) ecological model is useful for considering the context in which poverty exists. Poverty has profound effects on the home environment, family structure, and parenting. Poor families are at risk for physical and mental health, factors that impact family functioning and the life course of children (Caughy et al., 2008; Sobolewski & Amato, 2005). Concerns go beyond the immediate home environment and extend to neighbourhoods, schools, and child care (Ambert, 2006). We will now consider some of the consequences of poverty that may affect children and their families.

Effects on Families and Communities

The effects of poverty reach individuals, families, and communities. Poverty is associated with poorer health (Kerr & Michalski, 2005; O'Campo et al., 2008), lower participation in the labour force, family disintegration, and increased rates of suicide (American Psychological Association, 2005), and is a key obstacle to parenting capacity (Russell et al., 2008). Viewed from the ecological perspective, the effects of poverty are felt not only because of limited financial resources, but also because being in poverty almost always encompasses a lack of social resources, higher stress, and the quality (or lack thereof) of neighbourhoods where children grow up (O'Campo et al., 2008). For example, low-income neighbourhoods often have less access to services, poorer quality schools and child-care centres, more crime, greater pollution, and higher rates of drug use, and are coupled with high levels of violence, social disorder, and fear (Caughy et al., 2008). In addition, poor people have less sense of control over their life and work, suffer increased levels of stress and higher levels of depression (and face decreased mental and physical health in general), and have a poorer ability to take care of their children (Caughy et al., 2008). The stress felt as a result of poverty is chronic and strongly influences family well-being (McDaniel & Tepperman, 2007).

Effects of Unemployment on Parenting

Although many families who face poverty are working families (Beauschene, 2006), the adults in many poor families are unemployed. For all family members, unemployment has social and emotional consequences that add to the stresses of poverty. To begin with, unemployment is often a blow to self-esteem. Men tend to blame themselves, and they tend to be blamed by other family members. The unemployed man's presence in the home all day can cause strain for the entire family. He may be used to being the authority figure, the disciplinarian, and he may go to extremes to maintain this role with his wife and children. He may also be used to being the breadwinner, and the loss of this traditional role will increase the strain he feels.

While this scenario rings true in many cases, changing gender norms in breadwinner roles as well as widespread unemployment may minimize some of the psychological consequences faced by traditional breadwinners. A significant increase in stay-at-home-fathers and female breadwinners suggests that the preceding scenario may be shifting. In addition, some researchers argue that the 2008–2009 global recession that left many unemployed decreased the social stigma around unemployment (Fernandez-Arias et al., 2009). Nonetheless, social stigma is only one part of the stresses faced due to unemployment, and unemployment's very real financial, health, and psychological consequences continue to strain affected families.

Effects of Poverty on Children

It has long been argued that socioeconomic disadvantage experienced very early in life is more damaging than that experienced later in life (Lindjord, 2002). Newer studies find that the negative consequences of childhood poverty persist and affect adult well-being (Najman et al., 2010). This is particularly true when the poverty is of long duration, or when it occurs during adolescence (Najman et al., 2010; Sobolewski & Amato, 2005). The negative long-lasting effects of poverty are evident in the physical and mental health of children (Caughy et al., 2008; Najman et al., 2010). Najman et al. (2010) indicated that poor children experience less social support and have parents who are less responsive and more authoritarian. They are read to less frequently and have less access to books. As early as preschool, children in low-income families have increased behavioural and cognitive problems (Scaramella et al., 2008). In addition, children in long-term poverty are often more likely to experience such psychological consequences as anxiety and depression (Caughy et al., 2008).

In a comprehensive report entitled "Starting Strong II," the Organisation for Economic Co-operation and Development (OECD) identifies child poverty as a major challenge in the attempt to enhance the well-being and education of young children (Education Directorate, 2006). The report emphasizes the following:

> The reduction of child and family poverty is a precondition for successful early childhood care and education systems. Early childhood services do much to alleviate the negative effects of disadvantage by educating young children and facilitating the access of families to basic services and social participation. However, a continuing high level of child and family poverty in a country undermines these efforts and greatly impedes the task of raising educational levels. (Education Directorate, 2006, p. 206)

It is vital for early childhood educators to maintain the strength-based perspective when working with poor families. Many children from poor families, and poor families themselves, have shown remarkable resilience and an ability to overcome the significant odds against them. Effects of poverty are also mitigated by social support, community-based resources, quality schools, and high-quality child care.

Homelessness

While homeless people face many of the same risks and consequences as other poor people, educators are becoming increasingly aware of the devastation to family life caused by home-lessness. Life tends to be unstable and irregular for families living in poverty, which, all too often, leads to homelessness for families with young children.

The homeless are, not surprisingly, among the most destitute of the poor. Most of them have been poor or on the margins of poverty all their lives. Families are often homeless because of a lack of affordable housing, while some have left their homes because of domestic violence or abuse.

Mothers in homeless shelters report having lost control over their environment and their lives, and having difficulty balancing their own physical and personal needs with those of their children. They don't have control over the daily routine, and they are unable to be effective parents because of the interference of house rules and shelter staff. Homeless children change schools often and are sick more frequently than other children (Ambert, 2006; Varney et al., 2008). They may suffer from inadequate nutrition, and their parents are often too stressed to help and guide them (Ambert, 2006; Varney et al., 2008). Homelessness can only be described as an immense trauma that leads to the disruption of social networks, family roles and routines, and emotional stability.

Homelessnees is devastating at any age, but for younger children it is particularly disrup-tive. If we consider the developmental needs of young children and the importance of security and consistency in building trust and autonomy, it is clear that the instability of homelessness can be highly detrimental. In short, homelessness deprives children not only of a decent qual-ity of life, but also of most of their future opportunities.

Reducing Poverty

In the past, the poor were at the mercy of their families, communities, or charities for assist-ance. Since about the time of World War I, however, governments in the West have taken vari-ous steps to address the problem of poverty.

The "Report Card on Child Poverty" (Campaign 2000, 2009) concluded that Canada had made no progress in the last decade in reducing child poverty. The report outlined five major benchmarks that would be crucial to the elimination of child poverty in Canada:

- Increasing the availability of good jobs at living wages, raising minimum wages, facilitat-ing the inclusion of immigrants, and providing better protection through employment.
- Creating an effective child benefit system that provides enough income support to keep working parents, including single parents, out of poverty.
- Building a universally accessible system of quality early education and child care to sup-port optimal early development of children and enable parents to work or receive training.
- Expanding affordable housing significantly to end adult and family homelessness and enable parents to raise their children in healthy community environments.
- Renewing the national social safety net, with increased federal funding and increased accountability for provincially delivered social services.

The Role of Early Childhood Educators

Our deep-seated attitudes and beliefs about the poor will affect the way in which we understand both the problems of poverty and the short- and long-term solutions that we promote to deal with these problems. As members of a helping profession, we have an ethical obligation to accept and respect people regardless of their social or economic standing. Sorting out one's personal beliefs about people who are poor is an important first step.

Understanding and Empathizing

Providing support to children and families in poverty requires the ability to empathize with their difficulties. Try to imagine what young children might feel like when

- they can never be sure where they will sleep from night to night
- they go to a child care or nursery school, but don't know if they will be able to return the next day
- they have no space or toys to call their own
- they have no consistent routines, and may not have clean clothes or the opportunity to bathe
- they sense the feelings of hopelessness, despair, and frustration felt by their parents, and feel helpless themselves

Now try to imagine what it might be like for parents who may

- be embarrassed about being homeless
- be unable to give their children even the most basic and simple provisions (snacks, a hot drink, or 25 cents for a hot dog for lunch)
- feel isolated and alone
- have no links with or support from their community
- fear having their children taken away from them
- fear being perceived as neglectful or abusive parents
- fear being perceived as vagrants or lawbreakers
- know that many judge them and their children by their appearance
- feel unprotected and vulnerable
- have no privacy for intimacy with their partner

It is important not to stereotype homeless people or to make assumptions. The preceding lists may apply to many people in such a situation, but not to all. It is also wrong to assume that homeless families are dysfunctional. They are enduring highly stressful circumstances, and extended periods of homelessness can indeed lead to family breakdown. We must be very careful not to "blame the victims," but rather to understand the circumstances that lead to poverty and homelessness.

For many children who are homeless or poor, the child-care centre or other early childhood program can be a crucial source of stability and support. Recognizing the special needs of children and families in these circumstances can help staff meet these children's needs in a supportive and sensitive manner.

Understanding Homelessness from the Child's Perspective

When Jimmy lay down for his afternoon nap, he insisted on taking his favourite toy, jacket, shoes, hat, and snack with him. On some days there were so many belongings on his cot that there was no room for Jimmy. When the early childhood educator mentioned this to his mother, she learned that Jimmy's family had been evicted from their apartment; some nights they were staying with friends, and some nights at shelters. No wonder Jimmy was clinging to his belongings.

For children living in shelters, every hour can bring change, and that can be frightening. Use the information you have read in this chapter to try to imagine what special support you could provide. Think about routine care. Might the child need extra nourishment at meal and snack time? Might she need extra attention to help her settle down at naptime? Would it be helpful to have some extra clothing on hand should a change be necessary? Is it reasonable to assume that some children who live in shelters will be more hesitant to leave their personal belongings out of sight? Will these children sometimes require more individual time or small-group time than other children? A bit of extra thought and planning may go a long way to alleviate some of the stresses that homeless children may bring to the child-care centre.

Sensitivity Pays Off

Staff members at an inner-city child-care centre were well aware that most children were coming in hungry and that the centre provided most of their nutritional needs. With some extra funding, they started a program in which extra food was prepared for lunch and snacks, and children were encouraged to take food home for a snack for themselves and to share with their siblings. Early childhood educators were sensitive to the needs of these families. The program was especially successful because poor children were not singled out. All the children enjoyed having the opportunity to take home things that they made or received at the centre.

A homelike environment that contains many private areas and personalized space with pictures, photographs, and personal cubbies is important to all children but will be vital to those who lack these element in their lives outside the centre. Most important is the development of a trusting relationship with a staff member, who can anticipate some of the feelings associated with poverty and homelessness and who is willing to find many small ways to make children feel welcome, appreciated, and safe.

When we understand the long- and short-term devastation that poverty can bring to children and families, it seems clear that as professionals committed to the well-being of children, we must not ignore the need to advocate for ending child poverty in Canada. There are several organizations—local, provincial, and federal—that are committed to this. And at the end of this chapter we have included an exercise related to advocacy.

Supporting Parents of Poor and Homeless Children

Low-income single mothers often have fewer networks of support and are less likely to seek help from both professionals and informal support systems (Attree, 2005). Thus, early childhood educators play a role in supporting low-income parents in a nonjudgmental and dignified manner. As one parent in these circumstances noted, "The last thing I need is to come to a parent meeting and have someone try to teach me how to be a better parent." Little gestures, such as having coffee, juice, and a quiet place to sit for a while, can make all the difference. Practical supplies such as extra clothing, toys, books, and food for emergency use should also be on hand. Provision of snacks and meals might be a major factor in the selection of child care for families living in poverty.

Scenario

Low-Cost or No-Cost Activities

Several child-care centres working with disadvantaged children incorporated different ideas that would involve and benefit their families. One centre started a lending library of toys and books for children to take home in order to ensure that they offered stimulating, educational materials. Another centre organized an exchange of toys, clothing, and other belongings. Each family brought items they no longer used to trade for other items. Families were able to replenish toy, book, and clothing supplies while sharing resources with other families. Another centre accomplished the same thing by having a garage sale. Parents were able to purchase toys, clothing, and items for a token fee, and the centre was able to raise a few dollars to purchase art equipment. The common factor in all these activities was that families were involved at no extra cost and in a manner that did not differentiate between those who were poor and those who were able to make some kind of contribution.

It is important not to assume that poor or homeless parents do not want to or cannot be involved in the program. They can be asked, without placing pressure on them, if they want to accompany the children on a field trip or help with serving lunch. One problem is that parent meetings held during evening hours often require that parents pay for a babysitter. Meetings during afternoon hours, with child care and food provided—if this is possible—are more likely to be attended.

Sometimes the centre can be a focal point for meeting with other parents in similar circumstances, for providing information about services and resources, or for simply providing a meeting place that is safe and where parents will be accepted and respected. This can be a most meaningful form of support. More important, these strategies may become coping devices for the families involved. Providing parents with this kind of framework can result in a sharing of resources and mutual support.

> **Tips for Providing a Sense of Security to Young Children**
>
> 1. Provide a homelike environment with private areas and personal space.
> 2. Provide consistent routines and preparation for transitions.
> 3. Assure children that there is plenty of food at mealtimes.
> 4. Never use food as a reward, punishment, or play item.
> 5. Provide a consistent place for each child's cot at naptime and extra attention when needed to help children settle.
> 6. Provide an appropriate number of toy choices and help children decide.
> 7. Provide open-ended materials.
> 8. Ensure that each child receives some individual attention and that all children participate in small-group experiences.
> 9. Enlist volunteers (when appropriate) to provide more adult–child interaction.
> 10. Develop a relationship with the children by helping them to feel welcome, appreciated, and safe.

Beyond the Centre

At the beginning of this book we described the family as a system that affects and is affected by other systems in society. The well-being of children is ultimately linked to the well-being of the family, and the well-being of families is inextricably connected to such societal factors as employment, housing, neighbourhoods, child care, and social assistance. Increasingly, experts in early childhood are pointing out the need to go beyond caring for children and families within the confines of the centre and to advocate actively for the eradication of poverty.

Early childhood educators should keep abreast of progress on eliminating poverty on a local, provincial, and national level. (Check the websites recommended at the end of this chapter.) There are many organizations committed to reducing poverty in Canada—find one that fits your values and beliefs, whether it be a religious organization, a not-for-profit organization (such as the National Anti-Poverty Organization), or a charity. Early childhood educators could join advocacy efforts through their local and national professional organizations. As well, writing letters to editors, seeking media coverage, and writing to legislators about the problems of poverty are among the more specific strategies. Early childhood educator organizations might try to network with other professions, for example social workers, to develop a broad-based coalition, and could enlist community and business leaders to support the cause. As with any kind of advocacy and activism, early childhood educators must be well prepared and have accurate and up-to-date information at both the local and the national level.

Early childhood educators play a critical role in the lives of young children—all children, but especially children facing adversity. Along with awareness, educators need confidence in their abilities and the increasingly important role they play in the lives of children and families.

Conclusion

This chapter has explored the many dimensions of poverty and how each of these dimensions may affect families. Poverty has profound effects on family structure and parenting and puts every family member at risk. Families exist within a societal framework and are, therefore, affected by their neighbourhood, the available supports, and the quality of child care.

Caregivers can play a major role in providing support to children living in poverty and to their families. Regardless of our own experiences with poverty, our beliefs about its causes, and our opinions about dealing with it, we must acknowledge the urgency of the problem and the need to find solutions for the children in our care and the children of future generations as well.

Chapter Summary

- Despite Canada's wealth, 1.2 million children—that is, one child out of every six—still live in poverty.

- Children make up the largest group of poor in Canada. The rates of poverty in First Nations communities are higher than in any other group in Canada. As well, women, particularly single-parent women, tend to be poor.

- Poverty is a complex, multidimensional phenomenon that affects the physical and sociological health of individuals, parents, and communities at large.

- Poor children don't do as well as their peers on any measure of achievement or physical and mental health.

- Child-care services can provide support to parents by offering a comfortable, nonjudgmental space for parents to meet and share resources.

- Child-care services can support children who are poor by providing consistency, individual attention, and by being sensitive to some of the special needs of poor and homeless children.

- Early childhood educators should work toward the reduction or elimination of poverty on a wider system level, through individual advocacy and the combined efforts of organizations and associations that are committed to ending child poverty in Canada.

Recommended Websites

Myths about poverty:
http://childcarecanada.org/documents/child-care-news/04/08/poor-bashing-never-answer-ca

Addressing poverty:
www.kickaction.ca/en/national_antipoverty_organization_napo

www.campaign2000.ca

www.whypoverty.net

Child and Family Canada:
www.cccf-fcsge.ca

Child Care Canada:
www.childcarecanada.org

Stats & Facts, Canadian Council on Social Development:
www.ccsd.ca/factsheets

Videos/Films

Family Motel. 2007. 80 min. This NFB film concerns an immigrant family that is homeless in Ottawa. www.nfb.ca/webextension/family-motel

Exercises

1. Write one paragraph summarizing your feelings about each of the following:
   a) parents who bring their children to the centre poorly dressed and hungry
   b) parents who spend social assistance money to smoke, drink, and play bingo
   c) parents who are social-assistance recipients

   Now write a brief analysis of your own attitudes toward poor people.

2. Brainstorm ideas about how you could help a child feel safe and secure in your centre. Review the chapter, list all the ideas suggested, and then add your own.

3. Help a child create a personal space of his or her own by using a cardboard box big enough for the child to crawl into. Make the box comfortable with a pillow or rug, cut out windows and possibly a "door" for privacy. Take some pictures of the child, family members, and friends, and let the child paste them to the walls. Provide a flashlight, books or tapes, or other objects that will help make the child feel comfortable.

4. Provide a "personal bag" for every child in the program to store his or her treasures.

5. Research your community for resources that may be available for families living in poverty. Make sure to check the cost before recommending ideas (e.g., it may be better to recommend a babysitting co-op than paid babysitters).

6. Consider ideas for exchanges and sharing that the child-care centre could initiate or be a part of (e.g., clothing exchanges, buying bulk foods, making meals).

7. Check your local library or bookstore for books that may be suitable for children or their parents.

8. Check the Internet to find groups that advocate ending child poverty in Canada. What responsibility do early childhood educators have in addressing the problem of poverty in Canada?

A Death in the Family

chapter 14

Objectives

- To describe the impact that a death in the family has on family members.
- To explore how the grief process occurs for children and adults.
- To discuss the importance of helping children cope with a death in the family.
- To highlight the role of early childhood educators when a death occurs in the family.

> Sylvia was a 4-year-old girl whose father was tragically killed in a car accident. He had been a musician who performed in bands during evening hours and had played a major role in her care and nurture during the day. For several months, Sylvia would play "funeral" in the doll corner. It was a daily ritual, to which she would invite the other children in the child-care centre. One day Marie, the early childhood educator, said to her supervisor, "That child has a problem. She seems so morbid." The supervisor reflected for a moment. She had noticed that when Sylvia first began enacting the funeral, her face was tense and it was obvious that she was deeply distressed. As time passed, the funeral play became lighter, and Sylvia clearly enjoyed arranging flowers, singing, and telling the other children where to sit. In the end, the supervisor told Marie that Sylvia's play seemed a healthy and natural way of coping with her father's death.

Despite North Americans' long life expectancy, many children in preschool programs do in fact experience the death of a loved one. It could be the loss of a grandparent or, less commonly, a parent or sibling; the death could be the result of violence, accident, or illness. For many children, even the loss of a pet can be devastating. Responses to death are influenced, in part, by the nature of the relationship with the deceased. It would not be exaggerating to say that the experience of losing an intimate family member has a profound and pervasive effect on the entire family that often lasts for many years. In addition, religion and cultural beliefs play a major role in people's conception of death.

Discussing death often causes discomfort. In many parts of our modern world, deaths occur in hospitals, away from the family (Walter, 2010). Although there has been a movement toward hospice care, in search of a "good death," some authors suggest that societal discomfort with death is still evident in the way dying people are often treated (Walter, 2010). Many people today have never witnessed the death of a person, and just thinking about that image can be stressful. Death today is considered an unnatural event or accident (Walter, 2010). Television provides confusing images of death (Woodthorpe, 2010). Cartoon characters die yet regularly rise again for the next blow. News shows flash endless images of death, so much so that we may have become desensitized or fail to understand the true meaning of what is perhaps the most traumatic event in the course of a family's lifespan.

Perspectives

Glenna is an Aboriginal social work student at a community college. During a discussion of grief counselling, she described how death is explained to young children in the Stoney culture.

"In the old days, children were kept away from the person making his final journey. Children were not told about death. They were forbidden to attend the wake services and the burial grounds. They never looked at a deceased person.

"The purpose of not telling a child about death was to alleviate the disturbing emotions and to respect our traditions. It was said that a child's soul is sacred, and therefore children should not be near a dead person, for the dead may be in need of a holy soul to lean on. Once the soul has been dominated by the dead spirit, the child's spirit will be possessed through eternity. The only way to bring the child's spirit back into the body is for a powerful medicine man to perform a sacred ceremony, which our forefathers say isn't easy; only some are successful. Therefore, children were kept away from the dead person during the two nights and three days of the wake service and right up until after the body was buried.

"Nowadays, since we're living in a new generation and shifting into a new style of life, this kind of tradition can't be maintained. Some people who prefer to attend church services take their children with them. There a child learns about our Saviour, how He died and His promise of a new world, a paradise called Heaven where all the nations in this world will eventually meet. Children realize that the dead aren't living in the ground permanently, but are merely awaiting His calling.

"But for some who still practise the traditions, some things have changed. Upon the loss of a loved one, the eldest member of a family—someone well respected—is the one who does the explaining to the children. It must be done before the children can look at the deceased, or even before they hear about it from someone else. If children hear from another person, they say, they will have ambivalent feelings, and it will take a long time before the children accept the loss or heal."

Social Aspects of Death

Death often has an impact on the family life that goes beyond the members' emotional responses. If a spouse dies, the family income can decrease significantly. Many widows slide into poverty when their husbands die. Men often experience more difficulties since they typically rely on their wives for emotional support. Feelings of loneliness and social isolation and a perceived need for major changes in lifestyle often accompany the loss of a spouse (Anderson, 2010). A long illness before a death can deplete the family resources and take an emotional toll. The death of a grandparent can result in a number of changes in the family, particularly when the surviving grandparent cannot live on his or her own.

Unclear Norms Regarding Death

People sometimes don't know how to behave when there is a death in the family. In our society, there are few guidelines or rules concerning appropriate length of time for mourning, dress, behaviour, and remarriage (Anderson, 2010; Walter, 2010). Grief is allowed only at specific times, usually in private (Jenkinson, 2004; Walter, 2010). Some would say that society does not recognize the individual's right or need to grieve or the child's capacity to grieve (Murray et al., 2005). The lack of norms is even more noticeable for nontraditional families: Cohabiting partners or same-sex couples may feel that, although their grief is as intense as that of a traditional spouse, they lack the support of the community.

The death of an unborn child through miscarriage or stillbirth is another area where people are uncertain of how to respond. For the parents (sometimes only for the mother), the loss of a fetus may be as devastating as the death of any other close family member. The mother may experience extreme guilt along with many other emotions associated with grieving. The parents often feel isolated in their grief because family members and friends did not have a chance to know the baby, and therefore they do not feel the loss in the same way.

And whatever guidelines do exist have not kept pace with social changes, as illustrated in the following example.

Scenario

Who Goes to the Funeral?

Leslie had been divorced from Norman for two years. They had two teenage children, Anna and Peter. Norman remarried a year after the divorce and had a child with his new wife, but he maintained regular contact with his teenage children. Shortly after the birth of this new child, Norman was in a tragic accident and died. His children, Anna and Peter, were devastated and wanted their mother, Norman's ex-wife, to accompany them to the funeral. Norman's widow did not want Leslie to attend. Leslie felt that, even though she was the ex-wife, she, too, had lost the father of her children and her ex-spouse. "There is no acceptable way for an ex-wife to mourn," claimed Leslie.

Adult Psychological Responses to Grief

Kübler-Ross (1974) identifies five stages in the grieving process: denial, anger, bargaining, depression, and acceptance. Her work has been widely accepted in the field, and, although modified somewhat, it is also used to help understand what people go through when they experience the loss of a loved one (Quine & Pahl, 1987). The stages identified by Kübler-Ross have often been interpreted as distinct phases that succeed one another until the process of grieving is complete. But human beings rarely follow precise formulas, and this is especially true for people in acute emotional pain. Grief reactions are highly individual; they may occur in different sequences, and the components of the grief response can occur and reoccur in an unpredictable fashion (Anderson, 2010). Certain events can evoke strong emotions and grief years after the death has occurred. Bearing in mind the reservations about categorizing into stages, it might be helpful to understand some of the most salient components of responses to grief.

Shock and Denial

Shock usually refers to the initial reaction following the death of somebody close. Some refer to this stage as denial. Essentially, this initial response to a death involves feeling numb or not being able to believe that the death has occurred. One man said that as he was coming up the steps to his apartment after his wife's funeral, he was expecting her to be at the door so that he could tell her who attended. This response can be likened to a physical response of those in shock. The feeling of pain occurs only when the shock subsides.

Anger and Protest

The second stage of grief is described as that of anger, protest, or guilt. The anger is often directed at the person who died ("Why did you leave me?"), at the doctor or nurse who cared for the deceased ("They didn't do enough!"), at the person who caused the accident (e.g., drunk driver), or at oneself ("Why didn't I make sure he kept to his diet?"). In this stage of grief, the mourner may cry a lot, have a difficult time sleeping, and try to "bargain" to get the loved one back.

Bargaining

Bargaining is perhaps easier to understand before the death has occurred. Please directed at God, at the dying person, or at the doctor may include statements such as "Please just let him live to see his daughter graduate," or "Please let him live and we'll never fight again." These kinds of bargaining thoughts do occur more often before a death than after.

Depression and Despair

A period of despair or depression is common among those in mourning. This experience often involves feeling apathetic, being disorganized, and lacking purpose and direction. Behaviour sometimes regresses, and people in this stage of mourning may want to sleep excessively. Feelings of hopelessness and helplessness are common.

Adjustment and Acceptance

In the adjustment phase, people begin to feel a sense of hope and some mastery over their lives again. They begin to loosen the psychological ties with the deceased and to reorganize their lives. In this stage, people attempt to find ways to maintain the memories of their deceased loved ones while moving forward with their own lives. With this adjustment and with time comes acceptance.

Children's Responses to Death

Children's grief responses may be different from those of the adult (Webb & Doka, 2010; Willis, 2004). Their different cognitive abilities and relative lack of experience limit their understanding of death and thus their response to it. Concepts of irreversibility, finality, causality, and inevitability need to be understood to comprehend death fully (Webb & Doka, 2010).

In earlier generations, it was common for children to be present when a family member died, to participate in the funeral preparations, and to be involved in the funeral itself. Children in modern society, by contrast, do not have much opportunity to experience death naturally as part of the life cycle of families or in nature (Webb & Doka, 2010). They often live away from older relatives, and when deaths do occur they are often in hospitals, where children are not allowed to be present (Jenkinson, 2004). Children miss out on what happens and subsequently miss many of the rituals associated with death.

Scenario

The Naturalness of Death

An older student told the following story to a class of young early childhood students. "I grew up on a farm with my family and grandparents. When I was 3 and 4 years old, I always napped in the afternoons with Grandpa in the parlour. My grandfather died when I was 4, and, as was customary at the time, he was laid to rest in a coffin in the parlour for the three days prior to the funeral. On each of those three days, I crawled in with him to continue our tradition of napping together." The students were aghast at this tale, but the one who told it replied that at that time death was a natural thing handled in a natural way by all members of the family.

Scenario

Don't Hide Death from Children

Marylea had a 4-year-old and a 2-year-old when the family dog began to suffer from the effects of old age. Marylea and her husband thought the best course of action would be to put the dog to sleep before its suffering became unbearable. Unable to tell the children, they made the appointment, carried through, and then told the children that the dog had run away. For weeks, the two heartbroken children frantically searched for the dog. Marylea realized that she hadn't done anyone a favour, and that taking the easy way out wasn't always the best way.

Many adults find it difficult to explain death to children, either because they think children should not have to think about death or because their own conception of death is unclear. Yet adults often underestimate children's capacity to understand or empathize (Webb & Doka, 2010). Children often talk about death in a much less inhibited fashion than adults do, *until* they learn that death is not a topic for discussion or that it is improper. In fact, children are naturally curious about death (Way, 2010). They are fascinated by dead insects, they pretend to kill each other, and they may enjoy retelling morbid descriptions of worms eating the eyeballs of a corpse, for instance. This is children's way of learning about what happens, and about the irreversibility and permanence of death. When children are denied these opportunities, or when a dead pet is immediately replaced, they are deprived of an opportunity that helps them understand and cope with death.

Children's Developmental Understanding of Death

Babies and Toddlers

The way children perceive death depends largely on their developmental level (Way, 2010; Willis, 2004). Babies have no understanding of death per se, but from a very early age they will be disturbed by being separated from a family member to whom they had an attachment (Way, 2010), as evidenced in their behaviour (e.g., poor eating and sleeping, increased crying, more difficulty settling). Toddlers seem to relate to a deceased member of a family more in terms of missing someone who is no longer around rather than by attaching any particular meaning to death. Generally, children under the age of 3 sense an absence or miss a family person.

Preschoolers

Many preschoolers, on the other hand, understand death in specific, concrete terms (Himebauch et al., 2008; Willis, 2004). They typically use "one-variable thinking"—that is, they take one factor out of what has been explained to them and identify it as the cause of death.

Preschoolers cannot understand the finality of death and tend to believe that the dead person or animal will come back and be able to move again (Himebauch et al., 2008; McEntire, 2003). They lack time concepts, and researchers have suggested that the concept of death develops for children along with the concept of time. Children do not understand *forever*. They believe that death is reversible, and they talk about the deceased person as if he or she were still alive. Another characteristic of preschoolers is their fascination with details, which is sometimes disconcerting for adults, who view this as morbid curiosity. Typical questions children may ask include "How will Gramma be able to go to the bathroom?" "How will she stay warm?" "Does she have her glasses to see?" Such questions reflect young children's natural curiosity about all the concrete and practical aspects of death. Young children need to ask questions over and over again and to revisit feelings and thoughts through each new stage of development (Himebauch et al., 2008). It is through this repetition that they come to understand death.

> A student relayed the following story regarding her early experience with death:
>
> When my grandma died, my mom told me that her mother had "gone to work." I was 4 years old at the time and didn't really think about what that meant—it just meant that Grandma wasn't around to spend time with me. When I was in grade 1, my mom announced that she was going to work. I remember being scared and pretty confused—when Grandma went to work she never came back—but at 6, I understood a little bit more about death than I did when I was 4.

Young children may, egocentrically, assume they are responsible—that their thoughts and feelings have caused this event. Preschool children may also associate particular places with death. For example, they often think that hospitals cause death.

Is Death Forever?

A 6-year-old boy named Lucas watched a television drama in which the main character, a 9-year-old boy, died of AIDS. Lucas was moved by the show and asked his parents many questions about death and dying. Three weeks later, he was watching a weekly television serial in which the same actor appeared. Lucas couldn't understand how the boy could be dead and then alive again. Perhaps death didn't really last forever as his mother had told him. Lucas's mother realized that he was confused and that she'd have to explain death to him once again.

Preschoolers, like Sylvia in this chapter's opening vignette, often act out the funeral or dying in pretend play. Although this may seem morbid, it is a natural way of attempting to understand, to make sense of what has happened. Preschoolers may also exhibit what is referred to as the "short sadness span." They may be extremely sad when they hear of the death but then seem to forget about it shortly after, often while engaged in play. Then hours, days, or even weeks later, they will display signs of sadness again. These types of reactions are typical for this age group.

While the typical grieving stages described previously occur in children as well as adults (Willis, 2004), children often have specific responses that adults should be aware of. The shock or denial typical of the adult grief response may look like the child's inability to comprehend finality. "Mommy will come home" is something that would not be uncommon for a 5-year-old child to believe. A death in the family may cause certain bodily reactions, such as stomachaches, lack of appetite, headaches, or changes in sleeping habits. Loss may also evoke a sense of loss of security. As a result, preschoolers may become clingy or more demanding (Himebauch et al., 2008). Regression to earlier behaviour may also occur—for example, thumb-sucking, bedwetting, or the need for a security item (Silverman & Kelly, 2009). A child's anger is often directed at the loved one who died, and he or she may make such comments as "Mommy is bad for dying," or "I hate her."

Young children are also at risk of feeling responsibility or guilt (Silverman & Kelly, 2009), thinking, for example, "Daddy died because I was bad." Children who are beginning to understand the finality of death may be stricken with feelings of genuine panic, wondering who will love them and care for them. Children may also idealize the family member who has died. For example, a child may remember his mother as being "perfect in every way." This, of course, makes it very difficult for someone else to attempt to fill the role of the deceased person.

5- to 9-Year-Old Children

Children between the ages of 5 and 9 begin to understand that death is permanent and irreversible, but they think it only happens to others. For example, some children in this age group think that old people die because they cannot run fast enough when "Mr. Death" approaches (Silverman & Kelly, 2009). Children will still have fears about death. Children at this age are often very curious about details.

10 Years Old to Adolescence

About the age of 10, children come to understand the finality, irreversibility, inevitability, and causality of death (Balk & Corr, 2009; McEntire, 2003) because they are now beginning to think in abstract terms (Balk & Corr, 2009). They realize that death is a natural part of life. At this age, children are vulnerable to the effects of the loss and are also likely to understand the family problems that result from a death, such as the loss of income, a move to a new neighbourhood, and the effect of the death on other family members (Balk & Corr, 2009). Yet children at this age, like younger children, rarely have the resources, abilities, or independence required to give them some sense of relief from their grief. They cannot simply decide that they want to spend time with a friend, for example, and make arrangements on their own to do so. Such arrangements would require involving family members who are often too busy to respond to the requests of the child.

Grieving in Children

Young children may display three additional reactions. In the first stage, they test reality until they come to accept the fact that the person has died. For example, the child may continue to get Grandpa's fishing rod ready at the beginning of fishing season. In the second stage, children deal with memories. They may want to hear stories about the deceased and look at their pictures over and over. In the third stage, children may look for someone to replace the dead person. More than occasionally, a child might look for a family member or friend to take the place of the deceased. One mother related the story of how her 5-year-old asked the gardener if he could come and be the new daddy.

Many people believe that children should not be told or be given details of the death because it will upset them or they won't understand, or because they are trying to protect them (Balk & Corr, 2009; Jenkinson, 2004). Others believe that children will adjust more smoothly when they know, understand, and have the opportunity to cope (Hamilton, 1998). Grieving must be learned and practised. Furthermore, Goldman (1996) argues that information can help reduce the fear children may experience.

The Family Dynamics of Grieving and Mourning

Grief is not only a personal process, but a family one. Many things change in the family system with the death of a family member, including the family roles. Often an older (but sometimes not old enough) son takes on some of the father's role. Sometimes a grandparent or other relative will step in temporarily or permanently. The death will sometimes fan the flames of hostility and rivalries within the family. We have all heard horror stories about siblings fighting over their inheritance, for example. For professionals involved with grieving families, however, the most significant factor can be illustrated in the following anecdote, told by a 30-year-old woman.

Scenario

Can Those Who Mourn Comfort Each Other?

"I got along very well with my mother. She was always supportive of me, and as I got older, I was happy to offer a shoulder to cry on when she was in need. When my father died I thought it made a lot of sense for us to spend time together, since we both loved him dearly. But as time went on I felt that, rather than providing comfort to each other, we were getting on each other's nerves. Then I realized that we were both so involved in our own grief that we weren't able to reach out and provide each other with the support we both expected to receive."

In other words, we must remember that a death in the family will likely affect each member deeply and that it may be very difficult for family members, even when the relationship between them is strong, to provide each other with the support they require. This may have a negative effect on the parent–child relationship.

When children are reacting to the death of a loved one, their close family members are likely also in mourning. They may not be emotionally available or may be too preoccupied with their own grief to provide the children with the support they need. Sometimes, parents may even feel that children should be protected from the harsh reality of death and the grief it brings (Jenkinson, 2004). Or they might believe that the child would not understand even if the situation were explained, or that the child may ask the parents to respond to such inevitable, difficult questions as "Will I die?" or "Will you die?" When children ask the same questions over and over, parents assume they don't understand. This reluctance to explain or to confront the issue squarely can contribute to the child's confusion. Although children feel the death of a loved one intensely, their grief spans are short and intermittent. While it is uncommon to see adults act lightheartedly soon after the death of loved one, children do move in and out of mourning. They may be extremely sad, and then shift quickly into a play situation. Parents often misinterpret this behaviour as confirming the belief that children are less capable of feeling and understanding the loss. Attention-seeking behaviour and withdrawal are similarly misinterpreted. Yet the depth of the grief children experience should not be underestimated or ignored.

The Role of the Early Childhood Educator

When a death occurs in the family of one of the children in your care, there is much that you, as an early childhood educator, can do to help both the child and the family. In this instance, it is particularly important to understand how your own views and feelings about death can affect your ability to provide support (Holland, 2008).

Scenario

The Fear of Showing Grief

A class of early childhood students volunteered for a play program for young children with disabilities. One of the children in the program was Arial, a 4-year-old girl with cerebral palsy. This little girl was often sick, and she died after the sixth week of the program. The students decided to go to the funeral together; however, Valerie, the student who'd worked most closely with Arial and who had babysat for her family, refused to attend, feeling she couldn't handle it. After the service, the parents graciously thanked each student for coming and noticed that Valerie wasn't there. When they asked about her, one of the students explained that Valerie hadn't come because was afraid she'd find the funeral overwhelming. The parents looked surprised and replied, "What about us?"

Dealing with families who are grieving can often bring one's own grief issues to the surface. For example, one early childhood educator confessed that she had great difficulty dealing with a family who had lost a child. After counselling, this woman realized that she still had many unresolved feelings about her own miscarriage. Early childhood educators who possess this self-awareness will be better able to provide empathy and support to families, as well as concrete suggestions that will help parents deal with their children during this stressful and confusing time. Perhaps most important, parents will appreciate any extra efforts made by the early childhood educator to help their child at a time when their own grief has affected their ability to meet the challenges of parenting.

Examine Your Attitudes

The scenario about Sylvia at the beginning of this chapter indicates that some adults are uncomfortable discussing death. If this is the case with you, it could impede your ability to help others who are grieving. Early childhood educators working with children and families should be aware of their own feelings about death and dying.

Answering the following questions might help to clarify your own thoughts and fears about death. If your answers indicate a high level of discomfort with the subject of death, you may wish to consider this in the context of professional development. Open and thoughtful discussions with counsellors, religious leaders, friends, and family members often help to alleviate much of the fear and discomfort people feel about death.

- Does the topic of death frighten you, or do you find it interesting to speculate about death and what it means?
- Have you ever experienced the death of a loved one? If so, did you attend the funeral or did you avoid it?
- Do you think children should be sheltered from the reality of death and kept from attending funerals?
- Are you disturbed by the physical degeneration of a lingering death and by the intellectual degeneration that often accompanies old age? Or do you think death could be an interesting experience?
- Do you view death as a release from earthly suffering, or does the idea of not thinking or feeling after death frighten you?
- Would you prefer to be told if you had a fatal disease, or would you rather be kept in ignorance for as long as possible?

Supporting Parents

Early childhood educators, like everyone else, may feel uncomfortable in approaching the subject of death with a parent. Yet simply by offering condolences and expressions of empathy, they can help parents to feel supported. A simple exchange like "Hi, Mrs. Dixon, I was sorry to hear of your mother's death. This must be a difficult time for you. Please let us know if there's anything we can do to help you" is much better than avoiding the issue, as we are often tempted to do. Some parents may respond by talking about their feelings, while others may acknowledge this offer of sympathy with a simple thank-you or nod of the head.

Although early childhood educators are not therapists and should not attempt grief counselling, they can listen with empathy. If parents seem to require more than this, or even if they seem to need extensive periods of time to talk, they should be referred to religious or counselling agencies. If a grief reaction seems too prolonged or too intense, it may be better to consult with a professional counsellor. Again, educators need to be aware of their boundaries in working with parents.

Often, early childhood educators can help by taking care of the technical details. They may ask another parent to drive the child home or prepare snacks for the day. Sometimes when people are in crisis situations, every small detail seems like a tremendous burden. Having an extra pair of hands may be just as welcome as the emotional support early childhood educators can provide.

Helping Parents Help Their Children

Early childhood educators should understand how children may respond to a death in the family, and they should also understand how caring adults can help children to cope with death. Sharing this information with parents can be extremely important. Two points should be remembered, however. First, for many people death is a taboo subject or, at the very minimum, causes discomfort. Therefore, parents may not ask for information at a time when they need it most. Second, even if this information is shared with parents, their own grief responses may interfere with their ability to apply it. Therefore, the early childhood educator may need to communicate information in a variety of ways—for example, through modelling and discussions, or by providing books and pamphlets on the subject.

At the same time, early childhood educators may need to understand and empathize with parents who may not be able to interact optimally with their children because of their grief. The two main areas that parents may want information about from early childhood educators are (a) how to talk to children about death and (b) what to do about children attending the funeral.

Talking to Children About Death

Open communication is the most effective way to deal with death (Willis, 2004). When children are included in the grieving process and participate in associated rituals, they gain a better understanding of death (Jenkinson, 2004). Young children need rituals and tangible ways to express their grief. A common mistake adults make is assuming that children should not be exposed to discussions about death because it will upset them. However, when children are left out of these conversations, their imagination often takes over, and what they imagine may be more frightening than the truth. Therefore, when children are helped to understand how and why a person died, their fears may actually be alleviated. In addition, children should not be required to withhold their feelings (e.g., tears).

Many adults are unsure of how they should talk about death with children (Willis, 2004). Adults will inevitably bring to their explanation their own thoughts and feelings about the subject. Cultural and religious factors also play an important role in determining how we perceive death. Not only do we have to be aware of our own perceptions, we also have to take care to be sensitive to the various cultural contexts in which children and their families might be experiencing grief (Corr & Balk, 2009). The following points may serve as useful guidelines in many cases.

Explain Death as Part of the Life Cycle

Children seem to appreciate the logic when death is explained as part of the life cycle of all creatures and as something that is therefore inevitable. Many children's stories about animals, plants, and people support this theme. This explanation may help to curb children's fears and guilt—they may stop feeling that someone, either themselves or the bogeyman, was directly responsible for the death. Children do, however, need some assurance that it is unlikely they will die soon. It is truthful to tell children that usually people die only when they are very old, and that children (and their parents) will not be old for a long time.

Avoid Euphemisms

Adults often speak about delicate or taboo subjects by using euphemisms. That is, they use vague and inoffensive terms to substitute for the actual word. These ambiguous responses may create confusion or fear for the child (Edgar-Bailey & Kress, 2010; Fearnley, 2010). Death has been described to many children, for example, as "a long sleep" or "a long journey." If a grandmother's death was referred to as "a long journey," can you imagine how frightened a child might be the next time her mother goes on a business trip? Children may become fearful of getting sick if they were told that Granny died because she was sick. It is difficult for children to sort out the difference between serious and common illnesses. Therefore, early childhood educators would be best to talk about death using accurate words. Using *died* is more understandable than *passed away* or other euphemisms.

Encourage Talking

In a discussion of death with children, early childhood educators should bear in mind children's curiosity and fascination with details, and establish an environment in which children feel free to ask any questions they may need answered. It is acceptable for adults to admit that they don't have all the answers. Educators should try to answer children's questions as honestly as possible, even if the response is "I don't know" or "Some people believe that . . ." or "Let's ask your dad when he picks you up." Differences in religious or cultural beliefs may be handled in this way.

To prevent mixed messages, early childhood educators should maintain a dialogue with parents about what was said and what the child was told. Children do not need to understand the answers fully; just talking to them and letting them know that people will respond may be sufficient (Corr & Balk, 2009). Children need to know they can ask questions over and over again. Adults discussing death with children should bear in mind how much information children are able to integrate. Young children may create misconceptions about death. It may be helpful to stress certain points:

- The doctors could not prevent death.
- The person loved the child.
- The child is not responsible.
- The child is loved and cared for.
- All feelings are okay and the child may feel sad.

While children need the opportunity to discuss death and their fears about it, at the same time early childhood educators can encourage them to focus on the living and on the pleasant memories of the person they have lost. Reading and talking about books that deal with death can be an additional way for children to cope. Poling et al. (2008) suggest that children's literature is a place where children can seek consolation and gain recognition that death is a part of life.

Attending the Funeral

Often parents will ask early childhood educators whether they think the child should attend a funeral. Again, there will be differences of opinion based on culture, religion, and the particular circumstances of the families involved (Jenkinson, 2004; Silverman, 2009). We noted earlier that children often have vivid imaginations. Sometimes actually seeing a dead person or attending a funeral is much less frightening to children than the images they may create in their imagination. Fantasies of reunions or of dead people coming back to life are often minimized with funeral attendance. A funeral is an event full of tradition and ritual in most cultures and a time for family gathering (Ward, 2006), and children need rituals to help them cope (Corr & Balk, 2009).

Scenario

Saying Goodbye

Jonathan was 5 years old when his grandmother died. Although he knew she was very sick and had seen her the day before at the hospital, it surprised him very much when his mother told him that Grandma had died. His first question was "Are you sure she's stopped breathing and her heart isn't thumping?" His mother tried to assure him that the doctors had checked all this. Jonathan still felt very unsure and cried that he needed to see for himself before she was buried. His mother brought him to the funeral home before the service and was amazed at the coolness he displayed while looking at his deceased grandmother. He touched her hand and face and placed his small hand over her heart to check if it was still thumping. He nodded his head and said a prayer. As he and his mother were leaving, Jonathan asked if he could just go back and say one more goodbye on his own. Upon arriving home, the first thing he told his father was that Grandma was okay because he had checked everything. He had experienced a meaningful closure.

Seeing the mourners express their emotions may help children express their emotions as well. The funeral is a means of sharing memories among family and friends. Children can observe this and participate in the sharing of memories. Being part of this release may help children realize that they are not alone in their feelings.

Attending the funeral may also help children to say their final goodbye to a loved one, since this is typically the culturally accepted way of saying farewell. This culturally accepted ritual can be very important for children to participate in.

Scenario

Not Attending the Funeral Can Be Painful

In a discussion of death in an early childhood classroom, students were asked if they remembered attending funerals when they were young. Many students recalled the funeral as a sad but memorable experience. Others claimed that their most vivid memories were of not being allowed to go to the funeral, and of the resentment they felt for not getting the opportunity to participate in the final goodbye. Many of these students reported years later that the anger, sadness, and fears they felt about the person's death were heightened by their not attending the funeral.

Preparing for the Child's Attendance at the Funeral

Children attending funerals should be prepared in advance in age-appropriate ways (Silverman, 2009). They can be told what the funeral setting will look like, how people may be acting/grieving, and whether the deceased will be buried or cremated. Since the people who normally provide support for the child may be consumed by their own grief at the funeral, it may be appropriate for the child to be accompanied by an adult who is less directly and emotionally involved and who will be able to provide the child with support. Children are unlikely to be able to sit still throughout an entire service; they may need to leave to go to the bathroom, or to go outside to run around for a bit. Children need to know that it is okay for them to cry or to leave if they need to. If such arrangements can be made beforehand, the child is likely to benefit from the experience.

Remember that you, as educators, may also be experiencing death in a personal way and have your own feelings to cope with, as you will see in the following scenario:

Scenario

Grief Affects Us, Too

A part-time student who works in a child-care centre shared this story about the unexpected death of the mother of a 5-year-old boy. The boy had been in the centre since he was a baby, and his older brother had been there as well, so the news of the mother's death came as a shock; it was a traumatic event for all the staff. The centre decided to close for the afternoon of the funeral, and all parents were given advance notice of the closure. One father read the notice, became very angry, and demanded that that centre find alternative care for his 5-year-old. The student and her team partner stood in shock and did not know how to respond, which only made the father angrier. The student felt she hadn't handled the situation well, but commented, "I was dealing with a 5-year-old little boy who'd lost his mom, I was dealing with his dad who'd lost his wife, and I was dealing with my own feelings about losing someone who'd I interacted with every day."

Alternatives to Funeral Attendance

When children decide not to attend the funeral, they need to be supported in that decision. A caring adult can arrange a "special ceremony" for the child. For example, one child made a special scrapbook about his grandfather. Another made a bouquet to take to the grave; another planted flowers. Children often have their own ideas about how they want to remember a loved one, and a caring adult can help them to implement those ideas.

Helping the Children in the Centre

Most families will find comfort in the fact that their child's needs are being met by concerned and caring early childhood educators. A child who is mourning may require some extra attention, a few moments longer in the educator's lap, or extra flexibility at naptime and at other transitions during the day. Educators need to remember that the child may be reacting directly to the loss of a loved one, to a changed atmosphere at home, and to the parents' distress.

The stability provided by the centre's routine and the warm interaction with early childhood educators are extremely important. In addition, guidelines are listed below for early childhood educators to follow in helping children understand death and in working with children who are mourning the loss of a loved one.

Helping Children Cope with Death

1. Listen carefully to children as they talk about death. Try to understand their conceptions and misconceptions. When children do not talk, reassure them that you are available if they have questions or want to talk or just need a cuddle. We all avoid topics that we find uncomfortable, and a special effort needs to be made to ensure that we are not discouraging children, either through our body language or by avoidance of the subject altogether.

2. Try not to be overprotective of children. Whether it is seeing a dead bird or overhearing an adult conversation about someone who died, these experiences can be used to enhance the child's understanding of death.

3. In explaining death, avoid euphemisms such as *gone on a trip, lost,* or *sleeping.* Children take such terms literally and may become fearful of sleeping or going on trips, or, if it sounds beautiful, children may want to join the deceased person. It is best to use the terms *dead* or *died* and, if necessary, explain to the young child what that means in a physical sense. For example, "Grampa's heart isn't beating anymore; he can't breathe."

4. Support the attendance of children at funerals, unless there are religious or other factors that prohibit this. Ongoing discussion and collaboration with parents is necessary to clarify such a matter.

5. Be aware of children's short grief span, and ensure that this is not mis-interpreted as denial. Ensure that parents also understand how children grieve to prevent misinterpretation of a child's behaviour.

6. Be aware of hidden fears, such as Grandma dying in the hospital, which may cause the child to think he or she will die if hospitalized. Explain the circumstances of the death, such as a serious illness, old age, a car acci-dent, etc. Also, children need information and reassurance about what would happen and who would care for them if their parents died.

7. Consider developmentally appropriate information—give the child as much as he or she wants and is able to handle. Check regularly if the child needs or wants more (Invest in Kids, 2003).

8. While children should be encouraged to share their feelings, they should not be pressured to do so. Give children permission to feel sad or con-fused, or to cry if that is what they want to do, or to go and play if they want to. We must take care not to interpret a child's feelings incorrectly. For instance, a little boy may be crying because another child took the ball away from him. We must not assume that those are tears of sadness due to his uncle's death.

9. Provide children with many opportunities to express themselves through play or creative expression, such as art or music. Books and stories about

death that are developmentally appropriate should be available to but not imposed on children (Goodwin & Davidson, 1991). Parents may also find such resources valuable in explaining concepts to their child. Let parents know about any good, age-appropriate resources.

10. When adults working with children have firm beliefs about death and the afterlife, they must be cautious not to impose them on others. Children may come from families with very different belief systems, and early childhood educators must treat all of their beliefs with the utmost respect. Collaboration with the child's parents will be necessary, and early childhood educators should encourage them to share their beliefs with their children (Goodwin & Davidson, 1991). If you are unfamiliar with the specific traditions of mourning in a different culture, be sure to ask about them. Most people would rather be asked what is appropriate in their culture, and they will probably appreciate your interest. Parents may not always realize that your customs and beliefs differ from their own.

11. Remember that there is no universally accepted way to grieve and mourn, and that people vary widely in the time it takes to recover. In modern society we have few built-in rituals to help with our mourning, and there often seems to be a rush to "get back to normal." Families and children may need more time than is formally allotted (compassionate leave at work, etc.) to recover from their loss. The patience and ongoing support of those who care about the bereaved family will be appreciated.

12. Perhaps most important, you should remember the tremendous impact that a death in the family can have on every family member. Early childhood educators might want to go that extra mile for a bereaved family. For example, you could allow for extra flexibility in arrival and pickup times or agree to be flexible in the centre's rules in other ways that would make things easier for the grieving family.

Source: "Includes" material from Canadian Child Day Care Federation, n.d.Helping children undersatnd death. By G. Garvie. Resource Sheet No. 10. Ottawa: Canadian Child Day Care Federation.

Conclusion

The death of a family member usually begins a period of crisis in the lives of the surviving family members. The time following a death will be a time of mourning for all. Children may understand death in different ways than adults do and may behave in different ways. Early childhood educators must put the child's reactions into a developmental context to better understand and help children to cope. Children need rituals, so participating in ceremonies and traditions like funerals and memorial services can often help children overcome their fears and misconceptions about death. The early childhood educator can play a valuable role not only in providing support to children, but also in assisting parents in their interactions with their young children.

Chapter Summary

- Early childhood educators need to be aware of the impact that death has on all family members, especially children.
- It is important that early childhood educators understand grieving in children and adults.
- Early childhood educators can better understand children's reactions based on development.
- Early childhood educators should consider ways to help children cope and should assist parents to help their children as well.

Recommended Websites

Canadian Child Care Federation:
www.cccf-fcsge.ca

Health Canada:
www.hc-sc.gc.ca/index_e.html

Helping Your Child Deal with Death:
http://kidshealth.org/parent/positive/talk/death.html

Exercises

1. Discuss death and burial rituals with a number of different people from different cultural backgrounds. Compare their traditions and their beliefs with your own.

2. Discuss death and funeral attendance with a number of people. Do they have pleasant or unpleasant memories? Can they explain why? How has it affected their beliefs today?

3. Practise what you might say in response to a 3-year-old's questions about death. What if the same questions were asked by a 5-year-old? How would your answers differ?

4. If one child in your playroom experienced a death, what would your response be to the other children? Would you tell them? Would you talk about it? Would you let the parents know?

5. Check your local community for people who may be able to provide information or expertise in dealing with death (e.g., mental health agencies, funeral directors). Check whether the information is suitable for children under the age of 5 and whether the professionals working there have experience with young children. Many professionals specialize in grieving but may not have expertise in applying it to young children. Funeral directors also often have information specifically related to young children and families.

6. The resource sheet "Helping Children Understand Death," published by the Canadian Child Day Care Federation in order to aid parents, makes the following suggestion:

    > Touring a neighbourhood funeral home and/or cemetery can be an excellent way to give your child accurate information about what happens to the body after death and the funeral process. Many funeral directors are experienced in answering children's questions, and often parents find such a tour extremely informative and interesting as well.

    Discuss this with your classmates and colleagues. Would you consider this? Why or why not?

Violence and Abuse in the Home

chapter 15

Objectives

- **To examine different types of abuse and neglect of children.**

- **To examine the myths and characteristics associated with the perpetrators and the victims of abuse.**

- **To examine the role of the early childhood educator in monitoring and reporting abuse.**

- **To examine the role of the early childhood educator in preventing abuse.**

- **To describe strategies for supporting children who are neglected or abused.**

- **To examine the role of the early childhood educator in supporting families in which abuse and neglect occur.**

> After I saw the bruises on Johnny's buttocks, I thought I'd faint when his father walked into the room at the end of the day. I wanted to scream at him, "How dare you hurt this innocent child!" Instead, I took a deep breath and approached him as calmly as I could. "Good morning, Mr. Smith," I said. "Would you please come with me to Mrs. Atari's [the director's] office? There's something she'd like to discuss with you." I accompanied him to the director's office door; then I left. But I couldn't do anything when I got back into the playroom. I was trembling so much that I couldn't even speak.

The most difficult aspect of being a member of the early childhood profession is coming face to face with child abuse. Child abuse strikes at the very core of our professional commitment to children's well-being. It is in polar opposition to all we believe about how children should be nurtured, respected, and protected. At the moment when we discover that parents have hurt one of their children, the idea of being accepting and nonjudgmental can seem like nothing more than a meaningless theory. In many cases, the signs may be ambiguous and it may require a long process to discover abuse. This is a fundamental concern in child welfare intervention—there is no universal way to define abuse or maltreatment, nor is there one accepted framework for intervention (Stith et al., 2008; Ward, 2006).

Although in many jurisdictions adults are legally compelled to report incidences of abuse, educators must decide when it is appropriate to seek and provide families and children with additional support, either from the centre or from community resources, and when child protection is required. This process and decision can be agonizing for even the most seasoned professional.

Violence and abuse within the family are not new phenomena. Abuse and maltreatment have existed throughout history and across cultures (Child Welfare Information Gateway, 2006). Statistics suggest that 78% of reported instances of assault were allegedly committed by parents (Child Welfare Information Gateway, 2004). Sometimes it seems as if violence within the home is more prevalent in today's society than in the past. However, the increase may be attributed to the increase in attention abuse has received, in people's willingness to discuss it, and in the availability of better reporting procedures. We should note, however, that family violence is still under-reported (Stith et al., 2008; Vanier Institute, 2004) and that prevalence rates with children continue to be difficult to determine because children are dependent on others to detect and report on their behalf. Children younger than 5 are over-represented among young people living with domestic violence (Baker & Cunningham, 2007), and while the prevalence of abuse is reportedly four times higher for young girls, young boys are more likely to experience physical injuries (as opposed to emotional or sexual abuse) (Statistics Canada, 2006).

In this chapter, we will examine both abuse and neglect of children in the home and discuss their effects on the adults and children involved. Although the focus will be on violence directed toward children, any kind of violence and abuse within families (elder abuse, spousal abuse, sibling abuse) constitutes a serious problem with devastating and long-lasting effects on family members. It should also be clear that, even if children are not the direct victims, they are harmed as a consequence of any violent or abusive situation in a family. The chapter will close with a discussion of the role of the early childhood educator in relation to this very serious problem.

Below are some key points that will help deal with children who are exposed to violence:

- Ensure that you are up to date on policies and procedures for reporting abuse and protecting the children.
- When you think a child may be experiencing abuse but are not certain, consult with a peer or your manager, do not ignore your suspicions.
- Always report abuse promptly.
- Ensure that the child is provided with a nurturing and stable environment while in your care.
- Provide support to parents and provide information on community support services.
- Make certain that you have your own support network.
- involvement in with family violence can be emotionally draining for staff.

Defining Abuse and Maltreatment

To begin, we shall try to arrive at a clear and practical definition of the terms *violence, abuse,* and *maltreatment* since these words so often seem to be open to interpretation. What one person considers abuse (e.g., corporal punishment), another may consider an appropriate response to bad behaviour (Health and Welfare Canada, n.d.). Increased awareness of and sensitivity to cultural differences have raised many questions as to how to determine whether culturally sanctioned practices are legitimate forms of discipline (Ward, 2006).

Violence refers to action that is intended to bring physical harm to another person (Ward, 2006). These acts involve the use of force and intimidation. *Abuse* usually refers to a situation in which a more powerful person attempts to exert control over a less powerful person (Ward, 2006). Abuse includes any physical force that exceeds reasonable discipline. Abusers use threats and actions to maintain control over their victims, which results in physical or psychological harm to the child (Health and Welfare Canada, n.d.). *Maltreatment* refers to "intentional harm or endangerment of a child including unkindness, harshness, rejection, neglect, deprivation and/or violence (Berns, 2004, p. 160). *Neglect* refers to situations in which the child's needs are not met by the adult, which may interfere with the child's development.

Understanding Abuse

Different types of abuse have been defined in a variety of ways. Before looking at specific definitions, it's important to stress that one form of abuse seldom occurs in isolation. More often, two or more types of abuse occur simultaneously. Thus, although the categories of abuse can serve as guidelines, in certain cases we may need to use them in a flexible way (Berns, 2010). In addition, early childhood educators must be mindful that behaviours may be attributed to other factors, so it's important to consider the context and look for patterns of behaviour.

Abuse can be divided into the following categories:

1. *Physical abuse* means that deliberate force has been used on the child to cause physical harm. Physical abuse can occur with or without verbal abuse.

2. *Emotional abuse* involves depriving the child of affection, love, and acceptance. Verbal abuse, a common form of emotional abuse, entails belittling and humiliation. Emotional abuse may also include intimidation, exploitation, or terrorization.

3. *Sexual abuse* involves the sexual exploitation of individuals against their will. It may include touching, forcing the child to touch, or forcing sexual acts such as intercourse upon the child. It can occur by force, by tricking, or by threatening the child. It can include touching or non-touching (Berns, 2010), such as exposure to pornographic material or to the adult.

4. *Neglect* describes a situation in which the child's needs are not taken care of by the adult to such an extent that it interferes with the child's emotional or physical development (Health and Welfare Canada, n.d.). Physical neglect occurs when there is a failure to meet medical, dental, nutritional, sleep, or dress needs. Emotional neglect occurs when the child's needs to feel loved, worthy, and secure are not met. Neglect is the least likely of all forms of abuse to be reported (Berns, 2010; Health and Welfare Canada, n.d.) yet is the most common type of child abuse (Berns, 2010). Neglect typically receives less attention because it is less noticeable and the effects less obvious. Society continues to associate neglect with poverty (Berns, 2010), but neglect can exist without poverty.

Many documents are available that define and list indicators of abuse and neglect. The following example is from "Protocols for Handling Child Abuse and Neglect in Day-Care Services," published by Alberta Family and Social Services (2006). Indicators of abuse are given with descriptions of physical and emotional signs that may be detected in the child. Behaviours that you may see in the adult abuser are also listed. For instance, one of the most common signs of abuse or violence consists of the strained interaction between the abuser and the victim. An early childhood educator who knows a child well will usually notice if the child behaves strangely around certain adults, especially when the behaviour involves an obvious withdrawal from a person who is closely related to the child.

Child Abuse: What to Look For

Indicators of Neglect

The child may:

- be underweight, dehydrated, emaciated, or have a distended stomach
- show improvement of developmental delays following proper stimulation and care
- demonstrate signs of deprivation: cradle cap, severe diaper rash, diarrhea, vomiting, anemia, recurring respiratory problems
- be consistently dirty or dressed inappropriately for weather, or wear torn clothing
- often be hungry or thirsty
- often be tired or listless
- demand much physical contact and attention
- assume role of parent or adult in the family
- lack proper medical and dental care
- have poor hygiene
- have unattended medical or dental problems such as infected sores, decayed teeth, lack of needed glasses

The adult may:

- maintain a chaotic home life with little evidence of personal care routines
- not supervise child for long periods of time or not supervise when child is involved in potentially dangerous activity
- leave child in the care of inappropriate persons
- give child inappropriate food, drink, medicine
- consistently bring child early and pick up late
- be apathetic toward child's progress, be hard to reach by phone, and fail to keep appointments to discuss child and concerns
- overwork or exploit child
- show evidence of apathy, feelings of futility

Indicators of Physical Abuse

The physical signs might include:

- unexplained (or poorly explained) bruises and welts
- a number of scars in a regular pattern
- bruises of varying colours in the shape of an object (cord, rope, belt, buckle, clothes hanger)
- bald spots or missing teeth
- human bite marks
- unexplained burns, such as the following:
  - cigarette-shaped burns
  - immersion burns (e.g., glove-shaped, sock-shaped)
  - electric iron or burner-shaped burns
- unexplained (or poorly explained) fractures, sprains, dislocations, or head injuries
- inflamed tissue suggesting scalding
- symptoms of consumption of a poisonous, corrosive or nonmedical, mind-altering substance

The child may:

- be wary of physical contact with adults
- seem afraid of parent or other person
- be frightened in the face of adult disapproval
- be apprehensive when other children cry
- show extremes of behaviour–aggressive/withdrawn
- be over-anxious to please
- approach any adult including strangers
- be defensive about injuries
- have low self-esteem
- wear clothing that covers body even though the weather is warm
- not tolerate physical contact or touch
- run away often
- be unable to form good peer relationships
- be reluctant to undress when others are around

The adult may:

- be angry, impatient; frequently lose or almost lose control
- appear unconcerned about child's condition
- view child as bad or as the cause of life's problems

- resist discussion of child's condition or family situation
- view questions with suspicion
- use discipline inappropriate to child's age, condition, and situation
- offer illogical, contradictory, unconvincing, or no explanation of injuries
- show poor understanding of normal child development (e.g., may expect adult-like, mature behaviour from a young child)

Indicators of Sexual Abuse

Physical evidence of sexual abuse is rare. Often with young children, abuse is not intercourse but touching, which may leave no physical signs. Where physical evidence is present, it may be:

- torn, stained, or bloody clothing
- pain or itching in genital area or throat, difficulty going to bathroom or swallowing
- bruises, bleeding, or swelling of genital, rectal, or anal areas
- vaginal odour or discharge
- stomachaches, headaches, or other psychosomatic complaints

The child may:

- use language and make drawings that are sexually explicit
- fantasize excessively
- show fear of closed spaces
- resist undressing or diaper changes
- masturbate excessively
- exhibit seductive behaviour
- express premature or inappropriate understanding of sexual behaviour
- display inappropriate, unusual, or aggressive sexual behaviour with peers or toys
- be excessively curious about sexual matters or genitalia of others or self
- wet pants (in a previously trained child)
- soil pants
- have eating disturbances (over-eating or under-eating)
- have fears/compulsive behaviour
- have school problems or significant changes in school performance
- display age-inappropriate behaviour, pseudo-maturity or regressive behaviour, such as bed-wetting and thumb-sucking
- be unable to concentrate

- have sleep disturbances, such as nightmares, fear of falling asleep, and sleeping long hours

The adult may:

- often be domineering but emotionally weak
- suggest or indicate marital or relationship difficulties with adults
- indicate own social isolation, loneliness, especially as a single parent
- cling to child, both physically and emotionally; hold and touch the child in an inappropriate way
- tend to blame others for life's problems and child's sexual behaviour—may even accuse child of causing sexual abuse

Indicators of Emotional Abuse

Child's appearance may not indicate or suggest the extent of the difficulty. The child may appear clean, well-groomed and well-nourished. Child's facial expression and body carriage may indicate sadness, depression, timidity, or held-back anger.

The child may:

- appear overly compliant, passive, shy
- show episodes of very aggressive, demanding, and angry behaviour
- fear failure, have trouble concentrating or learning, and give up easily
- be either boastful or negative about self
- constantly apologize
- cry without provocation
- be excessively demanding of adult attention

The adult may:

- blame or belittle child in public and at home
- withhold comfort when child is frightened or distressed
- treat other children in the family differently and better, showing more acceptance and love and less criticism
- tend to describe child in negative ways: "stupid," "bad," "trouble-maker"; and predict failure for child
- hold child responsible for parent's difficulties and disappointments
- identify child with disliked relatives

Source: Alberta Human Services, "Protocols for Handling Child Abuse and Neglect in Child Care Services," January, 2006. Reprinted with permission.

Early childhood educators should try to find a publication that provides written guidelines and other information for their own use and use by others in the child-care centre. These are often available from local child welfare offices, which provide specific information related to local legislation. In addition, national associations and clearinghouses that disseminate information exist in both Canada and the United States. Documents such as the one quoted above are intended to be used only as guides. Many of the indicators listed above characterize children who are experiencing problems yet are not abused or neglected. Therefore, it is important to be tentative about conclusions and open to new information. It is particularly important to consult with local child welfare agencies or other specialists in child abuse when suspicions of abuse arise.

Why Abuse Occurs

In this section, we will attempt to highlight some common characteristics associated with child abuse. Note that some of the characteristics focus on attributes of the abuser, while others focus on social conditions that make abuse more likely to happen. Abuse involves an interplay of characteristics and events and typically not just one factor (Administration on Children, Youth, and Families, 2008).

Social Conditions Associated with Abuse

Statistics suggest that the majority of abuse occurs in low-income homes (Administration on Children, Youth, and Families, 2008; Child Welfare Information Gateway, 2006). This may occur due to the large number of stressors involved in living in poverty, but some researchers have suggested that such a disproportionate representation may reflect the fact that abuse in low-income families is much more likely to be reported than that in middle- or high-income families, possibly because low-income families are more likely to be involved with social service agencies, or they may have fewer support systems to rely on, or people may simply be more willing to report such families (Administration on Children, Youth, and Families, 2008).

Research indicates that children in single-parent homes are also at a higher risk (Ambert, 2009; Child Welfare Information Gateway, 2006). There are two plausible and interrelated explanations for this phenomenon, both of them based on the ecological approach. First, the single parent experiences a high degree of stress in meeting the demands of child-rearing alone. Second, stress levels are further aggravated because many single parents live in deprived economic conditions. This is but one example of how economic and social factors may interact to produce conditions in which the probability of abuse is high.

As discussed earlier, families move through life stages just as each individual does within the family unit. As children grow and develop, they may challenge parents and parenting skills in new ways. Parents' ability to cope may be compromised, which may be one factor leading to abuse (McDaniel & Tepperman, 2007). When families experience stress (e.g., poverty, single parenting), children's challenging behaviour may increase, further compromising parents' ways of coping (Ambert, 2009).

Other social factors associated with abuse are social values and norms of behaviour. Cultural traditions do exist that condone and even contribute to family violence (Este & Tachble, 2009). Such traditions are strong in societies in which men are taught that they are in control and have the right to control others, especially their wives and children (Este & Tachble, 2009).

Nita is a 32-year-old married woman with two preschool-age children. She shared this story in an early childhood class she was taking in the evenings.

"My parents emigrated from Lebanon and worked very hard to set up a business and raise a family in Canada. I have two older brothers and three younger sisters. We've always been a close family, keeping our religious and cultural heritage in this new country. Just like back home, my father was the undisputed head of the house—he demanded respect and obedience, he set out all the rules according to tradition, and he dished out the discipline.

"I can't say when the abuse started; I can always remember being hit by my father when something went wrong or when I was bad. I know that my brothers and sisters were beat up too, but we never, never talked about it, because it was something that happened at home and stayed at home. I do remember that my father began to abuse me sexually when I was 12 years old. I never told anyone; it was his right as the head of the house, or so we were told. I think my mother knew, because she started to ignore me and was really distant. He came to my bed at night until I was 16 and couldn't stand it any more. I ran away from home and the small community we lived in to the big city. I worked the streets for a few years—what the heck, I'd been doing it since I was 12, and now guys would pay me money and they were nice, too.

"One day I was in the welfare office and met this really nice guy named Nick. He was in bad shape, too, and trying to start all over, so we tried together.

"That was five years ago. Now we're married, Nick works full-time as a baker, and we have two children. Domenica is 19 months and Marguerite is 3 years old. I still see my family, except for my father. Funny, everybody knew what Dad was doing, and he was doing the same thing to my sisters.

"I haven't talked about this much and haven't got any professional help. Maybe someday I will. But one thing I know for certain is that those things will never, never happen to my children. I'll never let my children go through the hurt like I did, and I'll do anything to make sure that it doesn't happen. My hurting will never go away, but it will always be a reminder of what kind of parent I should be."

Personal Attributes of the Abuser

Abuse is a complex issue, and there is no one factor that leads to it but rather multiple sources of stress that affect parents' ability to provide for their children.

Many myths surround abusers and victims of abuse. The two most common myths are that abusers fit one particular profile and that their victims somehow asked for or deserved the abuse. Both myths are untrue.

Abusive adults do, in fact, come from every walk of life—from every cultural group, socio-economic level, and educational background. No single description or profile fits all abusers. They do, however, share some common characteristics.

First, abusers who use physical force tend to be male, and their victims tend to be women and children. Power continues to be the cornerstone for violence (Ambert, 2006), which may be attributed to a number of factors. Fathers have always been perceived as more authoritarian than mothers. When it becomes evident that the use of violence can be effective in gaining and maintaining control of both women and children, its use is perpetuated. Again, there may be cultural sanctioning of the use of force in abusing women or disciplining children (Ambert, 2006; Este & Tachble, 2009). Women, on the other hand, are more likely to engage in corporal punishment (e.g., spanking) (Ambert, 2006).

Possible explanations for why some mothers abuse their children or allow their children to be abused by their partners focus on the relative lack of power and control some women experience. Many women continue to live in situations in which they themselves are abused because they are financially dependent or have been socialized to believe that they cannot make it on their own (McDaniel & Tepperman, 2007). Women are also often socialized to believe that their relationship with their spouse is the most important thing that can happen in their lives and that they are responsible for its success (McDaniel & Tepperman, 2007). Although gender differences cannot adequately explain abuse, the socialization of men and women in our culture does contribute.

The second common characteristic of abusers is that they frequently have difficulty dealing with their emotions (Eshleman & Wilson, 1995). Men have been socialized to believe that displays of violence are normal and to be expected.

A third characteristic of abusers is that they often blame other people or external situations for the violence they cause (Drakich & Guberman, 1988). For example, stress, alcohol, work, a messy house, or noisy children may trigger a violent reaction when they arrive home at the end of the day.

High Stress Levels and Few Coping Mechanisms

Abusive adults, whether they are mothers or fathers, tend to be under a great deal of stress (Dixon, 2009). Stress may come from events at work, at home, or from any other source. In addition, abusive people have few resources for coping with stress (Guterman et al., 2009; Seng & Prinz, 2008). Abusers tend to be more socially isolated and have fewer connections (Seng & Prinz, 2008). They often lack access to good support systems, and even if they do they seem reluctant to use them (Health and Welfare Canada, n.d.). Lack of social support, inadequate means of coping with stress, and the perceived cultural support for the use of force in disciplining children can all contribute to the creation and perpetuation of abuse within families (Guterman et al., 2009; Seng & Prinz, 2008).

Part of the Abuse Cycle

Researchers have established that the majority of abusive adults were themselves abused as children. In addition, researchers have found that violence and family turmoil are reproduced across generations of mothers and daughters, in what some researchers believe to be an "emotional archive" of gendered violence (Kenway & Fahey, 2008). The rate of abuse among those abused as children is 30%, which is significantly higher than the 2% expected in the general population. It may be that children learn that violence is an apparently effective way to solve problems, or it may be that, as children, many abusive adults were made to feel unloved, unworthy, and unwanted (Health and Welfare Canada, n.d.). They perpetuate this self-perception when they become adults by abusing others, thus reinforcing to themselves that they are no good. Perhaps they had poor role models as children or they are unable to meet the needs of their child just as their needs were unmet by their parents (Dixon et al., 2009).

However, not all abused children go on to abuse their own children or spouses; and in fact, others suggest that there is not an increase in subsequent generations (Ambert, 2006). These studies conclude that the transmission of violence is complex and that many dimensions are likely relevant, not just that abusers were themselves abused as children.

Poor Parenting Skills

Abusive parents often think of parenting as stressful and have difficulty understanding the child's perception of the world (Stith et al., 2008). They may believe that they have little control over their children. When the parent uses force or violence to control, there are immediate short-term effects (i.e., the problematic behaviour ceases), but they do not consider the long-term negative effects. The child misbehaves again and the parent uses force to control the situation once more, with the amount of force possibly increasing. This often leads to the creation of more stress and less control in parenting, and before long, the cycle of abuse has become established within the home.

Abusive parents often have unrealistic expectations about their child's development and behaviour (Berns, 2010; Palusci et al., 2007). They demand physical, social, and emotional abilities that are well beyond the child's developmental stage (e.g., demanding that the toddler not cry when Mommy leaves or expecting a baby to sleep through the night). When the child does not display these expected abilities, the parents may feel further frustration or they may look upon abuse as the discipline necessary to ensure compliance. Inappropriate parenting is characterized as being based on parents' needs, and so they accordingly ignore the child's needs, do not provide basic care or support, and use extreme discipline methods (Berns, 2010; Palusci, 2008).

Relationship Problems

Sexual abuse is more likely to occur with family members than it is with strangers (McDaniel & Tepperman, 2007). In fact, it is far more common for children, especially girls, to be sexually abused by a person that they know and trust (McDaniel & Tepperman, 2007). There are some common characteristics of families in which sexual abuse occurs. The adult is usually isolated and has difficulty in relationships in general but predominantly in emotional and sexual relationships. As well, abuse is more likely to occur in families that are socially isolated and appear very close and traditional. They often have poor communication patterns and blurred boundaries between family subsystems, with role confusion or reversal. Parents in abusive homes tend to suffer from emotional deprivation and are therefore emotionally needy. Sexual abuse usually occurs in situations where there is some form of inequality; for instance, males typically abuse younger females.

Characteristics of Victims of Abuse

Vulnerability

Children who are subjected to abuse also display particular characteristics. They usually know their abuser and may have an emotional relationship with that person. In the case of sexual abuse, the abuser may be the only person to show the child affection, making the child more vulnerable to being taken advantage of. Children have been taught to obey and be polite to adults, and not to question their actions or behaviour. In addition, children are generally unable to protect themselves from an adult, particularly one using physical force. Many abused children do not have well-developed social and emotional relationships with other people. This lack of support makes them feel isolated. All of these factors leave the child highly vulnerable to abuse.

Special Needs

Research indicates that children who have special needs are more likely to be abused (Sullivan et al., 2009). This includes children who have developmental delays, physical disabilities, or chronic health problems, or whose temperaments make them difficult to raise (Sullivan et al., 2009). Children living in foster or adoptive homes and those living with blended families or single parents (especially when the child was not wanted) are also at a higher risk for abuse (Health and Welfare Canada, n.d.).

Witness to Violence

In the past, it was thought that children living in families with inter-parental violence were simply witnesses of the violence; however, it has been found that "children actively interpret, attempt to predict and assess their roles in causing the violence. They may worry about consequences and take measures to protect themselves both physically and emotionally" (Baker & Cunningham, 2007, p. 199).

Children may be the victims of abuse when they are directly involved in or when they are observers of domestic violence (Baker & Cunningham, 2007). Children who witness violence in the home are more likely to display aggressive behaviour, and witnessing parental violence can shape gender roles in young children. They may pick up messages from violence that shape their definition of what it means to be female or male, such as that men deserve to get what they want, or that women should be submissive (Baker & Cunningham, 2007). In addition, children who witness domestic violence can develop negative beliefs about themselves, become isolated from support, internalize the abuse, and come to believe that inter-parental violence is "normal" (Baker & Cunningham, 2007). One study noted that young children may be flooded with such emotions as anger, fear, or grief, and may cry, act out, throw temper tantrums, or demonstrate other behaviours that are disruptive and problematic (Baker & Cunningham, 2007). Often (although not necessarily) inter-parental violence is coupled with poverty and substance abuse, which can heighten the effects of violence (Baker & Cunningham, 2007; O'Campo et al., 2009).

Children have no ability to remove themselves from the situation. They are typically not cared for, either physically or psychologically. Such children no longer perceive the home as a safe refuge. Parents, experiencing their own struggles, may be less available to the child at a time when the child is likely in need of increased emotional support. Many parenting roles may be unavailable to the child when parents are concerned with their own basic safety, so neglect may be the result (Baker & Cunningham, 2007). In addition, children witnessing abuse between parents may wonder who can be trusted or loved. Children may not understand why their lives are different from others' or why they have family secrets, can't bring friends home, or have no one to protect them.

Children living with domestic abuse will often experience physical health problems, such as weight, eating, or sleeping problems; acting-out behaviours; low self-concept; anxiety; aggression; social isolation; or difficulties interacting with other children (Ambert, 2006). Children who live in high-conflict homes tend to respond to conflict more readily and with more intensity. Whereas boys tend to react more externally (e.g., with aggression and behavioural outbursts), girls tend to react with anxiety and depression. Children who have been abused often have an uncanny ability to adapt and to perceive the mood, feelings, and needs of significant others in their immediate environment and then act accordingly (O'Campo et al., 2009). Children have also been labelled as hyper vigilant—that is, constantly maintaining vigilance over their environment so that they are prepared. Although this may be adaptive at home, it may interfere with learning (e.g., in school where the child maintains vigilance over the environment rather than focusing on the task at hand).

Developmental Effects of Child Abuse

Exposure to violence in the home has long-term effects on child development (Ambert, 2006; Hornor, 2008). Children who have been exposed to sexual and physical abuse or high rates of inter-parental violence report lower IQs, lower reading ability, increased rates of depression, low self-esteem, and increased alcohol and drug usage in adolescence and adulthood (O'Campo et al., 2009). They may feel shame and isolation and be unable to talk to anyone (Hornor, 2008). The abuser may have told them to be silent, that no one will believe them anyway, or may have threatened them (Health and Welfare Canada, n.d.). Children have demonstrated increased rates of negative and aggressive behaviour, antisocial behaviour, withdrawal, depression, fearfulness, and disruptions in eating and sleeping patterns (Christoffersen & DePanfilis, 2009). They may also experience nightmares, bedwetting, difficulties controlling emotions, insecurity, fears, or anxiety (Christoffersen & DePanfilis, 2009).

While school-age children have the ability to develop coping mechanisms, preschool-age children are more limited since they have not yet developed the cognitive capacities necessary for problem-focused or action-oriented coping. They are in the stage of cognitive development where they make sense of the world through generalizations, basic levels of categorization, and concrete thinking, so instead of being able to cope effectively, they must rely on mental and behavioural disengagement (Baker & Cunningham, 2007). In addition, because they are still developing their language skills, they are hyper-attuned to nonverbal communication, such as tone of voice, noises, or crying (Baker & Cunningham, 2007).

Scenario

Stormy Monday

A new early childhood educator was starting in the child-care centre on a Monday morning. A 5-year-old who had just been dropped off by his mother began acting out. He threw his backpack and coat to the floor, kicked the articles around, lay down, and began to kick the floor. Other violent behaviour followed. The staff appeared to be watching but not reacting to this display. When the new educator questioned what was going on, the child's educator replied, "It's Monday." Further probing revealed that the child's mother had been a victim of spousal abuse for a long period of time. This was a typical display of behaviour for the child after having been home for two full days on the weekend and witnessing the violence.

Disruptions in development occur when children are victims of abuse. Infants may have difficulty developing a sense of trust when their parents are unable to provide consistent, predictable care (Wallach, 1997). Continual abuse produces chronic stress. Over the long term, children will have to deal with the loss of self-esteem, trust, and security in their family life and with the reinforcement of inappropriate means of dealing with stress and problems in their own lives. As discussed earlier, children may become hyper vigilant and overreact to threats or perceived threats in their environment (Hornor, 2008). Children often become passive as they learn that being quiet/invisible helps to avoid abuse (Gilbert, 1995). Regression is common, as are poor peer relationships (Gilbert et al., 1995).

The effects of abuse are far-reaching and have serious consequences on the child's future development, possibly resulting in criminal activities, mental health problems, or developmental delays (Currie & Widon, 2009). We know that victims of abuse are at a higher risk of becoming abusers themselves, since they take their unmet needs from childhood to adulthood (Ambert, 2006; Hornor, 2008). And we must not forget that child abuse may result in the death of children. By understanding more about the abuser and the abused, the early childhood educator may be better able to assist the family through this crisis by not prejudging the abuser or blaming the victim. Understanding in a more objective way may help the early childhood educator provide support to the child and to the family.

Supporting Families

Throughout this book we have tried to highlight the interrelatedness of the well-being of the child with that of the family. Indeed, from the standpoint of the early childhood educator, support provided to families is based on the belief that such support will directly or indirectly contribute to the well-being of the child. In the case of child abuse, however, the equation becomes more complex. Supporting a family in which child abuse is occurring often begins with reporting the family to the appropriate authorities. This step can lead to legal action against the abuser that culminates in a prison sentence or the removal of the child from the abuser's care. While many families who are helped by professional intervention may ultimately come to thank the person who first reported the abuse, it is unlikely that most perpetrators of abuse will be pleased initially. Regardless of how the parents view such intervention, though, when a child's psychological or physical safety is at risk, early childhood educators have a moral and legal responsibility to intervene.

Scenario

Divided Loyalties

A young mother and her daughter's early childhood educator developed an excellent relationship over the two years when Jamie was in the child care. The mother had worked hard to overcome many of the difficulties associated with being a single working parent and was committed to taking excellent care of her daughter. One day, she told the educator that her boyfriend had hit Jamie and that she was worried he would do it again. She asked the educator to promise not to tell anyone, since this was the first serious relationship she had had in several years. She was sure that once her boyfriend got used to having a young child around, things would work out and her dreams of getting married would finally materialize.

Of course, the early childhood educator has an obligation to monitor and report if the abuse continues, but we cannot ignore how difficult this may be. It helps in this and similar situations to remind ourselves that protecting children must be our primary consideration, but also that reporting is often the first step in the long and painful process of helping, healing, and breaking the cycle of abuse.

Examine Your Attitudes

Do you agree or disagree with the following statements?

- Anyone who abuses children should be locked away.
- A parent who knows that abuse is occurring but does nothing deserves to be punished.
- Victims of abuse deserve what they get.
- I would report child abuse only when I was absolutely certain that abuse was occurring.

With your instructor as moderator, organize a classroom debate on these questions and be prepared to defend your responses.

Dealing with the Early Childhood Educator's Emotional Response to Abuse

For people involved with early childhood care, abuse evokes many deep emotions. Some early childhood educators experienced abuse as children, or they witnessed abuse. Coming into contact with an abusive parent, or a parent who allows abuse to occur, can trigger unresolved anger or feelings of helplessness. When this happens, it is very important to recognize and discuss these feelings with a counsellor or therapist. Even after successfully receiving treatment, people who have been abused often carry psychological wounds that require treatment at various times throughout their lives.

For people who have not experienced abuse, it is sometimes difficult to understand or empathize with the abuser or the victim. Accepting someone who abuses children is not easy for anyone to do, but it is especially difficult for those people who have chosen a career in early childhood education because of their strong commitment to children.

There is no easy solution to this dilemma. We maintain that it is important to remember several points. First, many characteristics, events, and experiences may contribute to abuse (e.g., stress, lack of support). Second, there are people who abuse, then feel deep sorrow, remorse, or feelings of failure; however, they feel powerless to change their behaviour. Accepting the perpetrator of abuse does not mean that we accept the abuse itself; it only means that we try to see him or her as someone in need of help, and who has the potential to be helped.

It is also sometimes very difficult not to blame an adult who is either a victim of abuse or does not actively prevent the abuse from happening. "How can she be so stupid?" we say. "Doesn't she care about her children?" Again, while protecting the child has to remain our top priority, trying to empathize with the victim or to understand the circumstances surrounding the situation is also important. Imagine what it would be like to live with such fear. Try to imagine how it would feel to have no safe place to run to. Try to imagine being raised in a situation where violence is considered normal. These and other considerations may help in developing empathy and may also help counter negative attitudes we might hold against the adult.

Strong negative feelings toward the abuser, lack of sympathy for the victim, or even blaming the victim are common attitudes that interfere when working with families in which violence occurs. Once again, it is important to remind ourselves that developing empathy and understanding is a process that is an ongoing part of professional development.

Monitoring Potentially Abusive Situations

When an early childhood educator suspects that a child is being abused or neglected, he or she must monitor and document the situation consistently. Systematic monitoring will help establish patterns for symptoms of abuse or neglect that are not immediately obvious. It may be the pattern or change of behaviour that is relevant. For example, the appearance of a bruise may provoke further observation and monitoring but not necessarily a reporting of the incident.

We must also take care not to judge too hastily. For example, could the impression of neglect we have formed be due to something as innocent as the child's desire for autonomy or the result of a simple lack of time on the parent's part? A boy may choose to wear summer clothing, such as shorts and a sleeveless top, in the middle of winter. We may misinterpret his quest for individuality here to mean that he does not have access to the appropriate clothing or that the parent is not paying sufficient attention to the child's well-being. Similarly, if a little girl arrives with her hair uncombed and face unwashed, this may be a result of nothing more than the parents' morning rush to work. When a child, however, is dressed in such a manner consistently, or his or her hygiene is so neglected that it poses a health risk, this needs to be monitored closely. We must be careful to maintain our objectivity and ensure that we focus on behaviour or situations that pose a real risk to the child. A careful record of each sign of abuse, giving the date, time of observation, and an accurate/objective description of the behaviour or symptom will be a crucial component of the assessment.

Bearing in mind that the well-being of the child is our primary concern, we must point out that often, if abusers suspect they are being monitored, they may withdraw the child from the centre. This often prolongs the abusive situation, since it may then go undetected for some time before the next child-care centre observes a situation or pattern of behaviour. Therefore, early childhood educators must not let on that the child is being monitored or that abuse is suspected until they have determined a plan of action. Being polite and acting as if all is well may not be easy, especially in light of the professional training that encourages open and honest relations with parents. Sometimes, however, this sort of conduct may be necessary and in the best interests of the child. During this time, seeking out and providing information or access to community supports may be crucial for this family.

Early childhood educators see young children every day. They see them in interaction with many different people, observe them as they engage in play, and are often involved in their personal care routines. From this vantage point, they can observe many things about the child. Educators need to document information on an ongoing basis in addition to making day-to-day observations. By doing this, the educator can make comparisons. For example, the educator is in a position to determine whether the child is unusually passive or pinpoint when the change of behaviour began. In addition, educators typically interact with a parent or parents on a regular basis. These interactions may also provide information regarding the relationship. Documentation will always be necessary if early childhood educators plan to report their suspicions to the authorities.

Reporting Abuse

It is not uncommon for early childhood educators to fail in reporting abuse for fear of making an inaccurate report, due to the lack of physical signs of abuse, or due to the feeling that child protective services do not help families (Peter, 2009). Despite these factors, the obligation to ensure the well-being of all children under our care must not be forgotten. Early childhood educators must remember that a report is a way to express concern and is not necessarily an accusation.

Child welfare legislation varies from province to province in Canada and is federally mandated in the United States. All states have mandatory reporting laws whereby professionals are required to report suspected cases of abuse to the child welfare authorities (Rankin & Ornstein, 2009). In addition, legislation has been put in place that specifically protects individuals with disability at home or in care (e.g., the Persons in Care Act in Alberta). Failure to do so can result in charges being laid against the child-care worker. In some places, complaints may be made on an anonymous basis. The authorities will then investigate and take further action if required. Some jurisdictions will require that the callers identify themselves, and in some cases early childhood educators are not legally bound to file a report. The intent of child welfare legislation also varies. In some areas, practices and procedures are in place to keep children with their families. The U.S. Adoption Assistance and Child Welfare Act, for example, is federal legislation with the primary goal of keeping families together. Parents are given a period of time (e.g., 18 months) to make efforts to get their lives in order or risk losing their children (Rankin & Ornstein, 2009). Supports are provided to the family, and the child is removed only as a last resort.

In other areas, legislation is written to protect children's immediate safety. In cases of suspected abuse, the child is removed from the home as soon as possible. When the courts deem that the family is ready, the child is returned to his or her parents. Laws and procedures vary from place to place. It is critical that early childhood educators be aware of local policies in order to protect the children and themselves. The National Center on Child Abuse and Neglect in the United States and the National Clearinghouse on Family Violence in Canada coordinate and circulate information regarding child abuse. These organizations are good starting points for early childhood educators to obtain more information.

The following box consists of an excerpt from the Alberta Social Services Protocols (2000), which provides an example of reporting practices in cases of suspected child abuse.

Reporting Protocol

When a person suspects a child is abused or neglected, the person must immediately report the situation to Child Welfare Services. Any person who fails to report is guilty of an offence and liable to a fine.

A person must report to Child Welfare Services regardless of how the information was obtained and regardless of advice or direction not to report.

Provide:
- name, age, birth date, sex, racial origin, and address of child concerned
- names and addresses of parents or guardians
- names and addresses of the alleged perpetrator (if known) and any other identifiable information about that person
- full details of the incident or situation that precipitated your report. Try to be specific; include details, events, or behaviours that have caused concern. Include any previous dated documentation you may have collected.

No action will be taken against the person reporting unless the reporting is done maliciously or without reasonable or probable grounds for the belief.

Source: Alberta Human Services, "Protocols for Handling Child Abuse and Neglect in Child Care Services," 2000. Reprinted with permission.

Early childhood educators often worry about repercussions after they report suspected abuse. A report can lead nowhere or action may not be immediate. Patience, careful observations, and regular documentation can be most helpful in ensuring that this is not the case. In these situations, early childhood educators will require support from their peers and supervisors.

Responding to the Child's Disclosure of Abuse

It is probably an early childhood educator's worst nightmare when a child confides that a family member is doing bad things to him or her. How do you, as an educator, respond? We have seen what the professional response should be with regard to documenting and reporting, but how do you respond to the child in your care? Early childhood educators play an extremely important role in this situation. The child will have many needs at this time to which the educator will want or need to respond. At the same time, educators should be extremely careful when communicating with the child about abuse to ensure that he or she does not receive the wrong message or that words are not put into the child's mouth. The following box provides tips for the early childhood educator to use in this delicate balancing act.

Responding to a Child's Disclosure of Abuse

Remember these general guidelines:

1. Ensure that all children have the opportunity to form a meaningful relationship with a caring adult (Hornor, 2008). This can give children the opportunity to learn that there are people who care about them. Children may feel more comfortable about confiding in someone if this relationship is established.

2. If a child begins to tell you about an abusive incident, the first thing to do is to listen. It is very likely that the abuser will have told the child not to tell anyone because no one will believe them anyway. By listening, you will let the child know that what he or she has to say is important. Listening may be enhanced by taking the child to a quiet place, away from the group, where you can listen without interruption.

3. Let the child tell you what has happened in his or her own words. Do not put words into the child's mouth by asking leading questions (e.g., "Did he hit you with his fist?"). If the incident is to be pursued by social workers or police, it will be questioned if the child uses an adult's vocabulary to describe events (Corwin, 1995).

4. Let the child know that you believe what he or she has said. Children rarely lie or make up details about abuse, particularly sexual abuse.

5. Reassure the child. Tell him or her that it was a good thing to tell somebody. Reassure the child that you will do something to help.

6. Do not make promises to the child. This may well be the hardest thing for the early childhood educator to do. Because educators feel a strong emotional bond and want to protect children from harm, their first reaction is to promise the child that they will fix the situation. The professional must not promise the child that the abuse will not happen again or that she will not tell. Children will often begin their disclosure by saying that this is a secret and that they will tell it only on that basis. The early childhood educator needs to let the child know that she will only tell to make sure that the child is helped and will only tell certain people (e.g., "I need to tell the director or the social worker, but I won't tell your mom"). Because this is so difficult for early childhood educators to do, it is important that they be aware of this potential hazard and of what their response might be. The consequence of making and then breaking promises will be particularly devastating for the child who has already lost trust in adults closest to him or her. For the sake of the child, this must be avoided.

7. As difficult as this may be, it is important to remain calm and in control of your emotions. If you express disgust or horror, children may think they cannot tell you all the details or may interpret your reaction as your belief that the abuse was their fault (e.g., "How could this happen? How could someone do this to you?"). Acknowledge the information and the child's feelings without overreacting to the situation.

8. Involve the supervisor as soon as possible to determine what the next step will be. This may require that a report be filed or that the child welfare authorities be contacted. Knowing the local regulations beforehand and having documentation available will be helpful at this stage when emotions may be running high. Early childhood educators may also require support for themselves and shouldn't feel that they have to deal with this on their own. You can discuss your feelings with colleagues or friends without disclosing confidential information.

9. Document, document, document. Document information on an ongoing basis.

10. If there are signs of severe abuse, call the police or child welfare authorities without delay.

Providing Ongoing Support to the Child

After the initial disclosure, early childhood educators will have to be available to deal with the child for a long time to come. Sometimes disclosure is just the beginning of a long and stressful process for the child and the family. Educators must ensure that they provide care and support throughout this period. The child's environment should remain as stable and consistent as possible, with regard to both the physical setting and the routines and expectations. The child and family may be going through many changes, and a stable setting may be of the utmost benefit to the child at this time (Hornor, 2008).

Children in this situation may need to be exposed to good role models so that they learn how to behave in nonviolent ways. Children will need to have contact with supportive adults who listen and allow them to express themselves. Having opportunities for self-expression in alternative ways, such as through art, music, and play, will be beneficial as well. Again, in all of these strategies, early childhood educators must be cautious and sensitive about how they approach and react to the child.

Working with Other Professionals

In situations of abuse, several professionals are usually involved, and it is vital that they work effectively together. For example, doctors, social workers, psychologists, and counsellors may all be involved at some point. From the beginning, early childhood educators must understand the role that each professional plays. Will the child welfare worker keep you informed? Does the therapist want observational data from you? How would the parent like you to be involved and in what ways? Educators may be able to provide parents with resources and written materials (e.g., books, stories, videos) either for their own use or to share with their child. The level and type of support expected from the early childhood educator should be clarified. The nature and degree of involvement required may change over time. Therefore, frequent communication among the different professionals may be necessary.

Ongoing Professional Development

All early childhood educators would certainly agree that abuse and violence in the home is the one issue they hope never to encounter. Unfortunately, such incidents continue, and the likelihood of working with a child from an abusive or violent home is, therefore, also increasing. Educators can best assist if they are informed about local policies and practices—through discussion within the agency, through workshops, or through guest presentations—and are prepared for such situations. When educators are trained and prepared, they are better able to assist and be supportive at a time when emotions are high and likely to interfere.

Accessing Expert Help

Adults who abuse children are in need of professional help that is beyond the scope of the early childhood educator. In any situation, educators must recognize when outside intervention is required and be prepared to refer families to qualified experts. Highly qualified therapists who specialize in working with family violence have a good success rate in helping these families. However, the role of early childhood educators must not be undervalued because it is they who often have regular, front-line contact with children and parents.

Preventing Abuse

One of the key roles of the early childhood educator is the prevention of abuse. This may happen in a number of different ways. Many programs are available to teach children to protect themselves from potential abusers. They provide advice on how to say no, how to report that they were approached, and how to avoid dangerous situations. These programs or kits have excited much controversy. Some say that they are necessary; others adamantly insist that the protection of children should remain the sole domain of their parents or guardians. The potential hazard with the kits currently in use is that they are not all developmentally appropriate.

Scenario

Stop, Danger!

The director of a child-care centre recounted how she had reluctantly agreed to let an expert on preventing abuse speak to the children at her centre. The expert told the children that, just as a red light means "stop, danger," when someone touches you and it doesn't feel right, it's like a red light. The 4-year-olds listened intently. The next day, one of the early childhood educators came dressed in a red sweater. "Stop, danger!" exclaimed the children. They had understood that red means danger, and the rest had gone over their heads.

Conclusion

Early childhood educators can play a role in the prevention of abuse. They may act as role models for parents by demonstrating guidance, nonviolent discipline techniques, and ways of interacting with children. For example, they can demonstrate how to give the young child choices rather than expecting unquestioning compliance.

Early childhood educators can also help by being aware of children's family situation and of stressful events that might be occurring in their lives. Knowing, for example, that the father has recently lost his job can be the signal that the family may be under additional stress and therefore needs more support. Developing and maintaining good parent–early childhood educator relationships before crises occur will be of the utmost importance in helping families feel comfortable in divulging such information.

As an early childhood educator, you may be able to create an atmosphere in which parents feel that they can confide in you when they are on the edge. Sometimes just being able to let off some steam may be sufficient, but there will also be times when families need extra help. Being familiar with community resources, such as emergency shelters, relief homes, support groups, and telephone hotlines, may be useful. If abuse is associated with other problems, other support groups and services may also be pertinent. These are the times when you may be called upon to go that extra mile to prevent a crisis (e.g., stay late, check out resources). When good relations exist, early childhood educators can serve as an excellent support for children and their families.

Recent brain research sends a much stronger message about the effects of abuse and neglect on children in the early years. Research clearly shows that the early years are pivotal for healthy brain development. In addition, prolonged stress or anxiety can lead to differences in how children's bodies handle stress. Early childhood educators, then, provide responsive child care to meet not only children's developmental needs but also to ensure healthy brain development.

Chapter Summary

- Early childhood educators need to be aware of the different types of abuse so that they know what to look for and document.

- Early childhood educators should consider their own attitudes toward abuse and family violence so as to better understand and support children and families. They must also understand their role in preventing, documenting, and reporting abuse.

- Early childhood educators need to understand the characteristics of both abusers and victims.

- Early childhood educators must develop an understanding of abuse, neglect, and maltreatment as well as an understanding of the conditions leading to abuse, of both the perpetrator and the victim of abuse.

Recommended Websites

Abuse Help Guide:
www.helpguide.org/mental/child_abuse_physical_emotional_sexual_neglect.htm

Child Welfare Information Gateway:
www.childwelfare.gov

Child Welfare League of America:
www.cwla.org

Child Trauma Academy:
www.childtrauma.org

Exercises

Based on the information in this chapter, review the following scenarios and discuss what you, as a director of a child-care centre, should do regarding reporting, responding to the child, and supporting the family.

Scenario

1

Bonnie (4 years old) comes from a nice home. She attends the centre regularly, is well fed, and very well dressed. Her parents are reliable with their payments and follow up any of the centre staff's requests, but they have little involvement with the staff otherwise.

When Bonnie is at the centre, she is often apathetic and withdrawn. At other times, she will overreact or misbehave to get attention. One day, Bonnie confides in her early childhood educator that when she goes home, she always eats, sleeps, and plays in a closet so that she is out of Mommy and Daddy's way.

Scenario

2

Matt's mom, Mrs. Benning, is usually one of the last parents to pick up her child. She has to take a bus to the centre and then take two more buses to get home. She is often very rushed and hurries to get Matt ready as soon as she gets in the door.

One day, Matt wants to show her what he has done at the art centre. Mrs. Benning says that she has no time and tells Matt to hurry up. Matt deliberately moves very slowly toward his coat. Mrs. Benning becomes enraged and crosses the room, yelling, "I'll show you what slow means!" and proceeds to spank him on his bottom five or six times. She then gives him a firm shaking, grabs his coat, and drags Matt from the room.

Scenario

3

The staff members in the playroom for 3-year-olds have told you, the director, that Drew's mother has come late to pick her up three times this month. Each time, they could smell liquor on her breath. They ask you to stay in the playroom until she arrives this Friday after work. When she enters the room, it is obvious that she has been drinking, and she yells to Drew to hurry up because she's missing the party.

4

Elaine is in the midst of a difficult separation from her husband. Her 5-year-old son, Shaun, has been unusually quiet and very reluctant to talk about what is happening at home. Late one afternoon, when most of the children have left, Shaun and the early childhood educator have just finished reading a story about a family of bears when Shaun remarks that he wishes his home was like that. When the early childhood educator asks him why, he explains that he wishes he could see his dad more and talk to his dad on the telephone and— At this point, his mother walks into the room and stares at Shaun. Shaun has a look of absolute terror on his face, covers his head with his arms, and then runs from the room in tears. Elaine declares that the conversation is over and never to be brought up again, and then leaves.

Working with Families

part

3

Early childhood educators have long recognized the importance and relevance of working with parents. The need to maintain positive parent-early childhood educator relationships has been studied and well documented in the literature. Working with parents and families provides one way of promoting resilience—by helping to minimize risks (e.g., through parenting sessions, modelling techniques and approaches) and by strengthening protective factors (e.g., accessing community supports for families). This section provides theoretical and practical knowledge focused specifically on collaborating with parents.

Chapter 16 examines different perspectives on parent involvement. This examination provides a conceptual framework that will help early childhood educators reflect on their own beliefs and practices.

Chapter 17 examines the potential sources of conflict and tension that can exist between parents and early childhood educators. Guidelines for preventing and solving conflicts are presented, showing that recognizing tension and its sources should be the first step in resolution.

Chapter 18 provides practical suggestions for collaborating with parents and determining which activities are likely to be most meaningful to a particular group of parents. In addition, Chapter 18 provides guidelines for evaluating the success of parent-staff collaboration.

chapter 16

Understanding Parent Involvement

Objectives

- **To clarify the meaning of parent involvement.**

- **To discuss the concept of parent education.**

- **To discuss the issues related to parental influence and control.**

- **To examine the importance of continuity of care.**

- **To consider the importance of supporting and empowering parents.**

- **To view parent involvement in the context of the family systems and ecological models.**

"I was an early childhood educator and a director in a child-care centre for several years and thought that I was quite an expert on parent involvement. Then I had my first baby and joined the ranks of all the struggling parents who juggle work, child care, and family. Parent involvement took on a very different meaning for me after I became a parent myself."

(Janet, an instructor in an early childhood education program)

Working with families, especially with parents, is widely accepted among early childhood educators as "an integral aspect of the early childhood teacher's job" (Galinsky, 1990, p. 2). The National Association for the Education of Young Children includes guidelines to help early childhood educators establish reciprocal relationships with families (Bredekamp & Copple, 1997). In addition, the Canadian Child Care Federation (1991) continues to cite the critical importance of parent partnerships in practice. Most training programs for early childhood educators, and most early childhood textbooks, contain at least one unit on working with parents. As well, close relationships between early childhood educators and parents improve the quality of care (Baker & Manfredi-Petitt, 2004) and are important in the prevention of problems

(Wilson, 2010). After all, a tense relationship between early childhood educators and families can impact the quality of care, especially the ability to form strong relationships with the child (Baker et al., 2004).

Family-centred practice, strengths-based or relationship-based practice, partnership with parents, collaboration with parents, and *parent involvement* are but a few of the terms we see repeatedly in the professional literature. Yet many early childhood educators admit that working with parents is frequently the most frustrating part of their job and the aspect they feel most unprepared for (Eldridge, 2002; Wilson, 2010).

Before we accept that we should work toward partnerships with parents, we should be able to answer three basic questions:

- What specifically are we attempting to achieve in our work with parents?
- Why is it important to achieve these particular goals?
- How can we ensure that we will achieve these goals?

A historical perspective can reveal to us where many of today's assumptions come from. Sometimes we accept models that worked in the past but that may not be appropriate under today's social conditions. For example, a common strategy for working with parents in the 1960s was to make home visits. Many well-researched programs (Bromwich, 1981; Lombard, 1994) have demonstrated the effectiveness of early childhood educators' providing education and support to parents through regular home visits. Most of these programs, though, were designed to serve families whose children were at risk of school failure because of environmental factors or handicapping conditions. Although past and present interest in home-visiting programs indicates that they can be successful in some circumstances, they may be more difficult for staff or parents in many child-care centres. Most parents with children in child care work during the day, and it can be difficult for educators to be available for home visits in the evening.

In the same way, many model early childhood programs that were begun in the 1970s included a parent-involvement component in which parents would regularly participate in a preschool setting as volunteers or as paid aides (Katz, 1994). Although this strategy has many potential benefits, it may not be feasible for many working parents to attend a child-care setting regularly unless their work schedules are extremely flexible.

As responsible early childhood educators, then, we need to carefully evaluate both the appropriateness and the effectiveness of different ways of working with families. To do this properly, we have to examine the usefulness of each proposed strategy from the perspective of staff, children, and parents.

Defining Parent Involvement

Most of the literature on parent involvement relates to four main goals: (1) to educate parents, (2) to provide parents with the opportunity to influence or control the programs in which their children are involved, (3) to provide for the greatest possible continuity of care between home and centre, and (4) to empower parents, a goal that has recently gained attention in the early childhood literature (Couchenour & Chrisman, 2011; Powell, 1989).

Underlying the goals of parent involvement is the desire to support parents in their child-rearing roles, not to parent ourselves. We want to ensure that parent involvement will benefit everyone in the early childhood programs—children, parents, and staff alike.

Professor Lillian Katz, who is the editor of ERIC Clearinghouse on Elementary and Early Childhood Education, has been a dominant force in early childhood education for over two decades. She was interviewed about her views on parent involvement, and her thoughts are summarized here.

Many educators pay lip service to the idea that all parents know their children best, while unfortunately, we too often see results of parenting that indicate otherwise.

Early childhood educators have knowledge about what is best for children and should be using this knowledge in their interaction with parents. We must have confidence in our knowledge and understanding. Just as a teacher stands before a classroom because she knows more about the subject matter than the students do, early childhood educators should have some authority, based on their knowledge, that comes into play in their interaction with parents.

Although the relationship with parents is important, the primary consideration of the early childhood educator should be what is best for the client rather than what makes the client happy, and the two do not always coincide.

Professor Douglas Powell has been studying parent–child-care relations since the 1970s. In his 1989 book, *Families and Early Childhood Programs*, he discusses differing views on parent involvement. Powell points out that widely varied views of the parental role in child care can be found both among early childhood educators and among parents. The commonly used term *partnership* is itself open to interpretation. Powell suggests that parents have parenting potential that should be supported by their child's early childhood educators. According to this view, "collaboration with parents is based on mutual respect and a desire to empower parents with information and roles that strengthen control of the environment" (Powell, 1989, pp. 19-20).

Parent Education

Parent education is probably the oldest form of parent involvement. We can trace it back to the early 1900s, when day nurseries (the precursors of child-care centres) were first established to serve poor and needy families. Mothers were instructed about health and hygiene and about how to raise children in ways that would keep them from falling into lives of crime.

Parent education became extremely popular during the 1960s and 1970s with the development of "Head Start" programs, where family involvement and early childhood education were believed to make a big difference in the lives of children and families living in poverty. A number of parent education formats evolved, including group meetings, home visits, and attendance by parents (usually mothers) at the preschool to learn from the teacher appropriate ways of interacting with children. The primary focus of many of these programs was teaching parents to interact with children in ways that would promote children's intellectual development (Couchenour & Chrisman, 2008).

At the same time, many other kinds of parent education programs were being implemented. Nursery schools, churches, community centres, and other organizations were forming parent education groups. These groups were often inspired by the works of such psychologists as Ginnott (2003). They generally focused on communicating effectively with children, discipline, and related topics, and most of the parents attending were middle class.

Parent education programs have traditionally been directed at two audiences: one for the poor, disadvantaged, or at risk, and another for the middle class and affluent. In fact, parent education has often been imposed on people living on assistance, immigrants, teen parents, and single parents. In other words, receiving welfare benefits or a space in child care has been conditional on parents' attendance at parent education programs. These programs have largely provided instruction to parents and have focused on parenting. On the other hand, middle-class parent education has been voluntary and based on discussion rather than on instruction (e.g., discussions of sibling rivalry or techniques for guidance and discipline). More recently, there has been a movement to "normalize" parent education so that people understand that parenting can be challenging for all parents, and that all parents, from time to time, may need support.

Today, many early childhood educators believe that educating parents is an ongoing process that best occurs through regular communication rather in than formal education programs. However, both early childhood educators and parents have cited problems that can occur with attempts to educate parents in this manner (Shimoni, 1992a), and we will explore this in the next chapters.

The concept of parent education has been widely questioned in recent years. We will consider some of the key points in the following sections.

Does Parent Education Work?

While many parent education programs have undergone rigorous evaluation, we must be careful not to assume that all parent education programs have demonstrated their effectiveness. There is generally little evidence to support specific types of parent education (Couchenour & Chrisman, 2011). Although many studies have shown that parent education classes have influenced parents' attitudes or knowledge about child-rearing, there is much less evidence to support the claim that real changes occur in families as a result of parent education programs.

It is difficult to understand just what kind of parent education is effective, but there is some consensus that successful programs share the following characteristics (Couchenour & Chrisman, 2011):

- They are intensive and extensive. That is, successful programs usually extend beyond one year and involve frequent contact between early childhood educators and parents in a variety of formats.
- They are substantially funded. It is difficult to avoid the simple formula that quality programs are costly.
- They are conceptualized and implemented under highly qualified professionals in the field of early childhood development.
- They respond to parents' needs.
- They are managed collaboratively. Professionals using a deficit model of parenting are less effective than respectful collaborative approaches.
- They include open-ended discussion.

Educators may hire professionals to organize and implement parent education programs, they may use packaged programs (e.g., STEP—Systematic Training for Effective Parenting; and PAT—Parents As Teachers), or they may collaborate with programs offered through family resource centres or parenting programs to meet parent needs.

Does Parent Education Undermine a Parent's Confidence?

After performing in-depth interviews with many mothers of young children, it was concluded that the involvement of so-called experts in child-rearing has undermined mothers' beliefs in their own ability to raise their children. There have been suggestions that parent education is rooted in middle-class values, and that parents from different cultures and types of families may accordingly feel left out or devalued or marginalized (Couchenour & Chrisman, 2008).

Parent education does not have to undermine parents' confidence. The intention, in fact, is just the opposite—to help parents gain confidence in themselves and thereby become better parents. Awareness of the potential impact on parents' self-image and a sensitivity to and appreciation of different parenting styles will help early childhood educators ensure that parent education meets its goal.

Who Should Offer Parent Education?

Almost all the helping professions today engage in parent education. Nurses, psychologists, teachers, early childhood educators, social workers, clergy, and even people with no related professional background now offer parent education. In some ways this is a good thing, since families and family relations are the focus of many professions, and the different disciplines can enrich one another's perspective.

Scenario

Who Is Qualified?

Marsha, a recent graduate of an early childhood education training program, expressed the view that she did not consider herself qualified to be an educator of parents. "In my training I learned a lot about child development and about how to care for children in a group. But I'm not a parent; I haven't brought up my own children. I can't teach parents how to do their job."

The sort of discomfort Marsha felt over being asked to provide parents with guidance and advice when she was not a parent herself is common among inexperienced professionals. Nonetheless, early childhood educators can develop the confidence they need to think of themselves as a useful resource for parents. Some parents do readily look to early childhood educators for guidance about parenting. Other parents have a different view. The question, then, of whether early childhood educators should engage in parent education cannot be answered simply.

The concept of parent education has been criticized because it implies a one-way sharing of information: the "experts" provide the required information to the parents without ever asking for their opinion. Parents do, however, have a wealth of information about their children, and this knowledge is every bit as valid and important as the contents of child development textbooks (Gonzalez-Mena, 2009). The point is to develop interpersonal spaces that recognize that parents have something to offer as "sources of knowledge and bearers of cultural capital" (Bernhard & Gonzalez-Mena, 2005, p. 22). Therefore, many early childhood educators have come to prefer the phrase *sharing information* instead of *parent education* (Shimoni, 1992a) because *sharing* implies a two-way communication process. Therefore, in the next chapter, we usually refer to sharing information rather than to parent education.

Parental Influence and Control

The second goal of many parent involvement strategies is to acknowledge the rights of parents to control, or at least to influence, policies and programs that affect their children (Wilson, 2010). Families may be considered as "consumers" who have made a considerable investment in their children. More and more, in tuition-based early childhood education programs, parents expect to influence policies and how their children are cared for and educated (Couchenour & Chrisman, 2008; Wilson, 2010).

This is a very sensitive issue for many early childhood educators. Through education and training they have acquired values, beliefs, and a considerable degree of knowledge about what is good for the children in their care. They spend much time and effort developing programs for the children based on those beliefs. Letting parents share in decisions about the program is not always easy to do. For example, the following incident occurred not long ago in a child-care centre.

Scenario

Who Knows Best?

Marcy, the centre director, regularly scheduled large blocks of time for free play because she firmly believed it to be the most important learning opportunity for children. A group of parents expressed the concern that the children were not learning enough, and they pressed the centre to teach children their ABCs and numbers and to encourage worksheets. The parents were not convinced by Marcy's argument that play is the most appropriate way for very young children to acquire knowledge and skills. The staff members were upset that parents ignored their expertise, and parents felt that their views were not being respected.

This scenario illustrates one of the difficulties that might arise in parents' influence on centre programs. Early childhood educators have to be careful to articulate clearly which areas of programming cannot be compromised. Literature published by professional associations— for example, the National Association for the Education of Young Children (NAEYC), the Canadian Association for Young Children, and the Canadian Child Day Care Federation—are vital resources for staff whose beliefs and practices are being questioned. By sharing their concerns with parents and by showing their willingness to respond to parents' requests, early childhood educators can usually establish acceptable boundaries for parent influence on curricular decisions.

The involvement of parents in the decision-making process is complex, and professionals need to consider carefully which aspects of their program should be open to parental influence or control and how they can encourage parent participation in a way that will benefit everyone involved.

Continuity of Care, or "Creating Bridges"

With rapidly increasing numbers of very young children being away from home for many hours a day, one important concern for early childhood educators in their relations with parents is the difficulty children face in making the daily transition between two environments that may be quite different. "Continuity between home and centre" is a concept that has received much attention in the early childhood literature. Continuity of care involves the types and frequency of communication along with the congruence or degree of similarity between the home and the centre (Couchenour & Chrisman, 2008; Wilson, 2010). This has also been referred to as "seamless child care" (Baker & Manfredi-Petitt, 2004).

As early childhood educators, common sense tells us that most children need some assistance in these daily transitions, and that one way to bridge home and centre is to ensure that there is ongoing communication between parents and program staff (Baker & Manfredi-Petitt, 2004; Wilson, 2010).

Wendy, who worked for years as an early childhood educator before she became an instructor of early childhood students at a community college, made the following observation about continuity of care.

Scenario

One Definition of Continuity

"When people talk about the importance of continuity of care, they refer to grand notions of home and centre doing things in a similar fashion or responding to the child in similar ways. Educators like big phrases like 'continuity of care.' This is unrealistic. My job is to make the child feel welcome in the child care. Often he'll talk about something relating to his home—his sick goldfish, or his brother's new shoes. If I know a little bit about those things (from talking with his parents), it's easier for me to talk with him about them and make him feel more comfortable at the centre. It's that simple. That's what I mean by 'continuity.'"

Continuity for this early childhood educator meant nothing more complicated than ensuring that she knew enough about the child's home life that she could help the child make sense of his experiences throughout the day and feel more comfortable at the centre. Continuity, then, is based on principles of respect and mutuality.

Continuity of care can have added significance if children are experiencing stress in their home environment. This is reflected in the following remarks by Elizabeth, an early childhood educator.

Scenario

What You Need to Know

"You need to know things that happen in the children's homes. If Mom and Dad have suddenly split up, I think it's important that we know that. We don't want to know who or why, but it's important to know that maybe Daddy left or Mommy has gone for a while. That's important because it's going to affect the child's behaviour, and we need to know what kind of support the child will require."

If continuity of care, or seamless child care, is to happen at all, it presupposes that information about the centre will be taken home to the parents, and that information about the child's home life and family will be made available to the centre. However, such disclosure requires a level of trust and openness that may not always be present. Some parents feel very strongly that their private life is not a concern of the early childhood educator. The following remarks made by one mother are typical.

Scenario

One Parent's View

"Of course I'll inform the early childhood educator of any sudden change in our family life, but only the bare details. All families have ups and downs, and I don't want to feel pressured to discuss these with my child's educator. It's not that I don't trust her; it's just that I didn't choose her, as I would a counsellor or psychologist. So if my husband walked out on me, I'd mention that John was no longer living with us, but I'd leave it at that."

Other parents, though, do look on the early childhood educator as a prime source of support, as someone with whom they can discuss family concerns. Sometimes this kind of support leads to important actions, as the following scenario illustrates.

Scenario

Some Timely Advice

An early childhood educator asked to speak to a mother whose child seemed to be under a lot of stress. The mother tearfully related that she was indeed having difficulty with the child just then. The little girl had just turned 4, an age that the mother associated with excruciating memories of the abuse she experienced as a child. The educator listened attentively and encouraged the mother to go to counselling at a nearby centre for adult victims of child abuse. Several years later, the mother recalled how it was the caring early childhood educator who facilitated the beginning of a healing process for herself and her family.

It is easy to see by reading through these scenarios that there are different opinions about the meaning and importance of continuity of care. For continuity to exist, there must be an atmosphere of respect where both parent and early childhood educator are sensitive to each other's rights and values. This includes awareness of cultural values, traditions, and practices in all interactions with families. For this reason, we have listed some cautions that should be observed in planning for continuity of care.

Bridging Centre and Home: A Two-Way Street

1. For some families, privacy is a highly esteemed value. Deciding what is absolutely necessary to know about the family's life, and what is not essential, will help you to respect the privacy of the family.

2. Early childhood educators are not trained to be counsellors or therapists. Parents will often disclose highly personal information to the early childhood educator, who will then feel a strong desire to be helpful. However, knowing your professional limits is extremely important. Being able to refer parents to appropriate sources of support is part of the professional role.

3. Unfortunately, educators who believe in continuity of care often translate it to mean "This is the way we do it at the centre, and therefore parents should do it this way at home as well." Bridging home and centre has to be a two-way street. It may mean incorporating new ideas into the centre to bring it more into line with the way things are done at home, rather than the other way around.

4. Consider using varied types of communication, including both one-way and two-way communication.

5. Congruity of values and expectations between home and centre needs to be considered. Many factors may influence congruence (e.g., culture, income levels, education levels). These factors or differences need to be openly discussed between parent and early childhood educator.

Scenario

Cultural Conflict?

Pam's daughter attended a preschool program where it was decided that Halloween wouldn't be celebrated owing to the mix of different cultures represented at the centre. Pam and her daughter were disappointed, feeling that this not only denied them the opportunity for a fun celebration but also denied their Canadian culture, in which Halloween is a time to dress up and explore the community through trick-or-treating. Halloween for young children wasn't a religious or non-religious event; it was just fun.

Early childhood educators need to understand cultural diversity and how to support this diversity in their programs. Perhaps the most important resource, however, will be the parents and families themselves, who, along with co-workers, friends, and neighbours, can inform and advise child-care staff on how to enhance the continuity of care by incorporating diversity into the classroom (Gonzalez-Mena, 2009).

Empowering Parents

Scenario

Mother May Know Best

"When I had my first child, I was a young single parent. I thought I knew nothing about children, and I just waited for the early childhood educators to answer my questions and tell me what to do.

"When my little girl 'graduated' into the toddler room, I met Elcira, her early childhood educator, and continued to ask her questions. Elcira would listen to my questions, but then would say things like 'What have you been doing about that up to now? That seems to have worked well.' Sometimes she would ask me what I thought would be the best way. Other times she would recommend a book to read.

"At first I was annoyed with her. 'Can't she just answer my questions?' I thought to myself.

"Gradually, I came to understand that she was giving me the message that I really do know what is best for my child and that I could rely more on my own knowledge and intuition. That was an important thing for me to learn."

Empowerment is a term that has been used with increasing frequency in the helping professions (Addi-Raccah & Ainhoren, 2009). It denotes a move away from the traditional way of working with people, where an "expert" was assumed to know what was best for her or his clients (Addi-Raccah & Ainhoren, 2009; Couchenour & Chrisman, 2008). Empowerment is a process by which families and communities increase their influence and control over their own circumstances. In an early childhood setting, the empowerment approach includes the following:

- Understanding that families commit to their child's lifelong well-being
- Nurturing children and families to reach their full potential
- Creating a sense of mutuality
- Validating children and parents as an important part of community

This approach de-emphasizes the expert role and gives parents, in collaboration with professionals, the power to make and implement decisions that will be in the best interest of their children.

All the goals of parent involvement already discussed in this chapter can be pursued in a way that empowers parents. First, parent education can empower parents if it is done in a manner that goes beyond just delivering reams of advice and information. Parents will feel empowered to trust their own feelings and responses to their children. Second, parents can be empowered by actively participating in the early childhood programs at both the planning and implementation stages, where there is a genuine openness to parent influence. Third, parents can be empowered by many of the strategies that encourage seamless child care or continuity of care.

Goals of Parent Involvement
- To provide parents with information about their child's development and needs.
- To provide parents with opportunities to influence their children's programs.
- To foster continuity of care between the home and centre.
- To help parents be aware of what their own goals for their children are and to empower parents to realize these goals.

The Family-Centred Approach

More recently, the term *family-centred* has been used in early childhood care settings (Scott & Arney, 2010; Wilson, 2010). This represents a movement away from the traditional approaches, where the "expert" designs and implements interactions without input from family members. This movement has grown from respecting the rights of families and from the ecological perspective, which recognizes the multiplicity of factors that influence development. In addition, evidence suggests that involving families more respectfully and fully is beneficial to families and children (Scott & Arney, 2010).

> Family-centred practice is based on beliefs and values that (a) acknowledge the importance of the family system on child development, (b) respect families as decision makers for their children and themselves, and (c) support families in their role of raising and educating their children. (McBride, 1999, p. 62)

Family-centred, culturally sensitive care incorporates the following beliefs:

- Family is key in the lives of children.
- Each family has its own strengths, resources, and ways of coping.
- Each family must be respected without judgment or preconceptions.
- Cultural, ethnic, and religious diversity must be honoured.
- Programs must support families, and practices need to embrace diversity.

Defining and refining family-centred practice is an evolving process. Awareness of and access to community resources will be increasingly important in finding flexible services to meet the unique needs of children and families. Early childhood educators have a solid foundation and rich traditions of working with families from which to continue to grow and develop more family-centred practices. These approaches are not a new fad or phenomenon— they represent the best practices of early childhood educators and a new perspective on families.

Family-centred practice includes elements of a strengths-based approach that has also become more commonly used. In a strengths-based model, educators discover individual and family strengths and work with these unique talents and skills as one way to address unmet needs. The model also includes elements of relationship-based practice, a framewok that promotes optimal parent–child interactions through parent–educator relationships. When educators use this approach with parents to demonstrate behaviours and attitudes, it is assumed that these parents will feel more comfortable using the same approach to support their children. Relationship-based practice includes the ability to observe, the ability to be aware of your own values and beliefs and how those might impact others, the ability to be reflective, and the ability to be strengths based.

All in all, these conceptual frameworks provide educators with ways to focus on and emphasize strengths and functioning. And since the practices are built upon a foundation of respect, they are more commonly used with families with young children. They are also encompassed in practices associated with more specific approaches. For example, Reggio Emelia provides a framework for working with families based on their philosophical ideas, as does the Te Whariki Early Childhood Curriculum in New Zealand. Although specific practices may vary, the foundation of respect for families is similar in all approaches.

Partnerships

Quality child care serves the best interests of children and families in a partnership of parents, professionally trained care providers, all levels of governments, training institutions, and provincial, territorial, and national organizations that carry complementary responsibilities. Quality child care

- recognizes the role of the parent as the primary early childhood educator, and the role of the trained care provider as one who is supportive and enhancing to child and family.
- utilizes parent boards, advisory committees, cooperatives, etc. to maintain a philosophy consistent with the needs of the families served.
- ensures that parents/boards have access to ongoing board development and training to ensure effective management of the program.
- has a developed program philosophy and posted policies for behaviour management, safety/emergency procedures, and the reporting of suspected child abuse.
- shares resources among parents and care providers within a supportive and complementary environment.
- adheres to all applicable provincial/territorial legislation, with commitment to exceed legislation where possible.
- ensures that ongoing and annual program reviews/evaluations are conducted, both internally and externally, to ensure delivery of quality service.
- initiates and maintains positive liaison/networking with such community resources as schools, religious institutions, Native band offices, community boards and agencies, and professional associations.
- provides for an administrative office for use by the director, where confidential records of children and staff are kept.

Source: Canadian Child Care Federation. 1991. National statement on quality child care. Ottawa: Health and Welfare Canada. p. 14.

Conclusion

In order to work with parents in a way that supports and empowers them, early childhood educators should clarify their own goals for parent involvement, learn and understand what the parents' goals are, and work with parents to develop strategies that will foster those goals. You should be familiar with the entire family system, and with the other informal and formal systems with which the family interacts, in order to effectively consider all aspects included in an ecological approach. Whereas the preceding pages have provided some background to help you sort out and formulate your goals , the following chapters will look at the practical application of these ideas.

Chapter Summary

- This chapter has focused on the importance of working with parents and developing an understanding of continuity of care.
- We explored the concept of parent involvement as it relates to family systems and ecological models. Parent involvement has typically included four goals: parent education, parent control/influence on the program, parent empowerment, and provision of continuity of care or seamless child care.
- We examined parent education and issues related to parental influence and control. Early childhood educators need to consider the importance of supporting families and developing goals related to parent involvement.

Recommended Websites

Canadian Child Care Federation:
www.cccf-fcsge.ca

Centre of Excellence for Early Childhood Development:
www.excellence-earlychildhood.ca/home.asp?lang=EN

Child Care Information Exchange:
www.childcareexchange.com

Positive Behaviour Supports for Children:
www.pbsc.info

Videos/Films

Keys to Culturally Sensitive Child Care. 1995. 36 min. California Department of Education.

Exercises

1. In your own words, write a definition of the term *parent involvement.*
2. Ask two early childhood educators to give you their definitions of the term *parent involvement.* Summarize their responses in writing.
3. Ask two parents what they feel the term *parent involvement* means. Summarize their responses in writing.
4. Compare the responses of the early childhood educators and the parents you interviewed with your own definition. What are the similarities, and what are the differences? What do you think accounts for these?
5. Brainstorm a list of reasons you might have for making a home visit. What are some things you could do in advance to ensure a successful home visit? Discuss the ethical considerations involved in home visiting.

Resolving Conflicts and Tensions

chapter

17

Objectives

- To understand that conflicts and tensions may exist in some relationships with parents.

- To examine the sources of some of these conflicts.

- To discuss strategies that may help prevent or resolve situations where conflicts or tensions arise.

> One of the leaders in the field of early childhood education tells a wonderful story about how misconceptions develop between staff and parents. It was a bad day at the child-care centre: Two staff members were off sick and no relief staff were available. In order to maintain the approved adult–child ratios, Andrea worked a shift and a half without so much as a coffee break. Just five minutes before closing time, when only one tired little girl remained at the centre, the telephone rang. The girl's mother was calling to say that she would be tied up in a board meeting for another 30 minutes. The exhausted early childhood educator put down the phone and went to tell the child that her mother would be late. As the long 30 minutes drew to an end, the child curled up in Andrea's lap to look at a picture book. The mother walked into the playroom, glanced at Andrea, and remarked, "Boy, would I ever like to have an easy job like yours, where you can sit and relax in a rocking chair."
>
> (Adapted from Stranger & Beatty, 1984.)

Almost all parents want what is best for their children, and of course early childhood educators are also committed to their well-being. This common goal should provide a sound basis for developing a positive relationship between educators and parents, yet studies consistently substantiate what conversations with educators have suggested: that working with parents is often the most stressful component of the educator's role (Wilson, 2005). Given the diversity that exists among families and among staff, it is not unexpected that conflicts will arise.

Many early childhood educators describe parents as helpful, understanding, and cooperative, and they feel that their collaborative relationships provide one another with a major source of support. Sometimes, however, relationships between parents and educators are strained. Research suggests that three factors present barriers to parent involvement (Eldridge, 2002):

1. Awkwardness—early childhood educators often feel awkward in their attempts to initiate interactions, and families assume that they should not be asking for assistance in parenting.
2. Availability—parents may feel a sense of alienation from the teachers or the program (especially school-based) owing to their own negative experiences in school, and educators may not feel they have the skills or knowledge to offer parents.
3. Timing, conflicts, and mismatched schedules between parents and educators.

It can be frustrating when neither side really understands what is causing the discomfort or is willing to deal with it, which can in turn create further tension for both.

Although these conflicts are verbalized at times, most frequently they are not, making them even more difficult to understand or resolve. Early childhood educators need to expect that some conflict will occur and that avoidance is not the best solution. Instead, efforts must be made to resolve conflicts in mutually acceptable ways. Educators must be committed to initiating and nurturing relationships with parents (Gonzalez-Mena, 2002). In this chapter we will concentrate on identifying the sources of conflict between educators and parents. We will also emphasize the importance of good communication with parents in preventing and resolving conflicts.

Sources of Tension

Conflict is inevitable when early childhood educators and parents differ in their values and beliefs, cultural and religious backgrounds, and economic status. Educators may feel that parents do not value or appreciate them (Invest in Kids, 2010). Galinsky (1988) found that some parents subtly communicate the message that child-care workers play a secondary role in society; that is, parents leave their children at the centre so that they can be freed to do "real work."

Many of the tensions between parents and early childhood educators, however, may stem from simple logistics, and then conflict erupts over seemingly minor incidents (e.g., dirty clothing, lost items). Busy parents and busy educators are often not able to find suitable times for communicating, and thus misunderstandings arise. The end of the day tends to be a time when both parents and educators are stressed and tired, and the possibility of meaningful interactions may be limited.

Early childhood educators who are better trained and more experienced tend to be more positive about parents (Wilson, 2005), suggesting that training should include a focus on understanding and working with parents. When educators deepen their understanding of the sources of tension and conflict, they can then take steps toward ameliorating their relationship with parents. Let us now examine in more detail some of the common sources of conflict between parents and staff.

Mercy and her family immigrated to Canada seven years ago. As a young woman, she had completed her teacher training at a college and worked as a teacher in an elementary school. At present, she is employed as an early childhood educator in a child-care centre and has one of her own children in another room at the same centre. Here are Mercy's comments about potential areas of conflict between parents and staff at child-care centres.

"As a parent and a teacher, I was rather disappointed in the lack of awareness of some of the staff about cultural differences. Several children at the centre are from countries where the diet is very different from here. My children, for example, were used to spicy food and found some of the meals here literally hard to swallow. I was disappointed to learn that my child had been punished for not finishing his main course. His dessert was taken away from him.

"Some children at the centre had never seen a child with dark skin before. I was pleased with the way staff in the playroom talked to the children in a matter-of-fact way about how some people have light skin and some have dark skin. I would have liked, however, to see more toys and dolls and books that had pictures of visible minorities. On the other hand, I wouldn't want my child to be singled out in every possible discussion as a representative of a minority group. Staff members need to stress the similarities among all children and not just the differences.

"Sometimes I've felt that people assume I'm less educated than they are because of my skin colour and accent. I sometimes get tired of having things explained to me two or three times, or in 'easy English.' The truth is that I probably have more education than many of the people I work with and many other parents of children in the centre.

"There were no child-care centres where I lived in India. Grandparents often take care of the children while parents go to work, and often parents take the babies with them to work if they own their own business. I do remember, however, that there were excellent relations between the nursery school teachers and the parents. Most parents believe that teachers deserve a lot of respect and that if they treat the teachers well, the teachers will treat their children well in turn.

"I wear two hats—a parent of a child in child care and an early childhood educator in a child-care centre. Of all the strategies for enhancing relationships between parents and staff, I believe the most important one is mutual respect. I want my children's teachers to treat me as an enlightened and caring parent who may have different ways of doing things. As a staff member, I want parents to know that I'm committed to high professional standards and the well-being of their children. I'm open to their ideas and want to listen to them, but they need to understand that I'm not their personal nanny but an early childhood educator."

Preconceived Ideas

Parents often have preconceived ideas about early childhood educators, who also hold preconceived ideas about parents (Invest in Kids, 2010; Wilson, 2005). These ideas or prejudices may interfere with establishing or maintaining a good relationship. Here are examples of the common misconceptions that parents and early childhood educators may hold.

Parents: Early Childhood Educators Have an Easy Job

As the scenario at the beginning of the chapter shows, parents sometimes believe that early childhood educators have an easy job, thinking that all they do is play all day with children. They have little understanding of the factors underlying the educator's "easy" job—the planning, organizing, and preparation required in a group care setting. This may lead some parents to ask for small extras ("Could you braid her hair?" "Please try to find his blue snow pants"). They may not realize, for example, that on busy days clothing will sometimes not get changed or that toys will go missing. Parents who have never spent extended periods of time with groups of young children may truly not comprehend the nature of the job and may make mistaken assumptions about the educator's role.

Early Childhood Educators: Children Are Not the Parents' Priority

Early childhood students and professionals often question the legitimacy of parents leaving their children in child care while they take the day, or part of it, off. Many students are shocked when they hear tales of parents who use child care so that they can spend time without their child. However, they may not consider that this may be the only 20 minutes alone a parent has all day or night, that it is more efficient to grocery shop without a 2-year-old in tow, and that it is better to spend quality time after the parent has worked or done the grocery shopping. Sometimes the day off is better spent cleaning, studying, and organizing home lives so that the parent is free to concentrate on her or his children when they are at home.

Early Childhood Educators: Parents Treat the Child-Care Centre as a Dumping Ground

Some educators believe that parents treat the child-care centre as a "dumping ground." Parents, they reason, are free to drop off a sick child, to control the payment of fees, or to dictate the child's pickup time. Even though many centres have policies or guidelines stating that children should be in care for no more than 10 hours per day, parents choose the length of the day based on their needs.

From the parents' perspective, their hurried comings and goings may seem entirely reasonable. Parents are frequently rushed in the mornings; if they are to be on time for work, they have little time to linger at the child care's front door. The end of the day poses the same problem because the parent is often in a hurry to pick up other children or to get home and start supper. Some parents may simply be overwhelmed by day-to-day survival issues (Pelo & Davison, 2003). The parents may feel quite content with the level of care and the child-care centre itself, and thus feel that they really have nothing to report on or query at each arrival or departure. This lack of communication may be their silent message that all is well (for now, at least). Early childhood educators, however, see staff-parent communication as being very important and are frustrated when parents do not (Wilson, 2005).

Different Values and Beliefs

Conflict is bound to occur considering the divergent cultural backgrounds, approaches, styles, and values that can exist between early childhood educators and parents (Gonzalez-Mena, 2009). Parents and educators may have different values and beliefs about children and parenting, which may be based on their own experience, on how they were raised as children, or on cultural or religious background. Sometimes, we are not even aware that we have these ingrained beliefs until we are confronted with a belief or practice that is contrary to our own.

For example, if an early childhood educator truly believes that mothers should stay at home with their babies and toddlers, this idea may filter through in interactions with parents. Parents may be judged to be neglectful when their preschool-aged child arrives with his or her hair uncombed, face unwashed, and wearing a strange assortment of clothing. These aspects, however, may reflect nothing more than the morning rush, the parent's inability to engage in just one more battle to clean the child up, or the child's own quest for autonomy in the choice of clothes.

Prejudgments may also result from cultural or religious differences (Gonzalez-Mena, 2009; Pelo & Davidson, 2003). For example, parents who expect their child to be strong and independent may not spend a lot of time easing the child through the daily separation. Early childhood educators may judge these parents as cold and unloving, while the parents see themselves as teaching their children important values. Likewise, the parents who overprotect their children or always do things for them may be doing so in accordance with their cultural norms. Educators may make judgments about these parents without attempting to understand their actions in light of these considerations. Establishing a meaningful discussion when family backgrounds differ, then, can be a major challenge for educators (Bernhard & Gonzalez-Mena, 2005).

Cultural differences may also be relevant in parent–staff relations. Most programs orient parent education programs to mothers since they bear primary responsibility. This may cause difficulties where extended families are integral to parenting. North American values focus on independence and autonomy, whereas other cultures value interdependence and nurturing (Gonzalez-Mena, 2009).

Differences in Power and Status

Differences in perception of the professional status of child-care workers can be a source of tension. Parents often treat (or early childhood educators think they treat) child-care workers as nothing more than babysitters. Status, salaries, and working conditions in child care continue to be problematic across North America. Early childhood educators can feel inferior to parents or think that parents are uninterested in their observations or views, particularly in the area of developmental concerns (Wilson, 2010).

Some parents may never come to view the child-care staff as a resource (Wilson, 2010), and yet early childhood educators often have more training and applied education in child development than many parents have in their careers, including law, commerce, engineering, arts, and sciences. Parents' knowledge of child-rearing comes predominantly from family, friends, books, media, the popular press, and their own experience. Nevertheless, parents often consider that their sources of child-rearing information carry more authority than educator resources. This attitude can lead them to feel that two-way communication with educators is unnecessary, and educators can interpret this lack of sharing as a reflection of their lower status in the mind of the parent.

A Parent's Perception of Status

Elaine had two children who attended a child-care centre attached to the college where she worked as an instructor. When interviewed about differences in the status and power of child-care workers and parents, she had this to say: "I'm going to be honest with you. When I want something to happen for my children at the child-care centre, I wear my business suit, walk in holding my briefcase and looking very professional, and make it very clear that I expect to have my own way. But you know, even though I think my status as a professional exceeds that of the child-care worker, in the long run, it's the educator who really holds the most power. At the back of my mind I always know that if they don't like me, the staff might, probably not even consciously, take it out on my child."

Ironically, just as early childhood educators feel that the parent has the upper hand, it is not uncommon for parents to feel that educators do. Fear of criticism and of being judged can be a barrier to effective relationships (Pelo & Davidson, 2003). Parents may feel left out of the decision-making process when the "teacher" presents himself or herself as the expert (Wilson, 2010). Parents may fear the opinions or judgments of professionals, especially mothers looking for external validation of their parenting (Wilson, 2010). Fear of reprisal against their children may serve to silence parents. Who knows what really happens, a parent might think, when I'm not there? The following scenario vividly illustrates this fear.

Who Really Has the Most Power?

One father, who himself was a university professor specializing in early childhood education, published a letter to his daughter's teacher, saying all the things he couldn't say to her directly. The father commented that, in all our professional wisdom, we haven't made it safe for parents to communicate honestly.

"It has been a humbling experience, and a frightening one, for me to discover how little the accumulated wisdom in our professional literature really speaks to the circumstances of parents like me, parents who have discovered that the stakes are too high to open this particular conversation with this particular teacher. When I actually meet with her, I will temper my points, modulate my voice, tread so very carefully. Much will remain unspoken because I am so acutely aware of just how vulnerable my child is in this affair. My first agenda is the agenda of every parent: I must not make the situation worse. So where will parents' voices really be heard by teachers? Can parents' voices be heard in the professional literature without being encapsulated in someone else's study, framed by someone else's commentary; can parents be heard speaking on their own behalf? Sometimes they can, but still, not often" (Nuttall, 1993, p. 6).

Uncertainty About the Early Childhood Educator's Role

Lillian Katz, a leader in the field of early childhood education, has described the relationship between parents and early childhood educators as one of "endemic ambiguity" (Shimoni, 1992b). Uncertainty about the roles, rules, and boundaries between parent and educator is inevitable (Katz, 1980). In the same vein, Kontos and Wells (1986) have noted that early childhood educators suffer from a sociological disease called "role ambiguity." Are they really respected professionals, or could they be considered maids and nannies? Some parents seem to think the latter is more accurate.

Scenario

Respected Professional or Hired Help?

A parent had been complaining regularly to her daughter's early childhood educator about issues such as soiled clothing, missing items, and reports of being hit and bitten by the other children. These allegations were for the most part untrue, and the educator tried to explain the situation and reassure the parent that all was well. One morning, the parent arrived upset about yet another minor incident the preceding day. When the educator attempted to explain, the parent silenced her by saying that she was paying for service and that she wanted things to change. At that point her expectations were very clear. She expected to be treated as a consumer purchasing a service, and she believed she had hired the staff to provide that service.

Jealousy

Lack of clarity or agreement about roles can also lead to feelings of jealousy or rivalry on the part of parents. They naturally feel possessive about their children, but early childhood educators can also become attached to the children in their care. Competition for the child's affection can occur because children are likely to become attached to both the parent and the educator, and with each thinking they will be replaced by the other, both may become insecure (Gonzalez-Mena, 2009). Most often, it is the parent who worries about being replaced by the educator in the child's affection.

Scenario

Transference at an Early Age

A young educator was caring for a group of children who ranged in age from a few weeks to 12 months. One day a toddler, who had just begun to talk, very loudly and clearly called the educator "Mom" several times. When the child's mother arrived, the educator told her what had happened—and was surprised when the parent responded with tears instead of laughter.

Parents may have serious reservations about placing their child in care in the first place, and these feelings will be heightened if they feel they are missing any of their baby's firsts, or that the child's early childhood educator will replace them in their child's affection. This then increases any feelings of guilt or inadequacy they may have as parents, and feelings of jealousy or competition may result. Again, these negative emotions can usually be traced back to the original ambiguity about roles and responsibilities.

Discrepancy in Goals and Approaches to Learning

Parents and early childhood educators may also have different learning approaches. The most common discrepancy occurs in educational or developmental goals, when parents, concerned about achievement, want to see their preschool children "educated" (Pelo & Davidson, 2003). Parents do expect an educational focus (Liu & Yeung, 2000), and want their children to learn numbers and letters, likely in the same traditional learning style they recall having at school (e.g., sitting at desks, memorizing). Early childhood educators are also focused on learning, but this happens through play, discovery, and exploration. Parents may not understand or value a play-based, emergent approach.

These methods are not mutually exclusive, but instead represent different means of attaining the same goal of learning or development. The distinction may not always be apparent, however. Thus, the parent complains that the child "plays all day" rather than spending time learning. This discrepancy in perceptions of how children learn may lead to tensions if the parent believes that the early childhood educator is not fulfilling his or her duty to teach the child.

Another common example is the discrepancy between independence and interdependence. In some cultures, independence is instilled in the early years. This is often reinforced in child care, where children learn personal care and are rewarded for independence in these areas. Families who stress interdependence and helping others may find themselves in conflict with the centre staff members who believe that the parent babies the child.

Unclear Policies

Most child-care centres attempt to provide parents with as much information as possible, both during their initial orientation and on a daily basis. Nevertheless, conflicts still arise when parents claim that they were never informed about one thing or another. Parents may receive pages of policies and procedure information but not read it, or they may read it and not remember it. It is also possible that they will be given details at the end of the day when the only thing on their mind is getting home. This apparent lack of communication is quite common and can result in conflicts between early childhood educators and parents, either on a short-term or long-term basis (Wilson, 2005). The transition from home to child-care centre can be a stressful time for parents; therefore, it is probably not the best time to ask them to remember various details about centre policies.

Scenario

Unclear Policies?

A huge fluorescent green sign had been posted for a week on the front door of the child-care centre, reminding parents that fees were due on the fifth day of the upcoming month along with the penalty for nonpayment. On the morning of the 6th, some parents were informed that their children would no longer be able to attend because their fees had not been paid. All the parents affected responded with, "We didn't know."

Different Perspectives

The last set of differences revolves around the different world views or perspectives held by parents and early childhood educators. Katz (1980) discusses several distinctions between parenting and caregiving. Seligman (1991) discusses world views, focusing particularly on the interaction between early childhood educators and parents of children with special needs. The differences in world views may be more broadly applied to all parents who interact with early childhood educators and desire the best possible experiences for their children. The different views may lead to very different ways of interacting with children and hence cause tensions that are difficult to resolve.

Ascribed or Achieved Status

The first perspective involves whether one comes to care for children through an achieved or ascribed status (Seligman, 1991). Early childhood educators have chosen this career and have achieved their status by hard work and study. They then expect to enjoy the freedom and authority to practise in ways they choose. Parents, on the other hand, have what is known as an ascribed role—that is, one that is assigned to them by society rather than one they achieve solely through their own efforts. Parents also cannot choose what their children will be like—they have no control over their sex, temperament, abilities, or disabilities. In addition, there is no training—no guidelines or practice standards for good parents—as there is for professionals.

The discrepancy between an ascribed and an achieved role may be the cause of tension and conflict between the early childhood educator and the parent. For example, the educator may have more success in dealing with the child who presents behavioural problems because he or she has chosen to work with this type of child, has personal skills related to this type of work, and can go home after eight hours of work and leave the child with someone else. The parent, on the other hand, may not have chosen this child, may not have the specific personal skills needed to control the child, nor be able to leave the child after a long day long day of work and several exhausting hours of interaction.

Scope of Function

Katz (1980) refers to a similar distinction as differences in scope of function. On the one hand, parents have all-encompassing responsibilities in the family; everything is their business, and they are never off duty. Early childhood educators, on the other hand, have fixed hours, and their functions are more specific and limited in scope. These differences mean that the two sides look at their child-care responsibilities from completely different perspectives, and this can cause conflicts.

The Individual or the Group

A third perspective is called "universalism versus particularism" by Seligman (1991), or the difference in perspective between the parents, who focus on the individual child, and the early childhood educators, who focus on the group (Katz, 1980). For better or worse, parents are concerned exclusively with their own child and therefore have quite particular concerns. Parents may make demands for their child that inadvertently put other children at risk (Katz, 1980). For example, parents may choose to bring in a snack to which other children have allergies.

The early childhood educator, on the other hand, is concerned with all children under his or her care and must balance the needs of the individual within that group with the needs of the group as a whole. Sometimes this can be accomplished on an individual basis (e.g., each child is changed when wet or dirty), and sometimes this is best accomplished as a group (e.g., in drawing up snack and lunch schedules). When the focused perspective of the parent clashes with the broader outlook of the early childhood educator, there may be conflicts surrounding care.

Scenario

Why Should One Child Enjoy Special Privileges?

A child-care centre opened at 7:00 a.m. each morning, and children arrived steadily through to 9:00 a.m. One mother worked a late shift in a grocery store; this meant that she went to work later and arrived home later in the evening. She would let her son stay up until 10:00 or 11:00 p.m. so that she would have time to be with him. She would then let him sleep in until whenever he woke up and take him into the child-care centre between 10:00 a.m. and noon. The early childhood educators found this extremely difficult to plan around, since they did not know when he would arrive and felt that they could not leave the playroom until he did so. The child, in turn, found the arrangement trying because he often had to search to find his group in the morning and join them partway through an activity. He felt that he was missing out on the fun, and the other children had difficulty making room for him midway through their play. The parent's perspective was that she wanted to spend time with her son and fit care into her schedule, while the early childhood educators felt that the child should conform to the schedule everyone else followed in order to ease the child's transition into, and interaction with, the group.

Scenario

Children Insist on Being Treated Equally

One parent consistently brought in her 3-year-old child after the scheduled breakfast time. The child did not eat beforehand, so the parent and early childhood educators agreed that the parent could bring breakfast from home because it would be impossible for the centre to prepare it for him. This seemed to be a satisfactory solution until all the other children began asking for the same treatment. It seemed the arrangement created more problems than it solved.

In both these scenarios, the early childhood educators' view of group care has come into conflict with the parents' perspective of what is best for their child. When parents have not been involved in group-care settings themselves, the difficulties they are creating may not even be apparent to them. The potential for conflict here is obvious. While early childhood educators may find it difficult to accommodate the wishes of all parents, they should keep in mind that all children need a parent who cares about them more than anyone else.

Specific or Diffuse Functions

A fourth perspective centres around the context in which the child is viewed (Seligman, 1991). Early childhood educators usually see the child in only one setting, where they interact with peers and adults. Parents see the child in other settings, in interaction with a range of different people—especially extended family members and siblings. Sometimes the parent may not see the child function much within the peer group (i.e., with other children of the same age), but this is how the educator sees the child on a daily basis.

Thus, when the parent reports certain behaviour, skills, or abilities of the child, educators may find it difficult to believe because they have never seen the child act that way or in that setting. Likewise, the parents often cannot understand the educators' concerns about the child's interaction with other children. In both of these examples, the perspective from which each individual views the child provides the framework for the way he or she knows the child. The lack of opportunity to view the child in other contexts makes it difficult to understand the other person's view.

Scenario

It's All a Matter of Perspective

Judy's early childhood educator and mother were in the middle of an unpleasant conflict. Her mother did not want Judy to nap for more than half an hour so that she would not be up late at night. Her mother needed the time after 8:30 p.m. to devote to Judy's older sibling, who often required help with homework. The early childhood educator, however, found that with such a short nap, Judy was fussy and cranky for the rest of the afternoon. The mother's observations were quite different. On weekends, when Judy did not nap at all, she was fine until the early bedtime. It could very well be that, in the quieter home setting, Judy did not need a nap to cope with afternoon activities, whereas in the noisier, busier child-care centre, a nap was required. However, neither adult had the opportunity to observe Judy in both settings.

Intensity of Affection

Traditional views of professionalism have, as one of their cornerstones, objectivity and a lack of emotional involvement with clients (Katz, 1980). Recently this view has been criticized, however, because it does not take into account the mostly female-dominated professions, such as nursing, rehabilitation therapy, and early childhood education, in which warmth and caring are paramount (Baxter, 1998). However, the fact remains that many early childhood educators do feel somewhat uncomfortable with the emotional bond that often forms between themselves and the children in their care. Parents are expected to show affection to their children, but professionals are not. Attachment by early childhood educators can too often be interpreted as favouritism.

Professionals are trained not to become emotionally involved because to do so will affect their professional objectivity. Many human-service professionals find themselves in conflict because of this expectation. How does the nurse working with terminal patients not become emotionally involved with them? How does the professional working with children with special needs in a home setting not become emotionally involved? How does the child-care worker who interacts with young children all day, caring for their most intimate and personal needs, not become involved? The fact is that professionals *do* become involved because of the very nature of their work. The crux of the dilemma is this: It is difficult to give a child proper care without actually *caring for* that child. Parents who expect early childhood educators to be objective and detached and not become emotionally involved may find themselves in conflict when the child hugs the educator at the start of the day or expresses distress at having to leave the educator at the end of the day. These demonstrations of affection between child and educator may be misunderstood by the parent, and it may be difficult for the educator to understand this reaction.

Scenario

Role Jealousy

A parent had her 4-year-old daughter in a family day home operated by her sister, the child's aunt. The child would call the early childhood educator "Auntie Debbie" during the day and would often call her mother "Auntie Mom" in the evenings. The parent initially thought this was cute but then began to question it.

Katz (1980) discusses two other differences in relation to affection. The first is rationality. Society forgives parents a certain degree of irrationality when it comes to their children: They are expected to be "crazy" about their kids. This partiality is based on parents having an emotional attachment to their child, so they tend to treat their child as a special person. The early childhood educator, however, needs to be equally available to all children. If he or she acts differently with one child, the other parents interpret this as favouritism. In addition, parents become "ego involved" in parenting. When there is failure, of whatever sort, the parent might experience low self-esteem and guilt. Early childhood educators, on the other hand, are expected to be completely rational in their planning, observations, and interaction with the children in their care. Because they are not as emotionally involved, they can deal with failure in a more rational way.

These are the perspectives or world views around which parents and educators may experience tension and conflict. In most cases, parents and educators do not clearly perceive that a difference in perspective exists, and this makes understanding the inevitable conflicts that much more difficult. Both sides may then attempt to rationalize their feelings (e.g., "She doesn't like me" or "He doesn't like my child"). We believe that an awareness and recognition of these perspectives can facilitate the development of more positive relations. It doesn't mean that the "problem" is solved, but perhaps the early childhood educator may consider the parent's request from another perspective. For example, when educators recognize that it is natural for parents to advocate for their own children, it will be easier to think about complementary functions and about how educators and parents can work together in the best interests of the child without misinterpreting the parent's request.

Summary: Typical Sources of Stress and Tension in the Parent–Educator Relationship

1. Preconceived ideas:
    - Some parents believe that early childhood educators have an easy job.
    - Some early childhood educators believe that children are not really the parents' priority.
    - Some educators believe that parents consider the child care to be little more than a dumping ground for their children.

2. Different values and beliefs.

3. Differences in power and status:
   - Some parents find it difficult to view early childhood educators as professionals.
   - Both parents and educators can be uncertain of the early educator's role.

4. Discrepancy in goals and approaches to learning.

5. Different world views:
   - Parents have an "ascribed" role with children, while early childhood educators have an "achieved" role.
   - Parents and educators have a different "scope of function" in relation to child-rearing.
   - Parents will be chiefly concerned with their own child, while early childhood educators have to think about what is best for the children as a group.
   - Early childhood educators see the child functioning almost exclusively within the peer group (a "specific function"), while parents see their child functioning in a variety of situations—with siblings, with the extended family, and in other social circumstances (a "diffuse function").
   - Owing to their ties of natural affection, parents are thought to interact with their children in a way that is primarily emotional. Early childhood educators, on the other hand, are expected to react with the children in their care in a cool, rational manner.

6. Unclear policies
   - Policies that are in any way unclear or ambiguous are a potential source of conflict.

We have examined the many ways that conflicts and tensions can arise between parents and early childhood educators. While understanding the roots and sources of conflicts is an important first step in resolving them, this understanding needs to be followed by action. The remainder of the chapter will focus on general guidelines in preventing conflict or dealing with conflict when it arises. Chapter 18 will examine this further by outlining specific strategies.

Strategies for Dealing with Conflict

Techniques for Conflict Resolution
- Learn to expect conflict and realize that skills for resolving conflict must be learned.
- Understand that there may be differences in values and beliefs between the early childhood educator and parents.

- Provide parents with up-to-date written policies and guidelines.
- Keep parents informed and provide them with opportunities to become involved in the centre's program.
- Work to bring differences out in the open (rather than avoiding them).
- Attempt to resolve conflicts using a problem-solving approach in a way that makes it a win-win situation for the parent and the early childhood educator. Develop effective ways to communicate.
- Respect and learn about families' cultural and religious traditions.
- Recognize that each family is unique, and develop strategies that allow you to empathize with different families.
- Acknowledge resource limitations.

Examine Your Attitudes

Ask yourself the following questions, and write out your reply to each one.

- What do you think are the qualities of a good parent?
- What values and attitudes do you have regarding children and their needs?
- Being as honest as you can, try to define your attitude toward parents in general. Do you judge them harshly or leniently?
- What is your attitude toward discipline and punishment within the family? Have you known parents who were harsh disciplinarians and who favoured the use of corporal punishment, such as spanking? How did you feel about them?
- Does your attitude toward parents change based on any of the following factors: ethnic background, religious affiliation, income, or marital status?
- What behaviour do you associate with a caring attitude toward children?
- List all the characteristics of the type of family with which you would have the most difficulty working. Beside each characteristic, list the reason why you would find it troublesome. When you are finished, write a brief analysis of what this list tells you about yourself.

Examining the answers to these questions may help you recognize how you feel about parents and parenting. Once early childhood educators are aware of their own beliefs, they may take the first step in understanding and improving their relations with parents (Galinsky, 1988). Your beliefs or values will not necessarily be altered, but perhaps you will understand why your relationship with Harry's mother is not like your relationship with the other mothers. This examination may also make early childhood educators more effective by ensuring that the parents who require assistance the most are actually getting it.

Early childhood educators need to realize that conflict is inevitable in any relationship. Working through conflict may produce positive changes. Educators will need to deal with many different types of parents, and so they need to feel confident that they have the ability to resolve problems (Wilson, 2010).

Understanding Parents

First and foremost, early childhood educators need to be aware of their own beliefs, values, and attitudes and of how these may affect their interaction with parents (Gonzalez-Mena, 2002). They may then have to determine how they will continue to show respect for parents and interact with children despite differences of opinions and backgrounds.

Scenario

Achieving a Compromise

A young mother and an early childhood educator were at odds about toilet-training practices. The mother believed that children should be trained by the time they were 1 year old. Everyone in her family had been successfully trained by that age. The educator believed that children should be trained when they are developmentally ready, when they show interest, and at their own pace. The educator had difficulty understanding the mother's position until they discussed their beliefs and attitudes. Their different beliefs remained, but a compromise on practice was achieved.

Scenario

Unspoken Attitudes

An older early childhood educator in a baby room believed that mothers should really stay at home with their babies. That was the way that she had been raised, and that was the way she had raised her own children. Although she never expressed her views verbally, they were clear in her approach with the babies and mothers. She was often curt and cold to the parents, nonverbally communicating her lack of support for their actions. On the other hand, she was very cuddly and warm with the babies and viewed herself as the mother's replacement. Several of the parents complained to the director, claiming that the educator's need to be "a good mother" made her insensitive to the needs of the babies' real mothers. The real difference was in beliefs, and the educator's behaviour clearly portrayed her underlying attitudes about babies in child care.

Once early childhood educators become aware of their own beliefs in relation to parenting and families, they may also come to realize that the source of the conflict lies within themselves—that is, within these basic values and beliefs. This understanding will be the first step in helping to ease strained relations (Couchenour & Chrisman, 2011) and in developing more family-centred practices. The next step will be to discuss differences openly (McIntyre

& Phaneuf, 2008). This decision may then result in the use of problem-solving strategies. Once early childhood educators recognize the diverse nature of families, they may acquire more appreciation of different cultures and then involve parents accordingly.

Making Policies Clear

As we noted above, a centre's policies must be phrased in clear language and be communicated to the parents in a way they will understand. Here are a few guidelines to help in implementing this idea.

First, early childhood educators must initiate a thorough orientation meeting at which they review and explain to each parent the centre's philosophy, policies, and procedures, especially those that may be more contentious (Wilson, 2010). In this way, the parents will become aware not only of the policies but also of the rationale for each of them. They will also get to know the important people in the child-care centre, such as the director.

Second, early childhood educators can develop a policy manual for parents, which educators can give to the parents for their own reference. Updating and change will be required from time to time; when this occurs, parents should be kept up to date as well. Providing parents with this sort of information should reduce the potential for conflict at the centre. For example, parents will know beforehand that only certain snacks are allowed in the child-care centre, and they will understand procedures regarding clothing, lost items, and pickup times. Providing opportunities for parents to have input in developing and adapting policies may also serve to increase their willingness to work with early childhood educators and centres.

Informing and Involving Parents

The importance of two-way communication between parents and the centre is paramount. The more ongoing communication that occurs with parents and the more parents are informed and involved in the programs, the less likely it is that conflicts and tensions will arise. In addition to the guidelines presented here, Chapter 16 provides a number of strategies for enhancing communication and collaboration with parents on an ongoing basis.

Working Toward a Win-Win Solution

Resolving conflicts usually involves creating a situation in which both parties win. This begins with the understanding that conflict is highly likely and that avoidance is not the best solution. A problem-solving approach (i.e., be part of the solution, not part of the problem) rather than a power approach is usually more effective (McIntyre & Phaneuf, 2008). Ask yourself the following question: "What needs to happen so that the parent can walk out of here with her dignity intact and so can I?" If only one person wins, the other usually feels humiliated or victimized. Even though winning may feel good in the moment, it is rarely satisfying in the long run, if only because the conflict usually resurfaces in some other form. Early childhood educators need to act thoughtfully and develop relationships with parents based on professional rather than personal issues.

When a conflict does develop, early childhood educators need to adopt a problem-solving approach (McIntyre & Phaneuf, 2008; Wilson, 2005). Problem-solving strategies focus on solutions and resolutions, not on assigning blame. Such strategies may result in changing the situation (e.g., providing developmental information regarding toilet training), or recognizing that the situation will likely remain unchanged because of religious or cultural differences in child-rearing. This approach entails the following:

- Trying to remain calm and focusing on the situation.
- Not getting defensive and escalating the problem. When parents feel respected and in control, they are more likely to respond in a similar unemotional fashion. Remember that parents genuinely care about their children and attempt to do what is best for them, and that they may become passionate about issues concerning their child. Attempting to work with the parents toward this common goal is more effective.
- Clearly defining the problem.
- Allowing all participants to voice their perspectives.
- Reviewing relevant policies and procedures.
- Assuring parents that their voice has been heard.
- Working toward solutions for all.
- Informing all parties of resolutions.

Recognizing the absolute importance of family and working in respectful and supportive ways form the foundation of family-centred practice. This does not mean that early childhood educators must act in a subservient manner or apologize every time something goes missing. If an apology is warranted, provide it. If it is not, provide a clear explanation of what has happened. The parent may have to go home to reflect on the situation, but your manner of handling it without reacting emotionally or being defensive will help the process.

Respecting Cultural and Religious Differences

When conflicts or tensions result from cultural or religious differences, early childhood educators can do several things to bridge the gap for children and parents (Bernhard & Gonzalez-Mena, 2005; Perlman et al., 2010). First, they shouldn't make assumptions (Bernhard & Gonzalez-Mena, 2005). For example, all families may not be able to participate in centre activities in the same ways. Second, early childhood educators should seek information. Having factual information about traditions, beliefs, and their significance may lead to increased understanding. For example, appreciating why the child may be dressed in a particular way, eat certain foods, or demonstrate certain behaviours will enhance an educator's acceptance of difference. Most parents are willing to share their cultural heritage if they know that the educator desires and cares about the information and will use it to assist the child. Rising immigration rates across North America translate to a steady increase in the number of families with varied cultural backgrounds. This growing trend makes the acquisition of cross-cultural information by child-care workers more and more of a necessity (Perlman et al., 2010). There is a need to develop varied strategies for families with different linguistic or cultural backgrounds.

A third way that early childhood educators can respect cultural or religious differences is by asking parents to share information with staff, children, and other families. When children observe tolerance in their daily lives and have opportunities to view differences among cultures as interesting instead of as something to be feared or criticized, they, too, will grow in tolerance.

Developing Empathy

One of the most important reasons for writing this book was our desire to enhance the early childhood educator's understanding of the challenges faced by families today so that the educator is better able to empathize with families. It takes practice and commitment to develop empathy, but it is well worth the effort. There are several ways that this can be done.

The first way to develop empathy is fairly simple. Use the knowledge that you already possess and try to imagine what it would be like if you were in the same situation as the parent. What would it be like, for example, to go to work every morning having had no sleep because of a crying baby? What would it be like having to worry about where money for the next meal was coming from? What would it be like to lose an entire social network with the ending of a marriage?

Sometimes it is easier to empathize with people who are in the midst of a serious crisis or in unfortunate circumstances than it is with people who seem to be successful. Therefore, try to imagine also what it would be like for a mother of young children who has invested heavily in her career and is now struggling to juggle the demands of a job and family. Imagine the stress such a mother will feel when she has to be at work to negotiate a major contract she has spent months preparing and finds that her child has come down with chicken pox. Even if you think that a career should be secondary, try to consider this from her perspective, and imagine her frustration in such a situation.

A second way to develop empathy is to listen to and talk with people who are in similar situations. Talk to single mothers about the stresses in their lives; listen to fathers who are trying to be nurturing parents but have had no one in their own lives to act as a model.

A third and more sophisticated way of developing empathy is to find parallels in your own life that can help you identify with the feelings of parents. Suppose, for example, that you are having trouble understanding what it would be like for a new immigrant to Canada. Perhaps you can remember changing schools when you were little, or moving houses, or travelling in a foreign country where people did not speak the same language as you. In these and other ways, you may learn to empathize with parents rather than to blame or judge them.

Knowing Your Limits

All human-service professionals want to provide the best and most inclusive services possible. In keeping with this desire, early childhood educators must recognize the limits within which they work. They need to know when to say yes, when to say no, and when to refer to other resources. Furthermore, educators need to feel confident in saying no. They also need to recognize the stress of their chosen career and ensure that they have supports in place for themselves. As well, because it is so easy to create conflict unwittingly with parents and with others, they need to work within clear professional boundaries and limitations.

Scenario

Boundaries

Sam was an early childhood educator in the 4-year-old room. She began to babysit after work hours and on weekends for McKenzie, whose parents had just divorced and whose dad was really stressed. McKenzie often stayed after hours until Sam was ready to leave, and she also spent time at Sam's apartment. McKenzie would come in and tell the other children about Sam's place and what they did. Soon the other children began to ask if they, too, could come to Sam's house, but McKenzie told them that only she was allowed to go with her dad. The other early childhood educators began to feel that McKenzie was being favoured and thought that there might be something more between Sam and McKenzie's dad than just babysitting. The situation became more contentious when other parents expressed their belief that one child had special privileges, and also began to request after-hour care.

We can see in this scenario how the lack of professional boundaries in this all-too-common situation can lead to confusion and conflict, not just between parents and early childhood educators but between educators and children. The role educators play and the fact that they are typically caring people who want the best for the children in their care can lead to conflict and tension. Early childhood educators need to be aware of these potential areas of concern and deal with them in a proactive manner, before problems result.

As demographics change, so do the demands of communicating with different types of parents. In recent years, for example, students have posed questions related to communicating with older, more professional parents. It appears that many families with two professional parents have recognized the need and value of child care for their preschool-aged children—so much so, in fact, that educators have often expressed the difficulty in meeting the needs of these "demanding" parents. This perception may (or may not) be accurate, and of course educators will often need to cope with the requests of demanding parents of all varieties. Again, educators need to be reminded that parents typically have the best interest of their children at heart. Listening to parents is critical, and developing a relationship of trust and mutual respect can take time. When educators feel overwhelmed by these demands, they may wish to check out local supports and resources (e.g., community colleges) for courses that may assist them. For example, a course on effective communication, conflict resolution, or mediation techniques may be extremely helpful to your practice.

Conclusion

The early childhood profession has made great strides in the past decade in articulating the professional role of early childhood educators and teachers. Collaboration with parents is part of the definition of quality care. The National Association for the Education of Young Children (NAEYC) states the importance of teachers establishing and maintaining ongoing contact with families (Bredekamp, 1987). However, the conflicts and tensions described in this chapter often present obstacles to successful fulfillment of the early childhood educator's role. Understanding the sources of conflict and developing strategies to prevent and overcome them will ultimately enhance the relationship between educators and parents and benefit the children in their care.

Chapter Summary

- Early childhood educators must understand that conflict is inevitable in relationships. Rather than trying to avoid conflict, they must develop strategies and approaches to prevent and deal with it when it arises.

- Early childhood educators need to become familiar with the sources of tension that may occur when working with parents and then familiarize themselves with strategies and approaches to resolve conflict.

- Understanding the sources of conflict and developing strategies to enhance the relationship between educators and parents will benefit the children. Becoming aware of the different perspectives that parents and early childhood educators may have will also aid educators in their dealings with parents.

Recommended Websites

Canadian Child Care Federation:
www.cccf-fcsge.ca

National Association for the Education of Young Children:
www.naeyc.org

Videos/Films

Dinner for Two. 1996. 7 min. National Film Board of Canada.

Hyper Parents and Coddled Kids. CBC documentary.
www.cbc.ca/documentaries/doczone/2010/hyperparents

Exercises

1. Check your attitudes by completing the following checklist regarding your feelings about working with parents.

    As an early childhood educator, I . . .   YES   NO

    a) feel that parents are more work than help.

    b) feel stress when parents enter my playroom.

    c) prefer to work alone.

    d) compare siblings from the same family.

    e) feel threatened by parents.

    f) view parents as a great resource.

    g) enjoy having outside people in the room.

    h) hold certain beliefs about certain groups of people.

    i) feel that parents use television to babysit their children.

    j) feel that parents are not interested in their children.

    k) work better with a social distance between myself and parents.

    l) believe parents are irresponsible for letting children come to child care in inappropriate clothing.

    m) feel that a close working relationship with parents is necessary.

    n) feel that developing this relationship is part of my job.

    o) am pleased when all the parents leave.

    p) anticipate parent conferences with pleasure.

    q) use written communication to avoid face-to-face contact.

    r) feel that parents have resigned from their parental role.

s) feel that parents have their children overinvolved in activities.

t) enjoy working with parents.

Source: Adapted from a class exercise used at Grande Prairie Regional College in Alberta.

2. Identify your own areas of stress when working with families. List some of the factors outlined in this chapter that may help you or your colleagues work through some of these difficulties.

3. Read the following family situations, then

a) determine your attitude toward the parents described in each situation;

b) brainstorm ways to offer support to these families.

    i) Mr. and Mrs. Ban own their own small business and find it necessary to put in long days. It is difficult for them to spend time in their children's centre because of their business.

    ii) Mrs. Smith has not been seen at the centre for some time, and rumour has it that she has had a nervous breakdown. Her husband finally confirms this to be true. She is still interested in what happens to her daughter at the centre, but she is not ready yet for large groups or for attending meetings.

    iii) Wanda Green is a single parent and has expressed interest in attending parent meetings. She has no car, however, and would have difficulty affording the extra expense of a babysitter to attend.

    iv) Mr. and Mrs. Gupta are new to this country and have just enrolled their son in your centre. They have told him that he cannot participate in Halloween or Thanksgiving activities.

    v) Jack Reed would like to meet more parents of the other children. He has approached the early childhood educator but has been ignored each time he suggests a get-together.

    vi) Mona Perth is a very busy woman with three children and a full-time career. She feels that whatever happens during the day in the centre is the centre's problem and that the early childhood educators should handle it without bothering her.

    vii) For craft activities, the child care uses a variety of food, including macaroni, flour, dried vegetables, and fruits. One parent, Mrs. Earl, has a lot of difficulty with this since she is trying to teach her children to value what they have and is very involved in international relief. She believes that using food as toys is in conflict with her values.

5. Empathy exercise—For each of the following remarks, write down what feelings you think the parent may be experiencing:

a) I'm not sure what I'm supposed to do when I come to the centre for the day.

b) All my child does here is play. He never brings home worksheets or drawings.

c) My son teaches every song he learns here to everybody in our family.

d) The children are going on another field trip?

e) My child's soiled pants were sent home, and I'd just like to know why you didn't get him to the bathroom on time.

6. Who can you talk openly with when you are feeling upset about a parent? How does talking to this person help you?

7. How do you feel when parents are present in the room? How do you think the parents are feeling? List some ideas about what you could do to help parents and early childhood educators feel more comfortable and welcome.

8. Ask people from different cultural backgrounds what their approach to conflict and conflict resolution is. How will this information assist you in your work with parents?

Enhancing Parent– Staff Collaboration

chapter 18

Objectives

- **To provide guidelines for planning activities with parents.**

- **To suggest activities that are congruent with the goals of parent involvement.**

- **To highlight special considerations in planning collaborative strategies.**

> Cathy, a recent graduate of an early childhood education program, sighed in desperation after a parent meeting she had organized was poorly attended. "I don't know why I even bother," she said. "Parents just aren't interested in coming." At the same time, Adele, a parent who did not attend the meeting, was thinking. "I wish they [staff] would give me more notice about parent meetings. Three days isn't enough time for me to arrange a babysitter. They probably think I don't care."

The preceding situation is all too common. It shows why working with parents can be a frustrating experience—both for the child-care staff and for the parents themselves. If properly organized and carried out, however, collaborative ventures can communicate important information in both directions, can result in parents and early childhood educators working together for common goals, and can be fun. Several factors will influence the success of parent involvement activities. These include having a clear understanding of goals, having a repertoire of strategies and activities, considering the practical aspects beforehand, and having in place some way of evaluating the success of the parent involvement program on an ongoing basis. We refer to these considerations as the why, what, and how of working with parents and families. This chapter will focus on strategies to enhance parent involvement.

The "What and Why" of Parent Involvement: Clarifying the Goals

It seems appropriate that our discussion of strategies should begin with the process of clarifying goals. As early childhood educators, how we work with parents will vary greatly depending on our own beliefs and goals. It is important to understand where we wish to go before we determine how we will get there. For example, in the following scenario, a mature staff member admits that in the beginning of her career, her feelings influenced her more than her knowledge.

Scenario

Apprehension About Parents

"In the beginning, I couldn't bring myself to initiate a discussion with parents. I would quickly say hello and then busy myself with the children to avoid further contact. I knew I should be telling them about Johnny's artwork or about a new book we had in the centre, and asking them about his trip to his grandmother's over the holiday. But every time I tried, I was overwhelmed by the fear that they wouldn't really want to hear what I had to say."

It may be helpful to consider goals from the different perspectives of the child, the parent, the family, and the caregiver. Although it is common to think of goals in terms of one dimension only, the benefits of parent–staff collaboration often overlap. For example, if a parent accompanies a class on a field trip, it may benefit the children to have exposure to a new and interesting adult, and it will probably make the child of that parent feel very special indeed. Also, some staff members value the assistance that a parent can provide on a field trip. The goals of parent–staff collaboration may be seen quite differently by different participants. One mother made the following remarks.

Scenario

Just Showing Interest Is Important

"I always go to parent-teacher nights at school. I don't ever expect to learn very much because it's always so busy there and the teachers have so many parents to deal with. I go just so that the teachers will know that I care about Jimmy's education. Then I make a separate appointment to discuss any concerns with the teacher."

One might assume that the teacher's goal in holding a parent-teacher evening is to provide parents with information or an opportunity to discuss concerns. However, the parent's goal in this case was quite different: She simply wanted to show the teacher that she cared.

In Chapter 16 we presented an overview of the most prevalent goals of parent involvement: parent education, parent influence or control, and continuity of care. It is important to realize that any one activity can meet a number of goals.

Multiple Goals Covered by One Activity

When planning an "open house" evening for parents, siblings, and grandparents, staff members found they had different ideas about what goals could be accomplished by such an event. "This will give us a chance to talk informally about the importance of free play with parents," said one staff member (i.e., parent education). "It'll give parents a chance to see all the new community-resources pamphlets we've got on our bulletin board," said a second staff member (i.e., working within the ecological model). "My biggest concern is that parents feel welcome and able to make suggestions about the room arrangement," said a third (i.e., parent influence and control). "It'll be nice when parents see the new playground and can talk to their kids at home about it," said another (i.e., continuity of care). Janet, a parent who had come in late and overheard the conversation, smiled and remarked, "The goal for me will be to come to a place where I'll be served a cup of coffee while the kids are busy playing" (i.e., family-centred).

It is probably true that if an activity is designed to incorporate more than one goal, it is more likely to be well attended and well received than if the goals are too narrowly defined.

Start with the Children

Parent involvement activities can begin with early childhood educators' area of expertise—the children. Educators often have ideas, activities, and events that are appealing for young children and have sound developmental outcomes. Parents sometimes struggle with activities in which to engage their young children and might appreciate the opportunity to attend an event planned around the abilities and interests of their young child. This might include an arts and crafts evening, a family dance, or a family outing. These types of activities provide an excellent opportunity to communicate with parents while engaging children. It may be easier for early childhood educators to consider parent involvement from the starting point of what they know best.

From the Classroom to the Home

As a class assignment, early childhood students were asked to develop some type of presentation for parents. One group of students was especially apprehensive, so it was suggested that they plan something based on their own area of expertise. One member of the group, an accomplished singer, decided to record the songs sung in the program; she and the children could sing all the songs and the parents could take a tape home if they liked. The evening was planned, and turned out to be a hit. Many parents remarked that their child was often frustrated because he or she didn't know the words, but now they could all happily sing the child's favourite songs at home. Another student set up a "goop station" to coincide with departure time at the end of the day. She set out playdough, goop, and other sensory materials children could play with, along with easy recipes for parents to try at home. The children got to show their parents what goop was, and parents had the opportunity not only to experience the activity but also to replicate it at home.

Although singing may not be everyone's talent, early childhood educators often have many developmentally appropriate ideas, like the goop station, to share—and parents are usually thrilled to engage in and learn some of these ideas. It may be the perfect starting point for parent involvement activities.

Get Input from Parents

It is believed that parental time constraints are the major barriers to effective involvement (Duffy et al., 2010). Therefore, engaging parents early and appropriately is essential. Formulating the goals of parent–staff collaboration should always be done in conjunction with the parents. Early childhood educators need to provide opportunities to promote parents' choices and decision making (Wilson, 2005). It is very disempowering to have others decide what is best for you. In addition, there is little point in planning an activity if parents do not feel that it would be a valuable use of their time. Informal conversations, and seeking opinions using a questionnaire or a parent survey, may give you ideas as to the type, length, and scheduling of activities. For example, parents may be more willing to engage in social activities as fundraisers rather than having to commit to fundraising events through the year. When parents feel they have some input into activities, they will likely be more committed to them. This may also help the staff feel that parents are part of the process and have some input. If parents' responses are taken into account in the planning of activities, they may well be willing to increase their involvement. If a questionnaire *is* used to collect feedback on potential activities, bear in mind that, in responding, most parents will choose to support only those activities with which they are familiar; they will not have the benefit of discussion or of hearing about others' experiences with other options before they fill out the questionnaire.

Communicate Effectively with Parents

Effective communication is the framework for establishing and maintaining any kind of collaboration with parents. Although it seems logical that early childhood educators should be able to communicate easily with parents and adults, this is not always the case. In fact, in early childhood education programs, little training is directed at working with adults. Early childhood educators have been known to break out in a cold sweat at the very thought of interacting with parents. As we pointed out in Chapter 17, "Resolving Conflicts and Tensions," messages can be interpreted in unexpected ways. For example, when the caregiver remarks, "He's been so good all day," the parent might interpret that to mean, "I know how to handle him better than you do," leaving the parent feeling undervalued. But communication skills can be learned and can be improved, and early childhood educators can commit to further training in this area.

As we have repeatedly emphasized, good communication begins with self-knowledge—that is, with an awareness of one's own beliefs and values (Wilson, 2005). A good communicator is careful not to pass judgment and is open to receiving new information (Vuckovic, 2008). The ability to build effective communication with parents requires a rapport and a sense of trust. This serves as a foundation for all work with parents. In addition to self-awareness and a nonjudgmental attitude, good communicators acquire a repertoire of verbal and nonverbal behaviours (e.g., listening, paraphrasing) that facilitate good communication. Good communicators also learn to ask questions that provide direction for the conversation and solicit more information from the speaker. They do this with sensitivity and without prying.

An additional aspect of communication with parents is the use of technology. In a world increasingly connected by email and social networking, early childhood educators should consider multiple ways of communicating with parents. While virtual communication will not decrease the importance of face-to-face communication skills, early childhood educators can utilize things like email to enhance parent–staff communication (Liang & Chen, 2009; Miguez et al., 2009).

Since communication skills are so essential for effective work with families, it is recommended that early childhood educators continually assess and improve their skills in this area. Many continuing education programs hold courses and seminars in communication.

Communicate a Welcoming Attitude

As one element of effective communication, early childhood educators should ensure that parents feel welcome and know that their involvement is valued in an environment of acceptance (Halacka Ball, 2006). Even small things, such as how the room is set up and the way parents are greeted, can convey this message.

Scenario

Make the Centre Inviting

After hearing about a variety of different centres in a class on parent involvement strategies, a student realized that the parents of her children never came into her playroom. When she asked several of the parents why, they all said that they never felt welcome in the playroom. The lockers and sign-up sheets were in the main entrance, and the parents perceived the door to the playroom as the cut-off point. After the caregiver moved the sign-up sheet inside the door and made an effort to greet each parent and invite him or her into the playroom, many of them felt welcome.

Communication between staff and parents and parent involvement will occur more readily if parents feel welcome. Keeping parents informed and providing them with opportunities to participate, to share opinions, and to be involved in multiple ways will all serve to promote a welcoming partnership (Reedy & McGrath, 2010). Communication needs to be frequent, clear, and two-way as often as possible (Reedy & McGrath, 2010).

Ideas for Collaboration with Parents

Once staff members have reflected on their attitudes toward parents and their goals for working with them (and once they have the necessary communication skills), the stage is set for the development of a broad range of plans to implement parent-staff collaboration. We must stress, though, that there will always be a tremendous diversity in parents' interests and availability (Halacka Ball, 2006). Early childhood educators should consider the spectrum of needs evident in parents from various linguistic and cultural backgrounds and in parents with different levels of education. Therefore, we will outline a variety of ways to collaborate with them. These are presented as *ideas* that you may consider and discuss with colleagues. This list is not meant to be exhaustive but rather to provide a starting point or some new approaches to try. Rather than putting a lot of energy into one approach, consider as many options as possible, and then allow parents to choose or to offer feedback for future planning. It is not important to have perfect attendance for all approaches, but rather to have each parent involved in something on a regular basis. We begin with the kinds of activities that should be ongoing and almost automatic, and then we will consider strategies for collaboration that require additional thought and planning.

Verbal Communication

Daily Conversations

All early childhood educators attempt to greet children and parents each morning and at the end of each day (Invest in Kids, 2010). Children, especially young children, usually require assistance during these transition times, and educators often try to build this short interaction and conversation into their daily routine. This is the most common and frequent type of parent involvement activity (Wilson, 2005). These informal contacts and exchanges are also, perhaps, the single most important aspect of parent involvement (Reedy & McGrath, 2010). However, the intention to speak to each parent each day is not always as easy to carry out as it seems. Parents often arrive all at the same time, and one small disaster (e.g., wet pants, lost shoes, a crying child) can inhibit even the best of intentions. Parents are sometimes tired or stressed at the end of the day, just as educators are. Moreover, rotating shifts often mean that the child's primary caregiver is unavailable for discussion.

A 1991 study indicated that two-thirds of the communications that occurred were only 12 seconds in length (Wilson, 2005), and that almost 43% of the time there was no communication at all. Furthermore, the study suggested that most of the exchanges were social exchanges rather than a sharing of information that might lead to decision making. Therefore, while ongoing face-to-face interaction seems on the surface to be the best way to communicate, it often does not happen consistently or productively, so safeguards are needed to ensure that communication occurs regularly (Wilson, 2005). Early childhood educators should keep a record of conversations with parents and review this record periodically, perhaps at the end of every week. If regular contact has not occurred at arrival and departure times, educators should make other arrangements.

Phone Calls

Telephone calls can be an effective way of communicating, provided that they occur at a time convenient for both parties (Reedy, 2010). Staff should try to organize times when they are "covered" in the playroom and let parents know when it is convenient for them to take calls. Some parents enjoy receiving phone calls that are made simply to keep in touch and relate information about the child rather than just the bad news. One mother said that it made her day when she got a call from the centre with a funny story about her toddler's new accomplishment. Other parents may wish to communicate by telephone only if there is a specific need—for example, a request for extra clothing or in an emergency.

Written Communication

Not all communication with parents needs to be done face to face. Written communication can meet some of the objectives of parent–staff collaboration and can be used to reach either individual parents (e.g., through communication books) or groups of parents (e.g., through newsletters). The following ideas can serve as one- or two-way communication vehicles to (a) share information with parents, (b) provide a mechanism for parent input, or (c) help parents gain access to wider community networks.

Bulletin Boards

Bulletin boards can be an excellent way of making available for parents a wide variety of information, and they can also serve as an effective public relations tool for the program (Reedy & McGrath, 2010). Bulletin boards can relay information about the entire program or specific aspects of it; these boards can also include pamphlets from community agencies, book reviews, community events, and excerpts from magazines. Another part of the bulletin board can focus on centre activities, such as samples of children's artwork, photographs, information about daily activities, and lost-and-found notices.

We must remember that bulletin boards will be useful only if parents actually read them (Reedy & McGrath, 2010). Therefore, information should be presented in an organized and appealing manner—for example, by using pictures of the children to capture parents' attention (Essa & Young, 1994). The information should also be updated consistently. Parents may also have information they want to share on the bulletin board and should be welcome to make use

---

Ideas for Bulletin Boards

1. Provide a bright, colourful background—that is, cover the board with an eye-catching background colour or design. Trim the board with a contrast colour.

2. Choose a spot where parents will see the board every day, either near an entrance area or parent corner or near the sign-in sheet in individual playrooms.

3. Provide some type of sign so that parents know the information is specifically for them—for example, PARENTS.

4. Keep information current by displaying topics that have a direct effect on the children or families—for example, tips on summer safety or on coping with time changes. Make sure parents know when information has been updated or changed by using a new sign or a change of colour.

5. Provide information regarding upcoming family events in your community, especially if they are free.

6. Provide take-away information (e.g., pamphlets, articles, recipes) or a sign-up sheet so that you can make copies for those interested in the information.

---

7. Provide some humour in the use of pictures, cartoons, special messages, or thoughts for the day that would appeal to parents and bring a smile to their faces at the end of a long day.

8. Provide space for parents to post and exchange information with one another (e.g., child-care needs, interesting articles).

9. Attach a pen and paper to the board in case parents wish to jot down information.

10. Change information on a frequent and regular basis.

11. Avoid posting information that would more appropriately be delivered individually (e.g., overdue fees).

12. Avoid visual clutter.

13. Interactive boards that encourage parent input may help to connect families.

14. Displaying staff biographies or information will help families get to know individual staff members better and may serve as a way to share relevant information (e.g., education, experience). This may be an easy way to introduce new staff in the program or to highlight the accomplishments of existing staff (e.g., recipient of an award).

of it for this purpose. Whenever possible, early childhood educators should have translations available for parents who do not read English.

Parent Corners

As an extension of the bulletin board, many centres set up a parent corner with a bulletin board and a table for displaying information. This can be an effective way to communicate how much you value learning and the sharing of resources. A few comfortable chairs and a coffee pot can be a sign to parents that they are welcome to stay for a few minutes to look through the material. Even though the times parents are in the centre (usually for dropping off and picking up their children) seem rushed, sometimes they can be introduced to valuable sources of information during those few minutes. This may provide early childhood educators with a vehicle to provide information in sensitive areas without pointing fingers at a particular family, parent, or child.

Scenario

Unforeseen Consequences

A parent dropped off her two preschool-aged children at the child-care centre. On her way out, she noticed an advertisement on the bulletin board for a meeting of Alcoholics Anonymous, which was being held in the same building during the evening. This small, innocuous posting prompted her to attend the meeting. Twelve years later, when her new baby began at the same centre, she recalled fondly that the bulletin board had played a significant role in changing her life.

Parent corners may also provide sufficient space for parents to advertise (e.g., for lost items, for a babysitter exchange, for articles they want to sell). Offering space for this purpose may also encourage parents to share information and resources with other parents.

Scenario

An Exchange of Information

Students enrolled in an early childhood course on the family and the community were required to copy and read a number of journal articles on a wide range of topics. When one student had completed a module of readings, she decided to take them into her child-care centre and leave them on a table by the coat racks. She was amazed to see how quickly the articles were taken by the parents, and even more amazed to see parents bringing in other articles of interest to add to the collection. This exchange of articles provided the perfect opportunity both for early childhood educators to share with parents and for parents to share with other parents.

Ideas for a Parent Corner

1. Provide a special room, section, or corner for parents to call their own. This space should be well defined, easily accessible, and inviting to parents. In an infant centre, this space may be used as a convenient, quiet spot for mothers to breastfeed their babies throughout the day.

2. The area should include the parent bulletin board, comfortable adult-sized chairs or a sofa, a table, and coffee, if possible, so that parents are encouraged to stop and relax for a moment.

3. Start a parent information library in this area. Include books that may be borrowed and articles or pamphlets that may be taken home or copied for personal use. Community newspapers or magazines that focus on children and families could also be provided.

4. Set out a picture album of happenings in the child-care centre for parents to look at. Add new photographs or children's art regularly so that parents can stay up to date on daily activities. Make sure to represent all the playrooms and all the children.

Daily Notes

In many cases, brief notes sent home with the children can provide parents with very important information. Notes can take on a variety of forms and serve many purposes. Many parents of infants and toddlers will want to know how much their children ate and slept, and whether or not they had a bowel movement. Small, prepared, fill-in-the-blank notepads can facilitate this communication process. As the children get older, notes can contain other kinds of information, and the child may also wish to add a message with a picture or a scribble, again to enhance the communication. Parents of children with special needs may wish to stay updated on progress the child is making toward goals.

Example of a Daily Note

My Day

TODAY: Leanne was very busy playing at the water table with her new friend, Casey. She played with blocks, made a castle, and dressed up as a princess.

LUNCH: Leanne ate half a sandwich and some apple pieces, and drank two cups of milk.

TOILET: Leanne did not have a bowel movement today.

NAP: She napped for two hours. Leanne had a bit of trouble getting settled but slept soundly.

CAREGIVER COMMENTS: Do you think that if Leanne had a special cuddly or blanket, she might be more comfortable at naptime? Let me know if you have any other ideas.

When using daily notes, as with all other forms of written communication, staff should take into account whether the parents will be able to read English. In some cases, it may be possible to have a daily communication form in a bilingual checklist format. Then staff could check off the relevant entries in English and the parents would be able to read them in their own language. In programs for infants and toddlers, this information is often presented on a white/chalkboard so that information can be readily updated for parents.

Communication Books

Two-way correspondence can enhance communication in that parents and early childhood educators are seen as equals, both contributing valued information (Couchenour & Chrisman, 2011). A notebook that goes back and forth with the child provides the opportunity for the caregiver to write pertinent information to parents or to ask parents questions. Parents can then respond and ask staff any questions they may have. Topics may include eating, sleeping, a new accomplishment, and information about upcoming events. One drawback is that communication books can become a one-way vehicle for communication, going from the centre to home but with no information returning. Early childhood educators can enhance the two-way nature by asking questions, by seeking information or clarification on a matter of concern, or by asking parents to share details of the child's life at home (e.g., "Ken says that you went to the farm this weekend. What did he enjoy the most?").

Scenario

A Communication Aid

Two-year-old Miguel came home from the centre one day, looked at his mother, and said, "Boat." "Did you read a story about a boat today?" asked his mother. Miguel shook his head no. His mother tried several more guesses, but each time her guess was wrong, Miguel seemed more frustrated, so she tried to distract him. That evening she wrote in the communication book that Miguel had been saying "boat" and she wondered if the staff knew what he was trying to tell her.

The caregiver wrote back that they had gone to the swimming pool and had watched the canoe practices there. The next evening Miguel's mother asked him about the canoes, and both Miguel and his mother seemed highly satisfied with the conversation.

Communication books can be delightful for parents and staff, but they can also become a burden. Parents will vary in the enthusiasm of their responses, and they should not be judged if they do not write back. One mother was asked why she did not write in the communication book and responded as follows.

Scenario

Who Has the Time?

"After work I rush to the centre to pick up Kaitlyn, then to the after-school program to pick up the boys. Supper, playtime, dishes, baths, teeth brushing, and a bedtime story for each child leave me pretty exhausted by the time they've all gone to bed. I just don't have the energy to write in the book."

Some parents do not write in the communication book because they are concerned about the impression they will give by using poor grammar and spelling, so staff must demonstrate sensitivity in this area. When a parent does write in the communication book, it is vital for the staff to continue to respond.

Considerations for Communication Books

1. Provide children with a small notebook that will easily fit in their diaper bag or backpack.

2. Write legibly about the children's day, what they did, and how they responded to routines, such as naps, meals, or toileting. Include information about what parents will want or need to know, especially for younger children who may not be able to communicate this information. Remember, however, that older children may forget or answer every question from the parent with an "I don't know," so passing along information will still be considered useful. Include information about development or play.

3. Include questions for parents so that they know you want them to respond. Try not to ask too many questions, and phrase the questions in such a way that they require more than a yes or no in reply.

4. Ask parents for information about what they have done as a family, which will help you talk to the child and increase continuity of care.

5. Respect the parents' varying need or ability to write in the book.

6. Maintain confidentiality at all times.

7. Date and sign each entry.

Examples of Communication Book Entries

January 3, 2007

Martha: Jeff had a great time outdoors today. He was really interested in building a snowman, and said he wanted to build one at home to show you what he can do.

He ate a good lunch and napped for about an hour (must have been all the fresh air).

He's really coming along with dressing himself, especially his snow pants and boots. He's much less frustrated.

Jane [mother]: We haven't had time to build a snowman, maybe on the weekend. I have noticed that he is getting better at dressing; he doesn't give up as easily. Could you please make sure that he wears his hat outside this week? He seems to be getting a cold again.

January 9, 2007

Martha: We made sure that Jeff wore his hat and kept it on outside today. His nose was running quite a bit and he seems more tired than usual. He didn't sleep as long today—he woke up after a half hour all plugged up and couldn't get back to sleep. Hope he isn't getting another ear infection. He ate some of his lunch and played quietly for most of the afternoon.

Jane: Jeff seems to be feeling better. His grandma is visiting and would like to come and spend some time with him in the child care to see what he does there. I'll call to arrange a time with you.

Newsletters

Newsletters are a common means of sharing information with parents (Wilson, 2005). A newsletter provides a different format for sharing much of the same kind of information that can be available on bulletin boards in parent corners. The advantage, of course, is that parents can take the newsletter home and read it at their convenience. Newsletters are usually more effective when they have a personal touch and include entries from the centre director, board members, staff, and parents. Some parents will be interested in reading about child development, others may want ideas for birthdays or recipes, and stil others may be more interested in learning about the resources in their community, so it is important to have a good mixture of information (Couchenour & Chrisman, 2011). The best way to learn what parents want to read about is to ask them! It is also a good idea to find out whether the parents themselves would be willing to contribute or help in the production of the newsletter.

Having spots in the newsletter where children can be involved may enhance parents' interest and serve to improve communication between parents and children. One child-care centre's newsletter always left one blank page where children could draw a picture of something special that happened to them that week or on that day. When the newsletter arrived home, the child could describe the picture and event in more detail to the parent.

Alternatively, the newsletter could be sent out to parents via email, which some parents may prefer. This depends on parents' employment and if they prefer paper or digital documents in general. Early childhood educators can ask the parents what kind of newsletter they prefer and decide if it is worthwhile to email the newsletter via a distribution list.

Developing a website for the centre, which involves technological skills that more educators are acquiring, may be another means of providing parents with timely information. Working parents may have the time to browse a website regularly, especially if they know that information is updated regularly. As well, posting back issues on the centre's website could serve as a useful means of storing information for parents.

Considerations for Newsletters

1. Newsletters should be published and sent home on a regular basis.
2. Always include contact information about the child-care centre, including phone number and address. Another page can be more specific to a particular playroom or age group.
3. Include a title—something catchy or more personal than "A Monthly Newsletter." Ask parents for suggestions.
4. Use coloured paper if possible.
5. Try to have the information typed or keyboarded so that it is easier to read. Be sure to proofread it for spelling and grammatical errors.
6. Try to match the reading level or language to that of the parents. If language differences exist, try to enlist the assistance of an translator.
7. Get everyone involved in contributing information. Include the director, early childhood educators, cook, parents, and children.
8. Have a section where the children can draw a picture.
9. Have spaces for parents and community groups to add information as well.
10. Include messages from important people (e.g., the owner or director) and updates about the program and staff. A page dedicated to each playroom can serve to focus on the developmental needs of the children in each age group and particular noteworthy areas for parents.
11. Include activities, books, and toys that may be of interest to parents, and demonstrate the developmentally appropriate knowledge early childhood educators have.
12. Calendars of upcoming events and activities can be helpful for families in planning.
13. Provide digital copies via email or posted on the centre's website.

Example of Newsletter

[Catchy Title] *Small Town Crier*	*[DATE]* *March 2014*	**Page One**

A Note from the Director	Calendar of Upcoming Events
• review of policy • staff changes • room changes • welcome to new families	• meetings • potluck suppers • field trips
	Cook's Corner • new recipes • menu changes

Parent Contributions	Classifieds
• ask parents to share information, ideas, or concerns that would be pertinent to other parents • thank-yous	

Page Two

[Room Specific] *Toddler Tattler*	
Primary Caregiver's Contribution • update about what is going on in the room • requests for donations	**Children's Contributions** • pictures • stories • jokes • dictated "stories"

Parent Information *(related to parents with children in this age group)*
- courses/workshops (for parents and children)
- book reviews
- child development information
- ideas for "to-dos" with children
- coping strategies

Although bulletin boards, parent corners, and newsletters are usually considered strategies for sharing information with parents, other goals can be met at the same time. Parent participation in these activities furthers their influence at the centre. The information contained may help parents form their own networks of support and access wider-reaching community resources. Sharing information by these methods may very well assist parents in helping children bridge the distance between their child-care experience and their home experience. Reading about a field trip in the newsletter or learning about a new book or toy in the playroom helps parents communicate better with their children about daily experiences.

Internet-based Comunication

The past years have seen an explosion in Internet-based communication, particularly the use of social media. The potential for providing one- and two-way communication, resources, marketing, advertising programs, and a sense of community is endless. Educators appreciate the relative ease, currency, and cost efficiency associated with sharing information with parents in this manner, and parents appreciate the real-time information, the child-care program's responsiveness, and the readily available sources of support. However, caution must be exercised. Educators must be cognizant of their ethical responsibilities and remember that anything posted has the potential to be viewed by a worldwide audience. Administrators attempting to deal with their staff's appropriate use of social media (e.g., Facebook postings) are well aware of the cautions that may be required; for example, the Canadian Child Care Federation (CCCF) has developed guidelines for use of the Internet. Developing policies and rules may be a necessary first (and continuing) step.

Travelling Goodie Bags

Most children derive great pleasure from being able to share their experiences with their parents. A "goodie bag" that contains prized possessions from the child care may be a way of bringing a little piece of the centre home for an evening. For example, the children in one class each brought home a stuffed animal for the weekend, and then drew pictures or wrote in a journal about what they did over those two days. The pictures and writing were then shared in class. Family theme bags (Helm, 1994) involve more comprehensive planning of activities, songs, crafts, and stories around a particular idea, but they also give families an opportunity to spend some quality time together. Literacy bags that contain a story and a variety of associated literacy activities like songs, fingerplays, or art ideas may provide a means for parents to build on a child's interest. Portapacks (Wilson, 2005) consist of a small portable package of play materials that can be taken home or used in vehicles. These packs might include sensory objects (e.g., feely bags) or simple cause-and-effect toys. Goodie bags and family theme bags may have special merit for low-income families, where toys and books can be shared. The families could keep some of the items (such as playdough and craft supplies).

The goodie bag can be assembled by the child, and the caregiver can add to it according to her or his professional judgment. Sometimes child-care staff are concerned that the contents of the goodie bag will not be cared for or returned to the centre. It has been our experience, however, that families and children usually value this sharing and return the contents in good condition. And just as bringing a piece of the centre home can be enjoyed by children and their families, the reverse is equally important. Children are often thrilled to take a "piece of home" to the centre, in the form of picture albums of family as well as toys and objects.

But early childhood educators need to be cautious. If, for example, a family is in the throes of the divorce process, they might appreciate a book that explains divorce in language a child can understand. However, such a gesture may also be viewed as a criticism or an intrusion into family life.

Parents as Volunteers in the Child Care

In the 1970s, there were a large number of centres and preschools that relied on parent "volunteers" to participate and assist. Today the realities of work and family mean that it is much more difficult for parents to be involved in this fashion. However, with advance planning, parents may still be available to attend the centre. For example, many parents enjoy celebrating their children's birthday with their friends there. As well, parents can play a number of roles within the playroom—as a special helper, an extra guide for a field trip, or a guest speaker to talk about their job or a hobby (police officers and firefighters seem to be among the most popular). Early childhood educators should remember that children may have other special people in their lives who may be available to volunteer. A grandmother who will come and sing or a grandfather who reads to the children can be a welcome addition to the playroom, especially to the individual child. Parents need to feel welcome, and they may require sufficient notice to plan for such a day.

Scenario

Making It Easy

"I was really hesitant to spend time in the toddler room, since I'd never really spent time with little children except my own, and I've never been with a big group. But from the moment I walked in the room, the early childhood educators were so nice—they showed me where stuff was and let me spend time with Gabi until I was comfortable. Then it was suggested that I shift over to the housekeeping centre where many of the children played, including Gabi. They made it so easy—and now I'm not sure why I was so nervous!"

The benefits of parent involvement are clear. Parents can benefit from seeing and participating in their children's lives at the centre and from meeting their friends. This experience may also heighten parents' understanding of the complexity of the caregiver's role and the demands of the job. Moreover, early childhood educators can often learn much about the children by observing their interaction with their parents. Educators must remember, though, not to make hasty judgments based on a single observation of child–parent interaction. A parent might not feel comfortable enough to act naturally at first; therefore, the behaviour you see may not be at all typical. Because of the many demands on parents today, educators must not judge negatively those who are not able to participate in this way. Instead, the caregiver needs to find other opportunities or activities for involvement that are more suited to that parent.

Ideas for Parents Visiting the Room
1. Welcome parents and thank them for coming.
2. Provide parents with an information sheet that welcomes them and gives some directions about what they can do in the room.
3. Invite parents to hang up their coat with their child's and then to feel free to observe or follow their child to the activity of their choice.

4. If parents want to be assigned tasks, they may assist in the art area by making sure that children's names are on their work, by observing, and by listening to comments the children make.

5. Invite parents to join in any games, dramatic activities, or play that may develop, since the children will enjoy their participation.

6. Make sure that parents are enjoying their time in your playroom, and check regularly that they feel comfortable and at home.

Before- and After-Work Activities

For parents who are unable to come to the centre during daytime hours, activities before or after work may provide the only opportunity they have to be actively involved in the centre.

Scenario

Parent Activities Come in All Shapes

In discussing options for parent involvement, one student explained that in her centre, parents were expected to come in two Saturdays per year for a major cleanup and organizational day. The main rationale was cost saving—if parents didn't assist, extra fees would need to be gathered to hire cleaning staff. But the student explained that the day was a major social event for parents—they planned well in advance, had pizza, and had the opportunity to share with their child's caregiver and the parents of their children's friends. The event had been taking place for many years. It seemed clear that if parents could be involved in this type of activity, any type of activity could be successful with the right amount of planning.

Evening hours are often precious to staff and families, so early childhood educators should recognize their efforts to ensure successful evening events. Planning breakfast or lunch-hour events (e.g., in workplace centres) may be another alternative that better fits families' schedules. These activities may include celebrations, social activities, or speakers. Any of these events present an opportunity for fundraising. At a family picnic or carnival, parents won't be averse to paying a nominal fee if they know that the money will be used within the child-care centre. Parents may actually be more willing to contribute and be involved in a social event like this than in other fundraising activities (e.g., selling merchandise or tickets). Early childhood educators should always consider families' ability to pay and should choose other means of raising funds if this presents concerns for some children or families.

Celebrations and Social Activities

Social activities may include informal gatherings such as afternoon or evening tea or coffee parties, potluck suppers, or fundraising dinners (e.g., spaghetti nights, pancake breakfasts, barbecues). Parents may enjoy evenings planned around children's activities at the centre, such as art shows, or, if the children are old enough, performances of songs or plays. Even though some early childhood educators may have concerns about children performing, parents and grandparents treasure these moments.

Scenario

A Creative Idea

The director of a child-care centre was getting tired of constantly having to dispose of children's artwork and of cubbies filled to the brim. She decided to stage an "art show." All pieces of artwork were labelled and displayed. Families were invited to view the children's accomplishments and share refreshments and snacks. The children took great pride in showing off their artwork. The evening ended with each child leaving with his or her pieces of art—this alone fulfilled the director's goal for the evening, but the enjoyment experienced by the children and their families was a pleasant bonus.

Many preschool programs hold an evening where the daily program is simulated so that parents can actually experience "a day in the life of a child at the centre." "Special people" may be invited to attend, and even though fathers might be the most commonly invited guests, these can also included siblings, grandparents, cousins, and friends.

Holidays and special occasions are often good motivators for get-togethers between families and the centre. Halloween parties, Mother's and Father's Day celebrations, and cultural awareness evenings are often popular. Fundraising events such as games nights, cakewalks, or carnivals can provide families with a fun night out and at the same time give them an opportunity to support the centre. The ideas are endless, but you never know which idea will attract parents.

Early childhood educators need to arrange activities to fit parents' schedules and needs. For example, parents who need child care in the evening will be more likely to attend family events or activities that begin earlier in the day (e.g., at pickup time) or that have child care built in. However, parents with other young children at home will likely find these arrangements more difficult. Parent input will help guarantee a higher attendance rate. Educators should be careful to include diverse families in all events; for example, a Father's Day event or craft may serve to alienate those children who come from divorced families or single-parent homes. Ensure that children know they have the option of inviting a special person or of making the craft for that person.

Speakers

Engaging a speaker to discuss a topic of interest with a group of parents is one activity that is often well received. The speaker may be from a related profession, such as a doctor, nurse, psychologist, or social worker, or may be one of the staff. Sometimes early childhood educators do not give their own expertise enough credit, and the parents might very well prefer listening to the caregiver—who has daily contact with their children—discuss such topics as discipline or development. Many communities have parent programs that may be interested in partnering with the centre to provide speakers for an evening. In addition, educators should remember that parents themselves have a wealth of knowledge and information and may be invaluable as "guest" speakers. These events require considerable planning and input from parents to ensure that there is sufficient interest and ability to attend. Attendance may be improved by providing child care during the parent education activity.

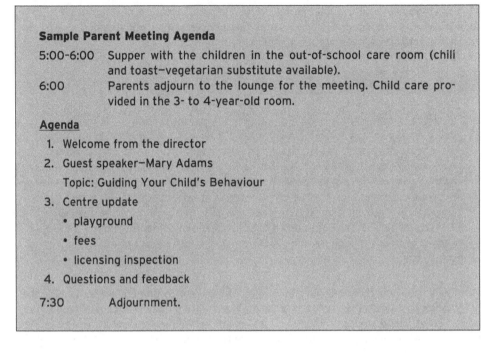

Sample Parent Meeting Agenda

5:00–6:00   Supper with the children in the out-of-school care room (chili and toast–vegetarian substitute available).

6:00   Parents adjourn to the lounge for the meeting. Child care provided in the 3- to 4-year-old room.

<u>Agenda</u>

1. Welcome from the director
2. Guest speaker—Mary Adams

   Topic: Guiding Your Child's Behaviour
3. Centre update
   - playground
   - fees
   - licensing inspection
4. Questions and feedback

7:30   Adjournment.

Home Visits

Home visits have traditionally been used as a form of parent–caregiver involvement (Wilson, 2005). Some educators note that there can be advantages to these visits. They can give the educator a very different perspective on the child and family. Children often talk about about the "time you came to my house!" long after the visit. If the intent of a home visit is clear, it can be a very positive strategy for building relationships. However, other educators have noted that they can be problematic. For example, some parents feel they are intrusive. Many families value the privacy of their home and are uncomfortable at the thought of a visit by an educator. Moreover, children may not understand the reason for the visit and misinterpret the intent. Early childhood educators have also observed that, given the demands of their work, the time required to visit the parents of all their children is unrealistic. For many reasons, then, home visits have waned in popularity and are seldom implemented these days, except in the case of children with special needs. If home visits seem like a worthwhile strategy, it is essential that the goals of the visit are clear to both staff and parents and that all parties are comfortable with the visit.

Scenario

Tension During Home Visits

"One day our daughter's preschool teacher came to our home for a visit. We lived in the same community and had been friends for some time before she became my daughter's teacher, so we were expecting a pleasant visit. My daughter felt strange calling her 'Mrs. Smith' instead of 'Sandy' and taking her on a 'tour' of her room. I felt that some of her questions weren't as casual and were about my parenting."

This anecdote highlights the boundary issues involved in home visits. Usually people who visit are friends, and a home visit by a caregiver can sometimes be stressful. The problem can be partially resolved by both sides having a clear idea of the purpose of the visit.

Parent Meetings and Conferences

Parent-teacher meetings tend to be more formal and are a way of ensuring that regular communication occurs. Just as the school system schedules regular meetings or interviews with parents, so do some child-care centres. Meetings can be called for a special purpose (e.g., to discuss a concern, to develop a joint plan for toilet training), or they can serve to update the parents on the children's experiences at the centre.

Parent meetings can be stressful for early childhood educators. Some staff actually freeze up at the idea of having to discuss problem behaviour with parents. Parents, too, can view the meeting with trepidation ("What bad news am I going to hear this time?") because of previous bad experiences that ended in misunderstandings (Nalls et al., 2009).

Good rapport and effective planning are essential ingredients for successful parent-teacher conferences. Conferences should always begin and end on a positive note (Nalls et al., 2009; Wilson, 2009). Effective planning also includes gathering documentation from other staff members, organizing the material to be shared with parents, and being prepared for questions from parents. It is just as important to listen to the parents' perspective as it is to make the points you want to convey.

Scenario

A Successful Conference

Jennifer, a caregiver, decided to ask Norman's parents to come in for a meeting. Norman had been so restless at naptime that the early childhood educators had had trouble settling him down for a sleep. When Jennifer discussed this with his parents, they said that bedtime at home had been difficult, too. Norman's parents thought he was having strange fears at night, which is quite usual for children around the age of 3. His parents had found that a nightly ritual of looking under the bed and placing a stuffed animal "on guard duty" seemed to alleviate his fears. The staff suggested that the parents bring the stuffed animal to the centre so that it could guard Norman at naptime as well. This input from the parents was most helpful.

Planning effective conferences with parents requires careful consideration—who should come, when they will come, what will be discussed, and how the discussion will be organized. This may be particularly important with parents from diverse cultural or linguistic backgrounds or when children present special concerns.

Considerations for Parent-Caregiver Conferences

1. Be prepared.
   - Consider which staff members would be the most appropriate to involve in the conference. These will most likely be the primary early

childhood educators, but consider including others (e.g., family members, professionals) as well.

- Familiarize yourself with the child and parent by reviewing the child's records.
- Have a clear idea about why you are holding the conference and what you hope to achieve.

2. Set the stage.

- Choose a time that is mutually convenient for both parents and staff. Try to ensure that no one is rushed, either getting there or during the meeting itself.
- Let the parents know what you'll be discussing ahead of time that so it won't come as a surprise and they have the opportunity to organize their thoughts and ideas.
- When the parents arrive, make them feel comfortable, provide adult-sized chairs in a quiet area, and offer refreshments if possible.
- Have all the necessary information with you so that you won't have to disrupt the meeting.
- Attempt to start every conference on a positive note.
- Begin with something personal about the child—an anecdote or a picture.

3. Lead the way.

- Inform the parents about the child's life at the centre by sharing, throughout the conference, observations, anecdotes, and specific examples of what the child is doing.
- Speak in plain, clear English. Avoid the use of jargon and terms with which parents may not be familiar.
- Listen to the parents and try to understand their perspective, their concerns, and their interpretation of what you're telling them. Be open to learning more about the child from the people who know him or her best.
- Present child behavioural problems as challenges requiring joint problem solving.
- Be prepared to offer parents ideas, resources, or referrals.
- Work out a plan of action with parents that will be in the best interest of the child, planning subsequent meetings or forms of communication if necessary.
- Close the conference on a positive note. Summarize what has been discussed and the plan of action, if there is one. Set a time to review progress, if necessary.
- Thank the parents for coming and for their input.
- Follow up after a few days with a note of thanks, a summary of the meeting, or a progress review.

Parent Boards

Many nonprofit child-care centres and nursery schools are run by a volunteer board of directors. The centre's director is accountable to the board of directors and reports to it regularly on all aspects of the centre, including finances, personnel issues, and programs. Often the board of directors consists of community members who have knowledge and talents in particular areas, such as accounting, fundraising, law, health, or human resources. When parents volunteer to be on the board of directors, their involvement gives them the opportunity to influence, and even control, the policies that govern the centre and its staff.

Parent boards can be difficult to manage. Early childhood educators may find it difficult to accept that they are accountable to people who are not trained in their discipline, and may feel that decisions, particularly about daily occurrences at the centre, should be made by people who have appropriate training. Sometimes, staff and parents may need to negotiate areas of control. For example, the parent board could be responsible for areas such as finances and public relations, while staff maintain control of the day-to-day activities of the centre. The division of duties may work in some programs, but not in all. Early childhood educators will need to be knowledgeable in their field and confident in their abilities to negotiate successfully with parent boards.

Parent Advisory Committees

Advisory committees have less power than boards of directors, and members may assume a variety of roles, from advising to helping with daily setup and snack time, with social events, or with hands-on assistance with the children in the classroom. All parents have the opportunity to be involved, but the type of involvement has been predetermined by the staff and is therefore usually very helpful indeed to the early childhood educators.

Beyond the Centre: Working with Wider Systems

Sometimes families require assistance and support that goes beyond the time limitations or professional boundaries of the early childhood professional. Many families have adequate support networks and can access required assistance without the help of the centre. However, for others, assistance provided by the centre in accessing community support networks can be invaluable (Daro & Dodge, 2009; Freeman, 2010).

Early childhood educators should be aware of the different types of resources their community offers. This knowledge will help them provide accurate information to parents about resources that can meet their particular needs. Parents' ability to make choices on their own must be respected, and sometimes the role of the caregiver is simply to provide information about existing resources so that the parents can independently decide what action to take.

There are a number of services in each community that provide support for a wide range of family or individual problems. When investigating and updating information related to community services, centre staff should gather specific and detailed information to ensure that their recommendations are appropriate.

Considerations for Community Resources

- Is the agency a self-help group run by people with similar problems, or is there professional support? For some parents, self-help groups are invaluable; but for others, professional counselling and guidance will be their only choice.

- Is there a cost for the services, and can the costs be claimed (e.g., through insurance policies or deducted from income tax)? Does the agency have a sliding fee scale where clients are charged according to their income? Providing alternatives may prevent the awkward situation of parents having to admit that they cannot pay for such a service.

- Does the agency have entrance criteria? Often agencies have to limit the number of people they deal with by imposing criteria based on age, disability, or type of problem. Sometimes the agency will openly state criteria, but in some cases guidelines will be vague and the early childhood professional will need to clarify.

- Does the agency have expertise in working with preschool children? Because most early childhood educators reading this book will be working with preschool children, a good question to ask is whether the agency has past experience in this area.

- What is the involvement with the early childhood professional? Some agencies work very closely with early childhood staff and invite observations and opinions from the educators who are with the children on a day-to-day basis. Other agencies will not be able to work in active collaboration with the centre or even to keep staff informed of what is happening. Depending on the organization, its structure and purpose, the nature of the problem, and the wishes of the family, the desirability of centre involvement will vary.

- How does one access the agency? Some agencies require a referral from a family physician, child welfare worker, or social worker. Other agencies are based on self-referral. A family in stress does not need to make extra phone calls. Finding out the appropriate way to access services and facilitating access may be helpful.

- Is there a waiting list? Some agencies have a waiting list of six months or more, while others will see people in crisis immediately. This information is vital to have.

- What kind of support does the agency offer? Some agencies provide group structures for people with problems, some work with families together, and some do individual counselling. Some offer "crisis intervention"—that is, short-term intensive support—while others may offer less intense support over a longer period of time. Many agencies offer a variety of formats.

Once the information is available, consider how best to pass it on to parents and how to assist them, if required, to "take that first step." You might display pamphlets from different agencies in the parent corner or on the bulletin board, write a short article in the centre's newsletter, or, through your personal relationship with parents, encourage them to seek outside assistance.

Making Collaboration Work

Even with the best intentions, early childhood educators who overlook certain considerations can hamper effective collaborative strategies, and sometimes this can result in parents' negative feelings toward the centre. Here are some considerations that should apply to the planning of all attempts to collaborate with parents.

Cultural Sensitivity and Inclusion

Sometimes, even though it may happen inadvertently, certain people are made to feel left out. The anecdote below provides an example.

Scenario

Be Sensitive to Multicultural Concerns

Staff at a child-care centre put up a poster in the parent corner that advertised a new indoor park in the city's downtown. The poster featured a photograph of people sitting on benches in a lovely area full of plants and flowers. The poster's written message was "Relax together in your garden." One staff member, who had attended a workshop on multicultural awareness, took a good look at the poster and remarked that its photo included no people of colour, no people in wheelchairs, and no elderly people. Everyone in the photo was well dressed, white, middle-aged, and appeared to be fairly well off. The staff member felt that the poster subtly excluded many people from feeling they had been invited to "relax together in your garden."

There is an increasing awareness that the words and pictures we use carry strong messages, and early childhood educators should be sensitive to this issue. Do the pictures and posters that invite parents to participate reflect the ethnic and economic diversity of parents in the centre? Do they reflect the different family structures, such as single-parent and step-parent families? Do they include parents and children with disabilities? Is the language level used suitable (e.g., little jargon)?

Some centres have made the effort to have their written material translated for parents who have difficulty with English. This is time-consuming and sometimes expensive, but when there is a commitment to the principle of inclusion, it is possible to find a way. Sometimes parents who are fluent in a second language are happy to help out, and immigrant-serving agencies are often able to assist as well.

Perspectives

Dianna is a 45-year-old mother of seven children. She was born and raised on a Blackfoot reserve and married into the Tsuu T'ina Nation.

"I come from a large family, five sisters and four brothers. My native language is Blackfoot. I attended boarding school from grade 1 to grade 10, and came to the city to finish high school. I've recently completed a diploma in social work and am working in child welfare on the reserve. From my experience as an Aboriginal person, and as a parent, I see much that early childhood educators can do to enhance the relationship between us. What I'm saying is undoubtedly influenced by my own experiences of racism and discrimination, my sense that mainstream culture is sometimes very apathetic concerning what has happened to Native people, and my feelings that I and my children have not always been free to express our opinions about our values and beliefs.

"The caregiver should be aware of the children's ethnic and cultural origin, including their history, extended family, and community. Early childhood educators shouldn't just read books, which are often written by whites, but should actually talk to tribal members. First, I would educate early childhood educators a bit about my culture so that they may better understand the Aboriginal lifestyle.

"These are some of the customs we watch for:

- We don't let children go outside after dark, because of the night spirits.
- We teach them patience and respect for elders.
- We teach them to respect and never abuse nature, for it has a life form in itself.
- We believe that children should never, ever be shamed, for shaming a human being is not acceptable in our culture.

"The caregiver should also be made aware of the communication patterns of the Native child. When Native children are asked questions, they often take time to respond. People sometimes think our children are dumb because they don't answer quickly. They don't answer quickly because we teach them to think carefully and formulate a precise answer before responding.

"Early childhood educators should know that, for many of us, grandparents and aunts and uncles have much responsibility for the children. In many cases, these extended family members take on lots of roles that you would assume belong to the parents.

"I would have been very happy to participate in activities in my children's child care, as I do in the schools today. Some of the activities I think suitable are storytelling by elders, organizing cultural days, taking children on nature walks, and demonstrating Aboriginal arts and crafts. I would also suggest that Aboriginal parents help the child-care staff design and decorate the child-care centre so that it reflects Native culture as well as the cultures of other children in the centre."

Imagine what it would be like to be invited to a parent–teacher conference at 5:00 p.m. on Christmas Eve, a time when your family has a traditional get-together every year. This happens all too often to families who celebrate their festivals and holy days at different times throughout the year. Several multicultural calendars are now available, and early childhood educators should ensure that parent activities do not conflict with special days from any of the religions and cultures represented at the centre. If in doubt, it is always better to ask than to plan without consulting parents.

Other Considerations

Bringing food to a potluck dinner may be a luxury that some families cannot afford. Attending a picnic with little to put in a picnic hamper may be so humiliating for some families that they may choose not to attend. Having to pay for child-care arrangements may make evening activities too expensive for some parents to attend. Even extra bus fare to attend an evening session may not be available. Awareness of the cost implications of parent activities is important to consider in planning.

One mother related the following incident.

Scenario

Be Considerate

"Last Wednesday I was invited to a parent discussion evening at the centre. I worked behind the cash counter until 5:00 p.m., rode home on a crowded bus, and quickly went through the children's supper, bath, and bedtime routine. Then I jumped into the shower, dressed, and ran out the door to catch the bus to the centre. When I got there I almost broke down into tears. The little chairs that the children sit on were arranged in a circle, and we (the parents) were expected to sit on them and listen to an expert tell us about reading stories to children."

In addition to location, the physical arrangements of the space in which parent activities are held should be given careful consideration. The arrangement of chairs can appear formal (in rows, as in a lecture), or the space can be arranged comfortably and informally.

One final and crucial consideration in planning collaboration with parents is the staff's time. Many early childhood educators volunteer time, after working for eight hours a day with children, in order to organize and attend meetings with parents. While their commitment to working with parents is honourable, it should not be taken advantage of. Educators need time to meet and plan, and need to either be paid for their work or given time off in lieu of it. Centre directors and staff need to balance the demands of the program with the physical and emotional well-being of the staff.

Evaluation

Evaluations of early childhood programs should be seen as an ongoing tool for improving the quality of the centre. In fact, what has come to be called "developmentally appropriate practice" requires that all programs be regularly evaluated (Goldstein, 2008). Many accreditation tools also expect evaluation of parent–staff collaborations. After all, this collaboration is an essential ingredient of a quality program and should be evaluated just as the other program components are.

Evaluation should be considered a means of gathering information and promoting discussion in order to help ensure quality care and good practice (Wright & Stegelin, 2003). Evaluation will also help staff and parents implement strategies that can lead to an enrichment of staff–parent relations and to successful collaboration between parents and staff.

Deciding What to Evaluate

Parent–staff relations, support for parents and families, and collaboration with parents are all multifaceted, subtle, but important aspects of a program. Therefore, determining how these should be evaluated and what information is to be collected should be the starting point in any evaluation. Early childhood educators must consider the many perspectives and variables when gathering and analyzing the data received.

Points to Consider

1. Consider the philosophies or beliefs of parents and staff.
2. Consider the different goals of parents, staff, and the centre.
3. Consider which aspects of collaboration should be evaluated, such as
   - timing (e.g., evenings, Saturdays, after work)
   - location (e.g., will parents have to travel back?)
   - child-care arrangements
   - parent versus family events
   - other considerations (e.g., length, time of year)
4. Consider who the stakeholders are.
5. Consider both parent and staff interests

Scenario

How Do You Measure Success?

A local association for children with special needs hosted a guest speaker who discussed sleeping disorders. The parents who regularly attended were not impressed by the talk since their children, for the most part, were older and past this developmental period. However, one new parent came to the meeting precisely because her 18-month-old child with special needs was experiencing major difficulties in sleeping. This parent was extremely grateful for the information and support that resulted from this evening. She left feeling confident that her severely handicapped son would be able to learn to fall asleep on his own.

To give yourself a clearer idea of what you feel your role is in collaborating with parents, complete the checklist below. Answer each question by using the following scale:

4 essential

3 moderately important

2 sometimes

1 never

As a caregiver, I believe I should . . .

1. Listen to what parents are saying.
2. Encourage parents to drop in.
3. Give parents an opportunity to contribute to my program.
4. Send newsletters home to parents.
5. Contact parents before a child begins my program.
6. Contact parents when a child does well.
7. Accept parents' views on child-rearing even if they differ significantly from my own.
8. Learn what objectives parents have for their children.
9. Learn about interests and special abilities of children.
10. Visit children at home.
11. Show parents examples of the children's activities.
12. Enlist parent volunteers for my program.
13. Encourage both mother and father to attend conferences.
14. Make parents feel comfortable when they visit the centre.
15. Include parents in plans for their children.
16. Try to be open and honest with parents.
17. Send notes home with children.
18. Keep both parents informed if parents are separated.
19. Consider parents as partners with the centre staff in the caregiving responsibilities.

Comparing scores with other early childhood educators will highlight differences in attitudes, comfort level, and skills in working with parents so that goals can be set for professional development and different parent activities.

The Benefits of Parent–Staff Collaboration

Different people often have different perceptions of the benefits of an activity, and any single activity may have different benefits for the participants. Early childhood educators may wish to consider the positive value for themselves as professionals, for parents, and for the child. When benefits are seen from multiple perspectives, goals may be seen as more worthwhile.

Benefits for the Child

- Children whose parents support the program are better motivated and their self-esteem enhanced.
- Children may feel more secure knowing that their parents trust and are involved with the centre.
- Parents and early childhood educators may develop realistic goals to maximize the child's growth.
- Parent involvement increases the children's self-confidence and makes them pleased and proud that their parents are interested in what is happening in their lives.
- Collaboration provides information and knowledge of cultural or religious influences that may allow for a better understanding of the children and their families.

Benefits for the Parents

- Collaboration strengthens families by helping them to have shared interests and goals and can give parents something to talk about or be engaged in with their children.
- Collaboration increases parents' self-esteem by making them feel more confident of their parenting skills.
- Access to resources and information helps parents develop knowledge.
- Parents form new friendships and develop supportive networks with other families.
- Parents have the opportunity to observe new or different parenting techniques.
- Parents can see other children the same age as well as their own children in the developmental context of their peer group, which may help them set more realistic goals.
- Parenting can be overwhelming—having a reciprocal relationship can provide parents with much-needed support.
- Parents may come to appreciate and value the efforts of early childhood educators.

Benefits for the Caregiver

- Collaboration provides another opportunity to find out more about the children they are working with, so they can develop more developmentally appropriate experiences.
- Early childhood educators have more time when a parent takes responsibility for certain jobs (e.g., snack preparation, fundraising, field-trip supervision).
- Having their work valued and respected is important to early childhood educators' sense of professionalism.
- When strong relationships are established, staff morale is improved.

One Activity, Two Different Goals

A child-care centre hosted a guest speaker for the evening. Parents arrived throughout the informal discussions and asked few questions, but after the meeting a lively debate ensued over coffee and doughnuts. One caregiver was quite upset at the low turnout and thought the late arrivals showed a lack of interest in the speaker. Another caregiver was pleased with the event since a significant number of parents did in fact attend (albeit not on time) and engaged in animated debate and socializing after the lecture. The first caregiver thought the goal of the evening was to provide information to the parents through the guest speaker. The second caregiver's goal was to provide parents with the opportunity to socialize with and support each other.

Clarifying criteria for success is an important part of evaluation. Early childhood educators need to bear in mind the vast differences in the parents' interest levels, their available time, and the ways in which they want to become involved. "Success" may not always be determined in terms of the number of parents involved in a particular event, but rather how the information can be used for change or improvement.

Father Participation

One child-care centre monitored parents' participation in scheduled activities for a period of several months. They noticed with concern that few fathers attended. One staff member commented that perhaps parent activities were more geared to mothers than to fathers; for example, every Mother's Day, children and staff hosted a tea party. This simple observation provided the impetus for staff to plan an activity geared specifically for fathers (e.g., soccer, hockey, video) once a month right after work. The activities were flexible enough that fathers could come and go according to their own schedules, and the children loved this time with someone special.

Conclusion

This chapter has made a number of suggestions for enhancing collaboration with and involvement of parents. The ideas in the following box can serve as a reminder. Staff and parents will have their own suggestions to add to this list.

The first step in planning successful parent–staff collaboration consists of understanding your own attitudes toward it and then making a commitment to its success. The next step consists of developing good communication skills and a repertoire of strategies that can be adapted to individual situations. With careful planning, sensitivity to parents' needs and concerns, and the assistance and input of parents, many positive results can be attained. To ensure that parent–staff collaboration is maintained over time, staff must continually evaluate their efforts. The next chapter highlights some of the questions that might be addressed in this ongoing evaluation of parent–staff collaboration.

Evaluation need not be too time-consuming, nor should it be very complex. If staff members are committed to an ongoing process of asking for, processing, and acting on the feedback they receive from families, their success at planning collaborative activities will likely increase. This ongoing dialogue with parents may well serve as the basis for each side getting to know one another better and thereby strengthening their relations. In addition, staff and parents will feel more comfortable when questions about collaboration are raised in accreditation review processes. Parents will feel more comfortable since they know the program and have input, and staff will have a better idea of where parents stand on issues affecting their child's care.

Chapter Summary

- In this chapter we have provided an overview of guidelines for early childhood educators to consider when planning parent involvement activities.
- We have also given an overview of a variety of different activities and strategies that might be used, including strategies to engage parents that begin with the child and communication strategies that will assist early childhood educators in working with parents.

- We reviewed the importance of evaluating staff–parent partnerships on an ongoing basis, and what evaluation is in the context of staff–parent partnerships.
- We explored different approaches to evaluating parent involvement, and we identified different factors to consider in interpreting results.

Recommended Websites

Canadian Child Care Federation:
www.cccf-fcsge.ca

Canadian Child Care Federation Workshop—Families Building Partnerships with Practitioners:
www.cccf-fcsge.ca/?s=families+building+partnerships+with+practitioners

National Association for the Education of Young Children:
www.naeyc.org

Exercises

1. Interview three parents about what types of communication they find to be the most effective and why.

2. Role-play the following scenario. It may be a good idea for the "players" to switch roles after their first performance to get the benefit of the other perspective.

> You are Ms. Renaud, director of the South East Child-Care Centre.
>
> Billy Blake, aged 4, has been in your centre about six weeks. He has adjusted well and appears to be an active, happy child. He participates in most activities, asks interesting questions, and particularly enjoys the block area and water play. He is less interested in the story corner, but seems really to enjoy playing with the other children. This morning when Mr. and Mrs. Blake dropped Billy at the centre, Mrs. Blake asked for an appointment to speak with you this evening. You don't know the Blakes well, but they seem pleasant and genuinely interested in hearing about what Billy does at the centre every day. Mrs. Blake is a lawyer, and her husband is a co-owner of a small construction firm.
>
> Draw up a plan for the best way of preparing for this appointment.

> You are Mrs. Blake, a lawyer with a large Edmonton firm. Your husband is co-owner of a construction company. Your son, Billy, aged 4, has been in the child-care centre for about six weeks. Although the child-care director, Ms. Renaud, and the staff seem pleasant and friendly and although Billy seems to enjoy his time at the centre, you and Mr. Blake have serious reservations about it. You don't think Billy is learning anything. He is a bright child and should be learning

to read and write–not just playing with blocks or at the water table all day. This is a competitive world; if Billy is to get into a good university, he must have a good start. These early years, when he is so eager to learn, are being wasted.

You have decided to talk to Ms. Renaud, the director, and this morning you made an appointment with her for when you pick Billy up this evening. (*Note:* Forget everything you know about the value of play, and don't make this easy for Ms. Renaud.)

3. Design a poster, brochure, or short video that explains the benefits that parent–staff collaboration offers for

   - the child
   - parents or families
   - early childhood educators

4. Interview parents and staff about a particular event or issue affecting them in the child-care centre. Gather the information first by using a random sampling and then by using a purposeful sampling. Compare the results. How are they similar and how are they different? Which type gave the most useful information?

5. Describe a situation in which you have worked with parents through sharing information and coordinating plans. How did you feel? How do you think the parents felt? What happened for the child?

6. Interview a family agency using the format suggested in this chapter (pp. 293–294). Present the information in a pamphlet form that would be practical for families to use.

7. The following information was taken from questionnaires that evaluated staff–parent involvement strategies. Based on this information, formulate some strategies and goals for your own program for the upcoming year.

   All seven staff responded. Of 40 parents surveyed, 38 responded. The responses were as follows:

   - Twenty-eight parents felt they did not know the staff very well.
   - Fourteen parents disliked evening meetings.
   - Thirty-five parents appreciated their children going on field trips.
   - Most staff members felt that field trips were not supervised well enough.
   - Thirty-seven parents needed care earlier than 7:00 a.m., and two needed care later than 6:00 p.m.
   - Seven parents enjoyed coming to the centre for lunch.
   - Nineteen parents were willing to contribute to snacks or lunch.
   - Some staff members did not know what to do when parents were in the room.
   - Some parents did not know what they were supposed to do in the room.

References

AADAC. 2010. Get the facts. Retrieved from http://www.aadac.com/87.asp

Addi-Raccah, A., & Ainhoren, R. (2009). School governance and teachers' attitudes to parents' involvement in schools. *Teaching and Teacher Education, 25*(6), 805-813.

Administration on Children, Youth, and Families. (2008). Child maltreatment. Retrieved from http://www.acf.hhs.gov/programs/acyf

Ainsworth, M. D., & Witting, B. A. (1969). Attachment and exploratory behavior in one-year-olds in a strange situation. In *Determinants of infant behavior IV.*

Alberta Children's Services. (2000). *Protocols for handling child abuse and neglect in child care services.* Alberta Children's Services.

Alberta Education: Aboriginal Services Branch and Learning and Teaching Resources Branch. (2005). *Our words, our ways: Teaching First Nations, Metis and Inuit learners.* Edmonton, AB: Ministry of Education.

Alberta Family and Social Services. (1990). *Protocols for handling child abuse and neglect in day care services.* Alberta Family and Social Services.

Amato, P. (2010). Research on divorce: Continuing trends and new developments. *Journal of Marriage and Family, 72,* 650-666.

Ambert, A. (2006). *Changing families: Relationships in context.* Toronto: Pearson Education Canada.

Ambert, A. M. (2005). *Divorce: Facts, causes and consequences.* Contemporary Family Trends. Ottawa: The Vanier Institute of the Family.

Ambert, A. M. (Revised 2005). Same-sex couples and same sex-parent families: Relationships, parenting, and issues of marriage. In *Contemporary Family Trends.* Ottawa: The Vanier Institute of the Family.

Ambert, A. M. (2006). *One-parent families: Characteristics, causes, consequences and issues.* Contemporary Family Trends. Ottawa: The Vanier Institute of the Family.

Ambert, A. M. (2009). *Divorce: Facts, causes and consequences.* Contemporary Family Trends. Ottawa: The Vanier Institute of the Family.

American Psychological Association. (2005). Effects of poverty, hunger and homelessness on children and youth. Retrieved from http://www.apa.org/pi/families/poverty.aspx

Anderson, A.L. (2002). Individual and Contextual Influences on Delinquency: The Role of the Single-Parent family. *Journal of Criminal Justice, 2002, 30*(6), 575-587.

Anderson, H. (2010). Common grief, complex grieving. *Pastoral Psychology, 59*(2), 127-136.

Arnett, J. J. (2010). Oh, grow up! Generational grumbling and the new life stage of emerging adulthood. *Perspectives on Psychological Science, 5*(1), 89-92.

Arnett, J. J., & Tanner, J. (2009). The emergence of "emerging adulthood": The new life stage between adolescence and young adulthood. In A. Furlong (Ed.), *Handbook of youth and young adulthood.*

Artz, S., & Nicholson, D. (2009). Documenting an integrated childcare program's Ability to Support At-risk Young Mothers and their Children. Retrieved from http://Dspace.library.uvic.ca:8080/handle/1828/1421

Artz, S., et al. (2007). From middle school to motherhood: The importance of collaborative approaches to changing girls' involvement in the use of violence. Paper presented at the Academy of Criminal Justice Sciences Annual Meeting, Seattle, March 13-17.

Åslund, O., & Grönqvist, H. (2010). Family size and child outcomes: Is there really no trade-off? *Labour Economics, 17*(1), 130-139.

Astor, R. A., et al. (2010). The influence of the second Lebanon war on Israeli students in urban school settings. In K. S. Gallagher et al. (Eds.), *International handbook of research in urban education.* New York: Taylor and Francis.

Ateah, C., et al. (2009). *Human development: A life-span view* (2nd Canadian ed.). Toronto: Nelson Education Ltd.

Attree, P. (2005). Parenting support in the context of poverty: A meta-synthesis of the qualitative evidence. *Health and Social Care in the Community, 13*(4), 330-337.

Auld, A. (2010). Children from military parents suffer fallout from PTSD: Study. *The Globe and Mail.* October 15, 2010.

Averett, P., et al. (2009). An evaluation of gay/lesbian and heterosexual adoption. *Adoption Quarterly, 12*(3), 129–151.

Bachman, H. J., & Chase-Lansdale, P. L. (2005). Custodial grandmothers' physical, mental, and economic well-being: Comparisons of primary caregivers from low-income neighborhoods. *Family Relations, 54,* 475–487.

Baker, A. C., & Manfredi-Petitt, L. A. (2004). *Relationships, the heart of quality care: Creating community among adults in early care settings.* Washington, DC: NAEYC.

Baker, L., & Cunningham A. (2007). Interparental violence: The pre-schooler's perspective and the educator's role. *Early Childhood Education Journal, 37*(3), 199–207.

Baker, M. (1997). Between breadwinning or caregiving: Fathers and Canadian divorce laws. *Lien-Social-et-Politique—RIAC, 37*(7), 63–74.

Balk, D., & Corr, C. (2009). *Adolescent encounters with death, bereavement, and coping.* New York: Springer.

Bank, L., Forgatch, M. S., Patterson, G. R., & Fetrow, R. A. (1993). Parenting practices of single mothers: Mediators of negative contextual factors. *Journal of Marriage and the Family, 55,* 371–384.

Bateman, N. (2006). What is a family life cycle? Retrieved from http://www.healthbanks.com/PatientPortal/Public/ArticlePromoted.aspx?ArticleID=HW5ty6171

Bauserman, R. (2012). A meta-analysis of parental satisfaction, adjustment and conflict in joint custody and sole custody following divorce. *Journal of Divorce and Remarriage, 53*(6), 464–488.

Baxter, J. (1998). A qualitative study of caregivers. Doctoral dissertation, University of Calgary.

Baxter, J., & Read, M. (1999). *Children first: Working with young children in inclusive group care settings in Canada.* Toronto: Harcourt Brace and Company.

Baydar, N., & Brooks-Gunn, J. (1995). Does a mother's job have a negative effect on children: Yes. In R. L. DelCampo & D. S. DelCampo, *Taking sides: Clashing views on controversial issues of childhood and society.* Guilford, CT: Dushkin Publishing Group.

Beattie, M. J. (2009). Emotional support for lone mothers following diagnosis of additional needs in their child. *Practice, 21*(3), 189–204.

Beaupré, P., Dryburgh, H., & Wendt, M. (2010). Making fathers "count." Retrieved from

http://www.statcan.gc.ca/pub/11-008-x/2010002/article/11165-eng.htm

Beauschene, E. (2006). Two wage-earners no guarantee against poverty. *Calgary Herald,* July 20, A8.

Beck, J. (1986). Problems encountered by the single working mother. *Family Relations: Journal of Applied Family and Child Studies, 35*(1), 113–123.

Bee, H., & Boyd, D. (2007). *The developing child.* Boston: Allyn & Bacon.

Bee, H., Boyd, D., & Johnson, P. (2006). *Lifespan development* (2nd Canadian ed.). Toronto: Pearson Education Canada.

Bengston, V. L., & Allen, K. R. (2004). The life course perspective applied to families over time. In: *Sourcebook of Family Theory and Research,* Chapter 19. Thousand Oaks, CA: Sage Publications Inc.

Benjamin, W., et al. (2008). Paternal work characteristics and father-infant interactions in low-income, rural families. *Journal of Marriage and Family, 70*(3), 640–653.

Benzies, K. I. (2008). Advanced maternal age: Are decisions about the timing of child-bearing a failure to understand the risks? *Canadian Medical Association Journal, 178*(2), 183–184.

Berk, L. E. (2000). *Child development* (5th ed., pp. 23–38). Boston: Allyn & Bacon.

Berkowitz, D. (2009). Theorizing lesbian and gay parenting: Past, present and future scholarship. *Journal of Family Theory and Review, 1*(2), 117–132.

Bernhard, J. K., & Gonzalez-Mena, J. (2005). When family priorities differ from program priorities. *Interaction,* Fall, 19–22.

Berns, R. M. (2004). *Child, family, school, community: Socialization and support* (6th ed.). Belmont, CA: Wadsworth.

Berns, R. M. (2010). *Child, family, school, community: Socialization and support* (8th ed.). Belmont, CA: Wadsworth.

Bibby, R. W. (2006). *The future families project: A survey of Canadian hopes and dreams.* The Vanier Institute of the Family. Retrieved from http://www.vifamily.ca

Biblarz, T. J. et al. (2010). How does the gender of parents matter? *Journal of Marriage and Family, 72,* 3–22.

Birkeland, R., Thompson, J.K., & Phares, V. (2005). Adolescent motherhood and postpartum depression. *Journal of Clinical Child and Adolescent Psychology, 34,* 292–300.

Blewett, J., & Lamb, M. (2008). Changing role of fathers in their children's lives. *Community Care, 1721*, 28-30.

Booth, A. L., & Kee, H. J. (2009). Birth order matters: The effect of family size and birth order on educational attainment. *Journal of Population Economics, 22*(2), 367-397.

Bowlby, J. (1951). *Maternal care and mental health*. Geneva, Switzerland: World Health Organization.

Bowlby, J. (1969). Attachment—*Attachment and loss: Volume I*. London: Hogarth Press.

Boyd, D., & Bee, H. (2009). *The expanded family life cycle: Individual, family, and social perspectives* (5th ed.). Boston: Allyn & Bacon.

Bradbard, M., & Endsley, R. (1980). The importance of educating parents to be discriminating day care consumers. In S. Kilmer (Ed.), *Advances in early education and day care* (Vol. 2). Greenwich, CT: JAI Press.

Bradley, J., & Kibera, P. (2006). Closing the gap: Culture and the promotion of inclusion in child care. *Young Children* (Jan), 34-42.

Bragadóttir, H. (2008). Computer-mediated support group intervention for parents. *Journal of Nursing Scholarship, 40*(1), 32-38.

Braithwaite, D. O., Bryant, L., & Wagner, A. (2004). Stepchildren's perceptions of the contradictions in communication with stepparents. *Journal of Social and Personal Relationships, 21*, 447-467.

Bredekamp, S. (Ed.). (1987). *Developmentally appropriate practice in early childhood programs serving children from birth through age 8.* (Expanded ed.). Washington, DC: National Association for the Education of Young Children.

Bredekamp, S., & Copple, C. (Eds.). (1997). *Developmentally appropriate practice in early childhood programs.* (Revised ed.). Washington, DC: National Association for the Education of Young Children.

Brom, D., Pat-Horenczyk, R., & Ford, J. D. (Eds.). (2008). *Treating traumatized children: risk, resilience and recovery.* Taylor and Francis Group.

Bromwich, R. (1981). *Working with parents and infants: An interactional approach.* Baltimore: University Park Press.

Bronfenbrenner, U. (1979). *The ecology of human development: Experiments by nature and design.* Cambridge, MA: Harvard University Press.

Bronfenbrenner, U. (1990). Discovering what families do. In *Rebuilding the nest: A new commitment to the American family.* Milwaukee, WI: Family Service America. Retrieved from http://www.montana.edu/www4h/process.html

Brooks, J. B. (2010). *The process of parenting* (8th ed.). Toronto: McGraw-Hill.

Brown, S., et al. (2009). The experiences of gay men and lesbians in becoming and being adoptive parents. *Adoption Quarterly, 12*(3), 229-246.

Brown, S., et al. (2010). Why don't teenagers use contraception? A qualitative interview study. *The European Journal of Contraception and Reproductive Health Care, 15*(3), 197-204.

Bruder, M. B. (2010). Early childhood intervention: A promise to children and families for their future. *Exceptional Children, 76*(3), 339-355.

Burrous, C., et al. (2009). Developmental history of care and control, depression and anger: Correlates of maternal sensitivity in toddlerhood. *Infant Mental Health Journal, 30*, 103-123.

Byrd, B., DeRosa, A. P., & Craig, S. S. (1995). The adult who is an only child: Achieving separation or individuation. In R. L. DelCampo & D. S. DelCampo, *Taking sides: Clashing views on controversial issues of childhood and society.* Guilford, CT: Dushkin Publishing Group.

Caltabiano, M., et al. (2007). Attachment style of foster carers and care-giving role performance. *Child Care in Practice, 13*(2), 137-148.

Campaign 2000. Retrieved from http://www.campaign2000.ca

Canadian Association of Mental Health. 2003. Retrieved from http://www.chma.ca

Canadian Child Care Federation. 1991. *National statement on quality child care.* Ottawa: Health and Welfare Canada.

Canadian Council of Social Development. (2007). Urban Poverty Project. Retrieved from http://www.ccsd.ca/pubs/pubcat/index.htm

Canadian Council of Social Development. (2010). *Families: A Canadian Profile.* Retrieved from http://www.ccsd.ca/factsheets/family

Canadian Perinatal Health Report. (2003). Health Canada. Retrieved from http://www.phac-aspc.gc.ca/publicat/cphr-rspc03/pdf/cphr-rspc03_e.pdf

Carbone, P., et al. (2010). The medical home for children with autism spectrum disorders: Parent and pediatrician perspectives. *Journal of Autism and Developmental Disorders, 40*(3), 317-324.

Carroll, J. S., Olson, C. D., & Buckmiller, N. (2007). Family boundary ambiguity: A 30-year review of theory, research and measurement. *Family Relations, 56*, 210–230.

Carter, E. A., & McGoldrick, M. (2005). *The expanded family life cycle: Individual, family and social perspectives.* Boston: Allyn & Bacon.

Case, A., Lin, I. F., & McLanahan, S. (2000). Educational attainment in blended families. Retrieved from http://www.thelizlibrary.org/liz/case_blended_families.pdf

Caughy, M., Nettles, S., & O'Campo, P. (2008). The effect of residential neighborhood on child behaviour problems in the first grade. *American Journal of Psychology, 42*(1), 39–50.

Center on the Developing Child at Harvard University. (2009). Maternal depression can undermine the development of young children. Working Paper No. 8. Retrieved from http://www.developingchild.harvard.edu

Chan, D., Lam, C. B., Chow, S. K., & Cheung, S. F. (2008). Examining the job-related, psychological, and physical outcomes of workplace sexual harassment: A meta-analytic review. *Psychology of Women Quarterly, 32*(4), 362–376.

Cherlin, A. J. (2009). The origins of the ambivalent acceptance of divorce. *Journal of Marriage and Family, 71*(2), 226–229.

Child Welfare Information Gateway. Retrieved from http://www.childwelfare.gov

Children of alcoholics: Are they different? Retrieved from http://www.alcoholism.about.com/cs/alerts/l/blnaa09.htm

Christoffersen, M. N., and D. DePanfilis. (2009). Prevention of child abuse and neglect and improvements in child development. *Child Abuse Review* 18: 24–40.

Chud, G., & Fahlman, R. (1995). *Honoring diversity within child care and early education: An instructor's guide* (Vol. 11). Vancouver: British Columbia Ministry of Skills, Training and Labour and the Centre for Curriculum and Professional Development.

Chute, Janet E.: Family, kinship, and social organization. In P. R. Magocsi (Ed.), *The Encyclopedia of Canada's Peoples* (Aboriginals: Algonquians/Eastern Woodlands). Retrieved from http://www.multiculturalcanada.ca/Encyclopedia/A-Z/a2/5

Citizenship and Immigration Canada. (2010). Retrieved from http://www.cic.gc.ca/english/immigrate/adoption/index.asp

Clark, W., & Crompton, S. (2006). Till death do us part? The risk of first and second marriage dissolution. *Canadian Social Trends,* Statistics Canada, Catalogue No. 11–008, Summer.

Clarke-Stewart, K. A. (1988). Evolving issues in early childhood education: A personal perspective. *Early Childhood Research Quarterly, 3*, 139–149.

Claxton-Oldfield, S., Goodyear, C., Parsons, T., & Claxton-Oldfield, J. (2002). Some possible implications of negative stepfather stereotypes. *Journal of Divorce and Remarriage, 36*, 77–88.

Cleveland, G., & Krashinsky, M. (1998). *Our children's future: Child care policy in Canada.* Toronto: University of Toronto Press.

Cohen, E., et al. (2010). Post-traumatic play in young children exposed to terror: An empirical study. *Infant Mental Health Journal, 31*, 159–181.

Coleman, M., & Ganong, L. H. (2004). *Handbook of contemporary families.* Thousand Oaks, CA: Sage Publications Inc.

Communicating with Parents and Students using Social Media. Retrieved from https://docs.google.com/presentation/d/1gva5ZcraGmNS9RyrOyXdUadAc9sTsVtHB5Sctk-nVlQ/present?pli=1&ueb=true#slide=id.p

Conference Board of Canada. (2005). *Decision time for Canada: Let's make poverty history.*

Conference Board of Canada. (2009). Child Poverty. Retrieved from http://www.conferenceboard.ca/hcp/details/society/child-poverty.aspx

Conference Board of Canada. (2010). How Canada Performs 2009: A Report Card on Canada. Retrieved from http://www.conferenceboard.ca/documents.aspx?DID=3526

Conger, K. J., Stocker, C., & McGuire, S. (2009). Sibling socialization: The effects of stressful life events and experiences. *New Directions in Child and Adolescent Development, 126*, 45–59.

Copeland, D. (2010). Psychosocial differences related to parenting infants among single and married mothers. *Issues in Comprehensive Pediatric Nursing, 33*, 129–148.

Copeland, D., & Harbaugh, B. L. (2005). Differences in parenting stress between married and single first time mothers at six to eight weeks after birth. *Issues in Comprehensive Pediatric Nursing, 28*, 139–152.

Corbin-Dwyer, S., & Gidluck, L. (2009). White mothers of Chinese daughters: Real mothers of real children. In S. Capporale Bizzini & A. O'Reilly (Eds.), *The personal to the political:*

Towards a new theory of maternal narrative (pp. 71–85). Selsingrove, PA: Susquehanna University Press.

Corr, C., and Balk, D. (2009). *Children's encounters with death, bereavement, and coping.* New York: Springer.

Corwin, D. L. (1995). How to recognize and prevent child sexual abuse. In E. N. Junn & C. J. Boyatzis (Eds.), *Annual editions: Child development.* McGraw Hill Companies.

Couchenour, D., & Chrisman, K. (2011). *Families, schools and communities: Together for young children* (4th ed.). Philadelphia, PA: Shippensburg University of Pennsylvania Press.

Couchman, R. (1994). From cloth to paper diapers and back: Reflections on fatherhood during two generations. *Transition, 24*(1).

Cox, C. B. (2010). *To grandmother's house we go.* New York: Springer.

Craine, J. L., Tanaka, T. A., Nishina, A., & Conger, K. J. (2009). Understanding adolescent delinquency: The role of older siblings' delinquency and popularity with peers. *Merrill Palmer Quarterly, 55*(4), 436–453.

Crowther, I. (2006). *Inclusion in early childhood settings: Children with special needs in Canada.* Toronto: Pearson.

Currie, J., & Widon, C. (2009). Long-term consequences of child abuse and neglect on adult economic well-being. *Child Maltreatment, 15,* 111–120.

Daly, K. (2000). *It keeps getting faster: Changing patterns of time in families.* Ottawa: The Vanier Institute of the Family. Retrieved from http://www.vifamily.ca

Daly, K. (2004). *The changing culture of parenting.* Ottawa: The Vanier Institute of the Family. Retrieved from http://www.vifamily.ca

Daly, K. (2006). *It keeps getting faster: Changing patterns of time in families. Contemporary family trends.* Ottawa: The Vanier Institute of the Family.

Danieli, Y. (1995). Who takes care of the caretakers? The emotional consequences of working with children traumatized by war and communal violence. In R. J. Apfel & B. Simon (Eds.), *Minefields in their hearts: The mental health of children in war and communal violence.* New Haven, CT: Yale University Press.

Daro, D., & Dodge, K. (2009). Creating community responsibility for child protection. *The Future of Children, 19*(2), 67–93.

Davis, K. (2000). Making blended families work. *Ebony* (July), 128–131.

DeAngelis, T. (2005). Stepfamily success depends on ingredients. *PA Online, 36*(11), 58. Retrieved from http://www.apa.org/monitor/dec05/stepfamily.html

Dearing, S. (2010). Poverty in Canada has increased as a result of the recession. *Digital Journal,* May 5, 2010. Retrieved from http://www.digitaljournal.ocm/article/291617

Deater-Deckard, K., Dunn, J., & Lussier, G. (2002). Sibling relationships and social-emotional adjustment in different family contexts. *Social Development, 11,* 571–589.

Deaux, K., & Bikmen, N. (2010). In A. Guinote & T. Vescio (Eds.), *The Social Psychology of Power* (Chapter 14, "Immigration and power," pp. 381–406). Guilford Press.

DeGarmo, D. S., Patras, J., & Eap, S. (2008). Social support for divorced fathers' parenting: Testing a stress buffering model. *Family Relations, 57,* 35–48.

Derman-Sparks, L. (2005). Teaching young children to resist bias. Washington, D.C.: NAEYC.

Devito, J., Shimoni, R., & Clarke, D. (2001). *Messages: Building interpersonal communication skills* (Canadian ed.). Toronto: Pearson Education.

Dickason, O., & McNab, D. (2009). *Canada's first nations: A history of founding peoples from earliest times.* New York: Oxford.

Dixon, L., et al. (2007). The co-occurrence of child and intimate partner maltreatment in the family. *Journal of Family Violence, 22*(8), 675–689.

Dokis, D. (n.d.). Cultural Studies Seminar I instructional manual (final draft copy). Mount Royal College Aboriginal Child/Youth Care Program.

Dorow, S.K. (2006). *Transnational adoption: A cultural economy of race, gender and kinship.* New York: New York University Press.

Drakich, J., & Guberman, C. (1988). Violence in the family. In Anderson et al. (Eds.), *Family matters: Sociology and contemporary Canadian families.* Scarborough, ON: Nelson.

Drummond, J., Kysela, G. M., McDonald, L., Alexander, J., & Fleming, D. (1998). *Risk and resilience in two samples of Canadian families.* Funded by Health Canada: Children's Mental Health Unit, National Health Research Development Program and Alberta Heritage Foundation for Medical Research.

Dubeau, D. (2002). Portraits of fathers. *Contemporary Family Trends*. Ottawa: The Vanier Institute of the Family.

Duffy, S., et al. (2010). First 5 Contra Costa report on parent involvement. Mathmatica policy research. Retrieved from http://eric.ed.gov/PDFS/ED510423.pdf

Dunn, J. (2004). Understanding children's family worlds: Family transitions and children's outcome. *Merrill-Palmer Quarterly, 50*(3), 224-235.

Dunn, J., O'Connor, T. G., & Cheng, H. (2005). Children's response to conflict between their different parents: Mothers, stepfathers, non-resident fathers, and non-resident stepmothers. *Journal of Clinical Child and Adolescent Psychology, 34*(2), 223-234.

Dunne, E. G., & Kettler, L. J. (2008). Grandparents raising grandchildren in Australia: Exploring psychological health and grandparents' experience of providing kinship care. *International Journal of Social Welfare, 17*, 333-345.

Dunne, G. (2001). Opting into motherhood: Lesbians blurring the boundariers and transforming the meaning of parenthood and kinship. *Gender and Society, 14*(1), 11-35.

Dupuis, T. (2007). Examining remarriage: A look at issues affecting remarried couples and the implications towards therapeutic techniques. *Journal of Divorce and Remarriage, 48*, 91-104.

Durand, T. (2010). Celebrating diversity in early care and education settings: Moving beyond the margins. *Early Child Development and Care, 180*(7), 835-848.

Dwyer, R. E. (2010). Poverty, prosperity, and place: The shape of class segregation in the age of extremes. *Social Problems, 57*(1), 114-137.

East, P. L., & Siek, T. K. (2005). Longitudinal pathways linking family factors and sibling relationship qualities to adolescent substance use and sexual risk behaviors. *Journal of Family Psychology, 19*(4), 571-580.

Ebling, R., et al. (2009). "Get over it": Perspectives on divorce from young children. *Family Court Review, 47*, 665-681.

Edgar-Bailey, M., & Kress, V. E. (2010). Resolving child and adolescent traumatic grief: Creative techniques and interventions. *Journal of Creativity in Mental Health, 5*(2), 158-176.

Education Directorate of OECD. (2006). *Starting strong II: Early childhood education and care*. OECD Publishing.

Edwards, O. W. (2003). Living with grandma: A grandfamily study. *School Psychology International, 24*(2), 204-217.

Elder, G. H. (1998). The life course as developmental theory. *Child Development, 69*, 1-12.

Eldridge, D. (2002). Parent involvement: It's worth the effort. In *Annual editions: Early childhood care and education 02/03*. Guilford, CN: McGraw-Hill/Dushkin.

Engel, M. (2002). Stepfamily resources. Stepfamily Association of America. Retrieved from http://www.marriagepreparation.com/stepfamily_resources.htm

Epstein, R., & Duggan, S. (2006). *Factors relating to parenting by non-heterosexual fathers (AKA gay fathers cluster)*. University of Guelph Father Involvement Research Alliance (FIRA). Retrieved from http://www.fira.ugeulph.ca

Erikson, E. H. (1963). *Childhood and society* (2nd ed.). New York: Norton.

Eshleman, J. R., & Wilson. S. J. (1995). *The family* (Canadian ed.). Scarborough, ON: Allyn & Bacon.

Essa, E., & Murray, C. (1994). Young children's understanding and experience with death. *Young Children, 49*(1), 74-81.

Essa, E., & Young, R. (1994). *Introduction to early childhood education*. Scarborough, ON: Nelson.

Este, D., & Tachble, A. (2009). Fatherhood in the Canadian context: Perceptions and experiences of Sudanese refugee men. *Sex Roles, 60*(7/8), 456-466.

Fanning, K. (2008). Blended families: Teens describe some of the challenges and rewards of living in a stepfamily. *Junior Scholastic*, February 11.

Favazza, P. C., & Munson, L. J. (2010). Loss and grief in young children. *Young Exceptional Children*. Retrieved from http://yec.sagepub.com/content/early/2010/01/12/1096250609356883.citation

Fearnley, R. (2010). Death of a parent and the children's experience: Don't ignore the elephant in the room. *Journal of Interprofessional Care, 24*(4), 450-459.

Fernández-Arias, E., et al. (2009). The multilateral response to the global crisis: Rationale, modalities, and feasibility. Inter-American Development Bank. Retrieved from http://idbdocs.iadb.org/wsdocs/getdocument.aspx?docnum=2029094

Fisher, J. (2011). Why use social media for your day care center. Retrieved from http://localchildcaremarketing.com/why-use-social-media-for-your-day-care-center

Flanders, J., et al. (2009). Rough-and-tumble play and the regulation of aggression: An observational study of father–child play dyads. *Aggressive Behavior, 35*, 285–295.

Fleury, R. E., Sullivan, C. M., & Bybee, D. I. (2000). When ending the relationship does not end the violence. *Violence Against Women, 6*, 1363–1383.

Fogden, S. (2006). Poverty in Canada: The new reality facing Canadians. Retrieved from Mapleleafweb.com/features/general/poverty

Fournier, S. and Crey, E. (1998). *Stolen from Our Embrace: The Abduction of First Nations Children and the Restoration of Aboriginal Communities.* Toronto: University of Toronto Press.

Freeman, R. (2010). Home, school partnerships in family child care: Providers' relationships within their communities. *Early Childhood Development and Care, 181*(6), 827–845.

Fremstad, S. (2010). *A modern framework for measuring poverty and basic economic security.* Washington, D.C.: Center for Economic and Policy Research.

Fuller-Thomson, E. (2005). Canadian First Nations grandparents raising grandchildren: A portrait in resilience. *International Journal of Aging and Human Development, 60*, 331–342.

Furstenberg, F. F., & Teitler, J. O. (1994). Reconsidering the effects of marital disruption. *Journal of Family Issues, 15*(2), 173–90.

Galinsky, E. (1981). *Between generations: The six stages of parenthood.* New York: Times Books.

———. (1987). *The six stages of parenthood.* Reading, MA.: Addison-Wesley Pub. Co.

———. (1988). Parents and teacher-caregivers: Sources of tension, sources of support. *Young Children, 43*(3), 4–12.

———. (1990). Why are some parent/teacher partnerships clouded with difficulties? *Young Children, 45*(5), 2–3, 38–39.

Gallagher, J. J. (1993). The future of professional/family relations in families with children with disabilities. In J. L. Paul & R. J. Simeonsson (Eds.), *Children with special needs: Family, culture, and society* (2nd ed.). Orlando: Harcourt Brace.

Gallo, A. M., et al. (2010). Health care professionals' views of sharing information with families who have a child with a genetic condition. *Journal of Genetic Counselling, 19*(3), 296–304.

Garanzini, M. J. (1995). *Child-centered, family-sensitive schools: An educator's guide to family dynamics.* Washington, DC: National Catholic Educational Association.

Garris-Christian, L. (2006). Understanding families: Applying family systems theory to early childhood practice. *Young Children, 61*(1), 12–20.

Gerstein, E. D. (2009). Resilience and the course of daily parenting stress in families of young children with intellectual disabilities. *Journal of Intellectual Disability Research, 53*(12), 981–997.

Gewirtz, A. H. (2007). Promoting children's mental health in family supportive housing: a community-university partnership for formerly homeless children and families. *Journal of Primary Prevention 28*, 3-4, 359–374.

Gilbert, K. R. (Ed.). (1995). *Annual editions: Marriage and family 95/96.* Guilford, CT: Dushkin.

Ginnott, H. (2003). *Between parent and child.* New York: Three Rivers Press.

Glossop, R., & Theilheimer, I. (1994). Does society support involved fathering? *Transition, 24*(1).

Gold, J. M. (2009). Negotiating the financial concerns of stepfamilies: Directions for family counselors. *The Family Journal, 17*, 185–188.

Goldenberg, I., & Goldenberg, H. (2008). *Family therapy: An overview* (7th ed.). Monterey: Thomson Brooks/Cole.

Goldman, J. L. 1996. We can help children grieve: A child-oriented model for memorializing. *Young Children 51*(6): 76–77.

Goldscheider, F., & Kaufman, G. (2006). Single parenthood and the double standard. *Fathering, 4*(2), 191–208.

Goldstein, L. (2008). Teaching the standards is developmentally appropriate practice: Strategies for incorporating the sociopolitical dimension of DAP in early childhood teaching. *Early Childhood Education Journal, 36*(3), 253–260.

Golish, T. D. (2003). Stepfamily communication strengths: Understanding the ties that bind. *Human Communication Research, 29*, 41–80.

Golombok, S., MacCallum, F., Goodman, E., & Rutter, M. 2002. Families with children conceived by donor insemination: A follow-up at age twelve. *Child Development, 73*(3), 952–968.

Gonzalez-Mena, J. (2002). *The child in the family and the community.* Upper Saddle River, NJ: Merrill Prentice Hall.

Gonzalez-Mena, J. (2009). *Strategies for communicating and working with diverse families.* Upper Saddle River: NJ: Pearson College Division.

Goodwin, C., & Davidson, P. M. (1991). A child's cognitive perception of death. *Day Care and Early Education, 19*(1), 21–24.

Graham, J. (2006). Family issues facts: A fact sheet for families and people who work with families. University of Maine Cooperative Extension.

Gray, B., & Robinson, C. (2009). Hidden children: Perspectives of professionals on young careers of people with mental health problems. *Child Care in Practice, 15*(2), 95–108.

Gregory, R. F. (2003). *Women and workplace discrimination: Overcoming barriers to gender equality.* New Brunswick, NJ: Rutgers University Press.

Gubernskaya, Z. (2010). Changing attitudes toward marriage and children in six countries. *Sociological Perspectives, 53*(2), 179–200.

Gugl, E., & Welling, L. (2010). The early bird gets the worm? Birth order effects in dynamic family model. *Economic Inquiry, 48*(3), 690–703.

Guterman, N., et al. (2009). Parental perceptions of neighborhood processes, stress, personal control, and risk for physical child abuse and neglect. *Child Abuse & Neglect, 33*(12), 897–906.

Haan, M. (2009). Birth order, family size and educational attainment. *Economics of Education Review, 29*(4), 576–588.

Halacka Ball, R. (2006). Supporting and involving families in meaningful ways. *Young Children, 61*(1), 10–11.

Halford, K., Nicholson, J., & Sanders, M. (2007). Couple communication in stepfamilies. *Family Process, 46*, 471–483.

Hamilton, J. (1998). *When a parent is sick: Helping parents explain serious illness to children.* Halifax, NS: Queen Elizabeth II Health Centre.

Harrigan, S. (1992). Places everyone. *Health* (November-December): 67–71.

Harrington, D., et al. 2010. The new dad. Retrieved from http://radioboston.wbur.org/files/2011/06/The-New-Dad-2011-embargoed-DRAFT-until-6_15.pdf

Hart-Byers, S. 2009. *Secrets of successful step-families.* Lothian Publishers Co.

Harvard Family Research Project. (2006). *Family involvement in early childhood education: Family involvement makes a difference: Evidence that family involvement promotes school success for every child of every age.* Number 1, Spring 2006. Battle Creek, MI: Kellogg Foundation. Retrieved from http://www.gse.harvard.edu/hfrp/pubs.html

Health and Welfare Canada. (n.d.). *Child abuse and neglect.* Ottawa: National Clearinghouse on Family Violence.

Helm, J. (1994). Family theme bags: An innovative approach to family involvement in the school. *Young Children, 49*(4), 48–52.

Helmes, E. (2009). Stereotypes of older adults: Does status make a difference? The Abstracts of the 44th Annual Conference of the Australian Psychological Society In: 44th Annual Conference of the Australian Psychological Society, 30 September—4 October 2009, Darwin, NT, Australia.

Henderson, T. L. (2005). Grandparent visitation rights. *Journal of Family Issues, 26*(5), 638–664.

Henry, P. J., & McCue, J. (2009). The experience of nonresidential stepmothers. *Journal of Divorce and Remarriage, 50*, 185–205.

Hertz, R. (2006). *Single by chance: Mothers by choice.* New York, NY: Oxford University Press.

Hetherington, E. M. (2003). Social support and the adjustment of children in divorced and remarried families. *Childhood, 10*(2), 217–236.

Hetherington, E. M. (2005). Divorce and the adjustment of children. *Pediatrics in Review, 26*, 163–169.

Higginbotham, B., & Adler-Baeder, F. (2008). The Smarts Steps: Embrace the Journey program: Enhancing relational skills and relationship quality in remarriages and stepfamilies. *The Forum for Family and Consumer Issues, 13*(3). Retrieved from http://ncsu.edu/ffci/publications/2008/v13-n3--2008-winter/higginbotham-adler.php

Higginbotham, B., & Myler, C. (2010). The influence of facilitator and facilitation characteristics on participants' ratings of stepfamily education. *Family Relations, 59*, 74–86.

Higginbotham, B., Skogrand, L., & Torres, E. (2010). Stepfamily education: Perceived benefits for children. *Journal of Divorce & Remarriage, 51*, 36–49.

Himebauch, A., et al. (2008). Grief in children and developmental concepts of death. *Journal of Palliative Medicine, 11*(2), 242–243.

Hinshaw, S. P. (2005). The stigmatization of mental illness in children and parents: Developmental issues, family concerns, and research needs. *Journal of Child Psychology and Psychiatry, 46*(7), 714–734.

Holland, J. (2008). How schools can support children who experience loss and death. *British Journal of Guidance & Counselling, 36*(4), 411–424.

Holtzman, M. (2006). Definitions of the family as an impetus for legal change in custody decision making: Suggestions from an empirical case study. *Law and Social Inquiry, 31*(1), 1–37.

Hope Irwin, S., & Lero, D. (2004). *In our way: Child care barriers to full workforce participation by parents of children with special needs—and potential remedies.* Wreck Cove, NS: Breton Books.

Hornor, G. (2008). Child advocacy centers: Providing support to primary care providers. *Journal of Pediatric Health Care, 22*(1), 35–39.

Howell, S. (2007). *The kinning of foreigners. Transnational adoption in a global perspective.* Berghahn Books.

Hughes, M., et al. (2009). Marital biography and health at mid-life. *Journal of Health and Social Behaviour, 50,* 344–358.

Hull, G. H., & Mather, J. (2006). *Understanding generalist practice with families.* Canada: Thomson Brooks/Cole.

Hutchinson, S.L., Afifi, T., and Krause, S. (2007). The family that plays together fares better: Examining the contribution of shared family time to family resilience following divorce. *Journal of Divorce and Remarriage, Volume 46, Issue 3–4,* pages 21–48.

Invest in Kids. (2003). *An institute for child care professionals working with high risk children.* Toronto: Invest in Kids.

Invest in Kids. (2010). Answers for professionals: The power of parenting. Retrieved from http://www.investinkids.ca/professionals/answers-for-professionals

Jaffe, M.L. (1991). *Understanding parenting.* Dubuque, IA: Brown & Benchmark.

Jain, V. (2009). Rich nation, poor nation. *Toronto Star,* November 20, 2009.

Janmohamed, Z. (2007). Building bridges: Lesbian, gay, bisexual, transsexual, transgender and queer families in early childhood education. Retrieved from http://www.childcareontario.org/bbridges/BuildingBridgesHandbook.pdf

Janzen, B. L., & Kelly I. W. (2012). Psychological distress among employed fathers: Associations with family structure, work quality, and the work-family interface. *American Journal of Men's Health, 6*(4), 294–302.

Jenkinson, S. (2004). Dying and children. *Interaction,* Spring, 24–26.

Johnson, R. (2010). How to support children with gay parents. *Gaylife.* Retrieved from about.com/od/gayparentingadoptio1/a/gayparent.htm

Johnston, J., et al. (2009). *In the name of the child: A developmental approach to understanding and helping children of conflicted and violent divorce* (2nd ed.). New York: Springer.

Jordan Institute of Families. (2002a). Working with children with parents in prison. *Children's Services Practice Notes, 7*(1).

Jordan Institute for Families. (2002b). Understanding and supporting foster children with incarcerated parents. *Children's Services Practice Notes, 7*(1).

Juby, H., Le Bourdais, C., & Marcil-Gratton, M. (2005). Sharing roles, sharing custody? Couples' characteristics and children's living arrangements at separation. *Journal of Marriage and Family, 67,* 157–172.

Kagan, S. L., & Neville, P. R. (1995). Parent choice in early childhood care and education: Myth or reality? *Research and Clinical Issues, Zero to Three* (February–March).

Katz, L. G. (1980). Mothering and teaching: Some significant distinctions. In L. G. Katz (Ed.), *Current topics in early childhood education* (Vol. 3). Norwood, NJ: Ablex.

———. (1994). Parent involvement—co-op style. *Young Children, 49*(1), 2–3.

Kauppi, C., et al. (2008). Development of cyber-moms: A computer-mediated peer support group to address the needs of young mothers. *Currents: New Scholarship in the Human Services, 7*(2). Retrieved from http://currents.synergiesprairies.ca

Kelly, J. B., & Emery, R. E. (2003). Children's adjustment following divorce: Risk and resilience perspectives. *Family Relations, 52,* 352–362.

Kemp, C. (2003). The social and demographic contours of contemporary grandparenthood: Mapping patterns in Canada and the United States. *Journal of Comparative Family Studies* (March).

Kenway, J., & Fahey, J. (2008). Melancholic mothering: Mothers, daughters and family violence. *Gender & Education, 20*(6), 639–654.

Kerr, D., & Michalski, J. (2005). *Income poverty in Canada: Recent trends among Canadian families 1981–2002.* London, ON: Population Studies Centre, University of Western Ontario. Retrieved from http://www.ssc.uwo.ca/sociology/popstudies/dp/dp05-02.pdf

Kilmer, R. P., et al. (2008). Siblings of children with severe emotional disturbances: risks, resources, and adaptation. *American Journal of Orthopsychiatry, 78,* 1–10.

Kim-Goh, M., & Baello, J. (2008). Attitudes towards domestic violence in Korean and Vietnamese immigrant communities: Implications for human services. *Journal of Family Violence, 23*(1), 647–657.

Kitzinger, S. (1978). *Women as mothers*. Glasgow: Fontana.

Kluger, J. (2006). The new science of siblings. *Time Magazine*, July 10.

Kontos, S., and Wells, W. (1986). Attitudes of caregivers and the day care experiences of families. *Early Childhood Research Quarterly,* (1), 47–67.

Kostouros, P. (2003). Major mental health systems. In D. Clark (Ed.), *Foundations of children's mental health*. E-text, Mount Royal College.

Kowal, A. K., Krull, J. L., & Kramer, L. (2006). Shared understanding of parental differential treatment in families. *Social Development. 15*, 276–295.

Kramer, L., & Conger, K. (2009). What we learn from our sisters and brothers: For better or for worse. *New Directions in Child and Adolescent Development, 126*, 1–12.

———. (1974). *Questions and answers on death and dying*. New York: Macmillan.

Kubler-Ross, E. (1969). *On death and dying*. New York: Macmillan.

LaBoucane-Benson, P. (2005). A complex ecological framework of aboriginal family resilience. Retrieved from http://www.cst.ed.ac.uk/2005 conference/papers/LaBoucane-Benson_paper.pdf

Lamb, M. (2010). *The role of the father in child development*. Mississauga, ON: John Wiley and Sons.

Lansford, J. E. (2009). Parental divorce and children's adjustment. *Perspectives on Psychological Science, 4*, 140–152.

Lawson, D., & Mace, R. (2010). Siblings and childhood mental health: Evidence for a later-born advantage. *Social Science and Medicine, 70*(12), 2061–2069.

Lebow, J., & Newcomb-Rekart, K. (2007). Integrative family therapy for high-conflict divorce with disputes over child custody and visitation. *Family Process, 46*, 79–92.

Leon, K., & Cole, K., (2004). *Helping Children Understand Divorce*. University of Missouri Extension. www.extension.missouri.edu/publications/DisplayPub.aspx?P=GH6600.

Lerner, R. M. (2003). *Concepts and theories of human development*. Mahwah, NJ: Lawrence Erlbaum Associates, Inc.

Lero, D., et al. (2006). Inventory of Policy Areas Influencing Father Involvement. Father Involvement Research Alliance. Retrieved from http://www.fira.ca/cms/documents/22/FIRA-Inventory_of_Policies.pdf

Lever, K., & Wilson, J. J. (2005). Encore parenting: When grandparents fill the role of primary caregiver. *The Family Journal: Counseling and Therapy for Couples and Families, 13*, 167–171.

Lewis, C., & Lamb, M. E. (2010). The development and significance of father-child relationships in two-parent families. In M. E. Lamb (Ed.), *The role of the father in child development*. Mississauga, ON: John Wiley and Sons.

Li, J. A. (2007). The kids are OK: Divorce and children's behavioural problems. RAND Labor and Population Working Paper No. WR-489. RAND, Santa Monica, CA. Presented at the Council on Contemporary Families.

Liang, P. H., & Chen, H. F. (2009). Early childhood teachers' use of E-communication notebook. In T. Bastiaens et al. (Eds.), Proceedings of World Conference on E-Learning in Corporate, Government, Healthcare, and Higher Education 2009, pp. 3355–3360.

Lindjord, D. (2002). Families and adversity in the faltering US economy: The misery goes on and on. *Journal of Early Education and Family Review, 10*, 4–5.

Little, L., Sillence, E., Taylor, A., & Sellen, A. (Eds.). (2009). Special issue of the *International Journal of Human-Computer Studies* on The Family and Communication Technologies. Microsoft Research.

Liu, W. P., & Yeung, A. S. (2000). Do parents get what they want from day care service? In *Elementary and early childhood education; EBSCO Research Database* (PS 028278) [Web].

Lombard, A. (1994). *Success begins at home: The past, present and future of the home instruction program for preschool youngsters* (2nd ed.). Guilford, CT: Dushkin.

Lopez, M. E. (2010). Valuing families as partners. Family Involvement Publications and Resources. Retrieved from http://www.hfrp.org/family-involvement/publications-resources?topic=5

Lowe, E. (2002). Netiquette. *Interaction, 15*(4), Winter 2002.

Lowenstein, A. (1999). Intergenerational family relations and social support. *Zeitschrift fur Gerontologie und Geriatrie, 32*, 398–406.

Mandell, N., & Duffy, A. (Eds.). (2005). *Canadian families: Diversity, conflict and change*. Toronto: Nelson.

Marshall, K. (2006). Converging gender roles. *Perspectives on Labour and Income, Statistics Canada* Catalogue no. 75-001-XPE, Autumn.

Marshall, K. (2009). The Family Work Week. Statistics Canada. Retrieved from http://www.statcan.gc.ca/pub/75-001-x/2009104/pdf/10837-eng.pdf

Martin, J. A., et al. (2009). Center for disease control and prevention. Births: Final data for 2006. *National Vital Statistics Report, 57*(7).

Masten, A. S., et al. (2006). Centre of Excellence for Early Childhood Development—Encyclopedia on Early Childhood Development. Published online March 15, 2006, p. 3.

Masurel, C., & Denton, K. M. (2001). *Two homes*. Somerville, MA: Candlewick Press.

Mayer, K. U. (2009). New trends in life course research. *Annual Review of Sociology, 35*, 493-514.

McBride, S. L. (1999). Family-centered practices. *Young Children, 54*(3), 62-69.

McDaniel, S. A. (2010). *Close relations: An introduction to the sociology of families* (4th ed.). Toronto: Pearson Education.

McDaniel, S.A., & Tepperman, L. (2007). *Close relations: An introduction to the sociology of families* (3rd ed.). Toronto: Pearson Prentice Hall.

McEntire, N. (2003). *Children and grief*. ERIC Digest ED 4755393. Champagne, IL: ERIC Clearinghouse on Elementary and Early Childhood Education.

McGoldrick, M., et al. (2010). *The expanded family life cycle*. Toronto: Pearson Education Canada.

McGuire, S., et al. (2010). Sibling experiences in diverse family contexts. *Child Development Perspectives, 4*(2), 72-79.

McIntyre, L. L., & Phaneuf, L. K. (2008). A three-tier model of parent education in early childhood: Applying a problem-solving model. *Topics in Early Childhood Special Education, 27*(4), 214-222.

McWilliam, R. (2010). *Working with families of young children with special needs*. New York: Guilford Press.

Medoff, M. (2010). The impact of state abortion policies on teen pregnancy rates. *Social Indicators Research, 97*(2), 177-189.

Mellor, S. (1995). How do only children differ from other children? In R. L. DelCampo & D. S.

DelCampo, *Taking sides: Clashing views on controversial issues of childhood and society*. Guilford, CT: Dushkin Publishing Group.

Mendez, N. (2009). Sexualities and the identities of minority women. *Lesbian Families,* 91-104. doi:10.1007/978-0-387-75657-8-5

Miall, C., & March, K. (2005). Social support for changes in adoption practice: Gay adoption, open adoption, birth reunions, and the release of confidential identifying information. *Families in Society, 86*(1), 83-92.

Miguez, R., et al. (2009). Using Web 2.0 Technologies in Early Childhood Education. Retrieved from http://www.educanext.org/dotlrn/clubs/aspect/new-lors/.../TELearn-09.pdf

Milan, A. (2003). Would you live common-law? *Canadian Social Trends*. Statistics Canada Catalogue No. 11-8, Autumn.

Milkie, M., et al. (2009). Taking on the second shift: Time allocations and time pressures of U.S. parents with preschoolers. *Social Forces, 88*(2), 487-517.

Minnis, H., et al. (2009). An exploratory study of the association between reactive attachment disorder and attachment narratives in early school-age children. *Journal of Child Psychology and Psychiatry, 50*, 931-942.

Mitchell, B. A. (2006). Changing courses: The pendulum of family transitions in a comparative perspective. *Journal of Comparative Family Studies, 37*(3), 325-343.

Mitchell, S., Foulger, T. S., & Wetzel, K. (2009). Ten tips for involving families through internet-based communication. Retrieved from http://www.naeyc.org/files/yc/file/200909/Ten%20Tips%20for%20Involving%20Families.pdf

Mo, J. (2010). Stress and resiliency in children living in families impacted by addiction. Retrieved from http://www.norlien.org

Mollborn, S., et al. (2010). How teenage fathers matter for children: Evidence from the ECLS-B. *Journal of Family Issues, 31*(5). Retrieved from http://online.sagepub.com

Morash, M., et al. (2008). Risk factors for abusive relationships. *Violence against Women, 13*(1), 653-675.

Morrissette, M. (2008). *Choosing single motherhood: The thinking woman's guide*. New York: Houghton Miffin Harcourt.

Morse, S. (2007). Single Mothers by Choice: A dumb sex? Institute of Marriage and Family

Canada. Retrieved from http://www.imfcanada. org/article_files/Single_Mothers_By_Choice.pdf

Murray, C. I., Toth, K., & Clinkinbeard, S. S. (2005). Death, dying and grief in families. In P. C. McKendry & S. J. Price (Eds.), *Families and change: Coping with stressful events and transitions* (3rd ed.). Thousand Oaks, CA: Sage Publications.

Najman, J. M., et al. (2010). Timing and chronicity of family poverty and development of unhealthy behaviors in children: A longitudinal study. US Library of Medicine. Retrieved from http://www. ncbi.nlm.nih.gov/pubmed/20472210

Nalls, M., et al. (2009). How can we reach reluctant parents in childcare programmes? *Early Child Development and Care, 180*(8), 1053–1064.

National Anti-Poverty Organization. (2003). The face of poverty in Canada: An overview. Retrieved from http://72.14.253.104/search?q=cache:n1 Vpsqx6CRIJ:www.napo-onap.ca/en/issues/face%2

National Institute on Alcohol Abuse and Alcoholism. (1990). *Children of alcoholics: Are they different?* Retrieved from http://pubs.niaaa. nih.gov/publications/aa09.htm

National Scientific Council on the Developing Child. (2004). Young children develop in an environment of relationships. Working Paper No. 1. Retrieved from http://www.developingchild.harvard.edu

National Scientific Council on the Developing Child. (2007). The science of early childhood development: Closing the gap between what we know and what we do. Retrieved from http:// www.developingchild.harvard.edu

National Scientific Council on the Developing Child. (2010a). Early experiences can alter gene expression and affect long-term development. Working Paper No. 10. Retrieved from http:// www.developingchild.harvard.edu

National Scientific Council on the Developing Child. (2010b). Persistent fear and anxiety can affect young children's learning and development. Working Paper No. 9. Retrieved from http://www.developingchild.harvard.edu

Nayyar, S. (20060. Focus on the 100 best-come-back moms. *Working Mother.* Retrieved from http://www.workingmother.com

News-medical.net. (2009, December 7). Children in military families suffer from more emotional difficulties compared to other American youths.

Nicholson, D., & Artz, S. (2006). Gentle hands: Assisting single parent teen mothers in raising their children. *Child and Youth Care Forum, 35*(5/6), 411–426.

Nuttall, D. (1993). Letters I never sent to my daughter's third grade teacher. *Young Children, 48*(6), 6.

O'Campo, P., Salmon, C., & Burke, J. (2008). Neighberhoods and mental well-being. What are the pathways? *Health and Place, 15,* 56–68.

O'Campo, P., et al. (2009). Partner abuse or violence, parenting and neighborhood influences on children's behavioral problems. *A practical guide to the evaluation of child physical abuse and neglect, 3,* pp. 335–351.

O'Donnell, X. (2008). Selected findings of the Aboriginal Children's Survey 2006: Family and community. *Canadian Social Trends, 86,* 65.

Olson, D. H., et al. (1983). *Families: What makes them work.* Newbury Park, CA: Sage Publications.

O'Reilly, A. (2006). Rocking the cradle: Thoughts on motherhood, feminism and the possibility of empowered mothering. Centre for Research on Mothering, Demeter Press. Retrieved from http:// www.yorku.ca/crm

Palm, G., and Fagan, J. (2008). Father involvement in early childhood programs: Review of the literature. *Early Child Development & Care, 178*(7/8), 745–759.

Palusci, V., et al. (2007). Changes in parenting attitudes and knowledge among inmates and other at-risk populations after a family nurturing program. *Children and Youth Services Review, 29.*

Pang, Y. (2010). Selecting appropriate assessment instruments to ensure quality transition services. *Early Childhood Education Journal, 38*(1), 43–48.

Parke, M. (2006). Are married parents really better for children? What research says about the effects of family structure on child well-being. Centre for Law and Social Policy, United States Department of Education, ERIC document 476114.

Patterson, C. J. (2009). Children of gay and lesbian parents; psychology, law and policy. *American Psychologist, 64,* 727–736.

Patterson C. J., Sutfin, E.L., & Fulcher, M. (2004). Division of labor among lesbian and heterosexual parenting couples: Correlates of specialized versus shared patterns. *Journal of Adult Development, 11*(3).

Pearson, J., & Kordich Hall, D. (2006). *RIRO resiliency guidebook.* Toronto: Child and Family Partnership.

Pelo, A., & Davidson, F. (2003). Partnership-building strategies. In C. Copple (Ed.), *A world of difference: Readings on teaching young children in a diverse society.* Washington, DC: National Association for the Education of Young Children.

Penzo, J. A. (2008). Understanding parental grief as a response to mental illness: Implications for practice. *Journal of Family Social Work, 11*(3), 323–338.

Perlman, M., et al. (2010). Promoting diversity in early childhood education? *Early Child Development and Care, 180,* 753–766.

Perry, B. (2010). Effects of maltreatment on the developing child: Relational poverty and vulnerability to abuse and neglect. Retrieved from http://www.norlien.org

Peter, T. (2009). Exploring taboos: Comparing male- and female-perpetrated child sexual abuse. *Journal of Interpersonal Violence, 24*:, 1111–1128.

Pinquart, M., & Teubert, D. (2010). Effects of parenting education with expectant and new parents: A meta-analysis. *Journal of Family Psychology, 24*(3), 316–327.

Planitz, J. M., & Feeny, J. A. (2009). Are stepsiblings bad, stepmothers wicked, and stepfathers evil?: An assessment of Australian stepfamily stereotypes. *Journal of Family Studies, 15,* 82–97.

Poehlmann, J. (2003). An attachment perspective on grandparents raising their very young grandchildren: Implications for intervention and research. *Infant Mental Health journal Volume 24, Issue 2,* 149–173, March/April 2003.

Poling, D. A., et al. (2008). Death sentences: A content analysis of children's death literature. *Journal of Genetic Psychology, 169*(2), 165–176.

Popkin, M. (2007). *Taming the spirited child: Strategies for parenting challenging children without breaking their spirits.* [Paperback]. New York: Fireside.

Portrie, T., & Hill, N. R. (2005). Blended families, a critical review of the current research. *The Family Journal: Counselling and Therapy for Couples and Families, 13*(4), 445–451.

Potter, D. (2010). Psychosocial well-being and the relationship between divorce and children's academic achievement. *Journal of Marriage and Family, 72,* 933–946.

Powell, D. R. (1989). *Families and early childhood programs.* Washington, DC: National Association for the Education of Young Children.

Pruett, K., & Pruett, M. (2009). *Partnership parenting: How men and women parent differently—why it helps your kids and can strengthen your marriage.* Cambridge, MA: de Capro Press.

Public Health Agency of Canada. (2007). Analyzing data collected by the community capacity building tool: A manual for users. Retrieved from http://www.phac-aspc.gc.ca/canada/regions/ab-nwt-tno/documents/UserManual-January2007_e.pdf

Quine, L., & Pahl, J. (1987). First diagnosis of severe handicap: A study of parental reactions. *Developmental Medicine and Child Neurology, 29,* 232–242.

Raffel, S. (1999). Revisiting role theory: Roles and the problem of the self. *Sociological Research Online, 4*(2). Retrieved from http://www.socresonline.org.uk/4/2/raffel.html

Rankin, J., & Ornstein, A. (2009). A Commentary on Mandatory Reporting Legislation in the United States, Canada, and Australia: A Cross-Jurisdictional Review of Key Features, Differences, and Issues. *Child Maltreatment, 14,* 121–123.

Rauch, P. K., Muriel, A. C., & Cassem, N. H. (2002). Parents with cancer: Who's looking out for the children. *Journal of Clinical Oncology, 20*(21): 4399–4402.

Reaching in ... Reaching Out. Retrieved from http://www.reachinginreachingout.com/aboutresilience.htm

Reedy, C., & McGrath, W. H. (2010). Can you hear me now? Staff-parent communication in child care centres. *Early Child Development and Care, 180*(3), 347–357.

Remennick, L. (2007). "Being a woman is different here": Changing perceptions of femininity and gender relations among former Soviet women living in Greater Boston. *Women's Studies International Forum, 30*(1), 326–341.

Report Card on Child and Family Poverty in Canada. (2009). Retrieved from http://www.campaign2000.ca

Riggs, D., et al. (2008). Negotiating foster families: Identification and desire. *British Journal of Social Work, 39,* 789–806.

Riggs, D., et al. (2010). Foster fathers and carework: Engaging alternate models of parenting. *Fathering, 8*(1), 24–36.

Rocca, K., et al. (2010). Siblings' motives for talking to each other. *The Journal of Psychology: Interdisciplinary and Applied, 144*(2), 205–219.

Roer-Strier, D. (1999). Coping strategies of immigrant parents: Directions for family therapy. *Family Process, 35,* 363–376.

Roer-Strier, D., et al. (2005). Fatherhood and immigration: Challenging the deficit theory. *Child and Family Social Work, 10*(4), 315–329.

Rosenthal, C., & Gladstone, J. (2007). Grandparenthood in Canada. Retrieved from http://www.vifamily.ca/library/cft/grandparent-hood.html

Russell, M., Harris, B., & Gockel, A. (2008). Parenting in poverty: Perspectives of high-risk parents. *Journal of Children and Poverty, 14*(1), 83–98.

Rutkin, A. (2010). Child custody and visitation. *Family Law and Practice*, Lexis, pp. 3–32.

Rutter, V. (2009). Divorce in research vs. divorce in the media. *Sociology Compass, 3*(4), 707–720.

Sauve, R. (2010). Canada job trends update: National and provincial labour markets. Retrieved from http://www.peoplepatternsconsulting.com/pub_can_job10.html

Savio Beers, L., et al. (2009). Approaching the adolescent-headed family: A review of teen parenting. *Current Problems in Pediatric and Adolescent Care, 39*, 216–233.

Scaramella, L. V., Neppl, T. K., Ontai, L. L., & Conger, R. D. (2008). Consequences of socioeconomic disadvantage across three generations: Parenting behavior and child externalizing problems. *Journal of Family Psychology, 22*, 725–733.

Schaub, M. (2010). Parenting for cognitive development from 1950 to 2000: The institutionalization of mass education and the social construction of parenting in the United States. *Sociology of Education, 83*, 46–66.

Schellenberg, G., and Maheux, H. (2007). Immigrants' perspectives on their first four years in Canada: Highlights from three waves of the longitudinal survey of immigrants to Canada. Statistics Canada. Retrieved from http://www.statcan.gc.ca/pub/81-595-m/2010084/e1-eng.htm

Schmidt, T. (2008). *Standing on my own two feet: A child's affirmation of love in the midst of divorce.* New York: Price Stern Sloan.

Schoppe-Sullivan, S., et al. (2008). Maternal gate-keeping, coparenting quality, and fathering behavior in families with infants. *Journal of Family Psychology, 22*(3), 389–398.

Scott, D., & Arney, F. (2010). *Working with vulnerable families: A partnership approach.* New York: Cambridge.

Seligman, M. (Ed.). (1991). *The family with a handicapped child.* Boston: Allyn & Bacon.

Seng, A., and Prinz, R. (2008). Parents who abuse: What are they thinking? *Clinical Child and Family Psychology Review, 11*(4), 163–175.

Shechner, T., et al. (2010). Relations between social support and psychological and parental distress for lesbian, single heterosexual by choice and two-parent heterosexual mothers. *American Journal of Orthopsychiatry, 80*(3), 283–292.

Shelton, K. H., et al. (2009). Examining differences in psychological adjustment problems among children conceived by assisted reproductive technologies. *International Journal of Behavioral Development, 33*, 385–392.

Shimoni, R. (1992a). Parent involvement in early childhood education and day care. *Sociological Studies of Child Development, 5*, 73–95.

Shimoni, R. (1992b). Endemic ambiguity: The role of caregivers in relation to parents of children in day care. Doctoral Thesis, University of Calgary.

Shimoni, R., Este, D., & Clark, D. (2003). Paternal engagement in immigrant and refugee families. *Journal of Comparative Family Studies, 34*(4), 555–568.

Silverman, P., & Kelly, M. (2009). *A parent's guide to raising grieving children: Rebuilding your family after the death of a loved one.* New York: Oxford.

Skolnick, A. S. (1992). *The intimate environment: Exploring marriage and the family* (5th ed.). New York: HarperCollins.

Smith, H., et al. (2008). Even in Canada? The multiscalar construction and experience of concentrated immigrant poverty in gateway cities. *Annals of the Association of American Geographers, 98*(3), 686–713.

Sobolewski, J. M., & Amato, P. R. (2005). Economic hardship in the family of origin and children's psychological well-being in adulthood. *Journal of Marriage and Family, 67*, 141–156.

Sobon, S. M. (2005). Blended families in three marriage enrichment programs. Social Consequences of Poverty. Retrieved from http://www.mapleleafweb.com/features/general/poverty/consequences.html

Statistics Canada. (2006). *Women in Canada: A gender-based statistical report.*

Statistics Canada. (2006a). Wives as primary breadwinners. *The Daily*, 23 August. Retrieved from http://www.statcan.gc.ca/daily-quoti-dien/0060823/dq060823b-eng.htm

Statistics Canada. (2006b). *Family violence in Canada: A statistical profile.* Ottawa: Statistics Canada. Catalogue no. 85-224-X.

Statistics Canada. (2008). *Canadian demographics at a glance.* Retrieved from http://www.

statcan.gc.ca/pub/91–003–x/91–003–x2007001–
eng.pdf

Statistics Canada. (2007a). 2006 census: Families,
marital status, households, and dwelling characteristics. *The Daily,* September 12. statcan.gc.ca

Statistics Canada. (2007b). *Snapshot of Canada:
Families. Canadian Social Trends.* Ottawa:
Statistics Canada. Catalogue no. 11–008: 39–40.

Statistics Canada. (2009). 2006 *Census: Family
portrait: Continuity and change in Canadian families and households in 2006: National portrait:
Individual.* Retrieved from http://www12.statcan.
ca/census-recensement/2006/as-sa/97–553/p15-
eng.cfm

Statistics Canada. (2010). Age group of child (12),
number of grandparents (3) and sex (3) for the
grandchildren living with grandparents with no
parent present, in private households of Canada,
provinces and territories, 2006 census–20%
sample data.

Steckley, S., & Cummins, B. (2008). *Full circle:
Canada's First Nations* (2nd ed.). Toronto: Pearson.

Stith, S., et al. (2008). Risk factors in child maltreatment: A meta-analytic review of the literature.
Children and Youth Services Review, 30(1), 79–89.

Stranger, C., & Beatty, T. (1984). *Seeing infants
through new eyes* (video). Washington, DC: National
Association for the Education of Young Children.

Strier-Roer, D., Strier, R., Este, D., Shimoni, R., &
Clark, D. (2005). Fatherhood and immigration:
Challenging the deficit theory. *Child and Family
Social Work, 10,* 315–329.

Strohschein, L. (2007). Challenging the presump-
tion of diminished capacity to parent: Does
divorce really change parenting practices? *Family
Relations, 56*(4), 358–368.

Strow, C. W., & Strow, B. K. (2008). Evidence
that the presence of a half-sibling negatively
impacts a child's personal development.
*American Journal of Economics and Sociology,
67*(2), 177–206.

Sullivan, P., et al. (2009). Maltreatment of children and youth with special healthcare needs.
Aggression and Violent Behavior, 14(1), 13–29.

Sweeney, M. M. (2010). Remarriage and stepfamilies: Strategic sites for family scholarship in the
21st century. *Journal of Marriage and Family,
72*(3), 667–684.

Szinovacz, M. E., & Davey, A. (2006). Effects of
retirement and grandchild care on depressive

symptoms. *International Journal of Aging and
Human Development, 62,* 1–20.

Tang, C. H., Wu, M. P., Liu, J. T., Lin, H. G., & Hsu,
C. C. (2006). Delayed parenthood and the risk of
Cesarean delivery: Is paternal age an indepen-
dent risk factor? *Birth, 33*(1), 18–26.

Tarin, J. J., Brines, J., & Cano, A. (1998). Long-
term effects of delayed parenthood. *Human
Reproduction, 13*(9), 2371–2376.

The Online Farlex Dictionary: http://legal-
dictionary.thefreedictionary.com/adoption.

Thiele, D., & Whelan, T. (2006). The nature and
dimensions of the grandparent role. *Marriage
and Family Review, 40*(1), 93–108.

Thomas, A., & Chess, S. (1977). *Temperament and
development.* New York: Brunner/Mazel.

Thomson, L., et al. (2009). Who's in our family?
An application of the theory of family boundary
ambiguity to the experiences of former foster
carers. *Adoption and Fostering Journal, 33*(1),
68–79.

Trawick-Smith, J. (2010). *Early childhood development: A multicultural perspective* (5th ed.). Upper
Saddle River, NJ: Pearson.

Tucker, C. J., & Updegraff, K. (2009). The relative
contributions of parents and siblings to child and
adolescent development. In L. Kramer & K. J.
Conger (Eds.), *Siblings as agents of socialization:
New directions for child and adolescent development, 126,* 13–28. Retrieved from http://www.
onlinelibrary.wiley.com

Turcotte, M. (2008). Parents with adult children
living at home. *Canadian Social Trends,* Statistics
Canada. Catalogue 11 (Spring).

Turecki, S., & Tonner, L. (1989). *The difficult child.*
New York: Bantam.

Turecki, S. (2000). *The difficult child* (2nd ed.).
New York: Bantam Books.

Turnbull, A., & Turnbull, H. R. (1990). *Families,
professionals, and exceptionality: A special partnership* (2nd ed.). Columbus: Merrill.

Ulrich, D., Gagel, D. E., Hemmerling, A., Pastor, V.
S., & Kentenich, H. (2004). Couples becoming
parents: Something special after IVF? *Journal of
Psychosomatic Obstetrics & Gynecology, 25,* 99–113.

Umberson, D., & Williams, C. L. (1993). Divorced
fathers: Parental role strain and psychological
distress. *Journal of Family Issues, 14*(3), 378–400.

Updegraff, K. A., Thayer, S. M., Whiteman, S. D.,
Dennng, D. J., & McHale, S. M. (2005). Relational

aggression in adolescents' sibling relationships: Links to sibling and parent-adolescent relationship quality. *Family Relations, 54*, 373–385.

Vanier Institute of the Family. (2003). *Profiling Canada's families II: Canada's first families* [online]. Retrieved from http://www.vifamily.ca/profiling/parti3.htm

Vanier Institute of the Family. (2010). *Families count: Profiling Canadian families.* Retrieved from http://www.vifamily.ca/node/371

Van Riper, M. (2007). Families of children with Down syndrome: Responding to a change in plans with resilience. *Journal of Pediatric Nursing, 22*(22), 116–128.

Van Velsor, P., & Cox, D. (2000). Use of the collaborative drawing technique in school counseling practicum: An illustration of family systems. *Counselor Education and Supervision, 40*(2), 141–153.

Varney, D., et al. (2008). Homelessness, children, and youth: Research in the United States and Canada. *American Behavioral Scientist, 51*, 715–720.

Vuckovic, A. (2008). Inter-cultural communication: A foundation of communicative action. *Multicultural Education & Technology Journal, 2*(1), 47–59.

Walberg, R., & Mrozek, A. (2009). Private choices, public costs: How failing families cost us all. *Institute of Marriage and Family Canada* (June).

Wald, E. (1981). *The remarried family: Challenge and promise.* New York: Family Service Association of America.

Wallach, L. (1997). *Violence and young children's development.* ERIC Digest. Champaign, IL: ERIC Clearinghouse on Elementary and Early Childhood Education.

Waller, M. (2009). Family man in the other America: New opportunities, motivations, and supports for paternal caregiving. *Annals of the American Academy of Political and Social Science, 624*(1), 156–176.

Wallerstein, J. S. (2005). Growing up in the divorced family. *Clinical Social Work Journal, 33*(4), 401–418.

Walter, T. (2010). Grief and culture: A checklist. *Bereavement Care, 29*(2), 5–9.

Ward, M. (2006). *The family dynamic: A Canadian perspective* (4th Canadian ed.). Scarborough, ON: Nelson Education Ltd.

Way, P. (2010). That isn't really how it works: Discussing questions of life, death and afterlife with bereaved children and young people. *Bereavement Care, 29*(2), 17–20.

Webb, N., & Doka, K. (2010). *Helping bereaved children: A handbook for practitioners* (3rd ed.). New York: Guilford Press.

Williams, R. H., & Vashi, G. (2007). Hijab and American Muslim women: Creating autonomous selves. *Sociology of Religion, 68*, 269–287.

Willis, C. A. (2004). Helping children grieve: Implications for directors and teachers. *Child Care Exchange,* September/October, 20–23.

Wilson, C. (2009). *Perfect phrases for classroom teachers.* New York: McGraw-Hill.

Wilson, L. (2001). *Partnerships: Families and communities in Canadian early childhood education* (2nd ed.). Scarborough, ON: Nelson Thomson Learning.

Wilson, L. (2005). *Partnerships: Families and communities in early childhood development* (3rd ed.). Toronto: Nelson.

Wilson, L. (2010). *Partnerships: Families and communities in early childhood* (4th ed.). Toronto: Nelson Education Ltd.

Wolf, L., Fishman, S., & Ellison, D. (1998). Effects of sibling perception of differential parental treatment in sibling dyads with one disabled child. *Journal of the American Academy of Child and Adolescent Psychiatry, 37*(12), 1317–1325.

Woodford, M. (2010). Same-sex marriage and beyond. *Journal of Gay & Lesbian Social Service, 22*(1/2), 1–8.

Woodthorpe, K. (2010). Public dying: Death in the media and Jade Goody. *Sociology Compass, 4*, 283–294.

Worden, J. (2009). *Grief counseling and grief therapy: A handbook for the mental health practitioner.* New York: Springer.

Wright, K., & Stegelin, D. (2003). *Building school and community partnerships through parent involvement* (2nd ed.). Upper Saddle River, NJ: Merrill Prentice Hall.

Wylie, M. (2000). Having it all: How equally shared parenting works. *Gender & Society, 14*(3), 485–487.

Yngvesson, B. (2010). *Belonging in an adopted world: Race, identity and transnational adoption.* Chicago: University of Chicago Press.

Zajonc, R. B., & Mullally, P. R. (1997). Birth order: Reconciling conflicting effects. *American Psychologist, 52*, 685–690.

Index